DATE DUE

THE
PERIGLACIAL
ENVIRONMENT

Past and Present

Arctic Institute of North America

THE PERIGLACIAL ENVIRONMENT

Past and Present

EDITED BY TROY L. PÉWÉ

MONTREAL   McGill-Queen's University Press   1969

Based on the Symposium on Cold Climate Environments
and Processes, VII Congress of the International
Association for Quaternary Research, held at Fairbanks, Alaska,
August 18-25, 1965.

PREFACE

Central Alaska is one of the best areas in North America for the study of the periglacial environment. It is relatively accessible and its low-altitude periglacial phenomena are well developed. Yet, despite its wealth of material and its interesting Quaternary history, few modern workers have had an opportunity to examine the region. The Alaskan Field Conference of the VII Congress for the International Association for Quaternary Research (INQUA), August-September 1965, provided such an opportunity. It was the first field conference of any magnitude to be held in an active periglacial area in North America.

In connection with the Alaskan Field Conference, a Symposium on Cold Climate Environments and Processes was held at the University of Alaska and at field locations from August 18 to 25. Leading research workers from many different parts of the world were thus able to study active and inactive periglacial phenomena, including ice wedges, solifluction deposits, loess, and permafrost, and to present and discuss papers on the periglacial environment.

The Symposium and Field Conference, which were organized by the present editor, included seventy people whose national affiliations represented Belgium, Brazil, Canada, Denmark, England, France, Germany, Iceland, Ireland, Italy, Japan, Mexico, Netherlands, Poland, Sweden, Switzerland, U.S.A., and USSR. The Symposium brought together workers whose disciplines included geology, botany, vertebrate and invertebrate paleontology, soil science, geochronology, physical anthropology, archaeology, and physical geography.

The present volume is an outgrowth from, but not a complete record of, the INQUA Symposium held in Alaska. Seventeen of the twenty-nine papers presented in Alaska are included. Six additional papers were later written especially for the volume by participants of the Field Conference. Two of the papers were not given in Alaska but were presented at the INQUA Congress held in Boulder, Colorado, in September 1965. After the Symposium, several of the papers were translated and many were extensively rewritten in order to present the subject with more clarity. The present volume represents thirty-three authors from eleven countries and discusses subjects from fifteen countries.

The volume has two major subdivisions: the first group of papers deals with processes and features in the present periglacial environment in areas from the Arctic and Subarctic to the Antarctic, including high mountainous areas in the Tropics. The second group deals with cold climate phenomena now found in temperate environments or in other areas which no longer have active deposits or landscapes, such as altiplanation terraces, but which were formed under periglacial conditions; these phenomena now exist as "fossil" features and are paleoclimate indicators.

The editor is very grateful for the aid he received from his co-workers in organizing the Symposium, especially for the support from Richard D. Reger and Lawrence Mayo. He wishes to thank the authors for their contributions and for their willingness to condense and otherwise modify their material as it became necessary. Thanks are extended to Sidney White, who, because of his long experience in Mexico, edited an early draft of Lorenzo's paper, and to André Cailleux for his pertinent comments on the French contributions in this volume. Linda Phillips and Nancy Voyles retyped all manuscripts, and Marcus Hoyer and Michael Bussard were very helpful in proofing and reproofing manuscripts and bibliographical citations for the papers. Publication was arranged jointly by the Arctic Institute of North America and McGill University Press, assisted by a small contribution by the National Science Foundation. Miss Margery Simpson, Editor of the McGill University Press, was very patient with the editor in the final reworking of the material into book form and provided constant advice and assistance.

Thanks are also extended to the officers of the VII INQUA Congress, especially G. M. Richmond and H. E. Wright, Jr., for their encouragement in the presentation of the Symposium and the compilation of the volume.

T. L. P.

Tempe, Arizona

CONTENTS

viii

THE PERIGLACIAL ENVIRONMENT

TROY L. PÉWÉ
Department of Geology
Arizona State University
Tempe, Arizona, U.S.A.

More than one hundred years ago, geologists and geographers mapping in southern England and Wales noticed surficial deposits of a structureless and rubbly character which could not have originated by processes then active. This unsorted heterogeneous debris has been referred to as "Head," "Coombe Rock," "Warp," and by other terms. Dines *et al.* (1940), in an excellent summary of British thought on the subject, pointed out that when it became apparent that this rubble was produced and transported by agencies not operating there at that time, the idea of former cold conditions was considered. Gradually, as more observations were made of arctic processes and surficial deposits, the striking similarity between them and those of south England and Wales suggested that some deposits in temperate areas were products of a formerly colder climate. Such a climate soon was ascribed to the time of continental glaciation in nearby areas. In this cold climate frozen ground developed and frost action became intensely active. Before the turn of the century, Blanckenhorn (1896) demonstrated that certain surficial deposits in Germany were probably the result of a frost climate rather than deposits of glaciers. Even before that, Kerr (1881) pointed out that surficial deposits in the eastern United States could be the result of intense frost action during glacial times.

In 1909 Lozinski introduced the term "periglacial" for the concept of a cold climate outside of the glacial border; specifically, the term "periglacial" referred to the area which bordered the continental ice sheet, its climate, and the features developed in this rigorous environment.

The term "periglacial" has not been accepted by all, although the concept is now firmly entrenched. Such terms as "sub-nival," "subglacial," "sub-gelid," and "frost-climate" have been suggested, but "periglacial" remains most widely used. No single definition acceptable to everyone concerned with studying the periglacial environment has been formulated inasmuch as workers differ in their opinions of the exact climate of the periglacial zone. For instance, Zeuner (1945) restricts the periglacial zone to that area underlain by permafrost or that area where the annual air temperature is 28°F or colder.

Others state that permafrost is not actually necessary for a periglacial environment, and that such a climate could include regions where permafrost is absent, but where a considerable number of freezing and thawing cycles occur annually. Although exact definition of the periglacial environment has not been developed, workers agree that it has a rigorous climate. The present writer considers all permafrost areas today to be in the modern periglacial zone.

The periglacial environment is characterized by frozen ground, intense frost action in fine-grained sediments, and considerable sorting of coarse materials. Therefore, mechanical weathering is accelerated, and ice growth is abundant in perennially and seasonally frozen ground. Local sorting of sediments and the formation of small-scale patterned ground are common. Water is concentrated in fine-grained surficial sediments by ice segregation. This concentration of water, when released, and the impeded infiltration of surface waters, because of impervious frozen subsoil, aid in downslope mass movement of debris. Growth of large masses of ground ice occurs in permafrost with the formation of tundra polygons and pingos. The periglacial environment has its own characteristic sequence of soil development (Tedrow 1962).

Frost action and actively aggrading glacier outwash streams produce wide areas of vegetation-free sediments subject to wind action. Thus, loess, aeolian sand deposits, and ventifacts are common phenomena in the periglacial environment. It is important to note that the periglacial area is not only of interest to geologists, but also to soil scientists, climatologists, botanists, zoologists, archeologists, and other scientists. Just as many geological processes are controlled or modified by varying climatic conditions, so are soil forming processes and the distribution of plants and animals affected by past and present cold-warm climate fluctuations.

In the years prior to the Second World War there was widespread recognition in Europe of the periglacial concept, with its associated frost phenomena. Unfortunately, most workers in the field had not investigated the modern arctic and subarctic conditions where the periglacial environment is currently active. Those workers who had polar experience were, for the most part, familiar only with conditions on subarctic and arctic islands—areas not representative of the modern periglacial environment in continental North America and Asia, and not representative of the Pleistocene periglacial conditions in North America and Europe.

Since 1944 a new era of periglacial research has been initiated, with a more systematic and detailed study of polar areas, the modern periglacial zone. Although Russia has long been actively studying permafrost, the United States and Canada have become involved in such research only in the two decades since the war. Scientists in Scandinavia are becoming more keenly aware of cold climate processes as they gain experience in the study of these phenomena.

With the rapid increase of Quaternary geology research in general, and with an increase of the conventional studies of inactive periglacial features in temperate latitudes, plus new knowledge from the polar areas, it is only logical that we should now be involved in a new, intensified era of periglacial research. The meetings of the International Association for Quaternary Research (INQUA) are rapidly becoming larger, indicating much greater scope of interest in the various aspects of the Pleistocene. World-wide studies of frozen ground and related phenomena are no longer restricted to Europe, as indicated by the highly successful First Annual Permafrost Conference in the United States in 1963 (NRC-NAS, 1966) and similar meetings in Canada. In 1954 there appeared the first issue of a new journal entirely devoted to periglacial research, the *Periglacial Bulletin,* which is published in Poland and now is in its fifteenth volume.

Even though there is increased activity in the study of Quaternary geology in polar areas and interest in periglacial research, there still remains a noticeable lack of communication and understanding between scientists in various disciplines. Most serious students of many aspects of polar research have not yet concerned themselves with the importance of their work as related to periglacial features in present temperate latitudes; and, as has long been the case, most workers in periglacial research have no experience in polar areas and thus are not aware of all the ramifications of the modern periglacial environment. However, progress is being made. Several recent summaries of periglacial research have been made (Smith 1949, Troll 1948, Washburn 1956, Markov and Popov 1960), and even more recent ones have been compiled for publication in the *Periglacial Bulletin* (Smith 1962, Black 1964, Cook 1964, Dylikowa 1964, Pissart 1964, Nangeroni 1964, Rapp and Rudberg 1964, Raynal 1964, Sekyra 1964, Waters 1964, Dylik 1966).

Only recently North American workers (Holmes, Hopkins, and Foster 1966, Péwé *et al.* 1965) demonstrated that pingos are widespread in the subarctic forests of interior Alaska and are not features restricted entirely to the rigorous climate of the arctic regions. Open system pingos are now thought to be growing actively in the present climate of central Alaska where the mean annual air temperature is from −1° to −2 °C, as compared to the −8° to −12 °C or colder in the Alaskan Arctic.

Permafrost is the common denominator of the periglacial environment, and it is practically ubiquitous in the active periglacial zone. In the inactive periglacial zone, permafrost features are eagerly sought as evidence to demonstrate formerly more rigorous climates. Today the extent of permafrost in the northern hemisphere is constantly being better understood (Fig. 1) (R. J. E. Brown 1969; Weidick, in press; Einarsson [Iceland], oral communication; Rapp 1969; Anderson [Norway], written communication; Swenson [Norway], oral communication; Popov 1965). We know that many mountain tops and bogs contain small patches of permafrost far beyond the limit of (south) areas currently mapped as underlain by permafrost.

Detailed study of permafrost temperature profiles reveal late Pleistocene and Recent climatic changes and show that not all permafrost is in equilibrium with the existing climate, but is a product of an earlier, cold environment. In some northern areas and probably along the southern border some existing permafrost is the product of an extinct colder climate (Lachenbruch, Green, and Marshall 1966).

A former periglacial environment is readily assumed if permafrost is demonstrated to have been existent in the past. The most positive evidence of past permafrost is the presence of ice wedge casts. Many periglacial scientists still are unaware that ice wedges represent more than the mere presence of permafrost, and are a specific climatic indicator. While permafrost is present and can be formed where the mean annual air temperature is about −1 °C, and ice wedges are known to exist in areas where the mean annual air temperature is −1 °C to −2 °C, we cannot conclude that ice wedges developed under these climatic conditions. Recent studies of ice wedges (Lachenbruch 1962, 1966, Péwé 1966a, b) reveal that a mean annual air temperature of −6° to −8°C is necessary for ice wedges to grow. Many periglacial workers still do not realize that the climate need not warm to a mean annual air temperature of more than 0°C for a long time to produce "fossil" ice wedges. The freezing and thawing characteristics of the ground are modified, as has long been known, by the texture and moisture content of the ground, as well as by many other intrinsic and extrinsic parameters. For example, in central Alaska, areas of "fossil" ice wedges occur in well-drained outwash gravel, while nearby the ice wedges in perennially frozen silt were not melted and still exist (Church, Péwé, and Andresen 1965).

Recent work on the habitat of existing ice wedges by scientists in the USSR (Popov 1965, Shumskiy and Vtyurin 1966) should be very useful as a further aid in interpreting fossil ice wedges. Original work by J. B. Brown (1966) and Sellmann (1966) on the geochemistry of ice

4

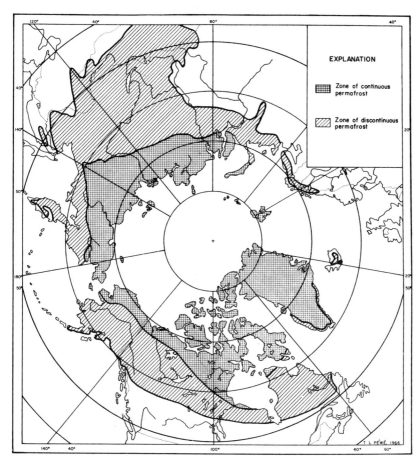

Fig. 1. Distribution of permafrost in the northern hemisphere. Sources: Alaska, T. L. Péwé; Canada, R. J. E. Brown, 1969; Greenland, Weidick, in press; Iceland, Einarsson, Iceland Industrial Research and Development Institute, written communication, 1966; Norway, Andersen, University of Oslo, written communication, 1966; Svensson, Lund University, oral communication, 1966; Sweden, Rapp, 1969; Mongolia and China, Shumskiy, P. A., *et al.*, 1955; USSR, Baranov 1956.

wedges and adjacent sediments will further permit us to understand the processes of the modern periglacial environment.

We commonly find in the periglacial literature that great importance is attached to the depth to which seasonal frost existed in the Pleistocene periglacial zone. If no information is available on the texture of the soil, moisture content, and vegetation and snow cover, as well as depth to the top of permafrost, little importance can be ascribed to the thickness of seasonal frost. Depth of seasonal frost in a small area in central Alaska today, for example, ranges from 1 to 6 metres (Péwé and Holmes 1964), depending upon the above named parameters.

Small-scale patterned ground, the result of sorting of the sediments by frost action, has received extensive study, especially in the laboratory (Corte 1961, 1962, 1966), and these quantitative data should be applicable to the study of now inactive forms. No satisfactory answer is yet forthcoming as to the origin of involutions (*brodelboden*), and therefore their importance as paleoclimatic indicators remains questionable. At present, many scientists still associate involutions with permafrost, with little or no supporting evidence. Again, data of soil types, moisture content, and other information are necessary before we can determine the definite answer as to the origin of these features.

Perhaps most periglacial deposits can be ascribed to solifluction, yet progress in understanding even the basic mechanics of solifluction and the climatic parameters necessary for solifluction is slow. The thorough study of solifluction by Washburn and associates (1965) will go a long way towards bettering our understanding of solifluction. The fine works of Williams (1957a, b, 1962), Rapp (1962), and Everett (1966) stress the important quantitative aspects of mass movement, and this information can be extended to include aspects of the Pleistocene environment all over the world.

A feature of which we need to know considerably more is the altiplanation terrace before we can use this landform as a paleoclimatic indicator. Rock glaciers are under detailed study, and we hope in the near future that fossil rock glaciers can be more readily used for paleoclimatic interpretation.

Although loess has been studied for more than 100 years, only few data (Péwé and Holmes 1964, Reger, Péwé, West, and Skarland 1965, Péwé, Hopkins, and Giddings 1965, p. 362.) are available for detailed evaluation of rates of accumulation or even of the environment in which modern loess forms.

Many of the papers in this volume present new information of the modern periglacial zone, information sorely needed for our thorough understanding of the paleo-periglacial zone. Perhaps of even more interest is the fact that many of the leading students of features in the Pleistocene periglacial zones of Europe and North America were able to spend many days of discussion and thought with fellow scientists familiar with the active periglacial processes in the continental periglacial environment of central Alaska.

When results of current systematic studies in the modern periglacial environment become available, and when this information is applied to the interpretation of processes in the Pleistocene periglacial zone, we shall be in a much more favourable position to reconstruct climatic conditions of the Pleistocene Epoch.

REFERENCES CITED

BARANOV, I. Y., 1956, Map showing distribution of permafrost in the USSR *in* Tystovitch, N. A., 1958, Izd. Ak. Nauk. USSR (in Russian).

BLACK, R. F., 1964, Periglacial studies in the United States 1959-1963: Biuletyn Peryglacjalny, nr. 14, p. 5-29.

BLANCKENHORN, M., 1896, Theorie der Bewegungen des Erdbodens: Deutsch. Geol. Gesell., Zeitsch., v. 48, p. 382-400.

BROWN, J. B., 1966, Ice-wedge chemistry and related frozen ground processes, Barrow, Alaska: Proc. Intern. Permafrost Conf., Nat. Acad. Sci.-Nat. Res. Council Pub. No. 1287, p. 94-98.

BROWN, R. J. E., 1969, Factors influencing discontinuous permafrost in Canada, p. 11-53 *in* Péwé, T. L., *Editor*, The periglacial environment: past and present: Montreal, McGill Univ. Press, 488 p.

CHURCH, R. E., PÉWÉ, T. L., and ANDRESEN, M. J., 1965, Origin and environmental significance of large-scale patterned ground, Donnelly Dome area, Alaska: US Army Cold Regions Research and Engineering Lab. Res. Rept. 159, 75 p.

COOK, F. A., 1964, Periglacial research in Canada: 1954-63: A selected bibliography: Biuletyn Peryglacjalny, nr. 14, p. 31-40.

CORTE, A. E., 1961, The frost behavior of soils: Part I, Vertical sorting: US Army Cold Regions Research and Engineering Lab. Res. Rept. 85, 22 p.

———, 1962, The frost behavior of soils: Laboratory and field data for a new concept: Part II, Horizontal sorting: US Army Cold Regions Research and Engineering Lab. Res. Rept. 85, 20 p.

———, 1966, Particle sorting by repeated freezing and thawing: Biuletyn Peryglacjalny, nr. 15, p. 175-240.

DINES, H. G., HOLLINGWORTH, S. E., EDWARDS, W., BUCHAN, S., and WELCH, F. B. A., 1940, The mapping of head deposits: Geol. Mag., v. 77, p. 198-226.

DYLIK, J., 1966, Problems of ice-wedge structures and frost fissure polygons: Biuletyn Peryglacjalny, nr. 15, p. 241-292.

DYLIKOWA, ANNA, 1964, Etat des recherches périglaciaires en Pologne: Biuletyn Peryglacjalny, nr. 14, p. 41-60.

EVERETT, K. R., 1966, Instruments for measuring mass-wasting: Proc. Intern. Permafrost Conf., Nat. Acad. Sci.-Nat. Res. Council Pub. No. 1287, p. 136-137.

HOLMES, G. W., HOPKINS, D. M., and FOSTER, H. L., 1966, Distribution and age of pingos of interior Alaska: Proc. Intern. Permafrost Conf., Nat. Acad. Sci.-Nat. Res. Council Pub. No. 1287, p. 88-93.

KERR, W. C., 1881, On the action of frost in the arrangement of superficial earthy material: Amer. Jour. Sci., v. 21, p. 345-358.

LACHENBRUCH, A. H., 1962, Mechanics of thermal contraction cracks and ice-wedge polygons in permafrost: Geol. Soc. America Spec. Paper 70, 69 p.

——, 1966, Contraction theory of ice-wedge polygons: A qualitative discussion: Proc. Intern. Permafrost Conf., Nat. Acad. Sci.-Nat. Res. Council Pub. No. 1287, p. 63-71.

LACHENBRUCH, A. H., GREEN, G. W., and MARSHALL, B. V., 1966, Permafrost and the geothermal regimes, p. 149-163 in Wilimovsky, N. J., Editor, 1966, Environment of the Cape Thompson region, Alaska, US Atomic Energy Commission, 1250 p.

LOZINSKI, W., 1909, Uber die mechanische Verwitterung der Sandsteine im germassigten Klima: Acad. Sci. de Cracovie (Cl. des Sci., Math. et Nat.) Bull., p. 1-25.

MARKOV, K. K., and POPOV, A. I., 1960, Periglacial phenomena on the territory of the USSR: Moscow University Press, Moscow, 290 p.

NANGERONI, GIUSEPPE, 1964, Rapports sur les études et les travaux concernant les phénomenes périglaciaires apparus en Italie de 1956 à 1963: Biuletyn Periglacjalny, nr. 14, p. 61-65.

NATIONAL ACADEMY OF SCIENCES–NATIONAL RESEARCH COUNCIL, 1966, Proceedings International Permafrost Conference, 11-15 November, 1963, Lafayette, Indiana: Nat. Acad. Sci.–Nat. Res. Council Pub. No. 1287, 563 p.

PÉWÉ, T. L., 1966a, Ice-wedges in Alaska: Classification, distribution, and climatic significance: Proc. Intern. Permafrost Conf., Nat. Acad. Sci.–Nat. Res. Council Pub. No. 1287, p. 76-81.

——, 1966b, Paleoclimatic significance of fossil ice wedges: Biuletyn Peryglacjalny, nr. 15, p. 65-73.

PÉWÉ, T. L., FERRIANS, OSCAR, NICHOLS, D. R., and KARLSTROM, T. N. V., 1965, Guidebook Field Conference F, Alaska, VII Intern. Cong. INQUA, 141 p.

PÉWÉ, T. L., and HOLMES, G. W., 1964, Geology of the Mt. Hayes D-4 Quadrangle, Alaska: US Geological Survey, Misc. Geol. Invest. Map no. I-394.

PÉWÉ, T. L., HOPKINS, D. M., and GIDDINGS, J. L., 1965, The Quaternary geology and archaeology of Alaska, p. 355-374 in Wright, H. E., Jr., and Frey, D. G., Editors, The Quaternary of the United States: Princeton Univ. Press, 922 p.

PISSART, A., 1964, Avancement des recherches périglaciaires en Belgique de 1956 à 1963: Biuletyn Peryglacjalny, nr. 14, p. 67-74.

POPOV, A. I., 1965, Editor, Underground ice, Issues I and II: Moscow University Press, Moscow, 218 p. and 184 p.

RAPP, ANDERS, 1961, Recent development of mountain slopes in Karkevagge and surroundings, Northern Scandinavia: Geog. Ann., v. 42, p. 71-200.

——, 1962, Karkevagge: Some recordings of mass-movements in the northern Scandinavian Mountains: Biuletyn Peryglacjalny, nr. 11, p. 287-309.

RAPP, ANDERS, and RUDBERG, STEN, 1964, Studies on periglacial phenomena in Scandinavia, 1960-1963: Biuletyn Peryglacjalny, nr. 14, p. 75-89.

RAPP, ANDERS, and ANNERSTEN, LENNART, 1969, Permafrost and tundra polygons in northern Sweden, p. 65-91 in Péwé, T. L., Editor, The periglacial environment: past and present: Montreal, McGill Univ. Press, 488 p.

RAYNAL, RENÉ, 1964, Recherches de géomorphologie périglaciaire en Afrique du Nord: Biuletyn Peryglacjalny, nr. 14, p. 91-98.

REGER, R. D., PÉWÉ, T. L., WEST, F. H., and SKARLAND, IVAR, 1965, Geology and archeology of the Yardang Flint Station, central Alaska Range, Alaska: Anthro. Papers, Univ. Alaska, v. 12, no. 2, p. 92-100.

SEKYRA, JOSEF, 1964, On the periglacial investigation in Czechoslovakia (1955-63): Biuletyn Peryglacjalny, nr. 14, p. 99-108.

SELLMANN, P. V., in press, Geochemistry and ground ice structures: An aid in interpreting a Pleistocene section, Alaska: Geol. Soc. America Spec. Paper.

SHUMSKIY, P. A., SCHVETZOV, P. F., and DOSTOVOLOV, B. N., 1955, Ice veins, p. 12-32 in Special applications of engineering geology in reconnaissance of underground veins in the regions of their occurrence: USSR Acad. Sci. Pub.

SHUMSKIY, P. A., and VTYURIN, B. I., 1966, Underground ice: Proc. Intern. Permafrost Conf., Nat. Acad. Sci.–Nat. Res. Council Pub. No. 1287, p. 108-113.

SMITH, H. T. U., 1949, Physical effects of Pleistocene climatic changes in nonglaciated areas: Eolian phenomena, frost action, and stream terracing: Geol. Soc. Amer. Bull., v. 60, p. 1485-1516.

———, 1962, Periglacial frost features and related phenomena in the United States: Biuletyn Peryglacjalny, nr. 11, p. 325-342.

TEDROW, J. C. F., 1962, Morphological evidence of frost action in arctic soils: Biuletyn Peryglacjalny, nr. 11, p. 343-352.

TROLL, CARL, 1948, Der subnivale oder periglaziale Zyklus der Denudation (The subnival or periglacial cycle of denudation): Erdkunde, v. 2, p. 1-21. (English translation by H. E. Wright, Jr., and Clarke Thomson, University of Minnesota, 1956).

WASHBURN, A. L., 1956, Classification of patterned ground and review of suggested origins: Geol. Soc. America Bull., v. 67, p. 823-865.

———, 1965, Geomorphic and vegetational studies in the Mesters Vig district, northeast Greenland: Meddel. om Grønland, bd. 166, nr. 1, p. 1-60.

WATERS, R. S., 1964, Great Britain: Biuletyn Peryglacjalny, nr. 14, p. 109-110.

WEIDICK, A., in press, Observations on some Holocene glacier fluctuations in West Greenland: Meddel. om Grønland.

WILLIAMS, P. J., 1957a, Some investigations into solifluction features in Norway: Geog. Jour., v. 123, no. 1, p. 47.

———, 1957b, The direct recording of solifluction movement: Amer. Jour. Sci., v. 225, p. 705-715.

———, 1962, Quantitative investigations of soil movement in frozen ground phenomena: Biuletyn Peryglacjalny, nr. 11, p. 353-360.

ZEUNER, F. E., 1945, The Pleistocene period: Its climate, chronology, and faunal successions: The Ray Society, London, 322 p.

FACTORS INFLUENCING DISCONTINUOUS PERMAFROST IN CANADA

R. J. E. BROWN
Division of Building Research
National Research Council
Ottawa, Canada

ABSTRACT. Discontinuous permafrost forms a broad transition between areas with no permafrost and the continuous zone. From a study of available literature and field observations over the past decade, the approximate distribution and nature of the discontinuous zone in Canada has been established. East of Hudson Bay, discontinuous permafrost extends from the Laurentide Scarp, north to about 58° north. Between Hudson Bay and the Cordillera it extends northwesterly in a broad band several hundred miles wide to include the northern portions of the provinces and the southern portions of the territories. In the Cordillera, permafrost occurs at high elevations south to the 49th parallel and farther. Climatic control of the broad pattern of permafrost distribution is borne out by its relation to mean annual air temperature. Between the 30°F and 25°F mean annual air isotherms permafrost islands vary from a few feet to several acres in extent, to a maximum of about 50 feet in thickness, having temperatures between 30°F and 32°F. Between the 25°F and 20°F mean annual air isotherms, permafrost is widespread, 50 to 200 feet thick having temperatures down to approximately 23°F. Permafrost is virtually continuous north of the 20°F mean annual air isotherm. Climate is responsible generally for the existence of permafrost but the distribution of individual islands is conditioned by variations in microclimate and terrain features such as relief, drainage, vegetation, and snow cover. The extent of permafrost fluctuates in response to changes in climatic and terrain features with time. The permafrost in Canada's discontinuous zone probably formed after the final retreat of Pleistocene ice sheets or post-glacial inundations, except in the unglaciated portion of the Yukon Territory where its formation was periglacial.

RÉSUMÉ. Les zones discontinues de pergélisol constituent une vaste région de transition entre les zones sans pergélisol et la zone de pergélisol continue. On a pu établir la nature et la distribution approximative de la zone discontinue au Canada par une étude de la bibliographie disponible et des observations sur le terrain au cours de la décennie écoulée. A l'est de la Baie d'Hudson, une zone discontinue de pergélisol s'étend au nord de l'escarpement du Bouclier laurentien jusqu'aux environs de 58° de latitude nord. Entre la Baie d'Hudson et les Montagnes rocheuses la zone s'étend vers le nord-ouest en une bande large de plusieurs centaines de milles qui englobe les parties septentrionales des provinces des prairies et les parties méridionales des Territoires du Nord-Ouest. Dans les Montagnes rocheuses, le pergélisol occupe certains endroits à haute altitude au sud du 49° parallèle et au delà. L'influence du climat sur la configuration générale de la distribution du pergélisol est confirmée par ses rapports avec la température moyenne annuelle de l'air. Entre les isothermes moyens annuels 30°F et 25°F, les îlots de pergélisol varient de quelques pieds carrés à plusieurs acres de superficie, atteignent jusqu'à 50 pieds d'épaisseur et ont une température allant de 30 à 32°F. Entre les isothermes 25°F et 20°F de température moyenne annuelle de l'air, le pergélisol est très répandu, d'une épaisseur atteignant 50 à 200 pieds, et sa température s'abaisse jusqu'aux environs de 23°F. Le pergélisol se présente de façon pratiquement continue au nord de l'isotherme 20°F de température moyenne annuelle. L'existence du pergélisol dépend généralement du climat, mais la répartition individuelle des îlots découle des divers micro-climats et des traits physiques du terrain, tels que le relief, le réseau d'écoulement des eaux, la nature de la végétation et la couverture nivale. L'étendue occupée par le pergélisol varie selon les changements affectant le climat et le terrain au cours du temps. Le pergélisol s'est probablement formé dans sa zone canadienne d'étendue discontinue après le dernier recul des calottes glaciaires du Pléistocène ou après les inondations post-glaciaires, sauf dans la partie non affectée par la glaciation du Territoire du Yukon, où la formation du pergélisol est antérieure à la période glaciaire.

CONTENTS

INTRODUCTION

Discontinuous permafrost forms a broad transition between areas with no permafrost and the continuous zone. The discontinuous permafrost zone is a product of Quaternary periglacial processes. It comprises the southern fringe of the circumpolar region affected by contemporary periglacial processes, and forms a broad transition between temperate and cold environments, displaying characteristics of both. Most of the permafrost territory in the western hemisphere is located in Canada, the discontinuous zone extending in a broad band more than 3,000 miles (5,000 km) from Labrador to British Columbia and Yukon Territory. From field observations and a study of available literature over the past decade, the approximate distribution and nature of the discontinuous zone in Canada has been established. This paper describes the present state of knowledge of the distribution of discontinuous permafrost in Canada and factors influencing it.

DEFINITION OF PERMAFROST

Permafrost, or perennially frozen ground, is defined exclusively on the basis of temperature, referring to the thermal condition under which earth materials (mineral and organic soils, and rock) exist at a temperature below 32 °F (0 °C) continuously for a number of years (Sumgin 1940, Muller 1945, Shvetsov 1959, Pihlainen 1963). Permafrost includes ground which freezes in one winter, remains frozen through the following summer and into the next winter. This is the minimum limit for the duration of permafrost; it may be only a few inches or centimetres in thickness. This definition includes "climafrost" (Radforth 1963) and the Russian term "pereletok" (Sumgin 1940, Muller 1945). At the other end of the scale is permafrost which is thousands of years old and hundreds of feet or metres thick. The mode of formation of such old and thick permafrost is identical to that of permafrost only one year old and a few inches or centimetres thick. In the case of the former, even a small negative heat imbalance each year results in a thin layer being added annually to the permafrost. After several thousands of years have elapsed, this annually repeated process can produce a layer of permafrost hundreds of feet or metres thick. Permafrost is not permanently frozen especially in the southern portion of the permafrost region where it is thin and close to thawing; it may dissipate after a few years' existence.

DEFINITION OF DISCONTINUOUS PERMAFROST

In the discontinuous zone, there are discontinuities or thawed zones in the permafrost. American and Russian investigators have defined the discontinuous zone in Alaska and the Soviet Union, respectively, on the basis of temperature, the temperature of the permafrost just below the depth of seasonal variation being above 23°F (−5°C) (Ferrians 1964, Bondarev 1959). There is not a sufficient number of ground temperature observations for Canada's permafrost region to enable a delineation of the discontinuous zone on a temperature basis. Until temperature readings are available, the discontinuous zone can be delineated only qualitatively on the basis of horizontal and vertical extent.

LOCATION AND NATURE OF THE DISCONTINUOUS PERMAFROST ZONE

From a study of available literature and field observations over the past decade, the approximate distribution and nature of the discontinuous zone in Canada has been established (Fig. 1). In the southern fringe, permafrost occurs in scattered islands a few feet (metres) to several acres (hectares) in extent, and a few inches (centimetres) to a few feet (metres) thick. Its temperature is only a few tenths of a degree below 32°F (0°C) and it is confined to specific types of terrain. Northward it becomes increasingly widespread and thicker. Its temperature is several degrees below 32°F (0°C) down to about 23°F (−5°C) and it is associated with a variety of terrain types.

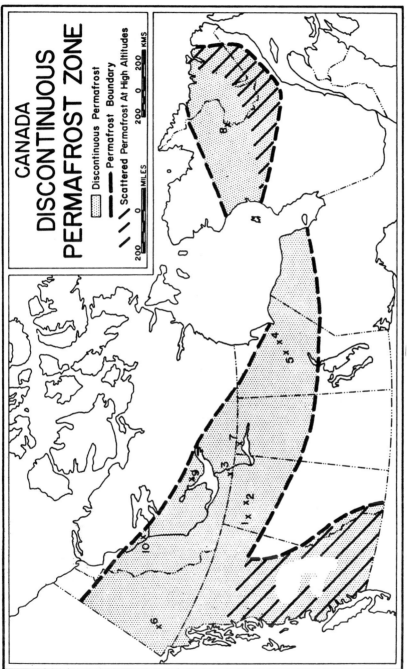

FIG. 1. Discontinuous permafrost map of Canada. (Numbers refer to ground temperature observations listed in Table 1.)

15

The southern and northern limits of this zone are known only approximately. The southern limit[1] refers to the most southerly occurrence of any known permafrost (excluding erratically distributed bodies of relic permafrost which occur at depth), and thus includes extensive areas where no permafrost exists. Similarly, the northern limit refers to the most northerly extent of areas that remain thawed throughout the year, this including areas where permafrost is widespread, occurring virtually everywhere beneath the ground surface.

There is little information on the southern limit of the discontinuous permafrost zone east of Hudson Bay. There are few field observations and the situation is complicated by the hilly to mountainous relief which provides many scattered areas at high altitudes suitable for the existence of permafrost. The authors of previous maps showing permafrost distribution in Canada have included the location of the continuous and discontinuous zones in Labrador-Ungava, but their locations were based largely on speculation, with little regard or knowledge of climatic and terrain conditions (Black 1950, Brown 1960). A more realistic estimate of the location of the discontinuous zone east of Hudson Bay was presented by Ives (1962). He postulated that the southern boundary of discontinuous permafrost probably lies as far south as the Laurentide Scarp which extends parallel to the north shore of the Gulf of St. Lawrence 15 to 30 miles (24 to 48 km) inland; permafrost should occur in the high mountains of Gaspé and New England, which rise above the tree-line south of the St. Lawrence River. Confirmation of this suggestion awaits field investigations, but the existence of permafrost at the summit of Mount Washington, New Hampshire (6,288 feet, 1,905 m), in the northeastern United States is well known.

West of James Bay, the presently known southern limit of the discontinuous zone lies at about 53° north in the vicinity of the Attawapiskat River, extending northwest to about 54° north in central Saskatchewan and about 56° north in Alberta. In the Cordillera, comprised of mountain ranges, plateaus, and intermontane valleys and trenches, permafrost occurs at high elevations south to the 49th parallel and even farther south into the United States. West of Hudson Bay, information on the distribution of permafrost is variable. In northern Ontario, field observations are scarce and are contained largely in botanical reports (Hustich 1957, Sjörs 1959a, b). Thus the southern limit of discontinuous permafrost may lie south of the above-mentioned 53rd parallel and could extend perhaps even to the south end of James Bay, at 51° north. The location of the southern limit of permafrost is

[1]The southern fringe refers to the southern portion of the discontinuous zone where the permafrost occurs in scattered islands.

known best in the prairie provinces where hundreds of field observations have been made in recent years (Brown 1964, 1965b). Observations in the Cordillera are limited, but the presence of permafrost is confirmed by its existence at high elevations in the western United States (Retzer 1965).

The northern limit of the discontinuous zone is even more difficult to ascertain than the southern limit without many field observations which are presently scarce in Canada. Speculation on the location of the northern limit of discontinuous permafrost (or the southern limit of continuous permafrost) east of Hudson Bay varies considerably. Black (1950) postulated that there is no continuous permafrost in Labrador-Ungava. Jenness (1949) suggested that the southern limit of continuous permafrost is located at about 60° north on the east coast of Hudson Bay extending southeast to Schefferville, Quebec, at 55° north and turning northeast to the Atlantic coast. On the basis of limited field observations from a variety of sources, Brown (1960) showed the northern limit of discontinuous permafrost forming a crescent roughly parallel to Jenness' boundary but lying closer to Ungava Bay in northern Quebec. Despite Black's earlier postulation, permafrost is probably continuous in the northern extremities of Labrador-Ungava. The most recent map of permafrost distribution in Labrador-Ungava shows permafrost to be continuous east and west of the Labrador Trough north of Schefferville (Ives 1962).

West of Hudson Bay it is suggested that the northern limit of the discontinuous zone extends from the vicinity of Churchill, Manitoba (58°46′N, 94°08′), northwest between Great Slave Lake and Great Bear Lake and into the Yukon Territory in the vicinity of Porcupine River at about 68° north.[2] For convenience the discontinuous permafrost zone can be separated into three subdivisions or regions: the subdivision east of Hudson Bay is termed the Eastern Region; the subdivision west of Hudson Bay to the eastern margin of the Cordillera is designated as the Central Region; the Cordillera is termed the Western Region.

INFLUENCE OF CLIMATE ON DISCONTINUOUS PERMAFROST

Climate is basic to the formation of permafrost and is one of the most important factors influencing the existence of this phenomenon. Of all the climatic factors, the temperature of the air is the most readily measured and most directly related to ground heat losses and heat gains.

[2]This coincides with the boundary between the discontinuous and continuous permafrost zones in eastern Alaska (Ferrians 1964).

Observations indicate the existence of a broad relation between mean annual air and ground temperatures in permafrost. Because of the complex energy exchange regime at the ground surface and the snow cover, the mean annual ground temperature is several degrees warmer than the mean annual air temperature. Local terrain conditions cause variations but a value of 6°F (3.3°C) can be used as an average figure. Many investigators have estimated the mean annual air temperature required to produce and maintain a perennially frozen condition in the ground (Brown 1963).

The southern limit of permafrost in Canada coincides roughly with the 30°F (−1.1°C) mean annual air isotherm (Fig. 2) (Thomas 1953). South of this isotherm, permafrost occurrences are rare and of small extent. North of the 25°F (−3.9°C) mean annual air isotherm, it is widespread and occurs in most types of terrain. On the basis of available field observations it is suggested that the northern limit of the discontinuous zone corresponds roughly with the 20°F (−6.7°C) mean annual air isotherm.[3] In the southern fringe between the 30°F (−1.1°C) and 25°F (−3.9°C) mean annual air isotherms, permafrost is restricted to the drier portions of peatlands and the slopes of these depressions because of the peculiar thermal properties of the peat. Isolated bodies of permafrost also occur on some north-facing slopes and at depth, but their distribution is erratic and usually they cannot be detected from surface features. South of the 30°F (−1.1°C) isotherm, permafrost occurs rarely, even in peatlands, because the climate is too warm. In the vicinity of the 25°F (−3.9°C) isotherm, the average value of the difference between the mean annual air and ground temperatures of 6°F (−3.3°C) obtains and the mean annual ground temperature is between 31°F (−0.6°C) and 32°F (0°C) in most types of terrain. Thus, permafrost is widespread because the climate is sufficiently cool.

Ground temperature observations are available from several locations in the discontinuous permafrost zone. At some stations where the difference is considerably greater than 6°F (3.3°C), the ground temperature measurements were taken at shallow depths well above the depth of zero annual amplitude (Table 1, Fig. 1).

In the Eastern and Western Regions there is a steady decrease in mean annual air temperature with increasing elevation which produces a vertical zonation in the distribution of permafrost. Although field

[3]If the American and Russian ground temperature boundary of 23°F (−5°C) between discontinuous and continuous permafrost applies in Canada, the northern limit of the discontinuous zone may correspond roughly with the 17°F (−8.3°C) mean annual air isotherm. Confirmation or rejection of this proposal awaits further field observations.

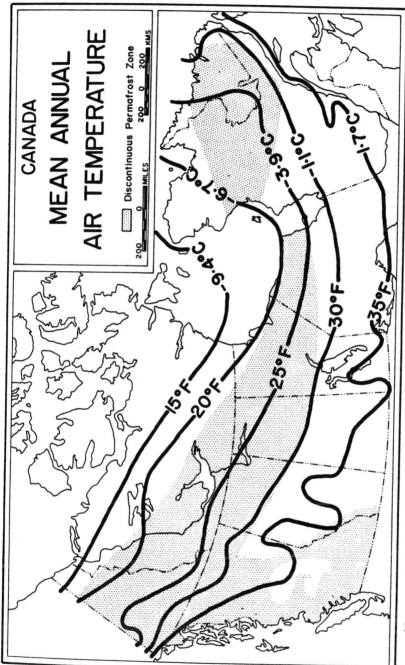

CANADA

MEAN ANNUAL AIR TEMPERATURE

▨ Discontinuous Permafrost Zone

MILES
200   0   200

KMS
200   0   200

-6.7°C

-4.4°C

-3.9°C

-1.1°C

-1.7°C

15°F

20°F

25°F

30°F

35°F

Fig. 2.   Mean annual air isotherm map of Canada.

TABLE I

MEAN ANNUAL AIR AND GROUND TEMPERATURES IN DISCONTINUOUS PERMAFROST ZONE OF CANADA

(Location of Stations Shown on Fig. 1)

Location	Mean Annual Air Temperature	Mean Annual Ground Temperature and Depth	Approximate Difference Between Mean Air and Mean Ground Temperatures
1. Keg River, Alberta (57°47′N, 117°50′W)	31°F −0.6°C	A few tenths below 32°F (5 ft) A few tenths below 0°C (1.5 m)	1°F 0.5°C
2. Fort Vermillion, Alberta (58°23′N, 116°03′W)	28.2°F −2.1°C	39.8°F (surface), 38.9°F (5 ft) (no peat) 4.3°C (surface), 3.6°C (1.5 m)	11°F 6°C
3. Fort Smith, Northwest Territories (60°01′N, 111°58′W)	26.2°F −3.1°C	Approx. 31.8°F (15 ft) Approx. −0.1°C (4.6 m)	6°F 3°C
4. Kelsey, Manitoba (56°02′N, 96°32′W)	25.5°F −3.6°C	30.5°F (surface), 31.5°F (30 ft) −0.8°C (surface), −0.3°C (9.1 m)	5–6°F 3°C
5. Thompson, Manitoba (55°45′N, 97°50′W)	24.9°F −3.9°C	31°F (surface), 32°F (25 ft) −0.6°C (surface), 0°C (7.6 m)	6–7°F 3.5°C
6. Aishihik, Yukon Territory (61°39′N, 137°29′W)	24.5°F −4.1°C	28.3°F (20 ft) −2.1°C (6.1 m)	4°F 2°C
7. Uranium City, Saskatchewan (59°34′N, 108°37′W)	24°F −4.4°C	31°F (surface), 32°F (30 ft) −0.6°C (surface), 0°C (9.1 m)	7–8°F 4°C
8. Schefferville, Quebec (54°49′N, 66°41′W)	23.8°F −4.5°C	30°F (25 ft), 31.5°F (190 ft) −1.1°C (7.6 m), −0.3°C (57.9 m)	6–8°F 3.8°C
9. Yellowknife, Northwest Territories (62°28′N, 114°27′W)	22.2°F −5.5°C	33.0°F (2.5 ft), 31.4°F (8.5 ft) 0.6°C (0.8 m), −0.3°C (2.6 m)	9–11°F 5.5°C
10. Norman Wells, Northwest Territories (65°18′N, 126°49′W)	20.8°F −6.2°C	26°F (50 ft), 28.5°F (100 ft) −3.3°C (15 m), −1.9°C (30 m)	5–8°F 3.5°C
11. Ottawa, Ontario (45°28′N, 75°38′ W)	41.6°F 5.3°C	47.1°F (20 ft) 8.4°C (6.1 m)	5–6°F 3°C

observations are few, it is assumed that the distribution of permafrost changes vertically up each mountain slope in response to the decreasing mean annual air temperature in the same manner as it changes horizontally from south to north through the discontinuous zone. Thus, permafrost occurrences are rare below the level of the 30°F (−1.1°C) mean annual air isotherm. Between the elevations of the 30°F (−1.1°C) and 25°F (−3.9°C) isotherms, permafrost is patchy, including islands in peat bogs and on north-facing slopes, and erratically distributed bodies at depth which are relict. Above the 25°F (−3.9°C) mean annual air isotherm, permafrost is widespread and found in various types of terrain; above the 20°F (−6.7°C) isotherm it is continuous.

Within the broad pattern of permafrost distribution imposed by air temperature, radiation is a climatic factor which produces significant effects. The amount of cloud cover is one factor affecting the amount of solar energy that arrives at the ground surface. Insolation totals are lower in the Eastern Region than at corresponding latitudes in the Central and Western Regions because of the higher incidence of cloud cover resulting from the maritime influence of Hudson Bay and the Atlantic Ocean. The effect of this regional variation on the distribution of permafrost has not been studied in Canada. In Alaska, along the Gulf of Alaska coast and southwest into the Aleutian Islands, heavy summer cloud cover is partly responsible for small isolated patches of permafrost occurring in peat bogs even where the regional mean annual air temperature exceeds 32°F (0°C) (Ferrians 1964).

Microclimatic factors are also very important in the distribution of permafrost in the discontinuous zone. Net radiation, evapotranspiration-evaporation, and conduction-convection are all elements of the energy exchange regime at the ground surface. Although they are climatic in origin, their contribution to the thermal regime of the ground is determined by the nature of the ground surface and thus can be considered as terrain factors.

INFLUENCE OF TERRAIN ON DISCONTINUOUS PERMAFROST

The distribution of permafrost in the discontinuous permafrost zone is related broadly to climate, as discussed in the previous section. Within this general pattern, local variations in the occurrence of permafrost, the extent of permafrost islands, depth to the permafrost table, and thickness of permafrost are caused by differences in terrain conditions.

Physiographic regions

The Canadian (Precambrian) Shield includes all of the Eastern Region and a belt several hundred miles or kilometres wide in the Central Region between the Hudson Bay Lowland and the Interior Plains (Fig. 3) (*Atlas of Canada* 1957). The terrain consists of rock knobs interspersed with poorly drained depressions. Soil cover on the rock knobs is generally thin or absent, consisting of till and other glacially deposited soils. The same soils occur in the depression and are overlain by peat. In the southern fringe of the discontinuous zone, permafrost islands occur in the better drained portions of bogs and peatlands. In the northern portion of the discontinuous zone permafrost is more widespread, occurring in other types of terrain. Variations within the Shield in Labrador-Ungava are described in the section on relief.

The Hudson Bay Lowland in northern Ontario and northeastern Manitoba comprises the smallest physiographic region of the discontinuous permafrost zone. It is a low, flat area, and beach ridges marking the limits of postglacial marine submergence are the only major relief features. Between river valleys, drainage is poor. Soils consist of thick peat deposits overlying marine clays and silts. Local microrelief features include spruce islands, palsas, peat plateaus, ridges, and hummocks. Permafrost occurs in scattered patches mostly in these better drained microrelief features (Sjörs 1959*a*, *b*, 1961).

The Interior Plains lie between the Precambrian Shield and the Cordillera in western Saskatchewan, Alberta, and northeastern British Columbia including the Mackenzie River valley. The relief is rolling with isolated highlands and the soils are predominantly fine-grained. In the southern fringe of the discontinuous zone, permafrost occurs in scattered patches in peatlands; further north it becomes more widespread.

The Cordillera or Western Region is mountainous with plateaus, intermontane valleys, and trenches. The distribution of permafrost is complicated by a vertical zonation with variations between north- and south-facing slopes, in addition to the usual increase in horizontal extent and thickness towards the northern portion of the discontinuous zone.

Glacial geology

The entire discontinuous permafrost zone was glaciated during the Pleistocene, except for the western portion of Yukon Territory (Fig. 4) (*Atlas of Canada* 1957). It is probable that permafrost formed initially during the cold period preceeding glaciation. While the area was ice-covered, the temperature at the bottom of the ice determined the thermal regime of the underlying ground. If the temperature at the bottom of an ice cap is 32 °F (0 °C), as generally suggested, previously existing permafrost in the underlying ground would dissipate over a long period

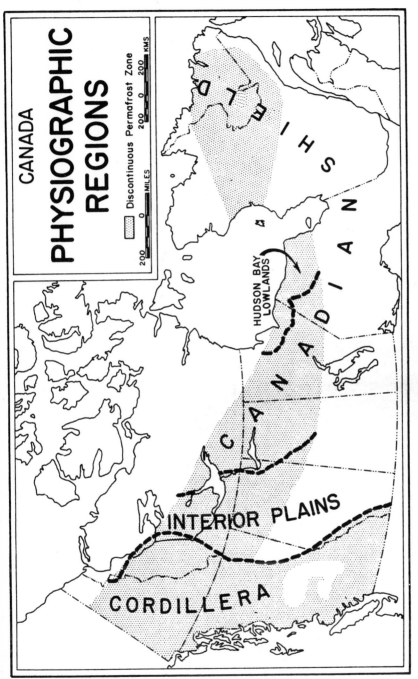

FIG. 3. Physiographic regions map of Canada.

CANADA

PHYSIOGRAPHIC REGIONS

Discontinuous Permafrost Zone

SHIELD

CANADIAN

HUDSON BAY LOWLANDS

INTERIOR PLAINS

CORDILLERA

24

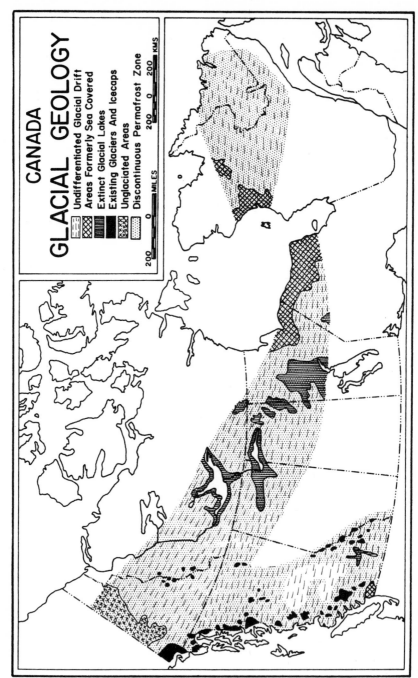

FIG. 4. Glacial geology map of Canada.

of time; new permafrost would not form during the period of ice cover. It is suggested that temperatures below 32°F (0°C) occur at the bottom of "cold" glaciers in arctic regions beneath which permafrost could be preserved or even formed. After glacial retreat, permafrost would form again in exposed areas but not beneath areas submerged by marine and lacustrine inundations. In fact, any permafrost formed under the ice or preserved from the cool period immediately preceding glaciation would dissipate beneath postglacial inundations (Lake Agassiz, Lake Athabasca, Great Slave Lake, Great Bear Lake). Permafrost would form in areas of marine and lacustrine submergence after the water bodies disappeared. In western Yukon Territory, which was unglaciated, the permafrost could have formed during the cold period at the beginning of the Pleistocene.

Thus, there is probably great variation in the age of permafrost in Canada depending on the glacial history of the area. The oldest permafrost could be more than one hundred thousand years old in the Yukon Territory and the youngest permafrost dating from the glacial period could be only a few thousand years old, such as in the centre of Labrador-Ungava where the last remnants of glacial ice melted only about 3,000 years ago.

Relief

East of Hudson Bay in the Eastern Region of the discontinuous permafrost zone, the relief is hilly to mountainous (Fig. 5) (*Atlas of Canada* 1957). The region is bounded on the south by the Laurentide Scarp which extends parallel to the north shore of the Gulf of St. Lawrence 15 to 30 miles (24 to 48 km) inland. North of this escarpment lies a complex mosaic of plateaus, uplands (massifs), ranges, and troughs. Elevations vary from sea level to 500 feet (152 m) along the Hudson Bay, Hudson Strait, and Atlantic coasts, to more than 3,000 feet (914 m) in the interior to more than 5,000 feet (1,524 m) in the Torngat Mountains in northeastern Labrador. Summits in the interior which rise to more than 3,000 feet (914 m) include the Otish Mountains (52°N, 70°W) and Mealy Mountains (54°N, 59°W). Little is known of the distribution of permafrost in this region. It occurs probably at high elevations south to the Laurentide Scarp (Ives 1962), that is, islands of permafrost in peat bogs in the zones bounded by the 30°F (−1.1°C) and 25°F (−6.7°C) mean annual air isotherms, and permafrost in various types of terrain above the 25° F (−6.7°C) isotherm. Ives (1962) postulates that islands of relic permafrost lying at depth could be encountered anywhere north of the Laurentide Scarp.

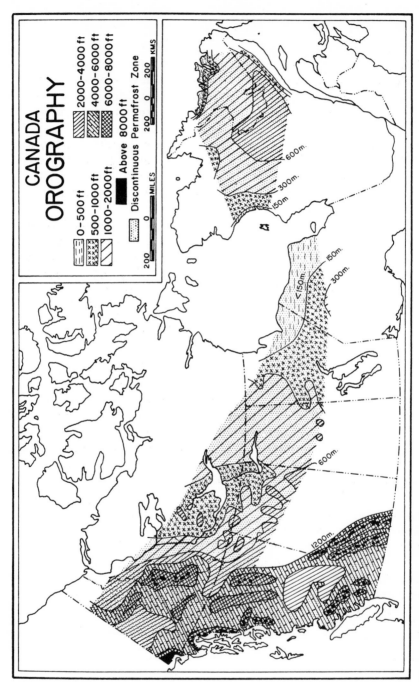

Fig. 5. Orography map of Canada.

The decrease of mean annual air temperature with elevation at the rate of about 1°F/300 feet (1°C/164 m) is illustrated by the situation at Schefferville, in the centre of the Labrador-Ungava peninsula. The mean annual air temperature in 1960 at the townsite (1,680 feet or 512 m above sea level) was 26.3°F (−3.2°C) (Davies 1962). On the nearby ridge summit 2,500 feet (750 m) above sea level where permafrost exists, the mean annual air temperature in 1960 was 23.5°F (−4.7°C). The ten-year average at the townsite for 1949-59 is 23.8°F (−4.6°C) and on the ridge summit it is probably about 2.5°F (1.4°C) less. Although the mean annual air temperature at the townsite is below 25°F (−6.7°C), the absence of permafrost may be caused by the lack of peat bogs with sufficiently dry conditions and high snowfall which counteracts the effects of low winter air temperatures. The thickness of permafrost on the ridge summit exceeds 200 feet (61 m).

There are few air temperature observations in the interior of the Eastern Region. Detailed terrain observations are also scanty. Thus, any discussion of permafrost distribution must be mostly speculative. Nevertheless Ives' map can be used as a basis for further investigations.

Between James Bay and the Cordillera in the Central Region, the relief is fairly subdued except for isolated highlands; in central Saskatchewan, Thunder Hills (2,230 feet or 680 m) and Wapawekka Hills (above 2,000 feet or 610 m); in central and northern Alberta, the Buffalo Head Hills (2,700 feet or 823 m), Clear Hills (3,600 feet or 1,097 m), Swan Hills (4,000 feet or 1,219 m), Birch Mountains (2,765 feet, or 843 m), and Cariboo Mountains (3,047 feet or 929 m). Permafrost occurs in peat bogs on the summits of the latter two highlands. The situation on the others is not known, although it is unlikely that there is permafrost on the above-mentioned highlands in Saskatchewan which are several hundred feet or metres lower.

In the Cordillera, the relief is mountainous. Elevations vary from 4,000 feet (1,219 m) to mountain peaks rising more than 10,000 feet (3,048 m) above sea level. The decrease of mean annual air temperature with elevation at the rate of about 1°F/300 feet (1°C/164 m) is illustrated by an example from southern British Columbia. The mean annual air temperature at the summit of Old Glory Mountain (7,700 feet, 2,347 m) at 49°09′N, 117°55′W is 28.4°F (−2.0°C). At nearby Rossland (3,305 feet or 1,007 m) it is 42.9°F (−6.1°C). At Garibaldi Park (49° 58′N, 123° 00′ W), permafrost occurs at about 6,000 feet (1,829 m) (Mathews 1955). At Cassiar, near the 60th parallel, no permafrost occurs at the townsite (3,500 feet or 1,067 m above sea level); just below 4,500 feet (1,372 m), permafrost is patchy and above 4,500 feet (1,372 m) it becomes widespread (Fig. 6). The mean annual air tem-

FIG. 6. Section of townsite of Cassiar (northwestern British Columbia) in foreground, 3,500 feet (1,067 m) above sea level—no permafrost. Mountain peak in centre background is about 6,500 feet (1,981 m) above sea level—permafrost begins just below 4,500 feet (1,372 m) above sea level. 18 September 1964.

perature at the town is about 26.9°F (−2.8°C), climatically in the southern fringe of the discontinuous permafrost zone. There are no peat bogs in the townsite which is located on the floor of a gravelly outwash filled valley, and no permafrost has been found there.

Along the Alaska Highway and branch roads south of Whitehorse, Yukon Territory (60°43′N, 135°05′W) permafrost occurs only in certain types of terrain—mostly peat bogs—up to 4,000 feet (1,219 m). It is improbable that permafrost occurs in the Interior Plateau of southern British Columbia because its elevation is less than 4,000 feet (1,219 m). Between 4,000 feet (1,219 m) and 6,000 feet (1,829 m) it appears that permafrost occurs in scattered patches (southern fringe), between 6,000 feet (1,829 m) and 8,000 feet (2,438 m) permafrost is probably discontinuous but widespread, and above 8,000 feet (2,438 m) it is probably continuous. The decrease in mean annual air temperature with latitude would result in decreasing elevations northward of the vertical zones.

Thus, by examining the orographic map in the *Atlas of Canada* (1957), it is possible to delineate approximately the probable locations of permafrost in the Cordillera.

Vegetation

On a regional scale the discontinuous permafrost zone lies generally within the boreal forest and subarctic forest-tundra transition (Fig. 7) (*Atlas of Canada* 1957). In Labrador-Ungava and particularly the Cordillera, there are extensive areas of alpine tundra above the tree-line. Here permafrost is either continuous or discontinuous but widespread.

On a more localized scale, no definite correlations have been found between vegetation species and the occurrence of permafrost. For example, tamarack grows on peatlands that have permafrost and on others that do not. Virtually all permafrost sites in the southern fringe have *Sphagnum*, but this species grows also in non-permafrost peat areas. Lichen grows both on permafrost sites and those having no permafrost.

The mechanisms that can cause permafrost to form in peatlands in the southern fringe appear to be associated with variations through the year in the heat exchange at the surface of the moss and peat (Tyrtikov 1959). During the summer a thin surface layer of dried peat having a low thermal conductivity prevents warming of the underlying soil. During the cold part of the year the peat is saturated from the surface, so that when it freezes its thermal conductivity greatly increases. Because of this the amount of heat transferred in winter from the ground to the atmosphere through the frozen ice-saturated peat is greater than the amount transmitted in summer in the opposite direction through

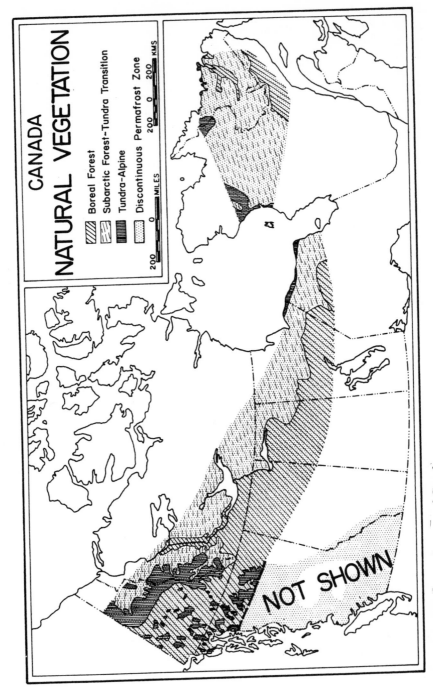

CANADA

NATURAL VEGETATION

- ⫽⫽ Boreal Forest
- ⫻ Subarctic Forest–Tundra Transition
- ▨ Tundra–Alpine
- ⋮ Discontinuous Permafrost Zone

200   0   MILES

200   0   200   KMS

NOT SHOWN

FIG. 7. Natural vegetation map of Canada.

the surface layer of dry peat and underlying wet peat. A considerable amount of heat is also required during the warm period to melt the ice and to warm and evaporate the water. The net result is a negative imbalance of heat and conditions conducive to the formation and preservation of permafrost.

Investigations have shown that the depth of thaw in peat areas is influenced mostly by the insulating cover of peat and moss; differences in thawing indices appear to have little bearing on the depth of thaw. It has been observed that the depth of thaw in peatlands at the southern limit of the discontinuous zone differs little from that in peatlands near the northern limit. Thawing indices (10 year averages) vary from 3,500 degree days in the vicinity of The Pas (53°49′N, 101°15′W) and Flin Flon (54°45′N, 101°50′W), both in Manitoba, to 3,000 degree days at Norman Wells, Northwest Territories, on the Mackenzie River at the northern edge of the discontinuous zone. The depth of thaw in peatlands throughout the discontinuous zone varies within the fairly narrow limits of about 1 foot 9 inches (53 cm) to 2 feet 9 inches (84 cm) averaging about 2 feet (61 cm) despite the range of 500 degree days of thawing (Brown 1964, 1965a).

Permafrost will form and persist in a peat bog as long as the moss and peat are not disturbed. Lichen and even the surface of the moss may be burned several times during the duration of the permafrost. At Chisel Lake, near Flin Flon, Manitoba, a fire in a peat bog burned the lichen and charred the top one inch (2½ cm) thick layer of the *Sphagnum*. The underlying *Sphagnum* and peat were not disturbed and the depth of the permafrost table remained unchanged. At Inuvik, Northwest Territories, located just north of the northern limit of discontinuous permafrost on the Mackenzie River, the removal of trees and brush caused little change in the depth of the permafrost table as long as the moss and peat were not disturbed (Pihlainen 1962).

Some observations have been made of the effects of microclimatic factors and the ground surface energy exchange components on the distribution of discontinuous permafrost. Studies at Norman Wells show that differences in net radiation and evapotranspiration are associated with variations in types of surface vegetation cover, and the depth and temperature of the active layer (Brown 1965a). At the Mer Bleue peat bog near Ottawa, Ontario, air temperatures are several degrees lower than on surrounding higher ground (Williams 1965). The same situation probably prevails in the discontinuous permafrost zone where similar differences result in permafrost occurring only in the peat filled depressions, but not in the surrounding terrain.

The density and height of trees are important aspects of the vegetation influencing the microclimatic effects of near ground surface wind velocities. Wind speeds are lower in areas of dense growth than in areas having stunted scattered trees or no trees. The movement of air represents the transfer of heat from one area to another. In peat bogs the trees are shorter and scattered, and there are numerous open areas which permit higher wind speeds and thus the movement of more heat away from these areas per unit time than from the high areas. Therefore, the possibility of slightly lower air temperatures and ground temperatures because of higher wind speeds is greater than in the high areas (Johnston 1963).

Drainage

The influence of drainage on the existence of permafrost is manifested by the thawing effect that moving or standing water has on permafrost. Along the Mackenzie Highway in northern Alberta, within the discontinuous permafrost zone, extends a 40 mile (64 km) stretch of wet reed and sedge meadows, the water table being either at or just below the surface. It is suspected that the numerous shallow ponds are fed by underground springs from adjacent sand and peat areas (Moss 1953). No permafrost has been encountered in this area because of the widespread poor drainage conditions resulting from the regional relief.

Net radiation

The exposure of sloping ground and the degree of slope determines the amount of solar radiation that will reach the ground surface. The nature of the ground surface influences the amount of solar energy that enters the ground from the atmosphere and affects the underlying permafrost. Some occurrences of permafrost in the discontinuous zone appear to be related to variations in net radiation.

The most obvious illustrations of the relation of permafrost distribution to differences in slope and net radiation occur in the Cordillera. There are numerous east-west oriented valleys in which there is permafrost on the north-facing slope but not on the opposite south-facing slope. Such a valley on the Alaska Highway is illustrated in Figure 8.

On a smaller scale, along the Mackenzie Highway in northern Alberta, permafrost has been encountered on the north-facing slopes of several east-west oriented river valleys tributary to the Hay River, but not on the opposite south-facing slopes. On an even smaller or microscale, otherwise unexplained patches of permafrost have been encountered at Thompson in northern Manitoba. About ten permafrost islands occur in areas having north-facing slopes of only 1° or 2°, which are

Fig. 8. North- and south-facing slopes of a valley at Mile 383.5 on the Alaska Highway in the Cordillera in British Columbia. The slope on the left is north-facing with spruce and poplar tree growth, ground cover of *Sphagnum* and permafrost at shallow depth. The slope on the right is south-facing with poplar and scattered spruce tree growth and no permafrost. 14 September 1964.

imperceptible on the ground or the aerial photographs. The difference between the amount of solar energy received by a north-facing slope of even this low angle compared to a horizontal ground surface or a south-facing slope, particularly when the sun is at a low altitude, is sufficient to contribute to significant differences in the ground thermal regime over a very long period of time (Johnston 1963).

The small patches of permafrost found beneath individual trees may be related to insolation. These patches appear to be related to the shading effect of the tree and may be only a few inches or centimetres thick. Isolated permafrost islands found in the banks of small stream valleys may also be associated with this shading effect. One such patch was found in the Yukon Territory south of Whitehorse, being the only occurrence of permafrost encountered on a 30 mile (50 km) section of road. It was found in a road cut in a small stream valley. The thick scrub willow growing on the banks of the stream possibly provided sufficient shading to promote the persistence of this one patch of permafrost.

Snow cover

Snow cover plays an important role in the distribution of permafrost in the discontinuous zone. A heavy fall and accumulation of snow in the autumn inhibits winter frost penetration and the formation of permafrost. On the other hand, a thick snow cover that persists on the ground in the spring will delay the thawing of underlying frozen ground. In any given area, the relation between these two situations will determine the net effect of the snow cover on the ground thermal regime.

On a regional basis, the southern limit of permafrost on the east coast of Hudson Bay is reported to be in the vicinity of Great Whale River, Quebec (55°17′N, 77°46′W), which is several hundred miles or kilometres north of the southern limit west of James Bay. Hudson Bay seems to have an appreciable effect on the amount of snowfall over the region immediately east of it, especially in the fall and early winter before this body of water becomes ice-covered. Examination of the snowfall records and maps reveals that the snowfall in October to December totalled 60 inches (152 cm) on the east side and only 40 inches (102 cm) on the west side. The insulation provided may help to explain the apparent discrepancy and the conspicuous jump northward of the southern limit of permafrost in crossing James Bay and Hudson Bay (Brown 1960).

Studies at Schefferville, in the centre of Labrador-Ungava, revealed the possibility of snow cover being a dominant factor in controlling permafrost distribution not only in the local area, but over large areas of the Eastern Region of the discontinuous permafrost zone. Variations in snow cover cause temperature variations in the soils far greater than those resulting from vegetation cover (Annersten 1963). Snow depth varies considerably from accumulating to depths of 8 feet (2.4 m) in sheltered tree-covered hollows to less than 1 foot (0.3 m) on exposed ridge summits. On the basis of snow depth measurements and ground temperature observations it was postulated that a snow depth of about 16 inches (40 cm) can be regarded as the critical snow depth for permafrost to survive. Beneath a greater depth no permafrost or a degrading condition prevails (Annersten 1963). Similar variations in snow depth prevail, presumably, in the Cordillera.

Detailed local studies of the influence of snow cover on permafrost islands are lacking. It has been observed, however, that the thickest permafrost in the Hudson Bay Lowland occurs in palsas on which snow cover is thin because of their exposure to wind. In the southern fringe of the permafrost region where permafrost near the surface is restricted to certain areas in peatlands, there may be significant variations in the thickness and duration of snow cover. It may be less in treeless or sparsely forested peatlands than in the densely wooded surrounding high areas. Towards the northern portion of the discontinuous zone, the relative effect of snow cover on the occurrence of permafrost probably diminishes, but it continues to influence the thickness of the active layer and the ground temperatures.

OCCURRENCE OF DISCONTINUOUS PERMAFROST

Southern fringe

In the southern fringe of the discontinuous zone, permafrost is restricted mainly to peatlands (Fig. 9). Other occurrences are associated either with the north-facing slopes of east-west oriented valleys, isolated patches in stream banks apparently associated with increased shading from summer thawing, or bodies, or relic permafrost lying below the depth of winter frost penetration whose presence is unrelated to contemporary factors. The peatlands vary in extent from several acres (hectares) surrounded by rock outcrops, as in the Precambrian Shield (Fig. 10), enclosed by knolls or ridges of mineral soil and of greater extent as in the Interior Plains (Fig. 11), or extending unrestricted for miles or kilometres as in the Hudson Bay Lowland. Microrelief in the peatlands ranges from hummocks 1 foot (0.3 m) high to peat ridges and plateaus which are 3 feet (about 1 m) high to palsas 10 feet (3 m) high.

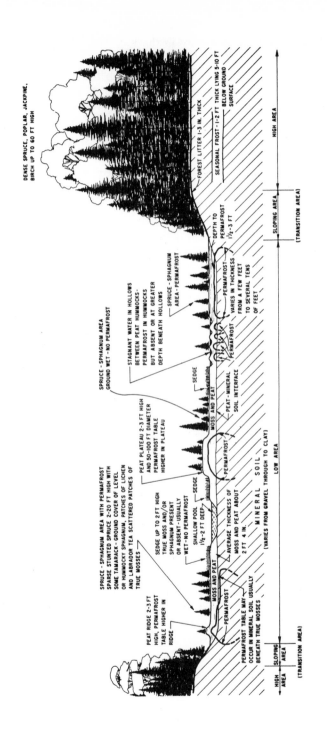

DENSE SPRUCE, POPLAR, JACKPINE, BIRCH UP TO 60 FT HIGH

FOREST LITTER 1–3 IN. THICK

SEASONAL FROST 1–2 FT THICK LYING 5–10 FT BELOW GROUND SURFACE

DEPTH TO PERMAFROST 1½–3 FT

PERMAFROST—VARIES IN THICKNESS FROM A FEW FEET TO SEVERAL TENS OF FEET

PERMAFROST

SPRUCE – SPHAGNUM AREA – PERMAFROST

SPRUCE – SPHAGNUM AREA GROUND WET – NO PERMAFROST

STAGNANT WATER IN HOLLOWS BETWEEN PEAT HUMMOCKS - PERMAFROST IN HUMMOCKS BUT ABSENT OR AT GREATER DEPTH BENEATH HOLLOWS

SPRUCE – SPHAGNUM AREA WITH PERMAFROST SPARSE STUNTED SPRUCE 2–20 FT HIGH WITH SOME TAMARACK - GROUND COVER OF LEVEL OR HUMMOCKY SPHAGNUM, PATCHES OF LICHEN AND LABRADOR TEA SCATTERED PATCHES OF TRUE MOSSES

PEAT PLATEAU 2–3 FT HIGH AND 50–100 FT DIAMETER PERMAFROST TABLE HIGHER IN PLATEAU

SEDGE UP TO 2 FT HIGH TRUE MOSS AND/OR SPHAGNUM PRESENT OR ABSENT – USUALLY WET – NO PERMAFROST

SEDGE

SEDGE

MOSS AND PEAT

PEAT – MINERAL SOIL INTERFACE

PERMAFROST

SHALLOW POOL 1½–2 FT DEEP

PEAT RIDGE 2–3 FT HIGH, PERMAFROST TABLE HIGHER IN RIDGE

AVERAGE THICKNESS OF MOSS AND PEAT ABOUT 2 FT 4 IN.

M I N E R A L   S O I L (VARIES FROM GRAVEL THROUGH TO CLAY)

MOSS AND PEAT

PERMAFROST

PERMAFROST TABLE MAY OCCUR IN MINERAL SOIL USUALLY BENEATH TRUE MOSSES

HIGH AREA

SLOPING AREA

(TRANSITION AREA)

LOW AREA

SLOPING AREA

(TRANSITION AREA)

HIGH AREA

Fig. 9. Profile through typical peat bog in southern fringe of discontinuous zone showing vegetation, drainage, and microrelief, and associated permafrost distribution.

36

Fɪɢ. 10. Peat bog in Precambrian Shield 26 miles (42 km) north of La Ronge, Saskatchewan, in the southern fringe of the discontinuous permafrost zone. It is about 600 feet (182 m) in diameter near the top of a hill flanked by a rock outcrop in the background. The tree growth on the bog is spruce up to 20 feet (6 m) high and the ground vegetation is *Sphagnum*, Labrador tea and scattered lichen patches below which is peat exceeding 7 feet (2.1 m) in thickness. Permafrost is 1 foot, 11 inches (58 cm) thick. 15 September 1963.

FIG. 11. Peat bog in Interior Plains 48 miles (77 km) south of Hay River, NWT.
The tree growth consists of scattered spruce up to 30 feet (9 m) high and the
ground cover is a mosaic of *Sphagnum* and other mosses, lichen, Labrador tea, and
marsh sedge. Peat varies in thickness from 4 to 8 feet (1.2 to 2.4 m). The depth to
the permafrost table is 2 feet, 3 inches (69 cm) and permafrost occurs in scattered
patches. The higher area has jack pine, spruce, and poplar tree growth and no
permafrost. 12 September 1962.

In the discontinuous permafrost zone, extensive peatlands are found in Labrador-Ungava, the Hudson Bay Lowland, northern Alberta, and along the Alaska Highway south of Fort Nelson, British Columbia (58°50'N, 122°35'W).

The predominant tree species in the peatlands is black spruce, with tamarack either mixed with the spruce or occasionally in pure stands, plus willow, alder, and ground birch. Tree growth is scattered and stunted, the tallest individuals growing to about 30 feet (9.1 m). On the surrounding higher areas, tree species include white spruce, jack pine, trembling aspen, balsam, poplar, and scattered white birch with willow and alder undergrowth. The tallest trees grow 80 to 100 feet (24 to 30 m) high in dense stands averaging about 5 feet (1.5 m) between trees. Extensive areas have been burned over. Following a fire, it appears that aspen is the main species to regenerate on medium- to fine-grained soils. Jack pine is the main post-fire species on sandy soils.

In the peatlands, the ground cover consists predominantly of *Sphagnum, Hypnum,* and patches of feather and club mosses, lichen, Labrador tea, and grass. There are also extensive wet sedge meadows. On the surrounding higher areas, the ground vegetation consists of berry plants, grass, Labrador tea, and a discontinuous cover of feather and club mosses, and lichen.

The peat in the peatlands is extremely variable in thickness ranging from a minimum of about 6 inches (15 cm) to a maximum of approximately 20 feet (6 m). In the Central Region, the average thickness for about 300 investigated sites was 3 feet 6 inches (1.1 m). The thickness of peat does not appear to be related to the area of the peatland; many extensive bogs exceeding one square mile (several square kilometres) in area have a peat layer less than 3 feet (1 m) thick in contrast to small enclosed bogs of only a few acres (hectares) with a peat layer exceeding 6 or 10 feet (2 or 3 m). The underlying mineral soil ranges from gravel to clay. The thickness of the peat and the depth of the permafrost table do not have any relation to the grain size of the soil.

In the peatlands, the areal extent of permafrost islands varies from a few feet (metres) to several acres (hectares). The depth to permafrost varies mainly from a minimum depth of 1 foot 6 inches (46 cm) to a maximum depth of about 3 feet (91 cm). At a few locations the depth to permafrost is as much as 5 feet 5 inches (167 cm). The thickness of permafrost varies from a minimum of only a few inches or centimetres (as few as 3 inches or 7.6 cm) to more than 20 feet (6 m). In Saskatchewan and Manitoba at 72 sites located between the 30°F (−1.1°C) and 28°F (−2.2°C) mean annual air isotherms in the southern fringe, permafrost varied from 3 inches (7.6 cm) to 5 feet 3 inches (1.6 m) in thickness, averaging 2 feet 8 inches (0.8 m).

There does not appear to be a correlation between the depth to permafrost and thickness of peat. In the Central Region, at 117 permafrost sites in peatlands, the permafrost was confined to the peat layers at 39 sites; the bottom of the permafrost layer coincided with the peat-mineral soil interface at 5 sites; the permafrost extended into the mineral soil at 49 sites; and at 24 sites the thickness of the permafrost was not determined, but it probably extended into the mineral soil.

Throughout the southern fringe ice occurs in the perennially frozen peat and mineral soil. Much of it occurs in the form of layers up to about 1 inch (2.5 cm) thick. It occurs also in the form of small crystals, pellets, other random inclusions, and as coatings around individual particles.

In the peatlands the vegetation consists primarily of two associations (Fig. 12):

(1) Sedge 1 to 2 feet (0.3 to 0.6 m) high, thin moss, predominantly of the feather and non-*Sphagnum* types, and scattered patches of *Sphagnum*. Trees are usually absent. These areas are almost always very wet.

(2) Thick, often very hummocky spongy *Sphagnum*, scattered occasional patches of lichen, Labrador tea, and scattered ground birch. Tree growth consists of scattered stunted black spruce, and some tamarack. Some of these areas are wet and some are fairly dry.

Permafrost is not encountered in the sedge areas nor in the wet *Sphagnum* areas, but it is encountered usually in the drier *Sphagnum* areas. At the edge of these areas, the permafrost table either dips downward very steeply or forms a virtually vertical face. Within the sedge and wet *Sphagnum* areas, peat plateaus elevated 2 to 3 feet (0.6 to 0.9 m) above the general level of the peatland surface are often present. These are usually drier, being relatively better drained, and permafrost is usually present.

No permafrost exists in the surrounding higher areas, the surface cover consisting of forest litter with patches of feather moss, lichen, and grass. These areas have good surface drainage but water tables are frequently high. The ground vegetation does not appear to provide sufficient insulation to preserve permafrost, although there is not sufficient water in the soil to inhibit the formation of permafrost. A decrease in the mean annual air temperature of less than 1°F (0.5°C) might be sufficient to maintain a permafrost condition in the high areas.

Islands of permafrost not associated with peatlands occur in several situations, frequently in river valleys. At Steen River in northern Alberta, a channel was cut across a meander diverting the river away from

Fig. 12. Peat bog in Interior Plains, 100 miles (161 km) south of La Ronge, Saskatchewan, showing two vegetation associations. In the treeless sedge areas peat exceeds 6 feet (1.8 m) in thickness and there is no permafrost. The spruce-covered islands are peat plateaus having a ground cover of hummocky *Sphagnum*, patches of lichen and Labrador tea. The peat exceeds 6 feet (1.8 m) in thickness and permafrost occurs in scattered patches. The depth to the permafrost table varies from 1 foot 6 inches to 2 feet 6 inches (46 to 76 cm) and the thickness of the permafrost from 2 to 3 feet (0.6 to 0.9 m). 12 September 1963.

the Mackenzie Highway. Permafrost was encountered in this cut at a depth of 12 feet (3.7 m) below the original ground surface and extended below the bottom of the 16 foot (4.9 m) cut.

Twenty miles (32 km) to the north on the same highway, permafrost was encountered at a depth of 8 feet (2.4 m) below the surface in a culvert excavation and extended below the bottom of the 16 foot (4.9 m) cut. At the Hay River crossing 60 miles (97 km) to the south, permafrost was encountered in a river terrace from the 6 to 10 feet (2 to 3 m) depth.

In the southern fringe of the discontinuous zone surface features commonly associated with permafrost, such as polygons, thermokarst hollows, solifluction lobes, and pingos, are either absent, obscure, or in fossil form. In fact, surface manifestations of permafrost both on the ground and on aerial photographs are rare or absent. Thus the presence of permafrost has to be inferred, usually from the vegetation and other terrain features as they appear on the ground and on aerial photographs. Figure 13 is an aerial photograph of a typical area in the southern fringe located in northern Alberta about 30 miles (48 m) south of the 60th parallel. The mean annual air temperature is about 28°F (−2.2°C). The air photo patterns and associated permafrost occurrences are as follows:

(1) Dark grey to almost black tone with grainy texture. This pattern occurs in scattered patches in the southern section of the photograph. In the north and along the river banks these areas are more extensive, exceeding one-half mile (0.8 km) in size. The lightest areas in the northeast corner are almost devoid of spruce and jack pine, being predominantly poplar and birch. In the northwest the high areas are predominantly spruce and jack pine; along the river banks spruce grows densely in almost pure stands. The maximum tree growth in these areas is about 50 to 60 feet (15 to 18 m). It is probable that no permafrost occurs.

(2) Medium grey tone with black specks and fine-textured patches up to one-third mile (0.5 km) in extent. These are spruce (black specks)-*Sphagnum* areas with moderate to imperfect drainage. Permafrost occurs 2 to 3 feet (0.6 to 0.9 m) below the ground surface unless its existence is prevented by excess water.

(3) Very light grey to almost white uniform area with faintly ribbed appearance that is slightly grainy—about one-half mile (0.8 m) long by one-quarter mile (0.4 km) wide. This is a spruce-*Sphagnum* area (enclosed mire) with scattered stunted spruce and thick hummocky *Sphagnum*. The light tone is caused by lichen, which produces the same tone and texture as the scrub growth on the adjacent airstrip (no permafrost). The presence of lichen indicates an old mire in which the soil is becoming increasingly mineralized. The living cover plus peat is 3 feet

FIG. 13. Section of Royal Canadian Air Force aerial photograph A15156-129 at Steen River in northern Alberta in southern fringe of discontinuous permafrost zone.

4 inches (102 cm) thick and the permafrost table is at a depth of 2 feet (61 cm) (Fig. 14).

(4) Light grey tone, fine-grained texture, uniform to blotchy areas are treeless or support very scattered, stunted black spruce. The light tone is produced by the predominance of marsh sedge. Drainage is poor, and permafrost is probably absent.

(5) Mixture of light grey and dark grey tones and fine to coarse-grained texture presenting a blotchy appearance. This is a mixture of small high areas and depressions having the vegetation associations described previously. There is probably no permafrost in the high areas, and none in the depressions unless they are fairly dry.

(6) Three small, dark grey uniform patches with fine-grained texture. The largest patch is about one-quarter mile (0.4 km) long. They appear to be *Sphagnum* peat plateaus supporting stunted scattered spruce. The peat is probably about 4 feet (121 cm) thick and the permafrost table about 2 feet (61 cm) to 2 feet 6 inches (76 cm) below the ground surface.

Northern portion of discontinuous zone

In the northern portion of the discontinuous zone, permafrost is not restricted to one type of terrain and is thicker than in the southern fringe. Fewer observations have been made than in the southern fringe but some information of the nature of permafrost distribution in this portion of the zone is available.

In the Eastern Region near Schefferville, permafrost exceeds 200 feet (61 m) in thickness on ridge summits which are climatically colder than the 25°F (−3.9°C) mean annual air isotherm (Fig. 15).

In the Central Region observations have been made at several locations. Between Thompson and Churchill along the Nelson River in northern Manitoba, permafrost is between 50 and 100 feet (15 and 30 m) thick, averaging perhaps 80 feet (24 m) having a mean ground temperature of 29°F (−1.7°C) to 30°F (−1.1°C). Two main vegetation patterns are evident on the ground and from the air (Fig. 16). One consists of grass- and sedge-covered depressions, generally very wet. Scattered pools of water are visible on the surface. Tree growth is practically non-existent. The other consists of a relatively dense spruce forest with a ground cover of hummocky thick *Sphagnum* and other mosses and lichen. These areas are generally 5 to 10 feet (1.5 to 3 m) higher than the adjacent depressions, and the boundary between the two is quite sharp. Permafrost does not occur under the wet depressions but appears to be extensive under the adjacent slightly higher spruce

FIG. 14. Airstrip on gravel ridge (no permafrost) in foreground at Steen River in northern Alberta. Dark area beyond airstrip is peat bog described as pattern No. 3 on aerial photograph in Fig. 13. Tree growth consists of scattered spruce up to 20 feet (6 m) high with ground vegetation of hummocky *Sphagnum*, lichen, and Labrador tea below which is peat to a depth of 3 feet, 4 inches (1.1 m). The depth to the permafrost table is 2 feet (61 cm) and the permafrost exceeds 2 feet (0.6 m) in thickness. 17 September 1962.

FIG. 15. Exposed ridge summit about 2,750 feet (838 m) above sea level near Schefferville, Quebec. It is situated above the tree-line and the vegetation is lichen-heath rock desert. Permafrost exceeds 200 feet (61 m) in thickness. May 1960.

Fig. 16. Aerial view showing two district vegetation patterns near Nelson River in Manitoba in the northern portion of the discontinuous permafrost zone. The smoother pattern in the middle of the photograph denotes sedge-covered wet depressions with no permafrost. The rougher pattern at the top and bottom denotes peat plateaus with permafrost. 7 October 1963.

covered area. The permafrost table slopes sharply down at the boundary of the two areas.

At Yellowknife on the north shore of Great Slave Lake, the thickness of permafrost is a function of the depth of overburden. Permafrost is not present in rock outcrops but extends to a depth of 280 feet (85 m) where the thickness of overburden approaches 60 feet (18 m). The overburden, consisting of lacustrine clays, is regarded as an insulating blanket that has preserved ancient permafrost. Thus the frozen ground must have extended into solid rock to depths at least greater than is presently known before the overburden was deposited. This occurred during a late glacial or Recent stage during which the level of Great Slave Lake was considerably higher than at present (Bateman 1949).

In the Cordillera, several observations are available which illustrate the permafrost situation in the northern portion of the discontinuous zone. About 90 miles (145 km) southeast of Dawson, Yukon Territory (64°04′N, 139°29′W), there is a peat bog in which permafrost occurs everywhere, even in wet areas and beneath pools of water (Fig. 17). Permafrost would not occur in a similar bog in the southern fringe because of the wet conditions. At Dawson the permafrost is about 200 feet (61 m) thick. At Elsa, about 100 miles (160 km) east of Dawson, permafrost occurs in the McQueston River valley, a broad outwash-filled glacial valley, to a depth exceeding 140 feet (43 m) and more with interspersed talik layers. Northeast of Dawson on the Peel Plateau, very close to the northern limit of the discontinuous zone, permafrost is probably nearly 1,000 feet (305 m) thick (Fig. 18).

CONCLUSIONS

Throughout the discontinuous permafrost zone in Canada there are considerable variations in climate and terrain. These in turn result in variations in the distribution and nature of the permafrost. The broad influence of climate on the formation and continued existence of permafrost is borne out by the location of the mean annual air isotherms relative to the distribution of permafrost. South of the 30°F (−1.1°C) mean annual air isotherm, permafrost occurrences are rare. Between this isotherm and the 25°F (−3.9°C) mean annual air isotherm, permafrost near the ground surface is restricted mostly to peatlands, other occurrences being erratic and at depth. Between the 25°F (−3.9°C) and 20°F (−6.7°C) isotherms, permafrost is discontinuous but widespread, and occurs in various types of terrain. North of the 20°F (−6.7°C) isotherm, permafrost is virtually continuous. This pattern occurs both horizontally with an increase in latitude and also vertically up the slope

48

Fig. 17. Peat bog 90 miles (145 km) east of Dawson, YT, in the northern portion of the discontinuous permafrost zone. Permafrost occurs everywhere in this bog even in wet areas and beneath pools of water. Beneath one pool 1 foot, 3 inches deep (38 cm), the permafrost table occurs at a depth of 3 feet, 6 inches (107 cm) beneath the water surface. 24 September 1964.

Fig. 18. Peel Plateau 80 miles (129 km) northeast of Dawson, YT, near the northern limit of the discontinuous permafrost zone. The depth to the permafrost table is about 1 foot, 6 inches (46 cm) and the permafrost is probably nearly 1,000 feet (305 m) thick. 23 September 1964.

of each mountain range in Labrador-Ungava and the Cordillera.

Within this broad framework of climatic control, local variations in permafrost conditions are related to variations in terrain. Thus, given a climate suitable for permafrost, the type of terrain determines whether or not permafrost will occur at a particular location. South of the 30°F (−1.1°C) mean annual air isotherm, permafrost cannot form or persist in any type of terrain. In the southern fringe between the 30°F (−1.1°C) and 25°F (−3.9°C) isotherms, it can form and persist in the drier portions of peatlands because of the special thermal properties of the peat.

North of the 25°F (−3.9°C) isotherm, permafrost occurs in various types of terrain, being no longer dependent on the presence of peat for its formation and persistence. It is related more closely to the climate and particularly the mean annual air temperature. The approximate difference of 6°F (3.3°C) between mean air and ground temperature applies, and the temperature of the permafrost is about 31°F (−0.6°C) to 32°F (0°C). Northward, the thawed areas decrease in number and extent and become isolated islands.

Through time many fluctuations have occurred in the areal extent, thickness, and temperature of the permafrost, in response to changes in climate and terrain. Since its initial formation, the permafrost in any area may have dissipated and reformed several times during periods of climatic warming and cooling. The glacial history has had a marked effect, the distribution of post-glacial submergence being particularly important. Changes in vegetation caused by fire, climatic succession, or encroachment in water basins all have pronounced local effects. The regime of the fall and accumulation of snow affect the ground thermal regime. The geothermal gradient also influences the ground thermal regime. It varies in different types of soil and rock and with changes in geologic structure. Its changes with time are significant also. Thus, the environment in which discontinuous permafrost exists is a complex dynamic system, the product of past and present climate and terrain features. The thermal sensitivity of permafrost is such that even small changes in climate and/or terrain will produce changes in the horizontal extent, thickness, and temperature of the permafrost.

In the past decade much knowledge has been obtained on the discontinuous permafrost zone in Canada. The southern limit of permafrost is being established and an increasing understanding of the factors influencing the formation and existence of permafrost is being obtained. There are still, however, large gaps. There are few observations in Labrador-Ungava or in the Cordillera. Information on the distribution of permafrost in the northern portion of the discontinuous zone is scanty. Ground temperature observations are very scarce. Of greatest interest to this conference is the place of discontinuous permafrost in the Quaternary and the relation of present discontinuous permafrost to that geological period. The next few years will doubtless see advancements in this line of study.

Note: The permafrost data in this paper were obtained prior to 1964. Information obtained during the past three years indicates that the discontinuous permafrost zone in Canada is somewhat larger than shown on the maps. The southern limit of the zone in the provinces of Ontario and Quebec extends to the southern end of James Bay. The northern limit of the zone lies between the 20°F (−6.7°C) and 15°F (−9.4°C) mean annual air isotherms. A new permafrost map of Canada, compiled by the author, can be obtained from the Division of Building Research, National Research Council, Ottawa, Canada (Order No. N.R.C. 9769).

REFERENCES CITED

ANNERSTEN, L. J., 1963, Investigations of permafrost in the vicinity of Knob Lake, 1961-62: McGill Sub-Arctic Research Papers, no. 16, p. 51-143.
BATEMAN, J. D., 1949, Permafrost at Giant Yellowknife: Trans. Roy. Soc. of Canada, v. 43, ser. 3, sec. 4, p. 7-11.
BLACK, R. F., 1950, Permafrost: Annual Report of the Board of Regents of the Smithsonian Institution for year ending June 30, Washington GPO, p. 273-301.
BONDAREV, P. D., 1959, A general engineering-geocryological survey of the permafrost regions of the U.S.S.R. and methods of construction in permafrost areas: Problems of the North, no. 3, p. 23-47. (This journal is translated by the National Research Council, Canada, and is available from the Council on subscription.)
BROWN, R. J. E., 1960, The distribution of permafrost and its relation to air temperature in Canada and the U.S.S.R.: Arctic, v. 13, p. 163-177.
——, 1964, Permafrost investigations on the Mackenzie Highway in Alberta and Mackenzie District: National Research Council, Canada, Div. of Building Research, NRC 7885, 27 p.
——, 1965a, Some observations on the influence of climatic and terrain on permafrost at Norman Wells, N.W.T.: Can. Jour. of Earth Sciences, v. 2, p. 15-31.
——, 1965b, Permafrost investigations in Saskatchewan and Manitoba: National Research Council, Canada Div. of Building Research, NRC 8375, 36 p.
——, 1966, The relation between mean annual air and ground temperatures in the permafrost region of Canada: Proc. Intern. Permafrost Conf., Nat. Acad. Sci.– Nat. Res. Council Pub. No. 1287, p. 241-247.
CANADA, 1957, Atlas of Canada: Dept. of Mines and Technical Surveys, Geographical Branch, 110 p.
DAVIES, J. A., 1962, A survey of two years' weather records in the Ferriman mine area (June 1959-June 1961): McGill Sub-Arctic Research Papers, no. 12, p. 76-96.
FERRIANS, O. J. JR., 1964, Distribution and character of permafrost in the discontinuous permafrost zone of Alaska: Procs. Canadian Regional Permafrost Conference: National Research Council, Canada, Assoc. Com. on Soil and Snow Mechanics, Technical Memorandum 86, p. 15-18.
HUSTICH, ILMARI, 1957, On the phytogeography of the sub-arctic Hudson Bay Lowland: Acta Geographica, v. 16, p. 1-48.
IVES, J. D., 1962, Iron mining in permafrost, Central Labrador-Ungava: a geographical review: Geog. Bull. no. 17, p. 66-77.
JENNESS, J. L., 1949, Permafrost in Canada: Arctic, v. 2, p. 13-27.
JOHNSTON, G. H., BROWN, R. J. E., and PICKERSGILL, D. N., 1963, Permafrost investi-

gations at Thompson, Manitoba: National Research Council, Canada, Div. of Building Research, NRC 7568, 51 p.

MATHEWS, W. H., 1955, Permafrost and its occurrence in the southern coast mountains of British Columbia: Can. Alpine Jour., v. 38, p. 94-98.

Moss, E. H., 1953, Marsh and bog vegetation in northwestern Alberta: Can. J. Bot., v. 31, p. 448-470.

MULLER, S. W., 1945, Permafrost or permanently frozen ground and related engineering problems: Strategic Engineering Study, no. 62, US Army, Washington, DC, 231 p.

PIHLAINEN, J. A., 1962, Inuvik, N.W.T.: Engineering site information: National Research Council, Canada, Div. of Building Research, NRC 6757, 18 p.

PIHLAINEN, J. A., and JOHNSTON, G. H., 1963, Guide to a field description of permafrost: National Research Council, Canada, Assoc. Committee on Soil and Snow Mechanics, Technical Memorandum 79 (NRC 7576), 23 p.

RADFORTH, N. W., 1963, The ice factor in muskeg: Procs. First Canadian Conference on Permafrost, National Research Council, Canada, Assoc. Com. on Soil and Snow Mechanics, Technical Memorandum 76, p. 57-78.

RETZER, J. L., 1965, Present soil forming factors and processes in arctic and alpine regions: Soil Science, v. 99, p. 38-44.

SHVETSOV, P. F., ed., 1959, Osnovy geokriologii: Akad. Nauk SSSR, v. 1, 459 p.

SJÖRS, HUGO, 1959a, Bogs and fens in the Hudson Bay Lowlands: Arctic, v. 12, p. 3-19.

———, 1959b, Forests and peatlands at Hawley Lake, northern Ontario: Contributions to Botany, National Museum, Canada Bull. 171, p. 1-31.

SUMGIN, M. I., KACHURIN, N. I., TOLSTIKHIN, N. I., and TUMEL, V. F., 1940, Obshcheye merzlotovedeniye: Akad. Nauk SSSR, 337 p.

THOMAS, M. K., 1953, Climatological atlas of Canada: National Research Council and Dept. of Transport, Canada, 253 p.

TYRTIKOV, A. P., 1959, Perennially frozen ground and vegetation, p. 399-421. In Shvetsov, P. F., Editor, Osnovy geokriologii; Akad. Nauk SSSR, v. 1, 459 p. (National Research Council, Canada, TT 1163).

WILLIAMS, G. P., 1965, Heat balance over saturated Sphagnum moss: Proc. First Can. Conf. on Micrometeorology, Toronto, 17 p.

UNDERGROUND ICE IN THE QUATERNARY DEPOSITS OF THE YANA-INDIGIRKA LOWLAND AS A GENETIC AND STRATIGRAPHIC INDICATOR

A. I. POPOV
Faculty of Geography
Moscow State University
Moscow, USSR

ABSTRACT. Polygonal-veined ice is an integral part of the Quaternary deposits in the northern USSR, Alaska, and Canada. It develops most actively in alluvial deposits, and therefore it is characteristic of the arctic and subarctic alluvial plains. The Yana-Indigirka lowland was not glaciated during the Quaternary, but considerable underground ice was formed in the sediments. Studying underground ice, we can assert that its extensive regional development and thickness are determined by the character of the flood plain conditions and sedimentation. Ice formation in the deposits of the arctic and subarctic alluvial plains is the most important lithogenetic factor determining original environmental conditions. The rates and trends of the tectonic processes can aid in judging the conditions of sedimentation and ice formation. Both the very presence of underground ice in the deposits and dimensions of the ice veins are indicators of the paleogeographic conditions of their formation. This gives a basis for using underground ice as a stratigraphic indicator too.

RÉSUMÉ. Dans le nord de l'U.R.S.S., de l'Alaska, et du Canada, la glace en veines polygonales forme une partie intégrante des dépôts quaternaires. Elle se développe activement dans les dépôts alluviaux et est donc caractéristique des plaines alluviales arctiques et subarctiques. Les basses-terres du Iana et de l'Indigurka ne furent pas englacées au Quaternaire, mais il s'y forma beaucoup de glace de sol dans les sédiments. En étudiant cette glace de sol, nous pouvons soutenir que son important développement régional et son épaisseur sont déterminés par le caractère des conditions de la plaine d'inondation et la sédimentation. La formation de glace dans les dépôts des plaines alluviales arctiques et subarctiques est le plus important facteur lithogénétique permettant de déterminer les conditions originales du milieu. Les taux et les tendances des processus tectoniques peuvent aider à juger des conditions de sédimentation et de formation de la glace. La présence de glace de sol dans les dépôts et la dimension des veines sont des indices des conditions paléogéographiques de leur formation. Ceci permet d'utiliser aussi la glace de sol comme indice stratigraphique.

РЕЗЮМЕ. Полигонально-жильный лед является неотъемлемой частью четвертичных отложений севера СССР и Аляски. Он наиболее распространен в аллювиальных отложениях и, следовательно, характерен для аллювиальных равнин Арктики и Субарктики. В четвертичный период Яно-Индигирская низменность не подвергалась наземному оледенению, а только подземному. На основании изучения подземного льда можно утверждать, что его значительное распространение и мощность определяются характером условий затопления пойм и осадконакопления. Подземное оледенение аллювиальных равнин Арктики и Субарктики является наиболее значительным литогенетическим фактором, определяющим их специфические черты. Темпы и направление тектонических процессов определяют условия седиментации и подземного оледенения. Наличие подземного льда в отложениях, а также размеры ледяных жил являются индикаторами палеогеографических условий их образования. Это также позволяет использовать подземный лед и как стратиграфический показатель.

CONTENTS

Underground ice can serve as a criterion for the origin of the deposits and also can be used for working out stratigraphic successions. With the present-day level of knowledge of underground ice, the genetic type called polygonal-veined ice is the most promising. Polygonal-veined ice forms extensive lattice works in the deposits as a result of frost cracking of the surface. Until now, underground ice was hardly ever used for the purpose of defining the genesis of the enclosing deposits.

Polygonal-veined ice is an integral part of the Quaternary deposits in the vast territories in the northern and northeastern parts of the USSR, as well as in Alaska and Canada.

As is well known, polygonal-veined ice develops most actively in alluvial, primarily in flood plain deposits, and, therefore, is mainly characteristic of the arctic and subarctic alluvial plains. Ice of this kind does not develop in alluvium alone, it also occurs in delta, bog-lacustrine, deluvial, glacial, and other deposits. In this paper, the term "underground ice" shall mean polygonal-veined ice only.

It has already been proven that the Asian northern plains never underwent surface mantle glaciation. During a long period of time only underground ice formation took place there. The Yana-Indigirka lowland is one of the regions where underground ice in the Pleistocene deposits is 40 to 50 and more metres thick (Fig. 1).

Following Bunge (1902), I think the underground ice here was formed in fractures in the ground, but unlike Bunge, who regarded ice as an epigenetic formation, I attribute to it the syngenetic growth accompanying sedimentation (Popov 1952, 1953, 1955). It is only the recognition of a syngenetic origin that makes it possible to explain the great vertical thickness of underground ice.

The extensive regional development of underground ice and its thickness are determined by the character of the flood plain conditions and sedimentation in an alluvial plain, under the conditions of a frigid climate with little snow, and of tectonic subsidence. However useful they may be, geological proofs of syngenesis are not sufficient, as such, to explain the origin of underground ice. It is necessary to have an idea of this process and of the conditions that determine it.

The process of syngenesis was at first understood to be the annual fastening in a permafrost layer (that adhered as a result of sedimentation) of a successive elementary ice veinlet that was formed when water froze in the frost crack in permafrost (Dostovalov 1952). Later it became clear that such a conception could not aid in explaining some peculiarities of ice structure and the enclosing deposits. A new explanation was suggested, based on the recognition of frontal growth of underground ice, that is, of its consecutive vertical increase on the whole surface of ice veins (Popov 1955, Romanovski 1959; Katasonov 1962, Gravis 1962).

Frost cracks are the cause of the initial polygonal network of vertical ice veins of small widths, consisting of elementary veinlets. As ice veins widen, the enclosing ground partly deforms and squeezes upwards, forming "ogives" (raised ridges of sediment) around the polygons. At a certain stage of the ice veins' expansion, the process of frontal growth begins functioning. At the same time, ice fills the cavity formed in the active layer along the frost crack zone as a result of diagenetic processes (mainly of shrinkage and contraction of the polygon edges in autumn) conditioned by physical differences between the vein ice and the overlying ground that began to freeze in winter. The ice vein that froze-in in this manner and penetrated into the active layer, reaching a certain maximum depth (determined by the depth of seasonal thawing of the ice), remains in this position, and does not grow upward any longer until new sediments are accumulated in a layer of such thickness as would provide for a new cycle of diagenetic expansion of the fracture zone and for a new "jump" upwards of the ice vein. As the ice vein grows upward as a result of the ground summer expansion, thawing deeper than the ice, the ground is pinched out, the ogives at the polygon

FIG. 1. Underground ice in the Pleistocene deposits on the Yana River, USSR. *Photograph by A. I. Popov.*

edges increase in number, and the intrapolygonal depression deepens, a small lake or a bog being formed there. The subsequent penetration of vertical veinlets into the fast-grown vein helps to widen it still further, to deform the enclosing sediments, and to deepen the depressions inside the polygons. Thus, the deformation of stratified deposits that is observed to occur at the contacts with ice veins does not originate in their frozen state (as is commonly understood), but in their thawed state in the active layer where the developing ice vein penetrates, and only later are they fastened by freezing. As a result of the ogives' expansion, either the plain stops being flooded, or the depth of the high water (and consequently its activity) significantly falls. It is mainly these that cause sedimentation and vein upward growth to stop.

Before new deposits accumulate, depressions in the polygons are filled with sediments and the flood plain regime is established again owing to tectonic subsidence. Then the whole cycle is repeated again.

In sections of the thick alluvial Pleistocene deposits, one can see catenas of ice veins that increase successively and cyclically creating syngenetic systems; and these, together with the peculiar deformation in the deposits, form rhythms. Such rhythms illustrate the cyclic character of sedimentation under certain tectonic conditions.

Hence, veined-ice formation strictly differentiates flood plain sedimentation and creates specific facies of polygonal flood plains. This is best confirmed by the regular lithological and facies changes that can be observed from the centres of polygons (both modern and fossil) towards the contacts with ice veins and by peat in the polygon centres. The amount of peat in ancient polygons in the sections and the morphology of ice veins and the contacts are indicators of whether, within some other cycle, the flooding of plains stopped or only lowered, in other words, whether the accumulation of flood plain alluvium ever stopped or only slowed down.

Thus, ice formation in the deposits of the arctic and subarctic alluvial plains appears to be the most important lithogenetic factor that predetermines quite peculiar facies environments. The morphogenetic criteria revealed enable one to judge the conditions of sedimentation and ice formation (which are closely interrelated), depending on the rates and trends of the tectonic processes.

Another problem to be considered is the use of underground ice as a stratigraphic criterion. The answer to this question depends to a considerable extent on the conditions of its formation, as well as the paleogeographic conditions it develops.

As is known, in the deposits of the old plateau ("edoma") within the Yana lowland, the horizontal thickness of ice veins is rather significant (up to 8 m to 9 m). At places their width exceeds the cross-sections of polygons enclosed between them.

The regular facies changes, from the centres of old polygons towards the contacts with wide ice veins, indicate that these ice veins were formed in very near-surface horizons, and that at the same time, as a result of their frontal growth, they immediately gained dimensions near to those observed now. The extension of polygons, therefore, was restricted by the sizes of the ice veins themselves.

Consequently, ice veins became so wide as early as the stage of their initial near-surface formation, but not as a result of thin ice veins being gradually widened owing to the successive intrusion of vertical ice plates that form in narrow frost cracks, as many investigators think. In the latter case, the morphological picture would have been different: sediments in the polygons would have been upturned at a distance of 4 m to 4.5 m when the ice grew; in reality, the edges of old polygons are deformed not more than 1.5 to 2 m, and often much less.

Hence, underground ice in the deposits of the divide plateau (40 m to 50 m above sea level) was formed under conditions that predetermined great widths of ice veins. Comparison with underground ice in younger deposits is particularly convincing.

Ice veins with great vertical thickness enclosed in the deposits in the second upper flood plain terrace (18 m to 25 m) are up to 3 m to 5 m wide. While in the deposits of the first terrace above the flood plain (10 m to 12 m), the ice veins extend vertically up to 8 m to 10 m and are up to 2.5 m to 3 m wide, in the modern flood plain deposits, the widths of ice veins do not exceed 1 m to 1.5 m. Thus, the widths of ice veins in younger deposits noticeably decrease. At the same time, no essential lithological and genetic differences between old and younger sediments can be observed. All these are clayey loam, sandy loam, and silt, having certain quantities of peat and belonging to the alluvial (flood plain) complex.

The nature and intensity of deformations in the deposits near ice veins (Fig. 2) of relatively young ages do not essentially differ from those near older veins: heavily deformed layers may occur near young veins, and in some areas slightly disturbed ones are observed near ancient veins.

Thus, with certain lithological similarity of the enclosing deposits, underground ice thickness varies in deposits of different ages (which depends, as is known, on the syngenetic alluvial thickness of the deposits). Ice vein widths also vary, and this is not thought by the writer to be adequately explained by earlier workers. In my opinion, the conclusion can be drawn that, during the process of formation of the

FIG. 2. Characteristics of deformation by layers of deposits between ice veins, Yana River. *Photograph by A. I. Popov.*

"edoma" series, there were especially favourable conditions for wide ice veins to be formed, and later, those conditions changed and became less favourable. I am prone to regard these changing conditions as the result of the joint influence of the climatic (temperature) factor on the one hand, and of the recurrently varying moistening of the accumulating sediments on the other.

The syngenetic growth of underground ice is conditioned by its frontal increase, as a result of diagenetic processes on the surfaces of the already existing ice veins, that is, of dehydration, with seasonal freezing of the active layer ground, mainly in the polygonal marginal parts, and with the formation of a cavity filled with ice. The higher the initial humidity of the ground and the more intensive its aridization, the higher the "contraction" effect, the wider the cavity between the two neighbouring polygons, and the wider the ice vein that is formed.

Wide ice veins appear in highly moistened and dusty deposits with peat and remain under water most of the summer period. Laidas, sors, and the like should be regarded as belonging to such facies of the flood plain; they are characteristic of near-deltaic conditions too.

Having emerged from under the water level by autumn and with the beginning of frost penetration, the moistened deposits rapidly and thoroughly dried, especially in the marginal sections of the earlier formed polygons. At the same time they diminished volumetrically, leaving open cavities above the underlying ice veins. As is known, slimy and dusty deposits containing organic matter are subject to the greatest volumetrical changes. It is in these cavities that new ice bodies appear, adding to the existing veins.

The formation of such wide veins, as in the edoma deposits, could take place under the conditions of a more distinctly continental climate than the present-day climate: only with rapid and significant drop of temperature of the over-moistened deposits is there a noticeable effect of ground "contraction." Under the present climatic conditions, in the Yana River flood plains and delta no such wide cavities can be observed; they do not exceed 0.5 m to 1 m.

The edoma deposits were formed within the vast ancient north Siberian alluvial plain, once extending as far as the boundaries of the Laptevykh and East-Siberian seas modern shelf, the present Novosibirsk Islands being the remainder. The vastness of this low-lying land that extended far north suggests the existence in the Pleistocene of a well-developed continental climate, and rather frigid at that, which is confirmed by paleontological data. During the same period, under the conditions of the tectonic setting of the plain, lattice works of thick ice veins were formed in the alluvium, the great widths of which were predetermined by the seasonal flooding regime and by the rigorous continental climate.

Thus, dimensions of ice veins are indicators of the paleogeographic conditions of their formation. This gives grounds for using underground ice as a stratigraphic indicator too.

The thick veins in the edoma deposits, up to 8 m to 9 m wide, are indicators of a rigorous, distinctly continental climate, and of open low-lying terrains representing a polygonal tundra landscape. Spore and pollen spectra from these sediments speak of evident predomination of pollen of grassy cold-loving plants.

This complex of sediments containing mammoth remains of the early type, large forms of the horse, as well as long-horned bison remains, must be regarded as belonging to the upper half of the Middle Pleistocene (Vangengeim 1961), though it may prove to be older.

Ice veins (up to 3 m to 5 m wide) exist in deposits of the second terrace and indicate that the climate on the plain was a little less continental, though still distinctly continental, and possibly less frigid.

The second terrace deposits, with remains of mammoth of the late type, of small forms of horse, and short-horned bison, must be referred to the Upper Pleistocene (Vangengeim 1961).

Ice veins (up to 2.5 m to 3 m wide) in the first terrace deposits indicate that the climate was noticeably less continental and less frigid than before. Remnants of mammals do not occur here, but a lot of wood relics and wood pollen, which speak of forest-tundra and sparsely-wooded taiga, do exist. By their age, the first terrace deposits are of the Early Holocene.

Ice veins (up to 1 m to 1.5 m wide) in the modern flood plain deposits correspond to the present climate and, therefore, to the landscapes of sparsely-wooded forest, forest-tundra, and, in the extreme north, of tundra. These are Late Holocene and Recent deposits.

As we see, major stages of the lowland development are confirmed with different vertical thicknesses of ice veins (which characterize the depths of the tectonic subsidence of the country), as well as with various widths of ice veins (that enable one to judge of paleogeographic and, in particular, of climatic conditions in those stages).

The Middle Pleistocene epoch in the north Siberian plain should be considered as the epoch of old "maximum" ice-vein growth.

The successive decrease of ice-vein dimensions from old to recent deposits makes it possible to fix the directed change of all those conditions from the Pleistocene up to the present, rather than to determine climatic and natural variations in general.

This change was related to both the climate becoming milder everywhere after the middle of the Pleistocene, and, perhaps particularly, to the change in the degree of its continentality because of the change in the position of the sea-coast line. Earlier I noted (Popov 1957) a relative constancy of the rather rigorous climate in the northeast of Asia. Owing to this, immense amounts of underground ice in the deposits have remained since the Pleistocene, and continuously formed as younger sediments accumulated. Now we can reaffirm this proposition, allowing for the general trend in the development of natural environments that has been revealed more distinctly through the underground ice structures.

REFERENCES CITED

Bunge, A., 1902, Einige wörte zur bodeneisfrage: Russian K. Min. Gesell. Verh., 2nd ser., v. 40, p. 203-209.

Dostovalov, B. N., 1952, On physical conditions of frost cracks formation and of the development of fractured ice in loose rocks: in coll., The study of permafrost in the Yakuts Republic, Ac. Sci. USSR Publ. H., p. 162-194.

Gravis, G. F., 1962, Ice veins in deluvial-solifluction deposits: Geogr. Probl. of Yakutiya, Yak., Yakutsk Publ. H., p. 107-112.

Katasonov, E. M., 1962, Cryogenous textures, ice and earth veins as genetic indicators of the Quaternary perennially-frozen deposits: in coll., Problems of cryology when studying the Quaternary deposits, Ac. Sci. USSR Publ. H., p. 37-44.

Popov, A. I., 1952, Frost cracks and the problem of fossil ice: Trans. of Geocryol. Inst., Ac. Sci. USSR, v. 9, p. 5-18.

――――, 1953, Features of lithogenesis of alluvial plains under the conditions of a frigid climate: Proc. Ac. Sci. USSR, Ser. Geogr., no. 2, p. 29-41.

――――, 1955, Origin and development of thick fossil ice: in coll., The materials for the fundamentals of the study on frozen zones of the earth's crust, Ac. Sci. USSR Publ. H., p. 5-24.

――――, 1957, History of permafrost in the USSR during the Quaternary: Herald of Mosc. Univ., Ser. Geol., Biol., Pedol., and Geogr., no. 3, p. 49-62.

Romanovski, N. N., 1959, An approach to the problem of formation of syngenetic fractured-veined ice: in coll., The glaciol. research during the IGY, no. 1, Ac. Sci. USSR Publ. H., p. 83-86.

Vangengeim, E. A., 1961, Paleontological grounding for the stratigraphy of the Anthropogen deposits in the north of Eastern Siberia: Trans. of Geol. Inst. Ac. Sci. USSR, no. 48, 181 p.

PERMAFROST AND TUNDRA POLYGONS IN NORTHERN SWEDEN

ANDERS RAPP and LENNART ANNERSTEN
Department of Physical Geography
Uppsala University
Uppsala, Sweden

ABSTRACT. A brief review is given of the present knowledge of permafrost distribution in Sweden, based on the occurrence of palsa mires and some few observations of perennially frozen ground in glacial deposits or in bedrock. The main part of the paper is a report of investigations of large polygonal patterns, interpreted as tundra polygons, formed by thermal contraction. They are generally situated on low ridges with a thin or no snow cover, in valley bottoms of the Padjelanta Basin and nearby valleys in the mountains of Lappland, northern Sweden. These polygon areas are at an altitude from 440 m above sea level to 900 m above sea level. Ground temperature measurements with thermistors down to a depth of 4 m indicate lenses of permafrost under such polygon areas but not in nearby depressions with a thick snow cover. Thin fossil ice wedges were observed in pits. The tundra polygons are interpreted as inactive and fossil during contemporary climatic conditions. In a brief discussion they are compared with similar forms in northern Norway and Alaska.

RÉSUMÉ. Se basant sur la fréquence des tourbières à palsen et quelques rares observations de sol perpétuellement gelé dans les dépôts glaciaires ou dans le bedrock, les auteurs donnent une brève revue des connaissances actuelles sur la distribution du pergélisol en Suède. La partie principale de la communication est un rapport d'enquête sur de grands dessins polygonaux, interprétés comme des polygones de toundra formés par contraction thermale. Ils sont généralement situés sur des crêtes basses à couverture nivale mince ou absente, dans les fonds de vallées du bassin du Padjelanta et les vallées voisines, dans les montagnes de Laponie, Suède du Nord. Ces surfaces polygonales apparaissent entre 440 m et 990 m au-dessus du niveau de la mer. Des mesures de la température du sol, au moyen de thermistors, jusqu'à une profondeur de 4 m, révèlent la présence de lentilles de pergélisol sous ces surfaces de polygones, mais non sous les dépressions voisines à épaisse couverture nivale. On a pu observer dans ces trous de minces coins de glace fossiles. Dans les conditions climatiques actuelles, on interprète ces polygones de toundra comme étant inactifs et fossiles. Dans une brève discussion, on les compare à des formes similaires de la Norvège et de l'Alaska.

ZUSAMMENFASSUNG. Zuerst wird eine kurze Übersicht über die Verbreitung des Dauerfrostbodens in Schweden gegeben, ausgehend von Palsamooren und einigen Observationen über Dauerfrost in Mineralerde und Felsboden. Der Hauptteil des Berichtes ist Untersuchungen grosser Polygonmuster in einigen Tälern des Padjelantagebietes, ein Hochland in Nord-Lappland, gewidmet. Die Polygonfelder sind in einer Höhe von 440 m bis 900 m ü. M. gelegen, entweder über der Baumgrenze oder auf waldfreien Tundraflecken mit dünner Schneedecke im Winter. Messungen von Bodentemperaturen mit Thermistoren bis zu 4 m Tiefe lassen Dauerfrostboden unter den Polygonen vermuten. Dünne fossile Eiskeile wurde an Aufschlüssen observiert. Die Tundrapolygone in Padjelanta sind unter den heutigen klimatischen Verhältnissen vermutlich fossil und inaktiv. In einer kurzen Diskussion werden sie mit gleichen Formen im nördlichen Norwegen und Alaska verglichen.

SAMMANFATTNING. En kort översikt ges av permafrostens utbredning i Sverige. Den representeras av palsmyrar. I några få fall har permafrost observerats vid borrnings—eller schaktningsarbeten i morän eller fast berg. Huvuddelen av artikeln är en redovisning av undersökningar i områden med stora polygonbildningar, här tolkade som tundrapolygoner (iskilspolygoner). De är belägna i breda dalbottnar i Padjelantabäckenet och närbelägna dalar i Lappland. Polygonområdena ligger på varierande höjd, från 440 m till 900 m ö.h., antingen ovan skogsgränsen eller på tundrafläckar i dalbottnarna. Typiskt är att de förekommer på mark med tunt snötäcke under vintern. Mätningar av marktemperaturerna med termistorer ned till 4 m djup tyder på förekomsten av permafrost under sådana polygonområden. Små fossila iskilar observerades i grävda schakt. Tundrapolygonerna i Padjelanta tolkas som inaktiva och fossila under nuvarande klimatförhållanden. I en kort diskussion jämföres de med liknande bildningar i nordligaste Norge och Alaska.

CONTENTS

FIGURE

INTRODUCTION

This paper is a short review of the present knowledge of permafrost distribution in Sweden and a report on current geomorphic investigations of some recently discovered areas with tundra polygons and permafrost. One of our main problems is that of the "Padjelanta type" of tundra polygons, their genesis and to what extent they can be used as surface indicators of either actual or former permafrost in northern Scandinavia and other marginal areas of the discontinuous zone.

Northern Siberia with its extremely cold winters is the heartland of the Eurasian zone of continuous permafrost. From there a zone of discontinuous permafrost extends westward along the coast of the Arctic Ocean to northernmost Scandinavia, with a lobe towards the south along the Scandinavian mountains and the rather continental areas to the east of them. This general trend of the permafrost zones[1] in northern Europe can be seen on small-scale maps, for example, those compiled by Black (1954), Brown and Johnston (1964), Maarleveld (1965), and Péwé (1968). It reflects the rule that permafrost is typically restricted to areas with very cold winters and a thin snow cover which permits deep penetration of frost into the ground.

Permafrost in palsas

The palsas are probably the most conspicuous surface indicators of permafrost in marginal areas. In Sweden they can be from about 1 m to 7 m high and generally from some few metres to 100 m or more in

[1]On recent permafrost maps two zones are distinguished—(a) the continuous and (b) the discontinuous—thus simplifying the three divisions of earlier maps (continuous, discontinuous, sporadic).

length. The core of permafrost in the interior of the palsas consists of frozen peat with or without ice layers (cf. Forsgren 1964). In many areas it also includes frozen updomed parts of the till or glaciofluvial substratum (Fig. 2 and text; cf. also Lundqvist 1962, p. 71, and Svensson 1962a, p. 222).

Figure 1 shows the approximate area of discontinuous permafrost in Sweden and is mainly based on the distribution of palsa mires. The border line is drawn according to a map by J. Lundqvist (1962, p. 15), with a slight revision in the northeast where the boundary in Figure 1 roughly follows the 68th parallel, to judge from local maps of palsa mires in the Vittangi-Soppero area, Sweden (Hoppe & Blake, 1963, p. 167), and in Enontekiö, Finland (Ohlson 1964, p. 152).

"Observations have shown that the mean annual air temperature is less than the mean annual ground temperature by about 2° to 5°C, depending on local conditions; the overall average is about 3°C" (Brown and Johnston, 1964, p. 67). The outer limit of palsa bogs in Sweden (Fig. 1) roughly coincides with the annual isotherm for −2°C (period 1901-30). But both these lines are very broad generalizations, so the closer relationship between air and ground temperature must be judged from measurements at the actual permafrost localities, taking into consideration not only air temperature, but also local relief, snow cover, soil type, vegetation, and drainage (Brown & Johnston, 1964, p. 66). These factors have a great influence on the existence and depth of permafrost.

Anyhow, it can be supposed that permafrost lenses also occur in bedrock or minerogenic loose deposits outside the palsa mires in a zone of discontinuous permafrost (Fig. 1).

Observations of permafrost by drilling and digging

Very little is so far known about permafrost of other types than palsas in Sweden. The topic has been discussed among Swedish geologists, geographers, and biologists since the 1920s or earlier, but mainly from indirect evidence.[2]

A compilation by Ekman (1957, p. 34 f.) summarizes some reports of permafrost found in drilling or excavating operations. The most remarkable of his examples is perhaps the permafrost locality on Mount Låktatjåkko west of Abisko (for location see Fig. 1). Drilling for water through bedrock was carried out in a mountain col at 1220 m above sea

[2]The present authors do not share the opinion expressed by E. Schenk in several papers (e.g. Schenk 1966) concerning string bogs as evidence of recent and fossil permafrost occurrence. We find no support for the hypothesis that string bogs develop by collapse of formerly permanently frozen bogs.

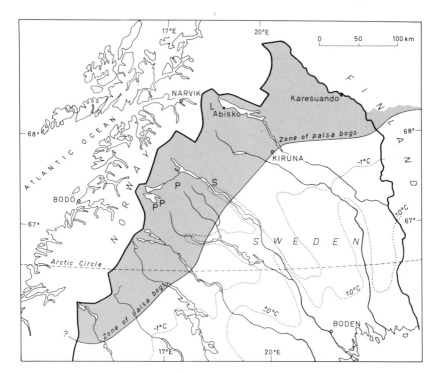

FIG. 1. Map showing the approximate zone of discontinuous permafrost in Sweden, as defined by the southern limit of the palsa region (mainly from J. Lundqvist 1962). Two isotherms for mean annual air temperatures from the period 1901-30 are included. L = Permafrost at Låktatjåkko. P = Areas of tundra polygons in Padjelanta. S = Tundra polygons at Lake Satisjaure.

Fig. 2. Small palsas, about 1 to 1.5 m high in a fen at Puolejokk, Padjelanta, about 750 m above sea level. The peat is only 20 to 40 cm thick, over a core of frozen dome-shaped sandy-silty sediment. *Photograph by A. Rapp, 1963.*

level. Abundant ground water came up when the hole reached a depth of 70 m, but on the following day the water was frozen down to 56 m. This indicates the presence of local permafrost at about 70 m, which is so far the greatest depth of frozen ground found in Sweden. Other indications of patches of permafrost reaching a depth of at least 6 m were reported during the construction of the railway in the Kiruna-Abisko area in the years before 1902. Thin lenses of possible permafrost have also been observed in construction work north of the Kiruna mine (Ekman 1957, p. 34). Similar observations have also been made at some excavations for water wells, etc., in scattered spots within the area marked with half-tone dots in Figure 1.

On the other hand, one case of rather deep permafrost in an area, such as the Låktatjåkko mountain, does not mean that permafrost is common nearby. For example, in the valley of Kärkevagge, located only about 5 km west of Låktatjåkko, no evidence of permafrost was found during a drilling project in July 1961 (Annersten, Tjernström, and Nilsson 1962).

A large number of holes were made with a Cobra drill along profile lines from low to high levels on the slopes, within an altitudinal belt from 725 to 950 m above sea level. Three of the profiles were on northeast-facing "cold" slopes, partly with fine-grained till and large solifluction lobes (Rapp 1961, p. 180 f.). Seventy-five drill holes were made to depths of 4 to 6 m. Thin layers of melting seasonal frost were drilled through in many holes close to remaining snow drifts, but at a depth of 2 m below the surface the ground temperature was positive (+0.1° to +3.3°C) at all check-points except one. The only negative temperature at 2 m was −0.1°C and evidently revealed a thin lens of melting frost. The last mentioned drilling was made on July 17.

From northern Norway, Svensson (1963) reports the following observations made in connection with tundra polygons. In several cases the ground in the polygons was not frozen in July, to judge from a number of test pits excavated to a depth of about 1 m (Svensson 1963, pp. 309, 322). "Official road authorities in this part of Norway have also supplied information that permafrost is not encountered in road construction, except in peat bogs. It therefore appears justifiable to regard the observed polygons as fossil" (Svensson 1963, p. 325).

B. Ohlson (1964) reports from the Enontekiö area in northern Finland that no permafrost is known there outside the palsa bogs.

TUNDRA POLYGONS AND PERMAFROST IN PADJELANTA AND SURROUNDINGS

As mentioned above, the palsa mires are regarded as indicators of rather weak permafrost and seem to require a mean annual air temperature of $-2\,^{\circ}$C or colder to develop and persist. Another surface indicator of permafrost is ice wedge polygons (or frost fissure polygons/thermal-contraction polygons/tundra polygons), but they require a much more severe climate to develop. Actively growing ice wedges in Alaska "occur, for the most part, in the continuous permafrost zone of northern Alaska, where mean annual air temperatures range from $-6\,^{\circ}$ to $-12\,^{\circ}$ .... Inactive ice wedges, no longer growing, occur in the northern part of the discontinuous permafrost zone of central Alaska, where mean annual air temperatures range from $-2\,^{\circ}$ to $-6\,^{\circ}$ or $-8\,^{\circ}$C; they have been found only in fine-grained silty sediments" (Péwé 1964, 1966). Some fossil ice wedges (ice wedge casts) also are present in central Alaska but are restricted almost entirely to coarse grained sediments (Church, Péwé, and Andresen 1965).

Recently some localities with large crack-like patterns on the ground have been discovered in mountain valleys in northern Sweden within the zone of discontinuous permafrost (Figs. 1, 3). The patterns are similar to true tundra polygons, either in a fresh or fossil form. In a current project we are making closer investigations of these forms, their origin and age and the climatic and ground conditions they indicate (Rapp, Gustafsson, and Jobs 1962).

The tundra polygons studied by us are very like those investigated by Svensson (1962a, b, 1963) in northern Norway, particularly the forms in upland areas (Svensson 1963, Figs. 5, 17, 21, 22).

Methods of investigation

The tundra polygons have been traced on vertical air photographs on an approximate scale of 1:30,000. In this scale, however, only the largest and most conspicuous polygons can be observed on the air photographs, so that a larger scale is preferable.

Some of the polygon areas have been checked on the ground, particularly the Puolejokk field. The studies there included detailed mapping of the fracture patterns, examination of the active layer (and the permafrost) by simple probing with an iron rod 1.5 m long, and in pits excavated by digging. Three excavations 2 to 2.5 m deep have been made in the frozen ground by digging and drilling with a Cobra drill. Ground temperature readings were made in summer, autumn, and late winter at 10 thermistor installations down to a depth of 4 m.

The ground temperature programme, methods, and results will be treated more thoroughly by Annersten under the section "Ground temperature measurements" in this paper.

A brief account of four polygon areas

The areas with tundra polygons marked in Figure 3 are the following:

(1) THE PUOLEJOKK FIELD (discovered on air photographs in 1962). (Fig. 3: two crosses south of *l* in Padje*l*anta). More than 50 scattered small subareas of tundra polygons on plateaus and ridges occur within an area of about 2 × 5 km. Drillings and ground temperature recordings show permafrost below the polygons but not in the gully bottoms which dissect the plateaus and are sheltered by snow (Figs. 4, 5).

(2) THE KISURIS FIELD (Fig. 3: two crosses southwest of Mount Akka). The polygons of this area were discovered in 1963. More than 40 subareas of tundra polygons of similar type and location as Field No. 1 have been checked on air photographs and on the ground, but the area probably extends further to the east beyond the existing coverage of air photographs on a scale 1:30,000 or larger. Excavations showed frozen ground at about 0.6 to 1 m below the polygons in late July of 1964 (Lund 1964). This may indicate permafrost of the same type as in the Puolejokk area.

(3) THE STALOVAGGE AND THE VIRIHAURE TUNDRA POLYGONS (Fig. 3: four crosses south of point 580 = Lake Virihaure). A few polygon fields were observed on air photographs and reported by Nordell (1965). No examination by digging has been made there.

(4) THE LAKE SATISJAURE TUNDRA POLYGONS (a cross east of Suorva in Fig. 3). A few polygons were observed and excavated in 1965 by E. Fridén (personal communication). They were 80 to 100 m from the western shore of Lake Satisjaure and were later covered by the artificially raised lake. Small fossil ice wedges occurred below the trenches (Fig. 8). Excavations in early August 1965 revealed the frost table at 0.9 to 1.2 m below the surface.

The altitude of this area is only about 440 m above sea level, but the cooling effect of the lake and the strong winds prevent the forest from growing and probably keep the snow cover very thin on the locality. Similar tundra areas[3] occur in valley bottoms and along the shores of

[3]Swedish scientists generally avoid the term "tundra" for describing the forest-free areas in the Scandinavian mountains above the timber-line. One of the reasons for this is that tundra is regarded as a non-mountainous, cold, and treeless area, with low relief. The present authors do not entirely share this view, but consider that ridges and plateaus above the timber-line in northern Scandinavia, with a low local relief and a tundra-like vegetation, can be called "mountain tundra" or "alpine tundra" in a similar way to the use of this term by American ecologists (e.g., Marr 1961, p. 75 ff.). There seem to be still stronger reasons, both topographical and ecological, for using the term "tundra" (tundra areas, tundra patches) for forest-free ground with low relief and severe frost action (not necessarily permafrost) in

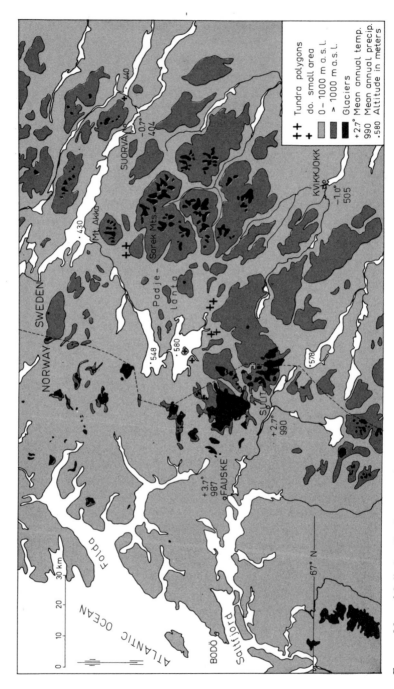

FIG. 3. Map of Sulitelma-Sarek area and surroundings, showing the rim of mountains with glaciers around the Padjelanta Basin. Mean annual air temperature and precipitation data are given for four weather stations. The areas of tundra polygons so far known are marked by crosses.

TABLE I
MEAN ANNUAL AIR TEMPERATURE (°C) AND ANNUAL PRECIPITA-
TION AT FOUR WEATHER STATIONS NEAR PADJELANTA*

Station	Altitude (m a.s.l.)	Air temperature (°C)	Annual precipitation
Fauske	15	+3.7° (1901–30)	987 mm (1936–42)*
Sulitjelma	151	+2.7° (1901–30)	990 mm (1901–30)**
Suorva	425	−0.7° (1901–30)	404 mm (1901–30)
Kvikkjokk	337	−1.0° (1901–30)	505 mm (1901–30)

*Fauske and Sulitjelma represent a maritime or western climate and Suorva and Kvikkjokk a more continental or eastern climate (Figure 3)
**From "Nedbören i Norge 1895–1943" (Oslo, 1949)

other lakes in Lappland, for example, Lake Torneträsk, which is 342 m above sea level (cf. Sandberg 1960, p. 18).

Physiography and climate

The Padjelanta area is north of the Arctic Circle at 67°N, 17°E. It is a rolling upland with broad valley bottoms and two large lakes, Virihaure and Vastenjaure, close to the Norwegian border (Fig. 3). The area forms a local basin about 40 km wide and 580 m to about 900 m above sea level, surrounded by high mountains with glaciers. The Sulitelma massif in the west reaches an elevation of about 1900 m, and the Sarek massif in the east (1900 to 2090 m) and other mountains almost close the basin rim in the south and north. This gives a local precipitation shadow, particularly for winds from the west and the east, and creates a rather continental type of climate, in spite of the fact that the nearest Atlantic fiords are only about 40 km away.

There are unfortunately no weather stations in the Padjelanta area. Some data from the nearest weather stations are given in Table 1 and Figure 3.

The period 1901-30 was chosen, as the Suorva weather station only made recordings in that period. In the period 1921-50 the mean annual temperature was slightly warmer in northern Sweden.

Extrapolated climatic data for Padjelanta, as shown on the maps in the *Atlas of Sweden*, indicate an average annual temperature of −3° to

valley bottoms or near lake shores in the northern Scandinavian mountains. By this definition the Puolejokk polygon field is a tundra area, and the Satisjaure is another.

−4°C and an annual precipitation of about 1,000 mm. The latter figure is very likely an estimate which is much too high, to judge from several observations:

(1) The general topography, which shows that Padjelanta is situated in a precipitation shadow.

(2) The absence of snowdrifts on levels up to 800 m as early in summer as the middle or end of July, when areas of the same altitude with 1,000 mm of precipitation still have a great many melting snowdrifts (e.g., the Riksgränsen area).

(3) The numerous traces of severe wind erosion on ridges and plateaus in the Puolejokk polygon field, indicating thin snow cover.

(4) The observation of only a very thin snow cover on ridges and plateaus in late winter in 1964 and 1965.

Permafrost in peat was observed at many localities in the area, either in the form of palsas (Puolejokk, Stalovagge, etc.) or in small bogs where the peat was completely frozen over, without individual palsas.

The whole area was covered by the Pleistocene ice sheets. The deglaciation probably occurred about 7,000 to 8,000 years BP. Glaciofluvial deposits of both coarse and fine-grained type from that period are common in the valleys. The bedrock consists to a large extent of marble and schist (Kautsky 1953), which crop out in many bare *roches moutonnées* and are probably the source of the till beds, which for Swedish conditions are unusually fine-grained.

The forest limit varies from about 600 to 650 m above sea level. The upper forest consists entirely of mountain birch (*Betula tortuosa*).

Fossil pine stumps (*Pinus silvestris*), on high levels indicating a former pine forest above the present forest limit of birch, have been found in this area, as well as in other parts of the Scandinavian mountains. J. Lundqvist (1962, pp. 13, 15) reports C^{14} dating of two pine stumps from Ruotevare northwest of Kvikkjokk (Fig. 3) and one from Lake Pieskehaure south of Padjelanta (578 in Fig. 3). The stumps were 6,400 to 6,800 years old BP.

In 1963 Eklöv collected a piece of pine trunk on the bottom of a shallow tarn on the Titirnjarka peninsula east of Lake Virihaure and just above the forest limit, about 700 m above sea level. The C^{14} dating of the trunk gave an age of 4,500 ± 80 BP (Olsson and Piyanuj 1965, p. 326, sample U-450).

The datings mentioned above suggest one or more periods of higher pine forest and a warmer summer climate than today in these areas, at least in the period 4,500 to 6,800 years B.P.

The Puolejokk polygon field

The area is marked with two crosses, southwest of Lake Virihaure (580 in Fig. 3). It is about 5 km long and 2 km wide and is in a broad valley bottom with many ridges and terraces of silty, ice-lake sediments, as well as till and coarse glaciofluvial deposits. The tundra polygons are on the exposed upper surface of ice-lake sediments or till but not in gravel. They are all above the forest limit and at an altitude from 670 to 900 m. Figures 4, 5, and 6 show the form and location of the polygon patterns.

The polygons generally have four or five sides and a diameter of about 10 to 40 m. They are rather irregular and in many cases one side is open; in other cases there are only single cracks in the ground. They occur on air photographs as dark lines surrounding a lighter central area. The polygon pattern is very conspicuous when seen from the air, because of the contrast between the low and dense vegetation (*Betula nana, Empetrum hermaphroditum* and *Salix* sp.) growing in the wind-sheltered trenches and the partly naked ground close by, which has only lichens, mosses, and some few *Empetrum* stands.

In the polygon flats are secondary, minor polygons of the non-sorted type, 0.5 to 1 m in diameter and with four to six sides (Swedish "jordrutor").

The width of the trenches in tundra polygons varies from about 0.2 to 2.8 m on the upper rim and 0.1 to 1.8 m in the bottom. The depth of the trenches is from 0.05 to 0.4 m. They have a thick humus layer and also a thickening of the podzol profile in the bottom (Fig. 7).

Besides the polygon trenches, two other features are prominent on many ridges, viz., the scars from wind erosion and the solifluction terraces (inclined non-sorted steps). Both features occur in large numbers and with striking regularity. Similar forms seem to occur in some polygon fields in Norway (cf. Svensson 1963, Figs. 17, 21).

Figure 4 shows some of the directions of the wind-eroded scars, taken from 45 direction measurements made by Gustafsson (1964). The predominant eroding winds come from the southeast, in contrast to the predominance of westerly winds in the mountain area in general. At this locality the mountain ridges of Kerkevare probably act as a shelter from west winds.

The non-sorted steps have vegetation-covered fronts (*Empetrum,* etc.) about 0.1 to 0.5 m high. They seem to be oriented normally to the southeast winds, with the overgrown fronts in the lee. They also seem to flow and extend laterally, moving obliquely downslope and not by breaking through the fronts. Their vegetation-covered fronts probably stay frozen longer in spring because of snow insulation, and thus force the solifluction to move sideways on the thawing, upper, flat part of the terrace.

In many of the subareas the solifluction lobes have deformed the tundra polygons and obliterated or partly filled the trenches, etc. This feature, together with the well-established brush vegetation in the trenches, indicates that they are at least several decades old. No bare or open trenches were observed, but narrow, open cracks about 1 cm wide could be seen in the moss cover on the bottom of some trenches (cf. Svensson 1963, Fig. 23).

Excavations in the Puolejokk polygons

Three large pits were made by Cobra drilling and digging. A large number of shallow pits were dug by hand across the polygonal trenches. The frost table at the beginning of August, 1963, was generally at a depth of 0.5 to 1 m. In all the areas with tundra polygons, frozen ground occurred at this depth but not in the ravines between the ridges. Not one of the three deep holes, drilled and excavated down to 2 to 2.5 m, revealed ice wedges or ice wedge casts of the same width as the trenches on the surface. Figure 6 shows a detailed cut in Area 10. Three thin cracks filled with medium sand and interpreted as fossil ice wedges by us were only up to 3 cm wide, which does not explain the much wider trench on the ground surface. Ice-filled cracks were also observed in the still frozen ground. They were only about 1 cm wide and about 70 cm from top to bottom, standing vertical and parallel to the polygon trenches. They showed that cracking still occurs, but perhaps only in the active layer.

Similar forms were observed in the two other excavated pits (Areas 1 and 12). In the excavations made by Fridén at Lake Satisjaure (Fig. 8), he observed what was interpreted as thin fossil ice wedges some few centimetres in width (for the grain-size composition see Figure 9).

The excavations thus indicated a weak cracking at the present time and a somewhat stronger cracking earlier, but the fossil ice wedges are not wide enough to explain the wide surface trenches.

Ground temperature measurements

A project for investigating the thermal regime of the area was initiated in the summer of 1963 (Annersten 1965). It was hoped that these investigations, together with geomorphological and stratigraphical investigations, would confirm the presence of any permafrost and also

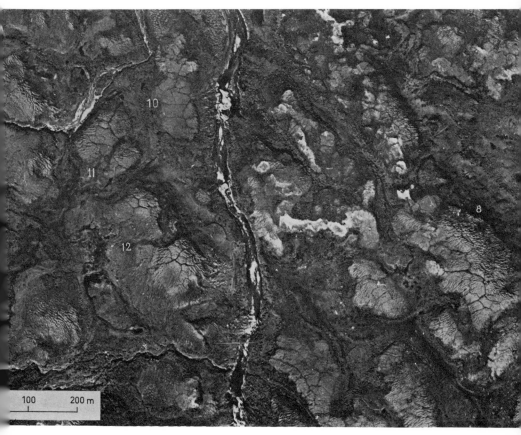

FIG. 5. Air photograph of polygon Areas 8, 10, 11, 12 (cf. Fig. 4). White scars from wind erosion occur in the centre. Parallel striations, e.g., near the arrow, are non-sorted solifluction steps.

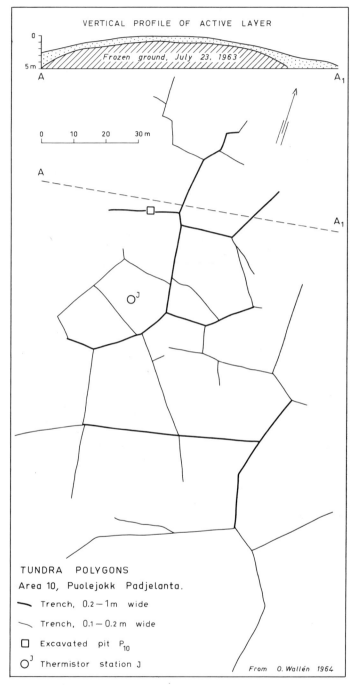

VERTICAL PROFILE OF ACTIVE LAYER

Frozen ground, July 23, 1963

0

5 m

A

A₁

0   10   20   30 m

A

A₁

Oᴶ

TUNDRA POLYGONS

Area 10, Puolejokk Padjelanta.

Trench, 0.2 — 1 m wide

Trench, 0.1 — 0.2 m wide

☐ Excavated pit P₁₀

Oᴶ Thermistor station J

From O. Wallén 1964

Fig. 6. Detail map and profile, Area 10, Puolejokk, Padjelanta. The trenches of these polygons are also visible in Figure 5.

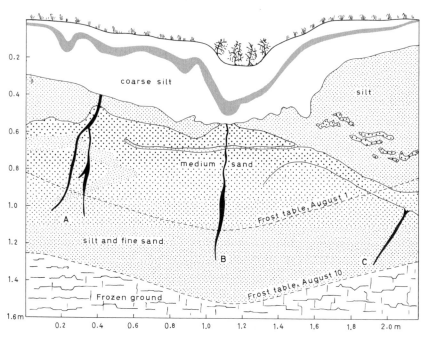

FIG. 7. Sketch from vertical cut across polygon trench in Area 10, Puolejokk, Padjelanta. Frost table influenced by the open pit. A, B, C are three features filled with medium sand and interpreted as fossil ice wedges. They were followed for about 1 to 2 m into the side wall and are oriented roughly parallel to the surface trench but are only 3 cm wide at their thickest part. Note the typical thickening of the podzol profile below the bottom of the trench (grey = the B horizon).

FIG. 8. Tundra polygons at Lake Satisjaure. The stake is 1.5 m long. *Photograph by E. Fridén, 1965.*

elucidate the conditions under which the polygonal pattern had been developed.

Ground temperature data were obtained from the thermistor installations within the Puolejokk area (Fig. 10). The light drilling equipment (Cobra drill, fitted with probing rods) limited the depth of installation to a maximum of 4 m. In each drill hole, four thermistors were installed and were spaced at 1 m intervals, the upper thermistor being situated 1 m below the ground surface. Disc thermistors ($R_{25} =$ 90 ohms) were used, and for protection they and the leads were enclosed in a plastic hose before installation.

The type of drilling equipment used had the advantage of causing minimum disturbance to the surface cover and soil. At some sites, however, the full depth could not be reached because of boulders or slumping in the drill hole. The successful installations were almost certainly due to the fact that the ground was frozen, as the holes could not be cased.

The readings from the thermistors were obtained by a Wheatstone bridge. The accuracy of the resistance reading gives an accuracy in temperature of $\pm 0.1\,^{\circ}$C, and the consistency of consecutive readings indicates that, including the accuracy of the calibration, no temperature deviated more than $\pm 0.2\,^{\circ}$C from the true value during the first year. Equilibrium temperatures were established by 2 days after installation.

The soil temperatures are shown as curves in Figure 10. The temperature data reveal that permafrost is present in all sites except Site C. The recorded temperatures at 4 m are not particularly low, however; they seem to pendulate between $-0.5\,^{\circ}$C and $-1.5\,^{\circ}$C. The active layer is usually 1.5 to 2 m thick. Site F probably has a somewhat thinner active layer of about 1 m.

The temperature maximum at the 1 m level seems in no case to be above $+5\,^{\circ}$C (except at Site C) and is for most sites probably one or two degrees below that value. The minimum temperatures at the same depth vary between $-5\,^{\circ}$C and $-7\,^{\circ}$C.

The comparatively rapid damping of the annual temperature wave indicates a low apparent diffusivity of the soil. The reason for the small temperature range at the 4 m level—about $1\,^{\circ}$C—is probably a high water content in the active layer and moisture migrations in connection with the freezing process in the silty sediments. No measurements of frost heave have been made, but there is reason to believe that this process must be prevalent within the area.

The temperature curves at Site C (Fig. 4), which is in a ravine between two sediment plateaus, show such anomalies as to make an interpretation based solely on heat conduction impossible. The thermal

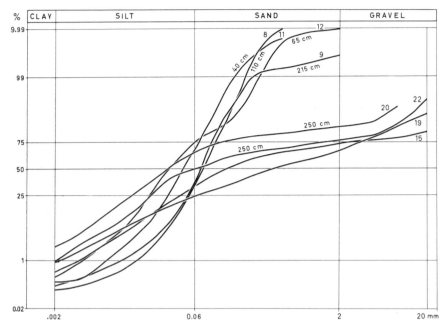

FIG. 9. Grain-size distribution in samples from the pit in Area 10, 40 cm to 250 cm below the ground surface, showing ice-lake sediments, resting upon till (20, 22). 15 and 19 from pit in Area 12*b*, Puolejokk, showing till material about 50 cm below the surface. As regards the areas, see Fig. 4.

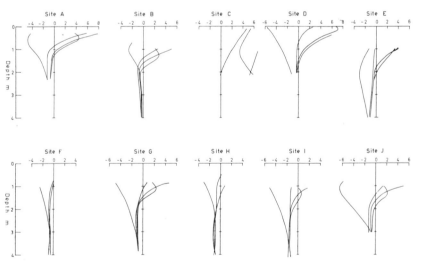

FIG. 10. Ground temperatures at ten sites near Puolejokk, Padjelanta. For the location of the installations, see Fig. 4.

regime of such ravines is probably to some extent dependent on convective heat transfer by running water and a more favourable winter climate resulting from considerable snow accumulation.

Summarizing the results from the temperature measurements, it is evident that areas which have the characteristic polygonal surface patterns are underlain by permafrost. As no temperature measurements could be made in the adjacent glaciofluvial deposits, it cannot be ascertained that permafrost is restricted to areas which show these surface features. But, as the physical properties of the soil must be of equal importance in developing the surface pattern, an area without this pattern does not necessarily mean that permafrost is absent. The temperature data indicate rather that scattered occurrences of permafrost must exist in the northern Scandinavian mountains, at least at wind-exposed sites and in areas with a reduced snow cover.

The temperature data also reveal that it will be difficult to explain the polygonal pattern solely as "thermal contraction cracks" (Lachenbruch 1962), as temperature measurements in recent polygons of similar size indicate temperatures in the soil far below those recorded in the Puolejokk area ($-20\,^\circ$C, versus $-7\,^\circ$C at the 1 m level). Extreme climatic conditions which could cause soil temperatures of even approximately this value have probably never prevailed in northern Scandinavia since the glaciation. It is likely that there are other contributory factors than just the temperature that are of significance in developing the polygonal pattern of the ground.

COMPARISON WITH ALASKA

A detailed map of the distribution of various types of permafrost in Alaska has been compiled and compared with the mean annual air temperature by Péwé (1966). Like northern Scandinavia, Alaska has both maritime and continental types of cold climate, but has a still wider range of mean annual temperatures.

Péwé's zone of continuous permafrost and active ice wedges has a mean annual air temperature from "about $-6\,^\circ$C to $-8\,^\circ$C on the south to $-12\,^\circ$C at Barrow on the north" (Péwé 1966). It is surprising that the highest air temperature in this zone is in the maritime west, coinciding with only $-4\,^\circ$C at the Bering Strait, but $-9\,^\circ$C at the Canadian border. The southern border of the zone with "weakly active to inactive ice wedges" roughly follows the $-2\,^\circ$C isotherm, but is closer to $-1.5\,^\circ$C in the west and $-3\,^\circ$C in the east.

Considerable parts of northern Scandinavia and Finland have a mean annual temperature colder than $-2\,^\circ$C, but permafrost seems to be more common at these temperatures in Alaska than in Scandinavia. If this is true, it may be due to differences in Pleistocene history. Scandinavia experienced total glaciation, and hence only postglacial permafrost, while in Alaska there was no glaciation, but permafrost existed over wide areas of interior and western Alaska in Wisconsin time, remaining as fossil permafrost (Péwé et al., 1965, p. 365), particularly under the widespread loess cover. Another possibility is difference in the present-day climatic, soil, or vegetation conditions.

The minimum ground temperatures in winter at the top of the permafrost are −3.3°C near Fairbanks and −4°C at Northway. They are estimated to be −3°C to −6°C in the Copper River Basin and suggested to be −10°C to −15°C at the northern border of the zone of inactive ice wedges. "Such ground temperatures probably rarely permit thermal cracking of the ice wedges; therefore, no or little ice is added to existing ice wedges and they can be considered dormant, relic, or inactive" (Péwé 1966).

The Puolejokk polygon plateaus in late winter, 1964, had ground temperatures at a depth of 1 m of about −3°C to −7°C, which would make the conditions in these localities comparable with those at Fairbanks or Cooper River Basin in Alaska. According to the views quoted above, this is not cold enough to result in the active growth of ice wedges.

DISCUSSION OF THE GENESIS OF THE POLYGONS

Two main alternatives for the origin of the polygons are considered here: thermal contraction cracks in permafrost and desiccation cracks. The large dimensions of the polygons, with the trenches 5 m to 40 m apart, do not agree with the generally much closer spacing of desiccation cracks. Some of the trenches occur in rather coarse material (e.g., in Area 12, cf. Fig. 9), with only a small proportion of clay particles. Such material is not likely to form wide desiccation cracks. The sand-filled wedge-like cracks observed in vertical cut (Fig. 7) are widest at about 1 m below the ground surface and do not reach up to the surface, two other facts which argue against the desiccation alternative.

The excavations and ground temperature measurements indicate that only a weak cracking resulting from thermal contraction is possible at present, and is perhaps restricted to the active layer. The fossil, sand-filled wedges indicate a somewhat stronger cracking earlier, but they are not wide enough to explain the much wider surface trenches of the polygons.

The trenches are probably increased in their width by other processes than ice-wedging:

(1) Running water has probably widened the trenches near the sloping sides of the plateaus, but not on the horizontal parts nor in the trenches lying parallel to the contours.

(2) The wedging action of roots may be another contributory factor but is of minor importance, as in many trenches there are only plants with small roots (*Empetrum*, etc.), and the trench forms are too regular to be created in this way.

(3) Wind erosion may possibly have widened the surface trenches, but only before they were colonized by plants.

(4) A filling in by lateral compression and flowing instead of slumping from above would tend to reduce the ice wedge casts and make them look more narrow than they once were. A well-developed root system in the sides of the trenches could keep the upper part of the active layer stable and permit a subsurface flow. The remaining thin layers of sand across the upper part of the sand-filled wedges form one of the indications which argue against such compression by "subsurface solifluction."

(5) A general frost heave of the whole ground when permafrost was first developed might have produced a large-scale crack pattern. This may be the explanation of some of the cracks on convex ridges and hummocks, but not on the horizontal surfaces, for example, the centre of Area 10.

CONCLUSIONS

Permafrost has been reported from the northern Swedish mountains, as well as from the areas east of them where palsas are the most conspicuous permafrost form. There are also localities with permafrost in bedrock and minerogenic loose deposits, although only a few such cases are known so far.

Other surface indications of permafrost in Sweden are the large polygons, here interpreted as tundra polygons. They show only very tiny, fossil ice wedges and narrow, vertical, ice veins, probably in the active layer. Permafrost has been checked by ground temperature recordings down to a depth of 4 m below such polygons in the Puolejokk field. Remaining ground frost in early August at a depth of about 1 m in the Kisuris and Satisjaure fields of tundra polygons indicates permafrost conditions there also.

The rather wide surficial polygon trenches were probably initiated by frost cracking and infilling, but were probably also widened through secondary processes—running water at the edges of sloping plateaus, the growth and wedging action of roots (?), frost heave (?), and possibly wind action (?).

Even if the permafrost still remains below an active layer of 1 to 2 m, the large polygons are probably fossil features or have been intermittently revived to a slight extent on rare occasions of very cold conditions.

ACKNOWLEDGEMENTS. The part of this paper entitled "Ground temperature measurements" was written by Dr. Annersten and the other parts by Dr. Rapp.

Financial support for the field investigations in Padjelanta were received from Längmanska kulturfonden, Stockholm, Matematisk-naturvetenskapliga fakultetens anslag för ograduerade forskare, Uppsala, and Sällskapet för Geografi and Antropologi, Stockholm.

Valuable oral information was received from Messrs. E. Fridén, P. O. Nordell, and other colleagues. Mr. N. Tomkinson checked the English text and Mr. V. Tiit and Miss K. Olsson drew the figures.

The maps in this paper have been approved for publication by the Geographical Survey Office of Sweden.

REFERENCES CITED

ANNERSTEN, L., 1965, Permafrostundersökningar i Padjelanta: Stenciled report, Geography Dept., Uppsala, 22 p.
ANNERSTEN, L., TJERNSTRÖM, L., and NILSSON, R., 1962, Sondborrning i talus och flytjord: Unpub. report, Geography Dept., Uppsala, 20 p.
Atals över Sverige (Atlas of Sweden). Sheets 25-6, 31-2: Svenska Sällskapet för Antropologi och Geografi, Stockholm.
BLACK, R. F., 1954, Permafrost: A review: Geol. Soc. America Bull., v. 65, p. 839-856.
BROWN, R. J. E., and JOHNSTON, G. H., 1964, Permafrost and related engineering problems: Endeavour, v. XXIII, 89, p. 66-72.
CHURCH, R. E., PÉWÉ, T. L., and ANDRESEN, M. J., 1965, Origin and environmental significance of large-scale patterned ground, Donnelly Dome area, Alaska: U.S. Army Cold Regions Research and Engineering Laboratory: Res. Report, 159, 71 p.
EKLÖV, A., 1964, Temperaturmätningar i ett område med förmodade tundrapolygoner: Stenciled report, Geography Dept., Uppsala, 20 p.
EKMAN, S., 1957, Die Gewässer des Abisko-Gebietes und ihre Bedingungen: Kungl. Sv. Vet. Akad.: s Handl. 4:3 ser. 6:6 Stockholm, 172 p.
FORSGREN, B., 1964, Notes on some methods tried in the study of palsas: Geogr. Ann. 46, p. 343-344, Stockholm.
GUSTAFSSON, K., 1964, Vindförhållanden i Puolejokks-Riddokjokks dalgång: Stenciled report, Geography Dept., Uppsala, 11 p.
HOPPE, G., and BLAKE, INGRID, 1963, Palsmyrar och flygbilder: Ymer, p. 165-168, Stockholm.
KAUTSKY, G., 1953. Der Geologische Bau des Sulitelma-Salojauregebietes in der Nordskandinavischen Kaledoniden: Sveriges Geol. Unders., Ser. C, 525, Stockholm, 228 p.
LACHENBRUCH, A. H., 1962, Mechanics of thermal contraction cracks and ice-wedge polygons in permafrost: Geol. Soc. America Spec. Paper 70, 69 p.
LUND, K. A., 1964, Undersökning av ett område med förmodade tundrapolygoner vid Snutjotisjokk: Unpubl. report, Geography Dept., Uppsala, 13 p.

LUNDQVIST, JAN, 1962, Patterned ground and related frost phenomena in Sweden: Sveriges Geol. Unders., Ser. C, 583, Stockholm, 101 p.

MAARLEVELD, G. C., 1965, Frost mounds: A summary of the literature of the past decade: Mededelingen van de Geol. Stichting. Nieuwe Serie, 17, Maastricht, 16 p.

MARR, J. W., 1961, Ecosystems of the east slope of the Front Range in Colorado: Univ. of Col. Ser. in Biology, 8. Boulder, 134 p.

Nedbören i Norge 1895-1943: Norges Meteorologiske Institutt, Oslo, 1949.

NORDELL, P. O., 1965, Deglaciationsstudier i södra Padjelanta.: Stenciled report, Geography Dept., Uppsala, 150 p.

NORSK METEOROLOGISK ARSBOK: Norges Meteorologiske Institutt, Oslo.

OHLSON, B., 1964, Frostaktivität, Verwitterung und Bodenbildung in den Fjeldgegenden von Enontekiö, finnisch Lappland: Fennia 89, 3. Helsinki, 180 p.

ØLSSON, INGRID and PIYANUJ, PIYA, 1965, Uppsala natural radiocarbon measurements V: Radiocarbon, v. 7, p. 315-330.

PÉWÉ, T. L., 1964, Ice wedges in Alaska: Geol. Soc. America Spec. Paper, 76, p. 124.

———, 1966, Ice wedges in Alaska: Classification, distribution, and climatic significance: Proc. Intern. Permafrost Conf., Nat. Acad. Sci.–Nat. Res. Council Pub. No. 1287, p. 76-81.

———, 1969, Editor, The periglacial environment: past and present: Montreal, McGill Univ. Press, p. 488.

PÉWÉ, T. L., HOPKINS, D. M., and GIDDINGS, J. L., 1965, The Quaternary geology and archeology of Alaska: in The Quaternary of the United States, VII Inter. Cong. INQUA, p. 355-374.

RAPP, A., 1961, Recent development of mountain slopes in Kärkevagge and surroundings: Geogr. Ann., 42, p. 71-200. Stockholm.

RAPP, A., GUSTAFSSON, K., and JOBS, P., 1962, Iskilar i Padjelanta? English summary: Ice wedge polygons (?) in Padjelanta, Swedish Lappland: Ymer, p. 188-202. Stockholm.

SANDBERG, G., 1960, Abisko: Sveriges nationalparker, Kungl. Domänstyrelsen, Stockholm, 40 p.

SCHENK, E., 1966, Zur Entstehung der Strangmoore . . . Zeitschrift für Geomorphologei 10, p. 345-368, Berlin.

SVENSSON, H., 1962a, Nagra iakttagelser från palsområden. English summary: Observations on palsas . . .: Norsk Geografisk Tidsskrift, 18, p. 212-227, Oslo.

———, 1962b, Note on a type of patterned ground on the Varanger peninsula, Norway: Geogr. Ann., 44, p. 413, Stockholm.

———, 1963, Tundra polygons, Photographic interpretation and field studies in north Norwegian polygon areas: Norges Geol. Unders. Arsbok 1962, Oslo.

SOILS OF THE OKPILAK RIVER REGION, ALASKA

JERRY BROWN
US Army Cold Regions Research and Engineering Laboratory
Hanover, New Hampshire

ABSTRACT. In the vicinity of the Okpilak River, northeastern Alaska
($65°25'$N, $144°00'$W), the manifestations of frost action in arctic soils are
of two general forms: (1) the surficial configurations or patterned
ground and (2) the morphological characteristics of the seasonally
thawed soil and the upper zone of perennially frozen ground. Approximately 55 types of soil conditions and surface features occur in an area
encompassing both the northern Brooks Range and the southern Foothill
Provinces. These include the genetic soils of arctic Alaska, numerous soil
conditions, and many of the common sorted and non-sorted circles, nets,
polygons, steps, and stripes. In both the glaciated and periglacial areas
sorted features predominate on the coarse-textured substrata.
    The arctic brown soils are distributed on the well-drained sites along
valley (longitudinal) traverses and across mountain (altitudinal) gradients. On a sequence of valley moraines, acid parent material is considered
more important than time and mesoenvironments in influencing the depth
and development of the characteristic brown solum. Weakening of the
soil-forming processes with increasing altitude is suggested in the mountains. In the valleys a podzol-like soil is observed in close proximity to the
arctic brown soils and in association with acid parent materials, dwarf
birch-heath vegetation, and protected microrelief positions. A peaty soil
associated with ice wedge polygons constitutes an organic terrain.

RÉSUMÉ. Dans le bassin de l'Okpilak, dans le nord-est de l'Alaska
($69°25'$N, $144°00'$W), les manifestations du gel dans les sols arctiques se
présentent sous deux formes générales: (1) des sols polygonaux (*patterned grounds*) et (2) les caractères morphologiques propres au mollisol
saisonnier et à la couche supérieure du pergélisol. Dans une région com-
prenant le nord de la chaine de Brooks et les "provinces" méridionales
du piedmont, on trouve environ 55 types de conditions du sol et de
caractères de sa surface: ces types comprennent les sols génétiques de
l'Alaska, de nombreuses conditions de sol et beaucoup de formes com-
munes, triées et non-triées: cercles, filets, polygones, marches et bandes.
Sur les substrats à texture grossière, les formes triées prédominent, à la
fois dans les régions glaciées et dans les régions périglaciaires.
    Les sols arctiques bruns se rencontrent sur les sites bien drainés, le long
des vallées et en travers des pentes montagneuses. Dans une succession
de moraines de vallée, on considère que l'influence de la roche-mère
acide est plus importante que le facteur temps et les "mésoenvironne-
ments" en ce qui a trait à l'épaisseur et au développement de ces sols
bruns caractéristiques. Dans les montagnes, on suppose un affaiblissement
des processus de pédogénèse en proportion de l'altitude croissante. On

observe dans les vallées un sol de type podzolique à proximité des sols bruns arctiques et associé à la roche-mère acide, à une végétation de bouleaux nains, et à des positions de microreliefs protégés. Une combinaison de sols tourbeux associés à des polygones à fentes de gel constitue un terrain organique.

CONTENTS

FIGURE

TABLE

94

PHYSICAL SETTING

Introduction

The soils of northern Alaska have been under investigation since the early 1950's. The major genetic soils and the processes of soil formation have been recognized and described (Tedrow and Hill 1955, Drew and Tedrow 1957, Tedrow et al. 1958, Douglas and Tedrow 1961, Hill and Tedrow 1961, Tedrow and Brown 1962, Ugolini and Tedrow 1963, Brown and Tedrow 1964). The relationships of these arctic soils to patterned ground and the cold environment are well documented, particularly for the Coastal Plain and Foothill Provinces (Drew and Tedrow 1962, Tedrow and Cantlon 1958).

In the Okpilak River region of northeastern Alaska, patterned ground, unstable soil surfaces, and a diversity of genetic and non-genetic soils result in a degree of soil complexity greater than is found on either the northern Foothills or Coastal Plain. The presence of altitudinal and longitudinal valley gradients in the mountains and foot-hills provides an opportunity to evaluate the relative importance of several factors of soil formation. This paper summarizes the results of investigations which were designed to provide information on soil genesis, morphology, and distribution in an area for which virtually no previous soils knowledge existed (Brown 1962b).

Geography and physiography

The study area lies within the region described by Leffingwell (1919) in his monumental and inspiring investigations of the Canning River region. For present purposes, the Okpilak River region is delineated as the area between the west bank of the Jago River and the east bank of the Hulahula River, a distance of some 25 km. The southern portion begins at the upper fork of the Okpilak River, 25 km south of the mountain front. The northern limit extends about 20 km beyond the mountain front. The area lies within the Mount Michelson and De-marcation Point quadrangles[1] (approximately 69°15′ to 69°35′N, 143°

[1] US Geological Survey topographic quadrangle maps, scale 1:250,000.

45′ to 144°30′W) (Fig. 1). Additional observations were made in the vicinity of Lakes Peters and Schrader (69°20′N, 145°00′W), Anaktuvuk Pass (68°05′N, 151°30′W), and Porcupine Lake (68°45′N, 146° 30′W) to supplement the soil studies in the Okpilak River region. The Okpilak River is headed by two valley glaciers located in the Romanzof Mountains of the northeastern Brooks Range. Their streams join to form the Okpilak River which then cuts a 3 to 12 m deep post-glacial canyon for a distance of some 7 km. The river flows through a wide U-shaped glacial trough past the mountain front into the southern Foothills or Anaktuvuk Plateau and eventually into the Arctic Ocean, about 110 km from its source.

Between the Jago and Okpilak rivers the mountain front is oriented in an east-west direction. It veers northwestward from the Okpilak to the Hulahula River. The mountains vary in altitude from 1,700 m above sea level at the front, to peaks of nearly 3,000 m southward in the Romanzof Mountains. Numerous snow-filled cirques and hanging and valley glaciers occupy these higher areas.

Among the major valleys of the area, the Okpilak contains the largest number of glacial features. Within the mountains, the valley walls are covered with lateral moraines and post-glacial alluvial-colluvial cones or fans that rise upwards of 150 m above the broad valley floor. North of the mountain front the valley is mantled by a series of end, recessional, ground, terminal, and lateral moraines, kames, and glaciofluvial outwash (Fig. 2). The East and West Okpilak lakes were glacially formed. Wide, braided river channels are constricted at the mountain front as the river passes northward through several low moraines. An earlier glaciation overspilled the 500 m high valley wall and covered the rolling uplands with a mantle of drift. Later glacial advances left lateral moraines on the ridges and walls of the valley. The Jago Valley contains large amounts of morainic materials and many small glacial lakes north of the mountain front. The Hulahula Valley possesses few glacial features at the mountain front, with an abundance of bedrock outcrops of mafic igneous rock.

The mountainous terrain for the most part is steep and has much slide rock and organic mats. Between 1,300 m and 1,400 m above sea level, flat, apparently unglaciated mountain benches are present. These benches, mantled by a thick, frost-shattered regolith, contain extensive areas of patterned ground and resemble the altiplanation terraces of interior Alaska.

The Lake Peters and Lake Schrader area, about 35 km west-south-west of the Okpilak River, is dominated by two large glacial lakes. Lake Peters is surrounded by high mountains and bordered by fans and

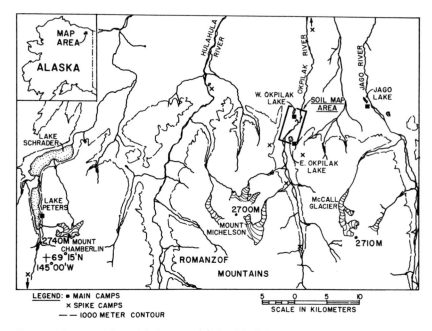

FIG. 1. Topographic and index map of the Okpilak River region, Alaska.

FIG. 2. Aerial oblique photograph looking south onto the Okpilak River valley and the adjacent uplands and mountains.

lateral moraines. Carnivore Creek, fed by a number of valley glaciers, empties into the south end of Lake Peters after flowing northward through a deep glacial trough for 12 km. *Roches moutonnées*, fans, and till occupy much of the valley of Carnivore Creek. Lake Schrader, north of Lake Peters and at the mountain front, has an east-west alignment. It is bordered by moderately sloping, till-covered uplands and by unglaciated mountains.

Glacial and bedrock geology

It is generally recognized that the Brooks Range supported a network of valley glaciers during the Late Pleistocene (Detterman *et al.* 1950). Valley glaciers descended northward from the Brooks Range and during earlier advances coalesced to form piedmont lobes. Bodies of drift and moraine from these older glaciations are found as far as 65 km north of the mountain front. At no time was there a continuous ice sheet in northern Alaska. More recent advances did not reach the mountain front.

Porter (1964) has established a Late Pleistocene chronology for the north-central Brooks Range based upon radiocarbon dating. The Itkillik glaciation with its four substages was correlated broadly with the classical Wisconsin glaciation. Three post-Itkillik advances, for which radiocarbon correlation was not made, are believed to be post-Hypsithermal and were restricted to the mountains. Apparently, very much the same glacial sequence is present in both the Okpilak and Lake Peters regions (Keeler 1959, Sable 1961, 1965, Kunkle 1958, Holmes and Lewis 1965). Brown (1962*b*, p. 137) noted that the degree of tussock development was not a reliable criterion for estimating relative ages of moraines. For example, in these studies the Jago Lake moraines (Itkillik or older) showed virtually no tussock development while outwash, dated at 2,830 years old, in Anaktuvuk Pass was well covered by cottongrass tussocks.

The Romanzof Mountains, through which the Okpilak River flows, contain an extensive system of valley glaciers between the Jago and Hulahula rivers. Sable (1961) demonstrated that the terminus of Okpilak Glacier has receded approximately 300 m, and that the lower part of the glacier has thinned approximately 50 m in the past 50 years. Sable concluded from these studies that the general shrinkage of valley glaciers in the Romanzof Mountains has occurred in the last half of the 19th and first half of the 20th century. These findings are in accord with observations made in the McCall Valley, a tributary valley of the Jago River (Keeler 1959).

The Romanzof Mountains are composed in part of a small granitic

99

batholith (Whittington and Sable 1948, Sable 1959, 1965). The granite is predominantly light-to-medium grey, coarse-grained rock with minor amounts of dark minerals. The granite is flanked on the south by the pre-Mississippian Neruokpuk Formation, commonly composed of a greenish chloritic schist. Younger rocks form the mountains to the north and include the Lisburne group, the Sadlerochit, Shublik, Kingak, and Ignek formations. Mafic igneous rocks are exposed along the Hula-hula River. The stratigraphy of the area is complex.

Vegetation

The area north of the crest of the Brooks Range lies wholly within the tundra region and is characterized by treeless and grass-like vegetation. The valley and upland slopes are frequently tussock-covered. The high mountainous terrain is a lichen-covered barrens of frost-shattered bedrock. In general, barrens conditions increase, and marsh and meadow types decrease with increased altitude (Spetzman 1959).

Cantlon (1961) divided the Arctic Slope into two zones: the arctic tundra (sea level to 1,200 m) and the arctic-alpine zone (above 1,200 m). Subzones of the former are littoral, typical, and shrub tundras. Two alitudinal belts are distinguished in the arctic-alpine zone; alpine tundra belt (1,200 to 1,800 m), and alpine desert belt (above 1,800 m). The typical tundra subzone and the two altitudinal belts are found in the study area (see also Malcolm 1959).

The typical tundra subzone is associated with July normal temperatures ranging from 6.7°C to 11.1°C. Cottongrass tussock and dwarf-shrub meadows are extensive. The alpine tundra belt, a discontinuous subzone most widespread in the eastern Brooks Range, has a flora of 120 to 150 species. Dwarf birch and berry-producing shrubs are of minor importance or are absent. The alpine desert belt occurs as a series of island-like peaks and shows a pronounced reduction in flora (10 vascular species) with the complete absence of shrubs and dwarf shrubs and the predominance of lichen barrens.

Climate

The climate of the Okpilak River region as well as the remainder of the northern Brooks Range is not well known. Summer climatic data (US Weather Bureau) from Barrow, Barter Island, and Anaktuvuk Pass are presented in Table 1 for a 5-year period. Compared to Anaktuvuk Pass in the central Brooks Range both the Okpilak River and Lake Peters areas are influenced by a more maritime climate, having nightly ocean fogs and overall lower temperatures.

COMPARATIVE SUMMER CLIMATIC DATA FOR BARROW, BARTER ISLAND, AND ANAKTUVUK PASS (1957-61)

	Average Monthly Temperature (°C)				Average Monthly Precipitation (mm)		
	Barrow	Barter Island	Anaktuvuk Pass		Barrow	Barter Island	Anaktuvuk Pass
1957							
June	0.8	0.8	9.3		27	5	15
July	4.1	4.8	10.8		20	24	33
August	5.6	7.8	10.0		35	41	33
September	-1.7	-1.1	0.1		28	76	47
4-month average	2.2	3.1	7.5	Total	110	146	128
1958							
June	1.2	2.3	11.2		20	4	145
July	3.5	7.4	12.1		15	4	31
August	5.9	7.3	9.2		20	4	26
September	1.9	2.6	0.8		40	18	15
4-month average	3.1	4.9	8.4	Total	95	30	217
1959							
June	1.1	-0.1	10.3		5	3	23
July	1.9	3.8	7.2		36	50	49
August	2.8	1.9	7.2		29	42	38
September	-1.0	-1.4	-0.8		29	3	5
4-month average	1.2	0.8	8.0	Total	99	98	115
1960							
June	0.8	1.1	7.3		7	13	33
July	3.1	3.3	9.2		5	18	36
August	1.2	3.3	6.4		37	17	29
September	-4.1	-1.4	-4.3		13	19	31
4-month average	0.3	1.6	4.7	Total	62	67	129
1961							
June	1.4	1.9	9.2		2	20	39
July	3.4	4.8	10.1		46	71	95
August	1.9	3.4	7.3		33	28	35
September	1.0	0.6	3.2		8	22	
4-month average	1.9	2.8	7.5	Total	89	141	(169)
Average for 5-year period	1.7	2.6	7.2		91	96	155

Conover (1960) estimated that the total annual precipitation may amount to 450 mm at the 600 m elevation along the slope of the mountains. In much of the Arctic about one-half of the annual precipitation occurs during the summer. Estimates from the author's field observations accounted for at least 150 to 200 mm of precipitation during the predominantly "snow-free period." In the Brooks Range the estimated snow cover of 850 mm usually disappears by late May or early June. Frequent light rain and snow storms are common throughout the summer months. At higher altitudes precipitation probably increases in the form of more frequent light rains, showers, and fog. Relative humidity is high throughout the mountainous region during the summer months.

July is the warmest month with mean temperatures varying locally from 5.6°C to 12.2°C. Maximum temperatures in the low 20s and minimum temperatures below −10°C are not uncommon during the summer. Mean annual temperatures approximate −9°C to −12°C. Consistent subfreezing temperatures are common by mid-September. Mean daily temperatures are below freezing for at least 8 months of the year. Conover (1960) estimated a decrease in temperature along the mountain front of 2.2°C per 300 m increase in altitude. Scattered temperature records and field observations of temporary summer snowlines substantiate a decrease of this magnitude (Tedrow and Brown 1962). The over-all summer climate can be extremely variable, but it is generally wetter and warmer than the coastal areas.

CRYOPEDOLOGY AND THE DISTRIBUTION OF SOILS AND SURFACE FEATURES

Manifestation of frost action in the soil

In the Arctic, the mechanical differentiation of soil material into sorted ground features, the occurrence of non-sorted surface configurations, the presence of buried organic layers in mineral soils, the existence and melting of massive ground ice, and frost action result in a lack of soil continuity and a diversity of microrelief configurations that are perhaps unequalled in any other climatic region of the earth. Smith (1965) noted that under the influence of an arctic climate moving soils were more common than stable soils. Nikiforoff (unpublished) portrayed the horizons of tundra soils as being mechanically restless as a result of horizontal and vertical movements year after year. Douglas (1961) stated that frost action is a special soil-forming process of the tundra.

Britton (1957, p. 30) aptly summarized the physical aspects of cryopedology in the following statements:

Cryopedologic processes include all mechanisms operative in the substrate that relate to the formation and degradation of permafrost, as well as all frost-cracking, -splitting, -churning, -stirring, -thrusting, and -heaving actions, induced either by expansion and contraction of frozen materials exposed to large temperature stresses, or to a repeated alternate freezing and thawing of surface materials. All such processes are products of the climate operating on materials consisting of anything from bedrock to boulders, and all size classes of materials to silts, clays, and organic layers. These materials are of varying water content, disposed on all gradations of slope, and variously blanketed by vegetation and seasonally by snow. Out of such complexes, intricate operations of unique combinations of processes produce characteristic minor relief features.

In the glaciated valleys and uplands and the older periglacial mountainous areas of the Brooks Range, cryopedologic processes produce microrelief features and complexities in soil morphology at a greater frequency than is encountered on either the Foothills or Coastal Plain provinces of northern Alaska (Brown 1962b, Tedrow and Brown 1965).

The fact that the mountain and valley terrains are mantled by frost features to such a degree may be partly explained in several ways:

(1) The valleys and uplands are covered with till, a highly heterogeneous material which is easily sorted (Corte 1959).

(2) The unglaciated mountainous terrain (approximately above 1,200 m) has probably been exposed to a longer period of frost activity than other comparable bedrock landscapes. Therefore, sorting and the development of patterned ground are more likely to be present.

(3) The strong relief in both the valleys and mountains favours solifluction and the development of surface configurations which are typical of areas of perennially frozen ground (Sharp 1942, Smith 1956, Washburn 1956).

The effects of frost action in the soils of the Okpilak River region are considered under two general forms: the surficial configuration or patterned ground, and the internal morphological characteristics found in the seasonally thawed soil and near-surface perennially frozen ground. Before discussing the individual soils and surface features, morphological examples of the effect of frost action in these soils are considered.

The instability of soils on slopes is manifested by soil terraces, lobate terraces, soil lobes, mudflows, stripes, and a variety of more nondescript microrelief features, all of which are gradational to some extent. Downslope movement of soil materials is enhanced by the presence of a perennially frozen substratum. These soils of the solifluction slopes possess no orderly profile characteristics. They present no systematic means of description, but all contain buried organic matter (Fig. 3).

The soils range from moderately well-drained to wet viscous masses. As the soil surface slowly moves downslope, organic matter is buried by a folding-under process which results in a lack of profile continuity. Frequently this buried material is traceable to the surface as one excavates upslope through the various microrelief features. The frontal portion is usually organic with the amount of mineral soil increasing upslope. The buried organic zone generally begins just above the base of the seasonally thawed soil.

Differences in the thickness of the seasonally thawed soil are common across small distances on both the solifluction slopes and level terrain. For example, in a raised mound the thawed zone could vary between approximately 45 cm in the centre of the mound and 25 cm in the adjacent trough. Differences in moisture content, thickness of organic surfaces, and microrelief account for these variations in the depth of seasonal thaw.

Evidence for recent fluctuations in the depth of thaw was observed on the south-facing slope above Porcupine Lake. The remains of a dead willow were found in an organic mat associated with a shallow depth of soil thaw and embedded in soil having a high ice content (perennially frozen ground). It is unlikely that the shrub grew to a height of over a metre in the present shallow depth of thawed soil. Therefore, a rise in the seasonal frost table was postulated. This rise could have been caused by a regional change in climate, a local shift in drainage, or an increase in the insulating quality of the organic mat. In any event, this reduction in depth of thaw demonstrates one aspect of the dynamic character of the wetter soil.

The non-sorted steps and stripes are cases of instability on gentle slopes. Relatively dry soil material often overlies buried organic surfaces. Such burials occur frequently in early spring when the mineral soil is close to saturation and the frost table is near the surface. However, all such burials are not of this type, particularly where the overburden is thick and cobbly.

Sorted nets (Fig. 4) and polygons demonstrate the lack of continuity of soil morphology on relatively flat terrain. In the trough virtually no fines are present for a depth of ½ m. This sorting may be attributed to the lateral and vertical segregation of particles (Corte 1963), although erosion of fines should not be completely disregarded. The desert pavement is another extreme soil condition. The pavement consists of a loose, coarse gravel devoid of fines. The amount of fines increases with depth. Downward migration of fines caused by repeated freezing and thawing may be responsible for this phenomenon, but the erosive effect of wind is also a contributing factor.

FIG. 3. Characteristic buried organic
matter in soils of the solifluction slope.

FIG. 4. Sorted nets on lateral moraine.

Frost scars, boils, peat rings, and the like are extremely common in all stages of development on the wet glaciated terrain. Cross sections of these show lateral burial of surface organic matter. The viscous mineral soil is displaced, first upwards and then outwards, by the "frost-churning process," resulting in the burial of surface organic mats. The soil adjacent to frost scars often contains vertical lobes and horizontal layers of the buried peat or poorly sorted pockets of cobbles.

Douglas (1961) discussed the buried organic horizons associated with wet tundra soils on level terrain. This universal presence of buried organic matter in tundra soils is thought to represent the result of a climatic change in which a cooler period caused the thickness of seasonally thawed soil to decrease. This decrease resulted in an increased soil volume which forced the upwelling of the mineral soil through the organic surface, and burial of the latter. Radiocarbon age determinations of these buried peats generally yield dates of between 8,000 and 10,000 years old (Douglas 1961). A radiocarbon date of one such buried peat layer from Anaktuvuk Pass yielded an age of 4,750 ± 100 years (Trautman 1963). Based upon observations in the glaciated regions of northern Alaska, the author believes that the occurrence of these buried surfaces and the present frost scars are related. That is, the buried organic matter is also the result of comparatively recent frost scar development.

The presence of ground ice and particularly ice wedges in the substratum similarly serves to produce disorder and instability in soil morphology. Numerous ice wedges are found in the peaty soils and in large melt-out polygons on peat-covered fans and slopes in the Okpilak Valley. Maximum melt-out of these ice wedges reaches depths of 3 m. As ice wedges increase in size, the soil mass is compacted and/or displaced, thereby distorting normal soil morphology. Ice-cored hummocks are also common.

Vesicular structure in the soil is frequently found under bare surfaces which are associated with various patterned-ground features. It consists of closely packed, spherical to ellipsoid voids of various sizes; the largest seldom exceeding 1 cm in width, occurring across a wide soil moisture range. This structure is difficult to observe when digging in the wetter soils since the soil mass flows readily resulting in the collapse of the vesicular cavities. The cavities may form as a result of evolution of air from soil water as freezing occurs and subsequent entrapment of the air in the soil mass. In his studies on desert soils, Springer (1958) produced similar vesicular structure by drying and wetting. Crocker and Major (1955) reported the same structure on bare to sparsely covered mineral patches on moraines near Glacier Bay. The soil mass associated with the vesicular structure usually exhibits a convex surface. Both convex surface and weakly developed vesicular structure were reproduced in the laboratory by repeated freezing and thawing of a nearly saturated soil sample obtained from an actual frost scar. The particle-size distributions of two soils exhibiting vesicular structure are shown in Table 2. In frost scars, granular aggregates are occasionally encountered under a thin mineral crust and over the zone of vesicular structure. A fine platy structure is also occasionally present in the surface horizon. Both may be caused by the formation and later melting of ice lenses.

TABLE 2
PARTICLE-SIZE DISTRIBUTION (%) OF
TWO SOILS EXHIBITING VESICULAR STRUCTURE

2–1 mm	1.0–0.5	0.5–0.25	0.25–0.10	0.10–0.05	0.05–0.002	<0.002
16	15	13	9	10	33	4
10	12	13	11	11	41	2

It is obvious from this brief discussion that a considerable segment of arctic soil morphology is the result of the alternate freeze-thaw processes that have occurred in the past and are presently active in these soils. Figure 5 summarizes some of these morphological characteristics. With this perspective, it is now appropriate to discuss the complex distribution of the soil and surface features in the Okpilak River region.

Types and distribution of surface features and soils

The subject of soil classification in arctic Alaska and the relationship to surface features has been discussed by Tedrow *et al.* (1958) and Drew and Tedrow (1962). The genetic soils include the lithosols and regosols, the well-drained arctic brown soils, the wetter glei tundra soils, and the organic bog soils. Detailed soil mapping in arctic Alaska is limited. Tedrow and Hill (1954, unpublished) mapped the soils of Umiat and four other areas, and based their classification upon lithology, origin of parent materials, and relative degree of soil drainage. Drew (1957) presented a soil map of the Barrow area and utilized the genetic soils, parent materials relative wetness, and stage of ice wedge polygon development in his legend. MacNamara (1964) has recently completed a soils map of the Howard Pass quadrangle (68°N, 156°W). For the present study it was considered desirable to systematically describe and map the numerous soils, soil conditions, and surface features for part of at least every major terrain component in the Okpilak River region.

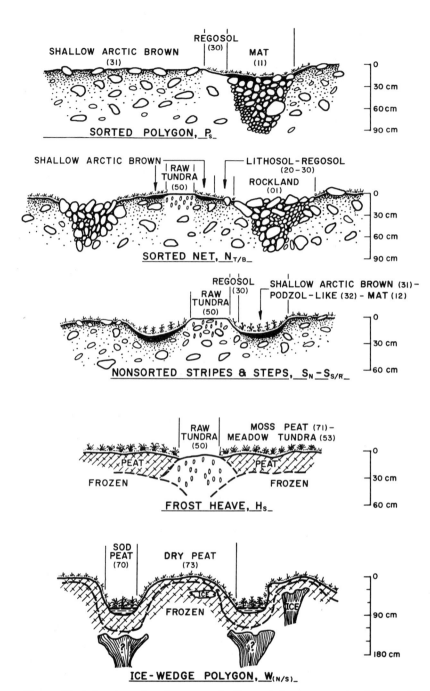

Fig. 5. Variations in surface features and soil morphology as a result of frost action.

These included the glaciated valleys and upland slopes and the un-glaciated mountain slopes and benches. A summary of this approach to mapping the complex soils environment follows.

The soils and surface features encountered in this region are pre-sented in Table 3. The arrangement is not intended to imply a genetic classification for either the soil or surface features. This legend is simply an expedient approach to the grouping and mapping of the numerous and often gradational forms of ground and soil conditions. Washburn's (1956) classification of patterned ground is employed for the majority of the patterns. The less regular and non-repetitious forms and surface markings are grouped in a miscellaneous category. The genetic soils and the previously undescribed soil conditions are arranged in eight groups. With the exception of the mats and alluvial-colluvial soils and soils of the solifluction slopes, these groups collectively comprise a soil drainage catena. Terms such as "raw" and "inundated" tundra are de-scriptive and do not imply processes of soil formation. Numbers alone, rather than terms, could easily suffice if soil terminology is considered burdensome.

The occurrence of these soils and surface features as determined by field studies is presented in Table 4. Usually three to five distinctly different soils occur within an individual surface feature. The table indicates the soils that may be anticipated within any one feature. The use of this table enables the extrapolation of a number of soil con-ditions from a limited number of symbols on the map.

In practice, mappable units are delineated by field observations and from aerial photo interpretation on an appropriate scale. Within each mappable unit the codes for the predominant patterns and soils are arranged in order of decreasing frequency. This approach, as applied to the Okpilak River region, northern Alaska, should satisfy recent criticism for the failure to map interrelationships of soils and microrelief in northern Alaska (Mikhailov 1961). A preliminary soils map of the Okpilak River region was prepared based upon this system (Brown 1962b), and a portion of it is presented in Figure 6. A brief description of the surface features and soils employed in the mapping is presented below. Photographs of the soils and surface features appear in another report (Brown 1966).

Surface features

SORTED NETS Central core of fines surrounded by narrow, non-vegetated border of rock fragments and developed commonly on both transported material (N_T) (Fig. 4) and disintegrated bedrock (N_B).

NON-SORTED NETS Raised centre, surrounded by depressed trench with non-sorted coarse material. Stone-centred nets (N_{SN}) consist of rubbly lichen-covered central areas outlined by vegetation in the protected depressed borders. On slopes

TABLE 3

MAPPING LEGEND FOR THE OKPILAK RIVER REGION, ALASKA

Surface features	Code	Soils	Code
Group A (after Washburn)		Rockland	01
		Mats and alluvial-colluvial substrata	
Sorted nets	$N_{T/B}$	Recent alluvium	10
Non-sorted nets		Mat on rubble and bedrock	11
Stone centred	$N_{SN/SS}$	Mat on well-drained substratum	12
Polygonal intergrade	N_P	Mat on poorly drained substratum	13
Sorted polygons	P_S	Stratified sediments	14
Non-sorted ice wedge polygons	$W_{N/S}$		
Sorted circles	S_C	Shallow soils on bedrock	
Non-sorted circles		Lithosol	20
Peat rings	R_P	Shallow arctic brown	21
Frost scars	$S_{F/FS}$		
Frost scar mounds	S_M	Shallow soils on transported materials	30
Inundated mounds	M_I	Regosol	30
Non-sorted steps	S_N	Shallow arctic brown	31
Non-sorted stripes	$S_{SI/R}$	Podzol-like soils	32
		Moderately deep, well-drained soils	40
Group B (miscellaneous types)		Normal arctic brown	40
		Arctic brown mull and humus carbonate	41
Solifluction mounds and terraces	S_T		
Hummocks	H_M	Tundra soils on wet mineral substrata	
Moss	$H_{P/PS}$	Raw tundra	50
Peaty mound		Upland tundra	51
Frost heaves	H_S	Inundated tundra	52
Silt oozes	H_R	Meadow tundra	53
Rubbly heaves	H_I	Organo-mineral tundra	54
Ice mounds	D_B		
Rock debris benches	P	Soils of the solifluction slope	60
Rubble pits			
Mudflows and slides	$M_{F/S}$	Organic soils	
Strangmoor and peat ridges	S_G	Sod peat	70
Levées	L	Moss peat	71
Trails	T	High moss peat	72
		Dry peat	73
		Bog	74

NOTES: /represents two different forms of same feature
Relatively dry moraine complex includes:

TABLE 4
OCCURRENCE OF SOILS WITH SURFACE FEATURES

SURFACE FEATURES	01	10	11	12	13	14	20	21	30	31	32	40	41	50	51	52	53	54	60	70	71	72	73	74
N_T	x	x	x	x			x	x	x	x				xx						x	xx			
N_S	x	x	x	x			x	x	x	x				xx						x	x			
$N_{SN/SS}$	xx			x										x								x	xx	x
N_P			x											x										x
P_S				x																				
W'_N																								
W_S	x			x					x	x							x							
S_C	x				x	x					x			xx			x		x	x		x	xx	x
R_P														xx	x	x	x	x		x	x			
S_F														xx	x	x	x	x		x	x			
S_{FS}														xx	x	x	x	x		x				x
S_M														xx	x	xx	x		xx	x		xx	xx	
M_I									x	x				x	x		x		x	x				
S_N		x	x											xx	x									
S_S				x										xx	x									
S_R	xx	x		x	x	x	x	x	x	x				x	x	x	x		x	x		x		x
S_T					x																			
H_M				x												x								
H_P		x		x	x		x		x					xx	x	x	xx	x	x	x	x			x
H_{PS}				x										xx						x	x			
H_S					xx	xx																		
H_R					xx	xx			x						x	x								x
H_I		x												x		x						x		x
D_B	xx	x	x											x						x				
P	xx	x		x													x	x	xx	x		x	x	x
M_F																								
M_S	xx					x								x	x		x	x		x			xx	
S_G	xx					x								x									xx	x

xx: Most frequently encountered soil for particular feature

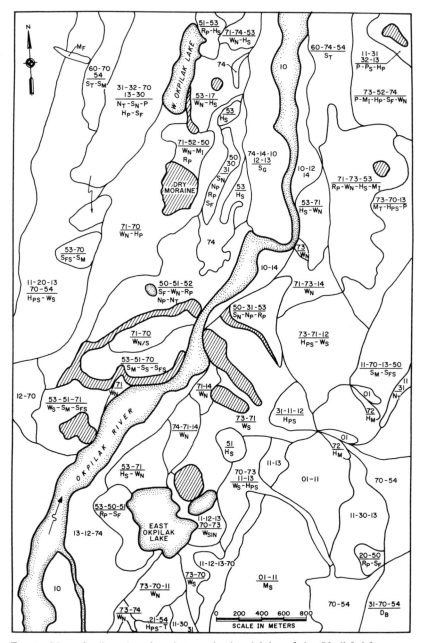

FIG. 6. Map of soils and surface features in the vicinity of the Okpilak lakes.

they elongate to form triangular islands of rock (N_{SS}). The polygonal intergrade (N_P) has a flat, raised centre and a weakly defined polygonal shape.

SORTED POLYGONS   Large polygonal-shaped, barren-covered, gravelly centre surrounded by a vegetated trough underlain by sorted gravels (P_S).

NON-SORTED, ICE WEDGE POLYGONS   Completely vegetated polygons, surrounded by narrow troughs which are underlain by ice wedges (W_N). Polygon edges may or may not be raised. Smaller, high-centred polygons are surrounded by deep, melt-out troughs both on flat terrain and slopes (W_S).

SORTED CIRCLES   Small, commonly less than a metre across, circular mineral core surrounded by a mesh of sorted coarser boulders (S_C).

NON-SORTED CIRCLES   Considerable variation among types with many gradational forms:

PEAT RINGS   Circular to oval wet mineral centres surrounded by ridge of peat or tussocks (R_P).

FROST SCARS   Circular to irregular-shaped exposures of mineral soil, usually covered by a network of desiccation cracks (S_F). On slopes, they become triangular in shape with vegetated centres but no frontal lobe (S_{FS}).

FROST SCAR MOUND   Gradational form on slopes with well-defined raised centre which is bare to completely vegetated (S_M).

INUNDATED MOUNDS   Raised, vegetated circular mounds underlain by either saturated mineral soil or peat and surrounded by wet marsh (M_I).

NON-SORTED STEPS   Elongated, bare mineral centres with conspicuous vegetated frontal lobe and vegetated depressed lateral borders (S_N).

NON-SORTED STRIPES   Elongated stripes of bare soil with only weakly expressed frontal lobes (S_S). On steep talus slopes, bare and lichen-covered stripes alternate (S_R).

SOLIFLUCTION MOUNDS AND TERRACES   This group constitutes many forms that do not lend themselves to grouping with other slope features. Common characteristics are: occurrence on wet slopes, conspicuous frontal lobe, bare mineral soil on upslope portion of feature, and folded-under organic matter in both the seasonally thawed soil and perennially frozen zone.

HUMMOCKS   Relatively small, raised feature on flat and sloping terrain. Moss hummocks (H_M) occur on steep, north-facing slopes. Peaty hummocks are circular, tussock-like, and have an organic core (H_P). Irregular hummock mounds on slopes (H_{PS}) are gradational to solifluction mounds.

FROST HEAVES

SILT OOZE, small, triangular mineral spots distributed irregularly between tussocks and hummocks (H_S).

RUBBLY HEAVES, mounds of fresh rubbly till recently heaved upward through a vegetated surface (H_R).

ICE MOUNDS, ice-cored mounds along river terrace, resembling miniature pingos (H_I).

ROCK DEBRIS BENCHES   Large mound-like features, crescent-shaped in the downslope direction and composed of talus and colluvium (D_B).

RUBBLE PITS   Pockets of rubble devoid of fines and vegetation on bouldery till (P).

MUDFLOWS AND SLIDES   Large, continuous flows of saturated, thawed soil on slopes with high frontal lobes (M_F). Bouldery slides occur on steep mountain and valley slopes (M_S).

STRANGMOOR AND PEAT RIDGES   Narrow, semi-continuous ridges of peat, principally on wet river terraces (S_G).

LEVÉES   Parallel bouldery ridges adjacent to deeply gorged stream channels on alluvial-colluvial fans (L).

TRAILS   Caribou and sheep trails criss-cross the entire landscape at close intervals (T). In the mountains, trails are marked by upturned exposed rocks in contrast to more stable lichen-covered rock.

Soils[2]

(01) ROCKLAND   Slide rock, talus, felsenmeer, and desert conditions, with shallow to no soil development (Pfg. 3).

[2] Depth to perennially frozen ground (Pfg.):
Pfg. 1   Shallow, approximately 30 cm;

Mats and alluvial-colluvial substrata

(10) RECENT ALLUVIUM   Recently deposited, unweathered alluvium on flood plains and fans (Pfg. 3).

(11) MAT ON RUBBLE AND BEDROCK   Thin partially humified organic mat on either glacial rubble devoid of fines or unshattered bedrock (Pfg. 3).

(12) MAT ON WELL-DRAINED SUBSTRATUM   Thin mat with organic matter in all stages of decomposition on well-drained, medium-textured mineral substratum with little evidence of further soil development; regosol intergrade (Pfg. 3).

(13) MAT ON POORLY DRAINED SUBSTRATUM   Wet peaty organic mat on a mottled grey substratum with little horizon differentiation and no flowing water; tundra intergrade (Pfg. 2).

(14) STRATIFIED SEDIMENTS   Distinct depositional layers of different-size mineral and organic materials as a result of deposition during frequent flooding (Pfg. 3).

Shallow soils on bedrock

(20) LITHOSOLS   Well-drained, loosely fragmented rock material with only faint colour development under a discontinuous organic mat (Pfg. 3).

(21) SHALLOW ARCTIC BROWN   Well-drained, coarse mineral material with thin, coloured B-horizon on shattered or glacially scoured bedrock (Pfg. 3).

Shallow soils on transported materials

(30) REGOSOL   Well-drained, predominantly sandy deposit with thin surface organic mat and virtually no horizon differentiation (Pfg. 3).

(31) SHALLOW ARCTIC BROWN   Well-drained soil with at least one distinct brown-coloured horizon (Pfg. 3) (Fig. 4).

(32) PODZOL-LIKE SOILS   Well-drained soil with thin and frequently discontinuous grey, A_2-horizon over a brown B-horizon (Pfg. 3).

Moderately deep, well-drained soils

(40) NORMAL ARCTIC BROWN   Well-drained soil with three distinct, ideally equi-dimensional horizons (A_1, B_{21}, B_{22}) and usually formed on transported parent materials (Pfg. 3).

(41) ARCTIC BROWN MULL AND HUMUS CARBONATE   Well-drained soils with thick, well-humified, surface organic layer and frequently on calcareous substrata (Pfg. 3).

Tundra soils on wet mineral substrata

(50) RAW TUNDRA   Imperfectly drained, olive-brown soil with conspicuous vesicular structure and no surface vegetation (Pfg. 4).

(51) UPLAND TUNDRA   Imperfectly drained, mottled, mineral soil, usually with some buried organic matter (Pfg. 2).

(52) INUNDATED TUNDRA   Water-saturated mineral soil with thin, wet surface peat on flat river terraces (Pfg. 4).

(53) MEADOW TUNDRA   Wet grey mineral soil with characteristic cottongrass-tussock vegetation and mat (Pfg. 1).

(54) ORGANO-MINERAL TUNDRA   Water-saturated profile with characteristic horizon composed of a mixture of finely disseminated organic material and silts, flowing water, and little mottling (Pfg. 2).

(60) SOILS OF THE SOLIFLUCTION SLOPE   No distinct, single soil profile, but a combination of characteristics such as buried organic matter, water-saturated mineral soil, unstable surface conditions (Pfg. 4) (Fig. 3).

Organic soils

(70) SOD PEAT   Thick, fibrous, tightly matted peat associated with flowing water on flats and slopes (Pfg. 2).

(71) MOSS PEAT   Accumulation of predominantly mossy plant fragments on poly-gonal ground and gentle slopes (Pfg. 1).

Pfg. 2   Moderate, approximately 60 cm;
Pfg. 3   Deep, generally greater than 90 cm;
Pfg. 4   Irregular, undulating, and generally between 30 and 90 cm.

(72) HIGH MOSS PEAT   Mossy peat layer on loose talus or perennially frozen substratum at higher altitudes and no flowing water present (Pfg. 4).
(73) DRY PEAT   Dry, fibrous, and woody peat generally on top of high-centred polygons (Pfg. 1).
(74) BOG   Thick, water-saturated, sedgy organic deposits along terrace bows and lake shores (Pfg. 2).

SOIL-FORMING PROCESSES

Well-drained soils

Investigation of the relatively stable, well-drained soil site often demonstrates the significance of one or more of the classical factors of soil formation. The glacial geology of the Brooks Range and southern Foothills, and particularly of the Okpilak Valley, provided an excellent opportunity for evaluating the influences of time and parent material upon soil development. Within a distance of some 45 km in the Okpilak Valley evidences of numerous glacial advances are present. Both the age and composition of the glacial and glaciofluvial deposits change along this north-south transect. In addition to this traverse, in which the factors of time and parent material were evaluated, studies were conducted to evaluate the changes in the well-drained soils with increasing altitudes. In this vertical direction, the climate was considered to be the primary variable. Numerous well-drained soil profiles were described and sampled across these vertical and longitudinal traverses for not only the Okpilak River region, but also the Lakes Peters and Schrader and Anaktuvuk Pass areas.

The dominant well-drained soil of the Alaskan Arctic has been termed "arctic brown" (Tedrow and Hill 1955). On the Foothills and Coastal Plain its distribution is limited to perhaps less than 1 per cent of the land surfaces. For the glaciated valley and frost-rived, mountainous terrains which produce better drained soil sites, this distribution increases to at least 10 per cent. The well-drained soils are reported to reflect the northward weakening of the podzolic process (Tedrow et al. 1958). The short, dry, cool, snow-free summers result in a reduction of biological activity and of effective leaching. Most of these well-drained soils have a persistent brown-coloured mineral horizon (Table 5, Fig. 7). In the valleys of the Brooks Range, and particularly in the Okpilak and Anaktuvuk valleys, a soil with a thin to discontinuous grey A_2 horizon was observed in close proximity to the arctic brown soil. Based upon morphological and chemical criteria this soil was considered podzol-like.

The data from these studies have already been presented in detail elsewhere (Tedrow and Brown 1962, Brown 1962b, Brown and Ted-

115

TABLE 5
DESCRIPTION OF ARCTIC BROWN SOIL

Horizon	Depth (cm)	Description
A_0	2–0	Thin raw organic mat consisting of lichens and dry mosses; gravels and cobbles common.
A_1	0–5	Dark reddish-brown to black well-decomposed organic with fines and gravels interspersed, wavy lower boundary.
B_{21}	5–25	Sandy loam, colours range from strong brown (7.5YR5/6)* to yellowish-brown (10YR5/6).
B_{22}	25–45	Sandy loam, colours transitional between B_{21} and C with brown (10YR4/3) to yellowish-brown (10YR5/4) colours common; carbonate crusts present on underside of cobbles; silt skins common.
C	below 45	Gravelly sandy loam; loose, pale brown (10YR6/3) to light yellow brown (2.5Y5/4); (Pfg. 3).

* Colour notations based upon moist conditions by Munsell colour charts

row 1964). In the majority of the arctic brown soils, there was no significant increase in free iron oxide below the first mineral horizon. All of the podzol-like soils showed a definite increase in free iron oxide in the B horizon. Free manganese showed no substantial trend in the arctic brown group of soils but increased with depth in the podzol-like soils. The pH values of both soils increased with depth; the most acid values were in the range of pH 4.5 to 5.0 in the upper solum to pH 5.0 to 6.0 in the lower solum and C horizon. Although carbonate deposits are commonly present on the underside of cobbles within the solum, values on the < 2 mm-size fraction are at times as low as pH 5.5. Carbon-nitrogen ratios indicated a range of 14 to 20 in the B horizon. No genetic accumulation of organic matter was noted in the B horizons of any of the soils. In the podzol-like soils cation exchange capacity and base saturation decreased with depth. Grain-size analyses indicated a clay content of generally less than 10 per cent, with coarseness increasing at depth. No significant clay weathering was noted in any of the soils, although abrupt mineralogical changes were. Radiocarbon analyses of organic matter in the A_1 horizon of a podzol-like soil from the Okpilak Valley yielded a date of 175 ± 75 years BP (Trautman 1963).

Field criteria for the rate and degree of soil formation have been based principally on colour development in the solum, thickness of the solum, and presence of the light-coloured A_2 horizon.

Unlike observations by Chandler (1943), Crocker and Dickson (1957), and Leahey (1947), a pedogenic function based solely upon increasing surface age was not substantiated in these longitudinal valley traverses of the Brooks Range. In most instances, variation in parent materials is more important than the time function. A solum of moderate thickness (25 to 35 cm) develops even on the young deposits when parent materials are acid and/or rich in iron-bearing minerals. Where, however, the till is charged with calcareous materials, the development of strong brown colours is apparently depressed, with the result that different aged surfaces yield weakly differentiated soils.

No positive correlation was found between the presence of the podzol-like soil and the time function. In the Okpilak River region, this soil occurred most abundantly on granitic glacial deposits of, perhaps, Itkillik age. In the Anaktuvuk Pass area, podzol-like soils were found on acidic glacial deposits which were radiocarbon dated at approximately 2,800 to 6,300 years old (Porter 1964). The lithology is considered more important than the time factor in the formation of both arctic brown and podzol-like soils in the northern Brooks Range. Great care should therefore be exercised in attempting to correlate glacial sequences with degree of soil development.

The distribution of both these well-drained soils, however, is often modified and controlled more by microrelief and vegetation than by lithology and time. Local prominences are subjected to wind abrasion during the snow-free period. This favours the perpetuation of a xeric, barrens vegetation and a discontinuous A horizon, conditions which result in reduced leaching, in free carbonates relatively close to the surface, and in a solum lacking strong colour differentiation. Frequently, the wind-blown barrens consist of lichen-covered, pebbly pavement. Arctic brown soils are common on the slightly elevated sites. The occurrence of podzol-like soil is favoured by the presence of depressed or protected microrelief and a continuous cover of dwarf heath vegetation. This commonly consists of *Betula nana, Salix* sp., *Vaccinium uliginosum, Vaccinium Vitis-idaea, Ledum palustre decumbens, Arctostaphylos alpina, Dryas octopetala, Empetrum nigrum, Carex* sp., and several species of *Alectoria, Cladonia,* and *Cetraria* (a biota commonly associated with podzol formation). These microdepressions are completely vegetated, accumulate more snow, and remain moist, a situation that favours more leaching.

The genetic authenticity of the A_2 horizon of the podzol-like soil remains a moot problem in northern Alaska. A contemporaneous depositional process, water or aeolian, is observed on similar sites on the north slope of Alaska. The strongest argument against such depositional origins in the present area is the absence of an organic accumulation or buried surface at the lower boundary of the A_2 horizon. It is difficult to postulate the deposition of a grey sandy layer over a brown mineral soil which would have had to be devoid of previous vegetation.

It is conceivable that the podzol-like soil represents the remains of a once widespread soil. Paleoclimatic analyses suggest several warmer periods in the time ranges under consideration (Porter 1964). A moister climate, a condition which would have enhanced the widespread formation of the podzol-like soil, has not, however, been substantiated. Subsequent truncation of the upper horizon by erosion and reduced leaching might account for the present distribution of arctic brown, podzol-like soils, and various intergrades.

Soil instability on these well-drained sites, principally caused by frost action, is not as extensive as it is on saturated soils. Weakly developed forms of circles, nets, steps, and polygons are, however, frequently associated with the arctic brown and podzol-like soils. The radiocarbon-dated sample of approximately 175 years for the A_1 horizon of a profile in the Okpilak Valley was associated with a non-sorted step. Formation of this horizon apparently took place in the period covered by the radiocarbon date. As evidenced by buried horizons associated with this frost feature, soil morphology within the soil pit suggested that the grey A_2 horizon was present prior to this average date.

Among the chemical processes operating during the development of both the arctic brown and podzol-like soils are increases in acidity, solution of carbonates, and a low-order mobilization and translocation of iron and manganese in the surface horizon of certain soils. Earlier it was shown that small quantities of iron, aluminum, and manganese were translocated with the arctic brown soil (Drew and Tedrow 1957). Mikhailov (1961) questioned that this represented an embryonic podzolization process. For at least some of these soils, it is evident that a process of translocation is in effect. It does appear, however, that the soil-forming processes present in these soils of the Brooks Range are somewhat similar to those processes operating in other low rainfall areas of northwestern North America (Kubota and Whittig 1960, Leahey 1947, Pawluk 1960, Rieger and Juve 1961, Wright et al. 1959, Day and Rice 1964).

The weakening of the soil-forming processes with increasing altitude was suggested in the study area (Tedrow and Brown 1962) (Fig. 8). Observations were made on the well-drained soils across vertical transects ranging from altitudes of 600 to 1,700 m. Soil colour and depth of solum were again the principal soil criteria utilized for determining soil development. Although the glacial deposits at lower altitudes probably

Fig. 7. Shallow arctic brown soil developed on alluvium.

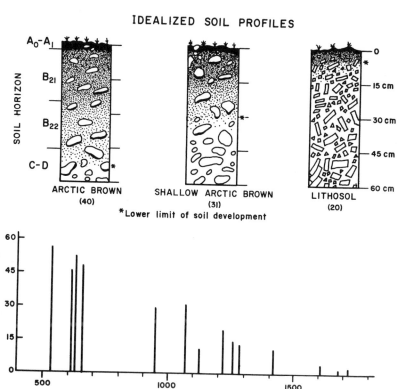

IDEALIZED SOIL PROFILES

ARCTIC BROWN
(40)

SHALLOW ARCTIC BROWN
(31)

LITHOSOL
(20)

*Lower limit of soil development

Fig. 8. Decreasing depth of soil development with increasing altitude in the Brooks Range (Tedrow and Brown, 1962).

represented considerably younger soil parent material than the unglaciated, higher mountainous landscapes, for all soils studied elapsed time was considered sufficient to reflect the morphology of a mature profile. With increased elevation, vegetation cover changes from a completely closed to broken mat of predominantly vascular plants to open cover with a predominance of lichens and mosses. On the gravelly glacial and stream deposits of the valleys the arctic brown soils have a solum thickness of about 50 cm. On the stable bedrock positions at 900 to 1,200 m there is a noticeable suppression of the soil-forming potential. At these altitudes the shallow arctic brown solum has a thickness of about 30 cm, and between 1,200 and 1,500 m a maximum of 20 cm. Finally at 1,700 m or so, the upper limit of stable soil sites, the soil consists of only 2 to 3 cm of discontinuous organic matter with virtually no characteristic brown soil colour in the mineral material. In addition to the decreased depth of solum with increasing altitude, the parent material is looser and coarser, and the A_1 horizon becomes less important with the B horizon dominant.

From these observations the general conclusion was drawn that the thickness of the solum as indicated basically by soil colour is a function of climate or of decreased temperature with altitudes. Even though the soil sites at higher altitudes may have been exposed to weathering for considerably greater time than those on the younger glaciated terrain, soil formation has not penetrated to the depths observed at lower altitudes. However, it should be mentioned that the secondary deposits, such as moraines, yield a deeper solum faster than a consolidated bedrock parent material, regardless of altitude.

Organic soils

In the Okpilak River Valley, a combination of organic soils and patterned-ground features constitute a limited area of organic terrain (Brown 1962a, b). The presence of these conditions warranted further investigation, since organic soils have not been investigated as extensively as the well-drained and tundra soils in northern Alaska. Ice wedge polygons in various forms of development and degradation dominate the tussock-covered tundra landscape (Fig. 9). The organic soils vary in composition and structure and include moss peats, sod peats, and secondary depositional accumulations of organic materials. The moss peat occupies the flat tops of the ice wedge polygons. The depth of seasonal thaw is limited to 25 to 30 cm (Fig. 10). As the width of the ice wedge trough increases, more and more of the trough area is occupied by a wetter sod-like peat. Water commonly stands in or

Fig. 9. Mosaic of polygon tops and troughs.

Fig. 10. Moss peat soil.

flows through these troughs. The flat, ice wedge polygons eventually develop into high-centred polygons and peaty mounds which result in a mosaic of marsh and moss peats as seen in Figure 9. The moss peat becomes a dry peat on these high-centred polygons with corresponding decrease in depth of thaw.

The modal site for the occurrence of the organic terrain is on the flat valley floor adjacent to the east side of West Okpilak Lake. Organic soils also ascend the gentle valley slopes and are observed on the uplands but are not associated with the ice wedge polygon sequence.

The vegetation of the moss peat soil is a dwarf shrub-heath type with various sizes of cottongrass tussocks. This includes *Eriophorum vaginatum, Ledum palustre decumbens, Vaccinium Vitis-idaea, Vaccinium uliginosum, Empetrum nigrum, Betula* sp. *Arctostaphylos alpina*, several *Carices*, and *Rubus chamaemorus*. Lichens include *Cetraria cucullata, Cetraria nivalis, Alectoria* (Black), *Thamniola vermicularis*, and *Cladonia* sp. *Sphagnum fuscum* is the dominant moss with *Dicranum* sp. and *Polytrichum* sp. present. The sphagnum species form the predominantly mossy substratum, although the finely divided layers may also consist of the remains of sedges and grasses. Tussock development is not as pronounced on the very wet, mossy sites as on the drier peats. The presence of *Rubus chamaemorus* is characteristic of this organic soil.

Ten organic samples were collected from five shallow profiles and one frost ooze of the type H_s. Six of the samples are from three profiles within a polygon 22 m in diameter. Two samples were from a profile situated on a high-centred peaty polygon located approximately 50 m south of this sampled polygon. A wet meadow tundra soil and an ooze, north of the main sample area, are included. These samples are described in Table 6.

For purposes of discussion and reporting of the results the samples are grouped according to physical appearance: the well-preserved, spongy moss samples (no. 31, 33, 34, 35, 38, 45) and the finely divided materials (no. 32, 36, 37, 46). Sample 39 is a mineral horizon of the meadow tundra soil.

The data presented in Table 7 indicate the acidic nature of moss peat and are typical of highmoor peats. The large loss-on-ignition values are characteristic of the mossy vegetation which constitutes the major part of the organic soil. The high ash contents are the result of mineral additions in the form of waterborne and airborne silts and sands. The cation exchange capacities agree with values for mosses and dry peats from other areas, as do the nitrogen and phosphorus levels.

In regions of perennially frozen ground, the frost table impedes

TABLE 6
MOSS PEAT PROFILES AND RELATED SOILS

Profile	Sample	Depth (cm)	Description
1	31	0–10	Dark brown (7.5YR4/5), well-preserved, moist, loose moss and shreds of cottongrass tussock; consistency grades into more matted moss at 8 to 10 cm. Principally *Sphagnum*.
	32	10–30	Wet, dark reddish-brown to black (5YR3/3 to 5YR3/1), finely divided organic material, little recognizable plant remains, darker at frost table (Pfg. 30 cm).
2	33	0–8	Black, loose, well-preserved moss peat with woody twigs and roots. *Sphagnum* and *Dicranum*.
	34	8–30	Black, well-preserved, wet mossy peat and organic shreds; somewhat more compact with depth (Pfg. 30 cm).
3	35	0–15	Dark brown to black, well-preserved moss peat, on raised edge of polygons with small tussocks. *Sphagnum* dominant, *Dicranum* present.
	36	15–30	Brown (7.5YR5/2), finely divided organic material with coarse sands and cobbles embedded in the organic matrix (Pfg. 30 cm).
	37	5–25	Dark brown, organic silt ooze from moderately polygonized moss peat area; few rounded cobbles embedded.
4	38	0–10	Brown moss mat between cottongrass tussocks. *Dicranum* and liverwort present.
	39	10–32	Grey, mottled silt loam with slight crumb structure immediately below the mat (wet meadow tundra) (Pfg. 32 cm).
5	45	2–8	Dark reddish-brown, coarsely fibrous woody peat from high-centred peaty polygon. *Dicranum* and *Polytrichum*.
	46	10–25	Dark brown, very finely divided, silty organic materials with some coarse sands (Pfg. 25 cm).

drainage. Water remains ponded in surface depressions and in polygon trenches. Under these conditions, ice wedge polygons and moss peat soils may develop on the subdued relief of the valley floor. As the organic surface thickens the insulating effect of the peat causes a reduction in the depth of the seasonally thawed soil. At first, the profile consists of a wet mineral substratum and a thin cover of moss and tussocks. This is represented by the wet meadow tundra profile 4 (Table 6). Where conditions are favourable for moss formation, the thawed zone soon becomes entirely organic as additions of organic

TABLE 7

PARTIAL CHEMICAL DATA FROM A MOSS
PEAT AND RELATED SOILS

Sample	Depth (cm)	pH	CEC* meq/100 g	Loss-on-ignition (%)†	Carbon (%)	Nitrogen (%)	Phosphorus (%)	C/N‡
31	0–10	3.8	116	92	46	0.98	0.093	47
33	0–8	3.8	108	92	46	1.1	0.099	42
34	8–30	3.4	101	90	47	1.3	0.096	36
35	0–15	3.7	102	90	46	1.5	0.15	31
38	0–10	4.0	88	76	39	0.85	0.11	46
45	2–8	3.9	108	79	40	1.7	0.19	24
32	10–30	3.6	85	82	51	1.4	0.068	36
36	15–30	4.1	31	44	29	0.85	0.092	34
37	5–25	4.2	52	65	43	1.6	0.088	27
46	10–25	3.6	70	51	29	1.7	0.19	17
39	10–32	4.6	7.4	7.6	4.7	0.22		21

*CEC = cation exchange capacity
†500C
‡C/N = carbon-nitrogen ratio

matter are made by the moss vegetation. Decomposition is slow in the cold anaerobic environment. The formation of peat associated with perennially frozen ground differs from the development of highmoor peats in regions of unfrozen ground. The modal peat of the flat terrain does not develop solely as a result of moisture from atmospheric precipitation, although P/E values are high with considerable fog and high humidity. Ponding is enhanced by the raised edges of polygons.

A source of nutrients is probably locally supplied to the peat through frost churning. Mineral and organic materials from the lower profile are circulated through the peat onto the surface as oozes. Cobbles embedded in the subsurface organic layers are further evidence of upward movements resulting from frost activity. Additional sources of nutrients are supplied by windborne silts and the breakdown of organic constituents as a result of mineralization. The frost churning is partly responsible for the fine division of organic matter.

The diagenesis of the moss peat soil is further demonstrated by the growth and the eventual partial thaw of ice wedges and massive ice lenses. As ice wedges grow, the volume of the total substratum increases. This results in the slight raising of portions of the developing polygon, particularly adjacent to the wedges. However, the polygon edges do not seem to be raised as much in peaty soils as in the wet mineral soils. This may be a result of the greater compressibility of the peat. Primary and secondary troughs of polygons develop on the tussock-covered surfaces. Ice wedges increase in size with time. The troughs broaden and become filled with water, and a bog vegetation develops. The flow of water enhances the deepening of the troughs by increasing the melting of the initial ice wedges. Slump occurs along the edges of the polygons and exposes new ice wedges and lenses. This deepening and broadening of the troughs eventually leads to the formation of a mosaic of high-centred peaty polygons. The tussock-covered, high-centred polygon is considerably drier than the weakly developed, low-centred polygon. Peat accumulation in the former is probably reduced. In a further stage in the degradation of the high-centred peaty polygon, peaty mounds may develop amidst a sod-like bog. These polygonal forms may therefore represent a sequence of events from weakly developed ice wedge polygons to high-centred peaty polygons to degraded peaty mounds.

CONCLUSIONS

A wide diversity of soils and patterned ground exists in the northern Brooks Range. This is attributed to the variety of parent materials, both glacial and non-glacial, to the extremes in relief, and finally to the arctic climate. Sorted features are common on flat terrain. Soil profiles lack horizontal continuity, primarily because of intense frost action and sorting. This is reflected in the difficulties encountered when attempting to map arctic soils. Complex mapping units are required if a detailed soils-patterned ground map is prepared.

Investigations of the well-drained mineral soils on different-aged surfaces fail to yield pronounced chronosequences of soil development, largely because of differences in parent materials. In these areas, frequently within a short distance of the northern tree-line, two distinct, well-drained soils exist side by side. In the valleys the arctic brown predominates, with the podzol-like soil present under certain optimum conditions of vegetation, microrelief, and parent materials. The present regional climate apparently favours the widespread distribution of the arctic brown. With increasing altitude the thickness of the well-drained solum decreases, a function of reduced temperatures and, in part, less physically weatherable parent materials. Peaty soils accumulate to a limited extent on the valley floors.

ACKNOWLEDGEMENTS. These studies were conducted in partial fulfillment of the requirements for the doctoral degree at Rutgers University and were aided by a contract between the Office of Naval Research, Department of the Navy, and the Arctic Institute of North America. Appreciation is extended to Dr. J. C. F. Tedrow for his role as thesis adviser and to Dr. Fiorenzo Ugolini, Dr. Edward G. Sable,

Dr. John E. Cantlon, and Dr. William Malcolm for their assistance in the field. The field support was provided by the Arctic Research Laboratory, Max C. Brewer, Director.

REFERENCES CITED

BRITTON, M. E., 1957, Vegetation of the arctic tundra: Biology Colloquium Proc. Oregon State College, Corvallis, Oregon, p. 26-61.

BROWN, J., 1962a, Organic terrain from a glaciated valley, northern Alaska: Proc. 13th Alaskan Sci. Conf., p. 159-160.

———, 1962b, Soils of the northern Brooks Range, Alaska: PhD thesis, Rutgers Univ., New Brunswick, New Jersey, 234 p.

———, 1966, Soils of the Okpilak River Regions, Alaska: US Army Cold Regions Research and Engineering Laboratory Res. Rept. 188, 49 p.

BROWN, J., and TEDROW, J. C. F., 1964, Soils of the northern Brooks Range, Alaska: 4 well-drained soils of the glaciated valleys: Soil Sci., v. 97, p. 187-195.

CANTLON, J. E., 1961, Plant cover in relation to macro-, meso-, and microrelief: Final Rept. Arctic Institute of North America, Grants ONR-208 and 212 (unpubl.).

CHANDLER, R. F., JR., 1943, The time required for podzol profile formation as evidenced by the Mendenhall Glacier deposits near Juneau, Alaska: Soil Sci. Soc. Proc. America (1942), v. 7, p. 454-459.

CANOVER, J. H., 1960, Macro- and microclimatology of the Arctic Slope of Alaska: Quartermaster Research and Engineering Center, Tech. Rept. EP 139, Natick, Massachusetts.

CORTE, A. E., 1959, Experimental formation of sorted patterns in gravel overlying a melting ice surface: US Army Snow, Ice, and Permafrost Research Establishment Res. Rept. 55, 15 p.

———, 1963, Particle sorting by repeated freezing and thawing: Science, v. 142, p. 499-501.

CROCKER, R. L., and MAJOR, J., 1955, Soil development in relation to vegetation and surface age at Glacier Bay, Alaska: Jour. Ecology, v. 43, p. 427-448.

CROCKER, R. L., and DICKSON, B. A., 1957, Soil development on the recessional moraines of the Herbert and Mendenhall Glaciers of southeastern Alaska: Jour. Ecology, v. 45, p. 169-185.

DAY, J. H., and RICE, H. M., 1964, The characteristics of some permafrost soils in the Mackenzie Valley, NWT: Arctic, v. 17, p. 222-236.

DETTERMAN, R. L., BOWSHER, A. L., and DUTRO, J. T., JR., 1958, Glaciation on the Arctic Slope of the Brooks Range, Northern Alaska: Arctic, v. 11, p. 43-61.

DOUGLAS, L. A., 1961, A pedologic study of tundra soils from northern Alaska: PhD thesis, Rutgers Univ., New Brunswick, New Jersey, 147 p.

DOUGLAS, L. A., and TEDROW, J. C. F., 1961, Tundra soils of arctic Alaska: Proc. 7th Intern. Soil Sciences Congress Comm. V, v. 4, p. 291-304.

DREW, J. V., 1957, A pedologic study of Arctic Coastal Plain soils near Point Barrow, Alaska: PhD thesis, Rutgers Univ., New Brunswick, New Jersey, 117 p.

DREW, J. V., and TEDROW, J. C. E., 1957, Pedology of an arctic brown profile near Point Barrow, Alaska: Soil Sci. Soc. America Proc., v. 21, p. 336-339.

———, 1962, Arctic soil classification and patterned ground: Arctic, v. 15, p. 109-116.

HILL, D. E., and TEDROW, J. C. E., 1961, Weathering and soil formation in the arctic environment: Amer. Jour. Sci., v. 259, p. 84-101.

HOLMES, G. W., and LEWIS, C. R., 1965, Quaternary geology of the Mount Chamberlin Area, Brooks Range, Alaska: US Geol. Survey Bull. 1201-B, 32 p.

KEELER, C. M., 1959, Notes on the geology of the McCall Valley area: Arctic, v. 12, p. 87-97.

KUBOTA, J., and WHITTIG, L. D., 1960, Podzols in the vicinity of the Necchina and Tazlina Glaciers, Alaska: Soil Sci. Soc. America Proc., v. 24, p. 133-136.

KUNKLE, G. R., 1958, Multiple glaciation in the Jago River area, northeastern Alaska: MSc thesis, Univ. of Michigan, Ann Arbor, Michigan, 41 p.

LEAHEY, A., 1947, Characteristics of soils adjacent to the Mackenzie River in the Northwest Territories of Canada. Soil Sci. Soc. America Proc., v. 12, p. 458-461.

LEFFINGWELL, E. DE K., 1919, The Canning River region northern Alaska: US Geol. Survey Prof. Paper 109, 251 p.

MACNAMARA, E. E., 1964, Soils of the Howard Pass Area northern Alaska; Special Report to Arctic Institute of North America. Rutgers Univ., New Brunswick, New Jersey, 125 p.

MALCOLM, W. McL., II., 1959, The genus *Carex* of the Arctic Slope of Alaska, an annotated species list and key: MSc thesis, Michigan State Univ., E. Lansing, Michigan.

MIKHAILOV, I. S., 1961, Soil studies in northern Alaska: Soviet Soil Sci., no. 2, p. 209-214.

NIKIFOROFF, C. C., Soils of Eurasian Arctic: Encyclopedia Arctica v, 6, Plant Sciences, Regional no. 13 (unpubl.).

PAWLUK, S., 1960, Some podzol soils of Alberta: Can. Jour. Soil Sci., v. 40, p. 1-14.

PORTER, S. C., 1964, Late Pleistocene glacial chronology of north-central Brooks Range, Alaska: Amer. Jour. Sci., v. 262, p. 446-460.

RIEGER, S., and JUVE, R. L., 1961, Soil development in recent loess in the Matanuska Valley, Alaska: Soil Sci. Soc. Amer. Proc., v. 25, p. 243-248.

SABLE, E. G., 1959, Preliminary report on sedimentary and metamorphic rocks in part of the Romanzof Mountains, Brooks Range, N.E. Alaska: MSc thesis, Univ. of Michigan, Ann Arbor, Michigan, 84 p.

———, 1961, Recent recession and thinning of Okpilak Glacier, northeastern Alaska: Arctic, v. 14, p. 176-187.

———, 1965, Geology of the Romanzof Mountains, Brooks Range, northeastern Alaska: PhD thesis, Univ. of Michigan, Ann Arbor, Michigan, 218 p.

SHARP, R. P., 1942, Soil structures in the St. Elias Range, Yukon Territory: Jour. Geomorp., v. 5, p. 274-287.

SMITH, J., 1956, Some moving soils in Spitsbergen: Jour. Soil Sci., v. 7, p. 10-21.

SPETZMAN, L. A., 1959, Vegetation of the Arctic Slope of Alaska: US Geol. Survey Prof. Paper 302-B, p. 19-54.

SPRINGER, M. E., 1958, Desert pavement and vesicular layer of some soils of the desert of the Lahontan Basin, Nevada: Soil Sci. Soc. Amer. Proc., v. 22, p. 63-66.

TEDROW, J. C. F., and BROWN, J., 1962, Soils of the Brooks Range, northern Alaska. I. Weakening of soil forming potential at high arctic altitudes: Soil Sci., v, 93, p. 254-261

———, and ———, 1965, Soils of arctic Alaska: VII International Congress INQUA, Boulder, Colorado, Abstract vol., p. 461 (paper in press).

TEDROW, J. F. C., and CANTLON, J. E., 1958, Concepts of soil formation and classification in arctic regions: Arctic, v. 11, p. 166-179.

TEDROW, J. F. C., DREW, J. V., HILL, D. E., and DOUGLAS, L. A., 1958, Major genetic soils of the Arctic Slope of Alaska: Jour. Soil Sc., v. 9, p. 33-45.

TEDROW, J. F. C., and HILL, D. E., 1954, Soil characteristics of the Arctic Slope of Alaska, a pedologic report: Boston Univ. Phys. Res. Lab. (unpubl.).

———, and ———, 1955, Arctic brown soil: Soil Sci., v. 80, p. 265-275.

TRAUTMAN, M. A., 1963, Isotopes, Inc. radiocarbon measurements III: Radiocarbon, v. 5, p. 62-81.

UGOLINI, F. C., and TEDROW, J. C. F., 1963, Soils of the Brooks Range, Alaska: 3 Rendzina of the Arctic: Soil Sci., v. 96, p. 121-127.

US Weather Bureau 1957-1961, Climatological data, Alaska, annual summaries: US Dept. Commerce.

Washburn, A. L., 1956, Classification of patterned ground and review of suggested origins: Geol. Soc. Amer. Bull., v. 67, p. 823-866.

Whittington, C. L., and Sable, E. G., 1948, Preliminary geologic report of Sadlerochit River area: US Geol. Survey, Geol. Inv. Naval Petroleum Reserve, no. 4, Alaska, Prelim. Rept. 20, 18 p.

Wright, J. R., Leahey, A., Rice, H. M., 1959, Chemical, morphological, and mineralogical characteristics of a chromosequence of soils in alluvial deposits in the Northwest Territories: Can. Jour. Soil Sci., v. 39, p. 32-43.

DISTRIBUTION OF SMALL-SCALE PERIGLACIAL AND GLACIAL GEOMORPHOLOGICAL FEATURES ON AXEL HEIBERG ISLAND, NORTHWEST TERRITORIES, CANADA

STEN RUDBERG
University of Göteborg
Göteborg, Sweden

ABSTRACT. A geomorphological map showing small-scale features is presented for a selected part of Axel Heiberg Island, Northwest Territories, Canada. The island, situated around 80°N, has a high relief influenced by folded (Mesozoic and Tertiary) sedimentary rocks. The climate is cold and semi-arid; the island is in part glaciated. The map was based on a contour map, the contours being used as sampling lines for localization of the mapped features. The map allows the following statements: Outcrops are few and mainly found in rock walls and other sites where erosion is active. Rock waste covers all higher slopes and is dependent on the rock in place. The fine material of the map is transported by wash. Glacial striae are found up to 240-250 m above sea level. Glacial deposits, mainly till, are found to 250-400 m and as isolated patches and erratics to 600-800 m. Valley trains and alluvial fans are important as are thin layers of wash deposits. Of the patterned-ground features the non-sorted forms are frequent in the areas of glacial deposits, while the sorted forms mainly belong to areas of coarse local debris. The capacity of present-day morphological processes is discussed, and results of mass movement measurements are given. The activity of running water is ranked as the most important and is tentatively connected with occasional heavy summer rains. The major forms of the landscape are strongly influenced by running water, far less by the extensive glaciation, proved by deposits and striae.

RÉSUMÉ. L'auteur présente une carte géomorphologique des formes mineures, couvrant une partie de l'île Axel Heiberg, dans les Territoires du Nord-Ouest canadien. Cette île, située au 80e degré de latitude, possède un relief élevé influencé par des roches sédimentaires mésozoïques et tertiaires plissées. Le climat est froid et semi-aride, l'île partiellement glaciée. Une carte en courbes de niveau a servi de carte de base, les courbes servant de repères pour la localisation des données recueillies sur le terrain. La carte permet les énoncés suivants: les affleurements sont rares et se trouvent sur des abrupts et à d'autres endroits où l'érosion est active. Le manteau détritique recouvre les parties supérieures des pentes et dépend de la roche en place. Le ruissellement emporte les débris les plus fins. On trouve des stries glaciaires jusqu'à 240-250 m au-dessus du niveau de la mer, des dépôts glaciaires, surtout du till, jusqu'à 250-400 m et, sous forme de taches isolées et d'erratiques, jusqu'à 600-800 m. Plaines alluviales et cônes alluviaux sont importants, ainsi que les dépôts minces de ruissellement. Les formes polygonales non-triées sont fréquentes dans les zones de dépôts glaciaires tandis que les formes triées se trouvent surtout dans les zones détritiques. L'auteur étudie la capacité des processus morphologiques actuels et présente les résultats de mesures de mouvements de masse. Il juge l'activité des eaux courantes comme la plus importante et essaie de la relier à de rares mais violents orages d'été. Les formes majeures du paysage sont fortement influencées par les eaux courantes et beaucoup moins par la vaste glaciation antérieure, dont les dépôts et les stries sont les indices.

SAMMANFATTNING. En geomorfologisk karta över småformer inom ett område på Axel Heiberg Island, Canada N.W.T., presenteras. Ön, som är belägen kring 80 breddgraden, har storkuperad terräng, påverkad av veckade mesozoiska och tertiära lager. Klimatet är kallt och semiaritt, ön delvis nedisad. Kartan har som underlag en kurvkarta, vars kurvor användes vid lokaliseringen av kartans detaljer i fält. Kartan visar följande: Hällar är fåtaliga och finns i branta väggar och på andra platser med aktiv erosion. Vittringsmaterial täcker sluttningarnas högre avsnitt och är klart bergartsberoende. Ytavspolning kan transportera kartans finkorniga vittringsmaterial. Isräfflor påträffas upp till 240-50 m ö.h., glaciala avlagringer, främst morän, upp till 250-400 och som isolerade fläckar och enstaka block till 600-800. Flodplan och alluvialkoner är viktiga, likaså tunna sedimentlager, härrörande från ytavspolning. Av frostmarksformer är de "icke-sorterade" vanliga i områden med glacialavlagringar, medan "sorterade" former främst tillhör områden med grovt vittringsmaterial. Kapaciteten hos recenta geomorfologiska processer diskuteras och mätningsresultat anges för massrörelser. Det rinnande vattnet bedöms som verksammast av processerna och förknippas försöksvis med förekommande kraftiga sommarregn. Landskapets storformer är starkt påverkade av fluviatila processer, vida mindre av den tidigare mera omfattande nedisning som räfflor och avlagringar omvittnar.

CONTENTS

INTRODUCTION

As a member of the Jacobsen-McGill expedition to Axel Heiberg Island, Northwest Territories, Canada in 1961, the author had, as his main duty, to make a geomorphological map. It was decided to make a large-scale map of a selected part of the Expedition area showing results (notably the small-scale results) of the morphological processes of the past and present, that is, the processes of a period of more extensive glaciation and a period of periglacial and glacial climate, the latter being the cold, semi-arid climate of the region today.

Somewhat similar maps have been made by the author and his students in the Swedish mountains (Rudberg 1962) and in the Canadian Arctic by Robitaille (1961) and by Saint-Onge (1964-65). The Axel Heiberg map, which is not yet published, is reported in two papers (Rudberg 1963a, b) which are partly used and quoted here. The purpose of such a mainly descriptive geomorphological map is the same as for other similar ones: to show the distribution of different features, their frequency, interrelations, and, possibly, in that way to give some information about the landform genesis. Such a map is a complement to other methods, both to the ordinary, comparative methods and to the quantitative measurements of the processes themselves. In a situation where it is impossible to get long-term observations about the processes the map might be a necessary complement. It is important that the area selected is representative.

Axel Heiberg Island (Fig. 1), situated between 78° and 81°N, is the second most northerly of the Canadian Arctic islands. Except for the northernmost tip, it belongs to the Alpine fold belt. The rocks of Triassic to Tertiary age are mainly shale, siltstone, sandstone, and quartzitic sandstone. These sediments are intersected by basic igneous rocks (gabbro, diabase, basalt), forming flows and sills. To the sequence also belongs gypsum of Upper Paleozoic age. The total thickness of the rock series is 11,000 m in the axial part of the basin. The folding is strong in the central part of the island, less in the western and eastern parts. The strike of the folds is from north to south and from northwest to southeast. The tectonic style is characterized by broad, open synclines and narrow anticlines in which are often found gypsum diapirs (Troelson 1950, Tozer 1960, Thorsteinsson and Tozer 1960, Thorsteinsson 1961, Kranck 1961, 1963, Fricker 1961, 1963, Hoen 1964).

Axel Heiberg Island is mainly a highland with mountainous relief, the highest summits reaching about 2,000 m. The highland is more pronounced to the west where the coast has the appearance of a fiord coast, at least in the southern and central parts of the island. The eastern slopes are in general more gentle, partly forming low plateaus, partly low plains.

The climate on the island can only be estimated by extrapolation from scattered weather stations in the Arctic archipelago, the closest being Eureka on Ellesmere Island and Isachsen on Ellef Ringnes Island. The monthly mean temperatures should be approximately: January-February −35° to −38°C; May-September −7° to −10°C; June-August +1° to +6°C, if June really has temperatures above freezing in the coastal areas. The number of days without freezing is probably less than 60. Reliable figures of precipitation are difficult to extrapolate as the variations between different stations are great and the variability quite high. As a whole the climate is dry, with highest figures 130 to 146 mm in a year (Resolute, Alert weather stations) and lowest 63 to 74 mm (Eureka, Mould Bay). One-third of the island is covered by glaciers. For climate see: Müller 1961, Thomas 1961, Wilson 1961, and the different climatological summaries from the weather stations.

The central part of the Expedition area (Fig. 1), chosen for the detailed geomorphological mapping, is situated around the inner end of the Expedition Fiord, the Expedition River, and the snout of the Thompson Glacier, an outlet glacier which drains the McGill Ice Cap, the largest on the island. The area has a representative geological sequence, including most of the series found on the island. The main

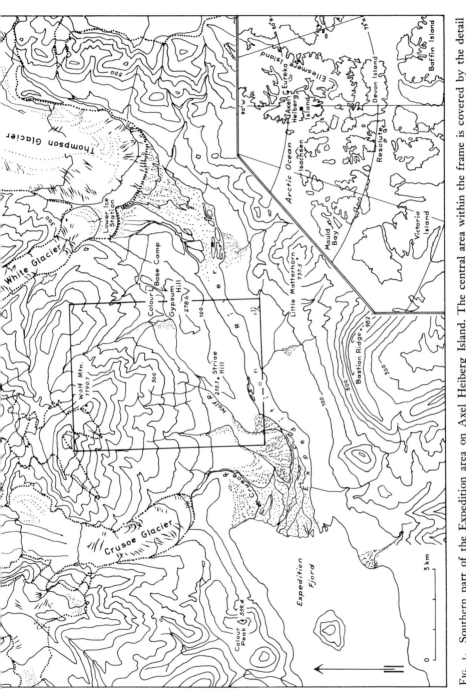

Fig. 1. Southern part of the Expedition area on Axel Heiberg Island. The central area within the frame is covered by the detail map (Fig. 2). Contour interval is 100 metres.

part of the area is a broad syncline with narrow anticlines at the western and eastern margin of the area, both of them with gypsum diapirs. The relief is high, including snow-free areas from sea level to close to 1,200 m above sea level. The central part is occupied by the broad Expedition River valley with outwash plains belonging to the Thompson Glacier and the White Glacier. Many smaller, mainly V-shaped valleys converge towards this large valley. The slopes are steep or medium steep, but flat areas occur. For a discussion of the geology see Fricker 1961.

The summer climate is known from meteorological observations at the Base Camp (within the area at 200 m above sea level) and at the Lower Ice station (at the snout of the White Glacier). The summer of 1961 was cold, with mean temperature for June of −0.4°C and with 50 days without freezing, of which only three occurred in June. The longest period without freezing was three weeks. The summer of 1963 was still colder (oral communication, F. Müller); the summers of 1960 and 1962 were definitely warmer. In July of 1962 no freezing at all occurred. The mean temperature for July was 6.6°C in 1960 and 8.7°C in 1962, compared with 4.8°C in 1961. The daily means in June-August of 1960 and at least June-July of 1962 were definitely higher than the normal means in Eureka and Isachsen. It is possible—but not stated—that these last-mentioned differences indicate slightly more favourable temperature conditions in the well-protected Expedition Fiord valley than in coastal areas. Snow patches existed definitely longer in these latter areas in 1961, and the first flowering is possibly somewhat later (Parmelee 1963). As to precipitation, the variations of 1960-62 are high, with the following figures for July-August (the 25th): 1960, 75 mm; 1961, 100 mm; 1962, 35 mm. If it is true that the summer season (at least 10 per cent more than the figures given here) accounts for about one-half of the annual precipitation, the Base Camp station would be ranked among the slightly more wet weather stations of the archipelago. The high figures for 1961 were caused by two single rainstorms, each of them giving about 30 mm in 24 hours. Similar wet conditions are also registered for other years in the firn stratigraphy investigated by Müller in an excavated ice shaft at the Upper Ice station (70 km from the Base Camp). The snow-melt in 1961 passed without giving much water, and almost all snow had gone at the end of June. As only few snow patches remained any longer, it is obvious that the redistribution by drifting had been of small importance that year (Havens 1961, 1963, Diem 1963, Müller 1963a).

Closed vegetation is nowhere extensive. Vegetation is mostly found only on some favourable soils, in stripes oriented in the strike of shale, following the details of the patterned ground, or forming scattered tussocks and tufts. Protection by vegetation, though not completely absent, is probably as a whole of restricted importance. No altitudinal zonation of geomorphological importance can be based upon vegetation.

As a whole, the central part of the Expedition area should be regarded as representative. However, no open coastal areas are included, and—for lack of time—no nunatak area.

MAPPING TECHNIQUE

The area chosen for mapping was, from a practical point of view, by far the best one. As a base for the field work the following was used: (1) a contour map (scale 1:25,000) based on aerial photographs and ground work; (2) aerial photographs of all the area in approximate scale 1:60,000; (3) aerial photographs of parts of the area in approximate scale 1:8,000 to 1:20,000. The aerial photographs showed many morphological features such as ice-wedge polygons, talus slopes, and more extensive areas of non-sorted stripes. They were, however, very insufficient, and detailed field work was necessary.

The exact localization of features observed during the field work caused some problem. The contour map and the aerial photographs were not detailed enough in many areas, and the compass was useless in this area not far from the magnetic pole. For these reasons the contour lines of the map were used as sampling lines, and their position was determined by aneroid barometers. The two end-points of the sample lines were a good control, being chosen at places easily recognizable on the map or aerial photograph, such as river beds or gully edges. The surveyors (the author and often an assistant) walked along the contours and pinpointed the features to be mapped by pacing distances as they went.

A map of this type gives the distribution of the different features and their local environment, but not always their frequency. In the last respect there are differences between features represented by dots and the small-scale features represented by individual symbols (e.g., sorted circles). In many cases such symbols tell that the feature exists, but tell nothing about the area covered.

A selected part of the map is published here as an example (Fig. 2).

MAPPED FEATURES

Outcrops

The term "outcrop" used in this report is restricted to sound rock not disintegrated by weathering. Outcrops of this kind have a low

Fig. 2. Map of periglacial features of part of Expedition River valley, southern Axel Heiberg Island, Canada.

Weathered material, fine	Gullies
Weathered material, coarse	Mud polygons
Till and other glacial deposits	Earth hummocks
Alluvial fans and valley trains	Nonsorted circles
Rock outcrops	Tundra polygons
Glacial striae	Terracettes
Talus	Nonsorted stripes
	"Up-slope" polygons

Sorted polygons	
Sorted stripes	
Lobes	
Lobes, built of stones and boulders	
Mud flows	
Direction of wind erosion	
Wind eroded surface	

0 1 2   4   6   8 km

frequency. They are found in the following clearly defined positions:

(1) Steep escarpments, generally connected with special rock types and with structures. Most cuestas and hogbacks are formed by layers of basic rocks. The majority of escarpments have talus slopes below and are in a stage of retreat and lowering. Some of the walls are quite small compared with the talus slopes. The wall forms are not analysed in any detail. Quite commonly there are talus slopes from which outcrops protrude as stacks far below the continuous cliff.

(2) Outcrops connected with active erosion. Outcrops of this kind are quite common and mainly result from running water. The marginal rivers along the glaciers (normal glacier drainage here) erode their channels actively. Signs of this are cliffs with ravines and chutes, the latter, at least, partly initiated by the undermining lateral erosion. Active erosion is also quite a normal feature in numerous small ordinary rivers with steep gradients. This erosion is almost exclusively connected with lateral erosion along the valley train, or in a slightly incised part of it. Water running over outcrops is not often seen, and real waterfalls are not frequent in spite of the steepness of the river curves. In its most typical form this lateral erosion occurs at the side of alluvial fans.

(3) Outcrops in other positions. Such outcrops are only common in shale areas and are found both on steep slopes, which are partly covered by scree (mainly the same angle of slope as the talus itself), and on gentle slopes and broad, rounded crests. The reason is probably a continuous removal of easily transported fine-grained rock waste. In the shale areas there is often no sharp limit between outcrops, and outcrops with a very thin cover of debris. At some distance or from the air, the rock structures are often discernible in detail, where only the weathered rock is observable from the ground. Outcrops of this latter type are probably slightly under-represented on the map. Similar outcrops in areas of sandstone or basic rocks are of small importance.

Rock weathering and rock waste

Of locally derived weathered material, the map distinguishes coarse fractions, mainly stones and boulders, and fine fractions, ranking from gravel to fine material. The reason for this grain size limit is the relation to the transporting processes, mainly rain and rill wash.

Typical of the sandstones and the quartzitic sandstones are boulder fields, sometimes with pieces of great size. The group of basic rocks (gabbro, diabase, basalt) have an intermediate position as one type forms boulder fields and the other sheets of gravel. The latter are the result of granular weathering, which is also combined with exfoliation and spherical weathering (Fig. 3). It is often found that the rock is rotten below a hard crust-like surface. Such crusts are found in the vicinity of polished surfaces with preserved striae. It is not definitely proven that the crusts and the striated surfaces form part of one and the same surface, but field evidences make it probable. The granular and the spherical weathering is remarkable in efficiency, to judge from "tor-like" residual forms found at the very edge of cuestas. The granular weathering is not investigated in any detail. In Scandinavia, granular weathering is not unusual in cold climates in basic rocks.

All the shales and siltstones form fine debris, except for inclusions of different types. The waste varies from splinters of gravel size down to fine material, silt, or maybe finer. The transition, if not obscured by wash, from one waste type to the other is often sharp. Each one of the thin beds may have its own type. The gypsum outcrops have crusts and do not generally seem to produce rock waste through mechanical weathering.

The limit between the two mapped types of weathered material is often sharp.

Generally speaking, weathering increases towards higher altitudes but without sharp limits. Boulder fields, for instance, are connected with suitable rock types and are found also at low altitudes. No clear zonation occurs with altitude, which is in accordance with the lack of good zonation in the plant cover. The increase in weathering towards higher altitudes is a problem: Is it due to higher frequency of short duration frost cycles during the summer, or mainly to higher ground moisture content during the same season? Is it mainly the latter? The higher parts of the slopes are more frequently situated above the base of the clouds and have more often a temporary snow cover in the summer. Well-preserved outcrops, also at lower altitudes, are generally found in "dry positions," such as hilltops, or on the edge of some cuestas, that is, in localities where the snow melts early and from which melt-water and rain drain away easily.

Areas with weathered rock are much larger than those with pre-served rock. Wide areas at low altitude are almost free of outcrops be-cause they are covered by glacial deposits. At high altitudes important boulder field areas are almost free of outcrops.

Glacial striae and direction of ice movement

Glacial striae were found at 40 localities within the mapped area, usually on diabase or gabbro and in a few instances on sandstone. Most of the localities were found in typical "dry positions," and all of them were at relatively low altitude, the highest being at an altitude of 240 to 250 m above sea level. Much of the striae was fairly well preserved as a fine polish with densely spaced microgrooves, but not all of it by far. Often the surface had to be dampened by melting snow before the striae could be appropriately studied, and in some cases the soil cover had to be removed. The main direction of orientation of the striae (measured in relation to distant terrain features) on flat rock facettes and in "free position" is from east-northeast or east. Though some influence from local topography is evident, main direction does not vary much within the area. On several outcrops two systems were observed, one from east-northeast and the other from east-southeast or southeast. In several cases the age relationship could be established (the older system may be found in a somewhat protected position in respect of the younger system). The system with the movement from a more southerly direction always proved to be the younger.

The main direction of striae (i.e., the older system) is in part close to the main direction of the Expedition River valley, but taken as a whole they diverge with a small angle. The younger system always forms a marked angle with the valley axis. In one site, close to the front of the Crusoe Glacier, the direction of striae is almost opposite to the present ice movement (Fig. 4).

Glacial striae were searched for at higher altitudes on the slopes, but without success. Either they have never existed, or they have been destroyed by the increasing weathering, or they have not been discovered, because the field work during the later part of the season did not fully permit the time-consuming search for striae.

Typical *roche moutonnée* forms are not frequent. They occur as small, rounded rock faces in the areas with well-preserved striae, and some small isolated, steep and well-rounded *roches moutonnées* were seen in the same area. Otherwise, they are few, and small *roches moutonnées* were obviously difficult to distinguish from forms resulting from spherical weathering in basic rocks. *Roche moutonnée* forms gave no more guidance about former glaciation than the information from striae.

Some of the outcrops showed glacial striations bending around steep *roche moutonnée* faces. A similar phenomenon is well known in Scandinavia where it is usually attributed to plastic deformation of the bottom layer of the ice.

Erratics of indisputably distant derivation were not discovered within the mapped area.

FIG. 3. Granular and spherical weathering in a dyke or sill of basic rock; this is a common phenomenon. Little Matterhorn in the background.

FIG. 4. View from the snout of Crusoe Glacier. Lateral erosion at work in the channel; notice the slumps. No remnants of older channels are visible outside the present one. On the nearest ridge, to the right just before the steep wall, outcrops with striae, showing ice movements from directions more or less opposite to the movement of the present glacier.

Till and other glacial deposits

The mapping of till deposits poses one of the more difficult problems because of the possibility of contamination, mainly by solifluction material. True till of the area is generally rich in fines and contains stones, not diverging from the local sandstone, gabbro, or diabase, and showing varying degrees of roundness. Some sorts of solifluction material, for example, from a shale area with sandstone layers, would exhibit very similar deposits. As to roundness, it can also be observed to be increasing from an upper scree slope to a lower solifluction slope. Difficulties might even be caused by small-scale mudflows or the very often observed thin alluvial deposits of shale material on top of other soils, also on those of till-like appearance. Examples are found on the map in a downslope direction from outcropping shale. As the contamination problem is not easily solved and was first observed only after some mapping had been done, a future revision of the map might reduce the till areas in some localities.

Till is distributed as follows: Lower parts of the slope up to 250-400 m are dominated by till. Waste from the local rock dominates completely the higher slopes and the investigated area as a whole. Mapped as till, however, are some important areas up to about 500 m above sea level, but they are more or less isolated, and the transition between till and rock waste is nowhere sharp in these sites. Above such till deposits are found small till patches or some scattered erratics (of local origin, not from distant areas) on sharp crests or at the edge of cuestas (and close to outcrops of different petrographic composition). The highest locality which gave evidence of former ice surfaces was found at about 800 m on the southwestern slope of Wolf Mountain.

The general distribution pattern of the till is characterized by an uneven upper limit, with isolated patches and tongues penetrating up the valleys. These tongues are better developed on valley sides which are situated in the lee position of the ice movment, to judge from the preserved striae. This can be taken as an argument in support of the interpretation of the field observations. The argument is, however, slightly weakened by the fact that the valley sides poor in till also are the steepest ones in accordance with the main structural elements, and steep slopes are more easily covered with local weathered material. Another feature in the distribution pattern is also worth mentioning. High isolated till areas are often found on flat convex parts of the slope, that is, in areas from which the transport by mass movement has been slow and to which very little rock waste has arrived from higher parts of the slopes.

On lower parts of the slope till must have been reworked by wave action. The highest upper limit is not stated, but marine shells are found up to 80 m above sea level (Müller 1963c). The lower parts of the slopes (up to about 40 m in certain sections) exhibit upper layers, made up of material rich in fines but with a thin layer of scattered stones at the surface. The layers, taken as a whole, are believed to be sediments deposited during stages of higher water level, but no interpretation is so far given to the presence of the stones. In some areas stratified sand and gravel below the fine material were shown in small ravines. As no opportunity has been given to complete the grain size analysis of the soil samples, a final revision of the lower parts at the till slope is possible.

The high content of fine material is probably the reason for the normal development of a hard, crust-like surface in areas with till and marine sediments.

Activity of running water

Results of fluvial erosion are shown by outcrops along valley trains or fans and by many small gullies and canyons. Evidence of fluvial deposition is striking. Aerial photographs show numerous alluvial fans of large size, even at the mouth of small valleys only 4 to 5 km long, and without any connection with glacial drainage (Fig. 5). Also small-scale features are very frequent: fans about 20 m in length, miniature deltas, water-transported material spread over large parts of shale slopes, and slope sections often below small gullies. In some cases a thin alluvial layer occurred as a cover over pebble material of a different petrographic composition.

The alluvial fans are generally continued in upstream direction by valley trains in the V-shaped valleys, even in very small ones (Fig. 6). Both the valley trains and the fans are mainly built of coarse material (stones and boulders often with imbricate structures). They are generally steep in the upper parts of the fans—about 10°. Steps and waterfalls are not common. The lower parts of the fans, at least of the larger ones, are generally composed of fine material. Parts of the fans might look old because of lichen-covered stones, but large areas are fresh-looking. A slight dissection of the fan deposits and the valley trains is a common feature. A strong dissection is not frequent, but there are alluvial fans which definitely are fossil forms and no longer in position of possible accumulation. The terraces at the upper end of the Crusoe River fan are interpreted as remnants of older fans.

Forms resulting from sorting processes, movement in situ, downslope movement

The units, weathered rock material and till, also form different units

Fig. 5. Typical fan of the Expedition area belonging to the small stream which crosses the Base Camp ridge in a gap. Length of the stream is only about 5 km; the fan is about 300 m broad; the angle of slope of the fan in several cases is rather steep—about 10°.

FIG. 6. Typical valley form, with interlocking spurs and straight valley sides, V-shaped and few outcrops. Valley bottom is occupied by a broad valley train· with a rather steep gradient (as in arid regions), but few real waterfalls. The material of the valley train consists of coarse gravel and boulders. Lateral erosion at the sides of the valley train is common. In the background Black Crown Mountain with an empty cirque.

of periglacial activity.

Low-lying areas, flat or gently sloping within the zone of till, marine sediments, and fine-grained alluvial deposits are characterized by cells and circles, polygons, and nets of different types and sizes showing insignificant sorting and no clear downslope elongation. The most conspicuous are the large ice wedge or tundra polygons. These are easily discernible on the ground in some localities, but in others their distribution is better studied from the air or from aerial photographs. The polygons are found in almost continuous sequences over long distances in areas of fine-grained sediments in the lower parts of the alluvial fans, or on the slope close to the outwash plain of the Expedition River. In most cases the pattern is irregular and is made up of cells of different sizes, some 10 to 40 m wide; some have 4, others 5 or 6 sides, others are irregular. A rectangular, rather regular pattern can occasionally be seen, but the single very good example was found outside the Expedition area. The furrow between the cells is about 2-4 m wide. No consequent difference in width was observed with certainty between polygons close to sea level and those at higher elevations. High-centre polygons were by far more common than low-centre polygons. Exact figures, however, cannot be given. Well-developed low-centre polygons, however, were not observed on the lowest altitudes close to the outwash plain.

The smaller forms are fissure polygons, mud polygons with bulging forms, and stone earth circles (terminology partly according to Washburn 1956). In this order they are found in a sort of succession from the lower sediment areas to higher areas with ordinary till. Earth hummocks are locally frequent, mainly on west-facing slopes and areas somewhat richer in vegetation. They are often densely spaced in small fields or in stripes more or less perpendicular to the contours. One single symbol has been used for features of eventually varying genesis, including such ones which obviously originate from a cellular pattern created by desiccation cracks or frost cracks.

Within the "till-zone" there are also forms indicating downslope movement or possible downslope movement. The most striking features are the non-sorted stripes which consist of raised ridges of almost bare soil separated by small rills which have a better vegetation cover. The rills act as waterways during snow-melt and rain. They do not, however, have a true dendritic pattern as ordinary rivulets, but extend downslope, more or less parallel to each other, only occasionally branching out or meeting. Another feature showing downslope movement is the terracettes, small stone earth flats with a front some centimetres to one or two decimetres high and generally covered with some vegetation. They occur frequently, isolated or in small groups, but are normally not well developed in this area with sparse vegetation. Sorted stripes (as sorted circles) are not often observed in the "till zone."

Also, forms resulting from swift or instant mass movement are locally present. Earth slides were observed, some of them looking rather fresh and evidently belonging to the summer season of 1961 or one of the previous years. They are a sort of bowl slide with a scar and an accumulation below. The accumulation may consist of "blocks" of soil, loosened from the cellular pattern of the dry upper layer. It also happens that the soil masses have been wet enough to slide away, down to the nearest river. The greatest earth slide was shallow, compared with the area involved. It is probable that the marked scar form is successively modified by small slides (in fact observed). The residual forms might easily be overlooked during mapping. This might be the explanation of the relative importance of the fresh-looking slides out of a total quite small number of observations. Also mudflows with *levées* are observed within the "till zone." They are, however, sometimes released higher up on the slopes, outside the zone in question.

The areas of weathered rock material—with generally higher altitudes, with more varying but normally steeper slopes, and great local differences in particle size of the soil cover—have patterned-ground features of mainly other types. The small cells and polygons described earlier are almost absent. In the shale areas there are, however, other types of small polygons. They occur in groups, are about one metre in size or smaller and are generally asymmetrically built, with a short steep slope facing upslope (Fig. 7). They are found probably in thin layers of shale debris and in the upper, slightly weathered parts of shale outcrops. Dug sections demonstrate strong upward bending of shale strata. In some groups of these shale polygons the cell pattern obviously revealed the fissure system of the bedrock. In the shale areas are also found large polygons, of size and form similar to the ice wedge polygons. They are formed in shale debris and obviously also in solid rock. They occur in small groups in flat areas, as on rounded spurs, but also on slopes. Otherwise the varying appearance of shale areas is caused more by running water than by mass movement and sorting processes.

Slopes in basic rocks with granular weathering have no typical patterned-ground forms, but they have in some places signs of wash processes as in shale areas (poorly developed miniature deltas).

On slopes where coarse-weathered material predominates (mainly boulder fields), forms are different. On flat areas or very gentle slopes sorted circles occur. Well-developed specimens are not very common, but are still found. On steeper slopes there are sorted stripes, often alternating with lobes. The typical lobes have boulder fronts and centres slightly richer in finer grain sizes. They are easily discernible at a distance when there is a colour contrast between the brown centres of the lobes and the grey or dark, more lichen-covered fronts. They are also easily visible when the ground has a thin snow cover. These lobes are formed as single features at the base of steep slopes of scree type, or they almost cover a whole slope completely (Fig. 8). In the latter case the slopes are slightly less steep than an active talus slope. The lobes can be traced on aerial photographs if they occur in large groups. These stone and boulder lobes are quite different in appearance from the well-known solifluction lobes of the tundra zone. Forms of this latter type are very rare in the mapped area, and are found only where the vegetation for some reason is more dense.

Talus slopes and talus cones are found below rock walls all over the area. That they are still actively fed from the wall is proved by stones and boulders on top of the covering winter snow. Mass movement within the talus slope itself seems often to be performed by mudflows. Their ways were particularly easy to observe when a partial snow cover still remained, giving contrast to the black snow-free *levées*. Mudflow activity was not directly observed. Nothing seems to have happened during the heavy summer rains (in contrast to gully erosion and formation of miniature deltas). It is more probable, though not verified, that the mudflows are released during the snow-melt when a high frost table still exists. Other signs of transport within talus or scree slopes were also registered. Water percolating between the stones transported small quantities of fine material during snow-melt. Below talus cone and escaping water rill accumulated small flats of fine-grained material. In a few investigated slopes a decrease in stone sizes was observed with depth, that is, a sorting similar to frost sorting. In the same sites it was observed that clear ice filled the interspaces between the stones, and that some of the stones were almost suspended in ice. If these conditions are normal, they give a hint of one possible mechanism of movement. The results of movement were also indicated by some scattered specimens of willow. The trunks were partly drowned by stones, the roots situated 0.5 to 2 m higher up on the slope than the superficial parts of the trunk.

Wind action and nivation

The direction of the eroding wind is indicated on the map. The indications of wind direction were polish on gabbro outcrops, grooves in gypsum outcrops, flutings in bare soil, and scars in vegetation cover. The arrows show that the eroding wind (the strongest?) with few

Fig. 7. Polygons in shale debris and solid rock, with a steep side facing up slope ("up-slope" polygons). Note geology hammer as scale in the central foreground. Crusoe Glacier in the background.

Fig. 8. Northern and northwestern slope of the Bastion. Below the steep wall is a typical talus slope. The rounded summit to the right is covered by solifluction lobes, each of them built of stones and boulders. Colour contrast is caused mainly by lichens at the front of the lobes.

exceptions is from the east or east-northeast from the direction of the broad Thompson Glacier valley. Local deflections are not pronounced, though there are slight deviations in a downslope direction on higher slopes. If the wind direction is compared with the distribution of earth hummocks, it is clearly seen that the well-developed areas of hummocks are found in typical lee-side positions. Large surfaces of naked soil are often found on the windward sides (only occasionally mapped). It is possible that the hummocks are developed in a sort of loessic deposits (Beschel, in press).

During snow-melt, wind-transported soil was found at a few places. Apart from this, snow drifting did not appear to have been of great importance within the Expedition area during the winter of 1961, as long-lasting snow banks were almost completely absent. Only one single case of active nivation was observed and measured in a small gully in till material. Nivation cirques were very few. In other parts of Axel Heiberg Island there were more remaining snow patches and signs of nivation, though not always very strong (Fig. 9).

CAPACITY OF PRESENT-DAY MORPHOLOGICAL PROCESSES: DISCUSSION

The results of rock weathering are obvious, with outcrops lacking over wide areas. We do not know, however, when this weathering started.

The slope processes of the area are mass movement and wash, of different intensity according to slope gradient. Even on gentle or medium-steep slopes, generally speaking, favourable conditions could be expected in the wet and soft upper soil layers in the "till zone" after snow-melt or in the boulder fields with the unstable positions of numerous stones. But there must be local differences. There are surfaces with signs of stability, surfaces with signs of movement, and surfaces without any special indications whatsoever. The latter predominate in the "till zone" and in large parts of the area with fine local material. Stable conditions are indicated by large surfaces with "soil cells" and polygons of all kinds. These generally do not show elongated forms on slopes, and it seems probable that at least the greater forms need a long time for their formation. Of the forms indicating downslope movements, larger areas are occupied by non-sorted stripes, several small but scattered areas of terracettes, and extensive and continuous areas by lobes and sorted stripes in the boulder fields. Rapid mass movement by earth slides and mudflows does important transport work in restricted areas. Their frequency is, however, low, to judge from the number of mapped sites, though it is possible that older earth slides have been

FIG. 9. Aerial view of a slope S of Rens Fiord, northern Axel Heiberg Island. Active nivation resulting in steep fans at the base of the slope. Between the nivation hollows are slopes with solifluction lobes.

overlooked during the field work.

The total area of gentle and medium-steep slopes with visible signs of mass movement is important, but no observations tell of any high total transporting capacity of the processes (e.g., lichen-covered boulders in the lobes). Talus slopes are formed below all rock walls. They are normally quite large compared with the height of the rock walls, and in numerous cases the free face is reduced to remnants, or has completely disappeared.

The first impression from the steep slopes is that the transporting processes are efficient. For further statements measurements are needed, but only a few were completed in 1961 during the snow-melt or in the time between late snow-melt and the first persistent snow cover. Measurements by means of lines of painted stones or stakes during the summer illustrate the following:

(1) Scree-slope east of Colour Lake: no movement.

(2) Lobe close to the shore: no movement.

(3) Slope slightly richer in fines north of Colour Lake: maximum movement 2 cm, mean movement 0.8 cm (16 stones observed).

(4) Slope, partly with fine soil on Base Camp Hill: 3 out of 8 stakes had moved 1 to 1.5 cm.

(5) Slope with sorted stripes close to Base Camp: 3 stakes out of 8 had moved 0.5 to 1 cm.

In Site 1, three buried willow trunks were tentatively used for measurements of movement. The length of the buried trunks, measured in the downslope direction from the root to the superficial parts of the willow, were 220, 55, and 205 cm, respectively, and the age 64, 40, and 67 years, giving a movement of 3.7, 1.4, and 3.0 cm in a year. The first specimen had the best tree-rings.

Rough measurement of fresh talus material and estimation of rock wall retreat were made at two localities.

In a site at Base Camp Hill stones and boulders from the rock wall had accumulated at the winter snow of the talus slope below. Material gathered from a defined area was estimated to correspond to a wall retreat of 1 m in 5,000 years. In a marginal channel near the snout of the White Glacier the weathering activity was very high during the snow-melt, at the very peak with stone falls and rock falls almost every minute. Some of the fresh-looking talus cones (the volume of which had been estimated in late snow-melt time) were removed during one of the heavy summer rains. If such removal can be regarded as a returning event (which seems probable) the wall retreat can be estimated at about 1 m in 200 years on an average for the wall investigated.

The measured rate of processes within the first group is low with the exception of Site 1, even compared with similar measurements from other areas. Some of the smallest figures obtained are perhaps accounted for by error in measurement. The wall retreat in the first-mentioned site is of quite normal order in comparison to other measurements (Rapp 1960, 1961, also the quoted figures). The wall retreat in the second site is unusually rapid. The few measurements so far obtained do not contradict the general impression obtained from the map.

The results of wash by rain (and melting snow?) are obvious in all areas with fine local material and also probably in the "till zone." The results are mainly observed when they are quite fresh. After a while the miniature deltas and the miniature mudflows seem to be incorporated in the ordinary ground, with poor vegetation or with desiccation cracks and cells. For that reason it is probable that the results of wash have been underestimated. The small fan symbols are used mainly for rather coarse material, as eventually existing lower parts of the fans with fine material are not easy to observe. During the heavy rains of 1961, new deltas and new small gullies were formed.

The activity of running water in the ordinary river-beds is of great importance because bedrock crops out along the valley trains and large fans, even at the mouth of very small rivers. A rough sort of grade, or partial grade in important sections, is indicated by the increase in gradient from the lower part of the fan to upper parts of the valley train —and this is in spite of former glaciation and recent uplift.

These obvious and widespread evidences of running water were at first somewhat a mystery, as the snow-melt passed without supplying much water to the rivers. The heavy rains in July gave the explanation, or one explanation. On these occasions, for example, the run-off of the small Wolf River partially filled its valley train and fan, the branches of the braided system changed position very suddenly, stones and boulders moved along the bottom, and large quantities of material were carried in suspension. Sediment-loaded water rushed down the small, usually dry rills in the adjacent shale slope. Large boulders, marked with painted numbers, in the marginal river of the White Glacier moved downstream and some disappeared altogether. A gabbro boulder approximately 120 × 70 × 70 cm in size moved a distance of 150-200 m.

Fluvial processes of this intensity during a rainstorm are probably caused by the almost immediate drainage, the result of a high frost table, large shale areas, the hard surface crust on till slopes, the scanty vegetation, and the superficial drainage on the cold ice bodies. It was mentioned above that rainstorms of this type are most probably normal climatological events; it is also probable, however, that they have been more frequent during the last decades (Müller 1963a). This is perhaps a warning against overestimation of the rain storm influence. In any case, if the weather conditions of 1961 were not too far from the normal ones, nothing else can give a better explanation of the obviously high intensity of fluvial processes than the heavy summer rains.

LANDFORM GENESIS: CONTRIBUTION TO THE DISCUSSION BY THE GEOMORPHOLOGICAL MAP

The map, alone and combined with other information, gives some ideas about the development of the relief.

Evidence of a former, more extensive glaciation is given by the glacial striae, till deposits, and most probably the uplift of the last 9,000 years. The striae, notably the youngest system, tell that the ice did not exactly follow the Expedition River valley but crossed it at an acute angle. As the direction of striae does not vary much from one place to the other in spite of the hilly topography, the ice must have been quite thick. The striae orientation tells that the radiation centre was somewhere to the east and later to the east-southeast, not in the area of the present McGill Ice Cap. No further statements about the centre can be made from the map area. Observations were, however, made on erratics and glacial striae in two other localities. On Schei Peninsula (east coast of Axel Heiberg Island) erratics from probably a long distance (e.g., red granite) were found together with striae from south or south-southwest up to about 400 m on diabase hogbacks. Also north of Rens Fiord (in the north) a few observations of striae from southeast and erratics were made. In both areas it is evident that they must have been invaded by an ice cover with centre outside the island. As a whole, the observations do not contradict the idea that the island was once incorporated in a large ice complex (Craig and Fyles 1961). The map material does not allow any definite statements as to whether there were one or two extensive glaciations.

The features of glacial erosion during this more extensive glaciation have not been mapped, except for the striae. As mentioned, the *roches moutonnées* are not perfect and are found only in very restricted areas. The typical rock floor of a glaciated area with *roches moutonnées* and hollows of all kinds is not found here, and lakes are very few. An exception is Colour Lake, which is a true rock basin (Müller 1963*b*). Also the large-size forms of glacial erosion are less common than could be expected. Outside the presently glaciated area only parts of the Expedition River valley and some valley sections to the south of it have a sort of U-form. The Expedition Fiord is also deep according to soundings (Müller 1963*b*). Empty cirques of the classical form are not found—at least no convincing examples. These could have been expected in view of the more extensive glaciations of the past and with regard to the other formerly glaciated areas. The reasons for this surprising morphology are probably complex, but a few comments may not be out of place.

It is probable that the typical rock floor forms either have never developed to the same degree as in other investigated areas or have been covered by younger deposits or have been destroyed by weathering. In proof of the latter ideas are the strong weathering of most rock types and rather continuous cover of till and alluvial deposits at lower altitudes, but this does not exclude the first alternative.

As to the cirque problem, it is possible that the cold glaciers of the area do not form ideal cirque glaciers. Existing small glaciers, most similar to the cirque glaciers, do not seem to have the typical broad bottom. They look more funnel-shaped or fluvial. Empty forms of this type are found outside the present glaciated area in positions where formation of small glaciers could have been expected as a reaction of intensified glaciation(s). The funnel shape indicates less pronounced erosion of the cirque bottom than in normal cirques. Back-wearing of the wall seems, however, to have been at work.

Ideas about the low frequency of good U-valleys in the formerly glaciated areas could perhaps be gained from valleys which are now filled with outlet glaciers. Some of them such as the Thompson Glacier valley or the Crusoe Glacier valley have (as concerns the visible parts) quite good U-forms with truncated spurs, straight sides, and rock walls with chutes and ravines. At least at the lower end of the glaciers strong erosion and rock wall formation is obviously caused partly by lateral rivers, which probably also initiate chute or ravine formation by undercutting (Fig. 10). In other glacier-filled valleys the described forms are less pronounced, and it is sometimes found that V-shaped valleys start almost immediately outside the present glacier front (Fig. 11). Remnants of a fluvial valley pattern are seen also within the glaciated area, as in a nunatak area and in non-glaciated tributary valleys. The lower end of the latter is often filled with glacier-dammed lakes.

To return to the problem: It is obvious that a fluvial valley pattern existed before the glaciation(s), and this pattern is not completely transformed even in the area which has been glaciated during a longer time than the "problematic" area. In this latter area it might have been stages with valley glaciers, but the stage preserved in the striae must have had the appearance of a more or less covering ice sheet. If the characteristic features of the glaciated valley in this climate are mainly caused by marginal processes, such forms should have had a long time

Fig. 10. Aerial view of the lateral channel west of Crusoe Glacier showing strong ravine erosion at work, possibly initiated by the undercutting erosion of the lateral stream (and glacier erosion?). Glacier movement from the right. The ravine erosion seems to have been at work for a longer time farther upstream, as compared with the glacier movement. The same observation can be made around other glaciers. In this special case a landscape sculptured by soft, fluvial erosion is obviously dissected again in a cycle caused by glaciofluvial erosion.

Fig. 11. Characteristic section of the mountainous, glacierized landscape of central western Axel Heiberg Island. U-shaped valley in front of glacier soon changes to V-shaped valley with valley trains and small fans at the bottom.

for transformation. Some of the rock walls of the mapped area, which are now in a stage of destruction, might be the last remnants.

This only tentative explanation gives a high supremacy to the fluvial processes also for the forms of the first order. This is, however, in accordance with the most active processes in the mapped area, with the active lateral erosion along valley trains, with the large fans, and with the rough stage of grade, partially reached even by very small rivers. This last statement is also still valid when the uplift has slowed down during the last thousands of years, which is possibly indicated by the dated levels (Müller 1963c), and eventually by the well-developed ice wedge polygons close to sea level.

Within large parts of Axel Heiberg Island the structural influence upon the relief is very high. In the mapped area this adaption is not always quite as good for landscape features of restricted size. Smaller details are obscured in till-covered areas and on slopes with local weathered material in a stage of slow solifluction movement.

The landscape on Axel Heiberg Island has, with its high influence of running water and also of rock structures, a surprisingly arid look. Similar forms are found in deserts on lower latitudes.

ACKNOWLEDGEMENTS. The research for this paper has been done with the financial support of the National Research Council of Canada, McGill University, and from different Swedish funds. The author wishes to acknowledge the help from several expedition members, notably the scientific leader, Professor F. Müller.

REFERENCES CITED

Arctic summary: A semi-annual summary of meteorological data from the joint arctic and other weather stations on the arctic islands, January to June, 1959— July to December, 1960: Dept. of Transport, Meteorol. Branch, Canada.
BESCHEL, R. E., 1966, Hummocks and their vegetation in the high arctic: Proc. Intern. Permafrost Conf., Nat. Acad. Sci.–Nat. Res. Council Pub. No. 1287, p. 13-20.
Climatological summaries for the joint arctic weather stations at Alert, Eureka, Isachsen, Mould Bay and Resolute, N.W.T., 1954-1958: Dept. of Transport, Meteorol. Branch, Canada.
Climatological summary, Alert, Mould Bay, Isachsen, Resolute and Eureka (N.W.T., Canada) 1955-1961: Dept. of Transport, Meteorol. Branch, Canada.
CRAIG, B. G., and FYLES, J. G., 1961, Pleistocene geology of Arctic Canada, p. 403-420 in Raasch, G. O., Editor, Geology of the Arctic: Proc. First Intern. Symp. on Arctic Geol., 1196 p.
DIEM, M., 1963, Climatological and glacial-meteorological studies in 1961, p. 111-116 in Müller, F., Editor, Axel Heiberg Isl. Research Repts., McGill Univ., Montreal, Jacobsen-McGill Arctic Research Expedition, Prel. Rept., 1961-1962, 241 p.
FRICKER, P. E., 1961, Geological report, p. 153-159 in Müller, B. S., Editor, Jacobsen-McGill Arctic Research Expedition to Axel Heiberg Isl., Prel. Rept., 1959-1960, 219 p.

——, 1963, Geology of the expedition area, western central Axel Heiberg Island, Canadian Arctic Archipelago: Axel Heiberg Isl. Research Rept., McGill Univ., Montreal, Geology I, 156 p.

HAVENS, J. M., 1961, Base camp weather stations, p. 143-146 *in* Müller, B. S., *Editor*, Jacobsen-McGill Arctic Research Expedition to Axel Heiberg Isl., Prel. Rept., 1959-1960, 219 p.

——, 1963, The 1962 meteorological program, p. 117-126 *in* Müller, F., *Editor*, Axel Heiberg Isl. Research Repts., McGill Univ., Montreal, Jacobsen-McGill Arctic Research Expedition, Prel. Rept., 1961-1962, 241 p.

HOEN, E. W., 1964, The anhydrite diapirs of central western Axel Heiberg Island: Axel Heiberg Isl. Research Repts., McGill Univ., Montreal, Jacobsen-McGill Arctic Research Expedition, Geology II, 102 p. with map.

KRANCK, E. H., 1961, Gypsum tectonics on Axel Heiberg Island, N.W.T., Canada, p. 147-152 *in* Müller, B. S., *Editor*, Jacobsen-McGill Arctic Research Expedition to Axel Heiberg Isl., Prel. Rept., 1959-1960, 219 p.

——, 1963, Tectonic of evaporite diapirs on Axel Heiberg Island, p. 133-138 *in* Müller, F., *Editor*, Axel Heiberg Isl. Research Repts., McGill Univ., Montreal, Jacobsen-McGill Arctic Research Expedition, Prel. Rept., 1961-1962, 241 p.

MÜLLER, F., 1961, The area selected for the glaciological studies, and accumulation and stratification, p. 143-161 *in* Müller, B. S., *Editor*, Jacobsen-McGill Arctic Research Expedition to Axel Heiberg Isl., Prel. Rept., 1959-1960, 219 p.

——, 1963*a*, Investigations in an ice shaft in the accumulation area of the McGill Ice Cap, p. 27-36 *in* Müller, F., *Editor*, Axel Heiberg Isl. Research Repts., McGill Univ., Montreal, Jacobsen-McGill Arctic Research Expedition, Prel. Rept., 1961-1962, 241 p.

——, 1963*b*, Depth sounding projects, p. 103-108 *in* Müller, F., *Editor*, Axel Heiberg Isl. Research Repts., McGill Univ., Montreal, Jacobsen-McGill Arctic Research Expedition, Prel. Rept., 1961-1962, 241 p.

——, 1963*c*, Radiocarbon dates and notes on the climatic and morphological history, p. 169-172 *in* Müller, F., *Editor*, Axel Heiberg Isl. Research Repts., McGill Univ., Montreal, Jacobsen-McGill Arctic Research Expedition, Prel. Rept., 1961-1962, 241 p.

PARMELEE, J. A., 1963, Mycological studies in 1961, p. 173-181 *in* Müller, F., *Editor*, Axel Heiberg Isl. Research Repts., McGill Univ., Montreal, Jacobsen-McGill Arctic Research Expedition, Prel. Rept., 1961-1962, 241 p.

RAPP, A., 1960, Talus slopes and mountain walls at Tempelfjorden, Spitsbergen: Norsk Polarinstitutt, no. 119, 96 p., 20 pl.

——, 1961, Recent development of mountain slopes in Kärkevagge and surroundings, Northern Scandinavia: Geog. Ann., v. 42, p. 71-200.

ROBITAILLE, B., 1961, Sur les travaux de géomorphologie effectués au cours de l'été 1960 dans le cadre de l'expedition, p. 171-177 *in* Müller, B. S., *Editor*, Jacobsen-McGill Arctic Research Expedition to Axel Heiberg Isl., Prel. Rept., 1959-1960, 219 p.

RUDBERG, S., 1962, A report on some field observations concerning periglacial geomorphology and mass movement on slopes in Sweden: Biuletyn Peryglacjalny, v. 11, p. 311-323.

——, 1963*a*, Morphological processes and slope development in Axel Heiberg Island, Northwest Territories, Canada: Nachrichten der Akademie der Wissenschaften in Göttingen, II. Mat.-Phys. Klasse, 1963, v. 14, p. 211-228.

——, 1963*b*, Geomorphological processes in a cold semi-arid region, p. 139-150 *in* Müller, F., *Editor*, Axel Heiberg Isl. Research Repts., McGill Univ., Montreal, Jacobsen-McGill Arctic Research Expedition, Prel. Rept., 1961-1962, 241 p.

Saint-Onge, D., 1964-65, La géomorphologie de l'isle Ellef Ringnes, Territoires de Nord-Ouest, Canada (map published, 1964): Étude Géographique, no. 38, Direction de la Géographie, Ministère des Mines et des Releves Techniques, Ottawa, 46 p.

THOMAS, M. K., 1961, A survey of temperatures in the Canadian Arctic, p. 942-955 *in* Raasch, G. O., *Editor*, Geology of the Arctic, Proc. First Intern. Symp. on Arctic Geol., 1196 p.

THORSTEINSSON, R., 1961, The history and geology of Meighen Island, Arctic Archipelago: Geol. Survey of Canada, Dept. of Mines and Tech. Surv., Bull. 75, I-XI, p. 1-19.

THORSTEINSSON, R., and TOZER, E. T., 1960, Summary account of structural history of Canadian Archipelago since Precambrian time: Geol. Survey of Canada, Dept. of Mines and Tech. Surv., Paper 60-7, 1960, 25 p. Also *in* Raasch, G. O., *Editor*, 1961, Geology of the Arctic, Proc. First Intern. Symp. on Arctic Geol., p. 339-360.

TOZER, E. T., 1960, Summary account of Mesozoic and Tertiary stratigraphy, Canadian Arctic Archipelago: Geol. Survey of Canada, Dept. of Mines and Tech. Surv., Paper 60-5. Also *in* Raasch, G. O., *Editor*, 1961, Geology of the Arctic: Proc. First Intern. Symp. on Arctic Geol., p. 381-402.

TROELSON, J. C., 1950, Contributions to the geology of Northwest Greenland, Ellesmere Island and Axel Heiberg Island: Meddel. om Grønland, bd. 149, no. 7, p. 1-86.

WASHBURN, A. L., 1956, Classification of patterned ground and review of suggested origins: Geol. Soc. Amer. Bull., v. 67, p. 823-866.

WILSON, H. P., 1961, The major factors of arctic climate, p. 915-930 *in* Raasch, G. O., *Editor*, Geology of the Arctic: Proc. First Intern. Symp. on Arctic Geol., 1196 p.

MINOR PERIGLACIAL PHENOMENA AMONG THE HIGH VOLCANOES OF MEXICO

JOSÉ L. LORENZO
Instituto Nacional de Antropología e Historia
México

ABSTRACT. Periglacial phenomena exist on the higher Mexican volcanoes as structural and textural soils but are restricted to small areas close to existing glaciers. Amorphous frost soils occur in the mountain pastures at lower altitudes but still above the tree-line. "Fossil" periglacial examples are very few and the amorphous frost soil type is absent in the "fossil" state. The scarcity of existing examples of periglacial phenomena, even near the glaciers, when compared with the even lesser number of fossil examples leads one to think that periglacial phenomena in tropical zone mountains, even though present, were never widespread. Their very existence was controlled by the topoclimate existing at the glacier border. The periglacial phenomena in Mexico today are typical of the daily climatic fluctuation instead of the seasonal fluctuation. In the past, similar conditions probably also existed.

RÉSUMÉ. Les formes périglaciaires que l'on rencontre actuellement sur les volcans mexicains les plus élevés sont cantonnées, en ce qui concerne les sols structurés et les sols à texture, dans la proximité immédiate des glaciers existants. On trouve les gélisols amorphes dans la zone à végétation herbacée, au dessus de la zone à végétation arborée. Les faciès périglaciaires fossiles laissés par les types de sols mentionnés sont peu nombreux et, présentement, on n'a pas trouvé trace de cas de gélisols amorphes fossiles. Le nombre peu élevé de ces phénomènes actuels, même au voisinage des glaciers, se compare au nombre de leurs manifestations fossiles connues, d'où l'idée qui, si les formes périglaciaires que nous offrent les montagnes tropicales sont notables, leurs dimensions, toutefois, ont toujours manqué d'amplitude, leur présence étant déterminée par le topoclimat régnant sur une frange restreinte autour des glaciers, proportionnellement à l'aire de glaciation reduite. Notre hypothèse s'enrichit si l'on considère que les phénomènes périglaciaires actuels résultent d'un processus de fluctuation climatique de type plus quotidien que saisonnier, ce qui nous ferait admettre, pour les temps anciens, un processus de glaciation qui relèverait d'un ensemble de facteurs climatiques aux caractéristiques locales fortement accentuées et bien circonscrites.

RESUMEN. Las formas periglaciales que en la actualidad se encuentran en los volcanes más altos de México, estan restringidas a las cercanías inmediatas de los glaciares que todavía existen en lo que concierne a suelos estructurales y texturales. Los suelos congelados amorfos se encuentran en la zona por encima del límite de vegetación arbórea, ocupando la zona de vegetación herbácea. Los restos de formas periglaciales fósiles del tipo de suelos estructurales y texturales son pocos y, por ahora, no se han encontrado restos de suelos congelados amorfos fósiles. La escasez actual de estos fenómenos, aun en las inmediaciones de los glaciares, al ser comparada con los tambien escasos restos fósiles conocidos, lleva a pensar que las formas periglaciales en las montañas tropicales, aunque conspícuas, no tuvieron gran extensión y su presencia estuvo normada por el topoclima existente alrededor de los glaciares, en forma de franja, proporcional al área glaciada pero nunca de gran tamaño. La hipótesis se amplia cuando consideramos que los fenómenos periglaciares de la actualidad son típicos del proceso de fluctuación climática diaria y no estacional, con lo cual, en el pasado, es permisible admitir un modo de glaciación semejante, atribuible a los elementos de un clima regional especial, muy circunscrito.

CONTENTS

FIGURE

INTRODUCTION

The present study is an attempt to direct the attention of specialists to the periglacial phenomena which exist in Mexico. The glaciology, glacial geology, and periglacial geology or cryopedology of the tropical and equatorial regions have been studied by some authorities but, in the author's opinion, not adequately where the American continent is concerned. As a result, the geological stratigraphy and the paleoclimatology of the horizons where evidence of early man has been found in Mexico are either completely unknown or have so been presented as to give rise to serious confusion.

A study of the works of Cailleux and Taylor (1954), Lliboutry (1956, 1957, 1961), Magnani (1962), Sekyra (1960), Tricart (1963), and Troll (1955, 1958), together with 30 years of mountaineering—including the invaluable instruction obtained during expeditions with Sidney E. White to the Popocatepetl and Iztaccihuatl volcanoes from 1949 to 1959, and during field work directed for the Glaciological Section of the Mexican National Committee for the International Geophysical Year in 1958 (Lorenzo 1964)—attracted my attention to the existence of periglacial phenomena in Mexico.

White (1962, p. 49, 61) noted the presence of sorted stripes and stone stripes on Iztaccihuatl. These, together with so-called mudflows in the same place (White, p. 52), are undoubtedly periglacial phenomena. Lorenzo (1961, p. 8-9) described elsewhere a group of hydrolaccoliths on Nevado de Colima and these, together with the other features mentioned above, form the complete published list of known periglacial phenomena in Mexico.

Only Troll has published anything about periglacial phenomena in tropical mountains. His examples are in the tropical part of the Andes, between latitudes 9° and 17° south (Troll 1958, p. 43-7) and on Kilimanjaro and Kenya (Troll, p. 48-53) between the Equator and 4° south. His illustrations are confined to "structure soils" which, in view of their geographic location, would perhaps be better described as equatorial rather than tropical, the term he uses. He also makes a point of mentioning subtropical mountains, these being those peaks which lie between the 20th and the 42nd parallels north, and the 25th and the 30th parallels south (Troll 1958, p. 28-9, 34).

Since Lliboutry (1956, 1957, 1961) principally concentrated on areas in Chile near the 31st parallel, the periglacial phenomena he notes are not really tropical in character. The same applies to similar features which Magnani (1962) describes in southern Argentina, between the 28th parallel and the Patagonian ice sheet.

In the northern hemisphere, Sekyra (1964) has worked only as far south as the 39th parallel, while Cailleux and Taylor (1954) mention only examples from regions even further north; the same is true of Tricart (1963).

Obviously, a more systematic study of both fossil and present-day periglacial phenomena in the tropics is needed, since only by comparing these aspects are scientists likely to reach a better understanding of the mechanics of cold climate processes during the Pleistocene. At the same time, however, further knowledge of present-day climatic conditions also is required to achieve this objective.

AREA DESCRIPTION

Within an area delineated by the Pacific Littoral, the coast of the Gulf of Mexico, and the 19th and 20th parallels north, lies a major volcanic chain, the Mexican Volcanic Axis (Foshag and Gonzalez 1956, p. 355). At one end it is derived from the Chapala-Acambay Fault (Fig. 1), this being in effect an offshoot of the San Andreas system, and, at the other, is a continuation of the Clarion Fault which, in its continental aspect, was given the name Humboldt Fault (Mooser 1963, p. 242). Along this zone of weakness volcanic activity has produced great peaks, among which Citlaltepetl (5,680 m), Popocatepetl (5,452 m), and Iztaccihuatl (5,286 m) still possess glaciers (Lorenzo 1964). Zinantecatl or Nevado de Toluca (4,609 m), Matlalcueytl or Malinche de Tlaxcala (4,461 m), Nauhcampantepetl or Cofre de Perote (4,282 m), and Nevado de Colima (4,180 m) show traces of having been covered with ice during the Late Pleistocene (Fig. 1).

During some winters snow may cover the summits of the glacierless volcanoes for a few days, but these conditions rarely last for more than two weeks. Unfortunately, very few high-altitude meteorological observations indicative of the type of climatic conditions governing these areas have been made. There do exist, however, the calculations of White (1954, Fig. 6), obtained by inference from conditions registered in surrounding lower areas together with observations made by mountaineers and by himself, and also the scanty information obtained on Altzomoni (4,100 m), a small peak which lies between Popocatepetl and Iztaccihuatl where, from 1957 to 1958, a year of rainfall was measured. The rainfall figures obtained here do, however, diverge seriously from the estimates of White, since the latter postulated a winter precipitation slightly less intense than the summer one. The Altzomoni information, on the other hand, indicates that 68 per cent of the total annual rainfall takes place between June and September, and only 2.6 per cent occurs between December and March. The fact that clear skies are much more common in winter must be taken into account; the accumulation of snow will diminish and the rate of thawing increase.

It should be emphasized that Altzomoni would, in fact, be classified as semi-arid, since its rainfall over the 12 months in question totalled only 623 mm. This is even more important to note in view of the fact that the climatic inferences drawn to date about conditions at high alti-

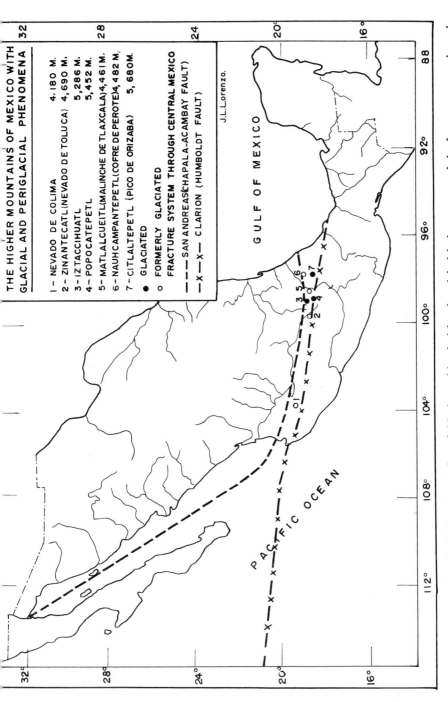

THE HIGHER MOUNTAINS OF MEXICO WITH
GLACIAL AND PERIGLACIAL PHENOMENA

1 – NEVADO DE COLIMA   4,180 M.
2 – ZINANTECATL (NEVADO DE TOLUCA) 4,690 M.
3 – IZTACCIHUATL   5,286 M.
4 – POPOCATEPETL   5,452 M.
5 – MATLALCUEITL (MALINCHE DE TLAXCALA) 4,461 M.
6 – NAUHCAMPANTEPETL (COFRE DE PEROTE) 4,482 M.
7 – CITLALTEPETL (PICO DE ORIZABA)   5,680 M.

● GLACIATED
○ FORMERLY GLACIATED
— — FRACTURE SYSTEM THROUGH CENTRAL MEXICO
             (SAN ANDREAS-CHAPALA-ACAMBAY FAULT)
—x—x— CLARION (HUMBOLDT FAULT)

J.L.Lorenzo.

GULF OF MEXICO

PACIFIC OCEAN

Fig. 1. Map indicating the higher mountains of Mexico with glacial and periglacial phenomena and the fracture system through the country.

165

tudes were based on the data of Robles Ramos (1944), obtained at 3,551 m, where total annual rainfall was 1,368 mm. Unfortunately, temperature readings at Altzomoni cover only five months, that is, March, April, May, June, and July 1958, and even with best intentions information of value cannot be derived from them. As a result, it is not possible to include here the corresponding seasonal and daily temperature distribution in isopleths, nor a table of frost alternation frequency and its annual distribution, even though these factors are so important for an understanding of the prerequisites for periglacial conditions.

Notwithstanding the lack of meteorological observations, there is no doubt that periglacial phenomena occur above the upper limit of arboreal vegetation (3,900 m) on the glaciated mountains. These features increase in number in the zone of herbaceous flora above, and are very frequent in the uppermost parts, devoid of all vegetation save lichen. They are encountered most often in the immediate vicinity of the glaciers themselves.

If 4,700 m is taken as the average lower limit for present-day glaciers, permafrost, which not only undergoes seasonal oscillations but, in this region, marked daily ones as well, appears above 4,600 m whenever surface material and slope-angle are favourable. Glacierless areas, from this point up to the summits, exhibit a wide variety of periglacial phenomena.

During unusually severe winters, the highest non-glaciated mountains are covered with snow. As a result, minor periglacial phenomena, albeit of a superficial character, occur there.

In summary, the three highest mountains in Mexico, that is, those which are still glaciated, possess permafrost today. Its existence depends on the gradient and the presence of finely fragmented rock and/or cineritic material. Moreover, its behaviour is influenced by daily and seasonal variations in temperature. Since the three mountains concerned are all extremely steep sided and considerable areas of them are covered with volcanic ash, permitting water to penetrate rapidly and deeply, it is not surprising that periglacial phenomena are rare.

GENERAL STATEMENTS

Structure and texture soils (Troll 1958, p. 43) are confined to the immediate vicinity of the glaciers. Amorphous frost soils, much less conspicuous (Troll 1958, p. 92), appear above tree-line. These observations lead us to endorse Troll's opinion that "farther towards the Equator, in the mountains, the lower limit of structure soils has a definite course and rises and falls with the forest border and tree line and specially the snow line" (Troll 1958, p. 95). This is certainly true, but with special reference to Mexico at least the lower limits of structure soils follow the upper boundaries of mountain pastures (Troll 1955, p. 193: "Gras- und Kräuterfluren des Hochgebirges") and amorphous frost soils extend down to the upper limits of arboreal vegetation.

Thus, glacierless mountains higher than 4,000 m would not possess structure and texture soils but only amorphous frost soils. This agrees with what has been observed so far. It is remarkable that nearly all the forms of periglacial phenomena occur only within the immediate vicinity of the glaciers themselves.

The scarcity of both periglacial phenomena and their fossil remains suggests that periglacial conditions on tropical mountains were never extensive, although they certainly existed. Then, as now, they would appear to have been occasioned by the climate in the vicinity of the glaciers rather than by any major climate change. This implies that sufficient rainfall existed to give the glaciers a positive balance at the summits of the mountains, provided that temperatures dropped below 0°C. This is enough to insure that peaks of only just over 4,000 m may support glaciers that extend for more than a kilometre (Lorenzo 1961, p. 7).

This sort of glaciation, however, would not appear to be of the type that produces a periglacial zone equal in extent to the area covered by the glaciers themselves. It would seem more as if these extended well into the foothills where the climate was not periglacial. This glaciation would be caused by an increase in rainfall in the upper regions, accompanied by a drop in temperature below 0°C in areas below 4,000 m.

If, as appears to be the case, the glaciers on the mountains of Mexico are fed during the rainy season (i.e., in summer), then this is a peculiar situation. The very existence of glaciers there is dictated by the mountain height and whether there exists, in addition, a large enough area to support them, and whether this area is above the 0°C isotherm line. A drop of the 0°C isotherm and a rise in precipitation is therefore necessary for the glaciers to extend beyond their present limits and for others to form on mountains which at present are glacierless. Such conditions are definitely not typical of glacial maxima, which are dry, but rather of the periods immediately preceding or following them. This means that in tropical areas a double set of features may occur, dating from the period before and from the period after glacial maxima but not from the maxima themselves. This is supported by the fact that the periglacial phenomena do not seem to have the extreme form that is the usual result of widespread glaciation. They are, in fact, very sparse and of local extent.

The periglacial phenomena recognized in Mexico and which may be illustrated here are next discussed, with modern present-day forms first, probable subfossil forms next (although the age of all of these is in doubt), and truly fossil forms last. The significance of some of these is uncertain, and it must be stressed that tropical periglacial conditions do produce atypical forms.

The first consideration is that of examples of striped ground (Troll 1958, p. 30) or stone stripes (Sekyra 1960, p. 144) or striated soils (Cailleux and Taylor 1954, p. 51-2), and which Lliboutry (1957, p. 144, 1961, p. 217) has divided, according to the size of the stripes and the distance between them, into "Petite Période" and "Grande Période" types.

Lliboutry (1956, p. 213) may be more correct—since he regards them as resulting from the same effect as the "Penitentes"—than Troll (1958, p. 30-2) who attributes them to aeolian activity.

Figure 2 illustrates an example in which stripes and micro-ridges and osteoles are combined, discovered on Nevado de Toluca at 4,210 m one week after a heavy snowfall. The size of the stripes is characteristic of those of the "Petite Période." An example of stone stripes of a type which in this area would be considered the "Grande Période" variety was found low down on the eastern flank of Ayoloco Glacier on Iztaccihuatl at 4,700 m. Another example was located near the south-eastern edge of the northern glacier of Citlaltepetl at 4,800 m and showed stone stripes of the "Grande Période" type.

Several examples are known in Mexico of the features referred to variously as "pattern soils," "polygonal soils," "net soils," as seen in the interior of the crater of Popocatepetl (Fig. 3, at left of photograph). The "net soil" is clearly defined by the snow, and in no way can be interpreted as other than a natural phenomenon.

Miniature stone polygons (Fig. 4) occur at 4,640 m on the east side of Iztaccihuatl below the Crater Glacier.

A buried glacier has been located and is mentioned because Lliboutry (1957, p. 144) believes these are periglacial phenomena. This particular example is at the bottom of Northern Glacier on Iztaccihuatl at 4,700 m. The stratification it displays makes it certain that it is not a regenerated glacier. Blockfields are numerous; many are active and the vegetation covered ones are fossil.

The next group of features to be illustrated are called "step on

Fig. 2. Stripes and probably micro-ridges at 4,210 m, January, 1965, after heavy snowfall on Zinantecatl. Mittens are 25 cm long.

Fig. 3. Crater of Popocatepetl (5,000 m). On left side of the inner crater a patterned soil is seen. April, 1958.

slopes." Unfortunately, it is not always clear that this is what is photographed since the type of grass characteristic of this area, named "zacaton" (*Stiipa ichu*), grows in clumps and these break up the line of steps. Figure 5 on the northeast side of Iztaccihuatl at 4,100 m shows steps on the left side. On the right side of the figure, however, appear features similar to hummocks. These are due, in this particular case, to the presence of water which seeps out and has altered the flora in the immediate vicinity.

A phenomenon which Sekyra (1960, pl. III-2) has named "weathering by regelation and aeolic action" can commonly be encountered where the soil contains sufficient fine fractions. The example here occurs on the north side of Popocatepetl at 4,050 m.

Not only a good example of steps on slopes, but also at the top, gelifraction niches are found on the southwest side of Iztaccihuatl at 4,100 m.

A very good specimen of a frost-split rock (andesite), shown in Figure 6, occurs on the same side of Iztaccihuatl. At the same place, a vertical section through stone polygons occurs (at centre left). In some instances frost spheroidal fragmentation has been confused with stones on edge around a rock fragment. In the case illustrated, the laminar structure of the fragmented rock, raised by convection of periodic freezing and thawing, results in a stone polygon.

Figure 7 shows possible ice wedge casts and involutions along the Mexico-Puebla Toll Highway. If this is the correct interpretation, these would be of exceptional interest since they are at only 2,730 m, low down on the mountain known as Teyotl (4,600 m), north-northeast of Iztaccihuatl. Probably ice fractures in fluviatile sands with clayey filling occur on the northeast side of Iztaccihuatl at 3,750 m.

Figure 8 illustrates one of the five cryolaccoliths discovered at about 3,570 m on Nevado de Colima. The word "cryolaccolith" is used in preference to "hydrolaccolith" since the features in question are caused by ice. Nevertheless, the use of "lithos" in either case cannot be justified, since objects specifically not containing stones of any sort are being considered.

Using observations made over several years as a mountain guide, to the following account about periglacial phenomena not dealt with so far in this short summary may be added needle ice (pipkrakes) that may occur beneath slabs or flat rocks anywhere above 4,400 m. During cold and wet periods, needle ice may be observed in the same context at lower altitudes. Vertical stones occur in the now silted-up Chalchoapan glacial lake, lying at 4,700 m on the northwest side of Iztaccihuatl. Stripes of the "Petite Période" type with an east-west alignment are

FIG. 4. Stone polygons, Iztaccihuatl, May, 1959, at 4,640 m. Lens cap in middle is 8 cm.

FIG. 5. Steps on slopes. Hummocks at centre right, Iztaccihuatl, 4,100 m. May, 1959.

Fig. 6. Vertical section through stone polygon and spherical exfoliation at left side, Iztaccihuatl, 4,000 m. June, 1965.

Fig. 7. Ice wedge and involution. Northeastern slopes of Iztaccihuatl, 2,730 m. Mexico-Puebla Toll Highway. April, 1963.

Fig. 8. Cryolaccolith, Nevado de Colima, 3,570 m. May, 1965.

commonly encountered above tree-line in barren, sandy areas after snowfalls and during the subsequent thawing process. The rarity of turf-hummocks (Thufur) may be attributed to the fact that they usually occur on meadow land, which does not exist in the higher zones where periglacial conditions prevail.

GLACIOLOGICAL IMPLICATIONS

Thus, the number of periglacial features whose existence has been demonstrated here is considerable. Those which exist today provide a measure of what must have existed in the past when the mountain glaciers covered a wider area. White (views expressed in personal communication) considers that even when the glaciers retreated beyond their present boundaries, the zone of periglacial conditions surrounding them was not reduced proportionally, but remained as it is at present.

Periglacial conditions observed in different places at elevations of about 4,000 m all seem to be relatively recent in origin; the cryolaccolith of Nevado de Colima, for example, opens up a wide field of speculation about the nature of tropical glaciation. It also demonstrates that the subject should be studied more intensively. During the last century and the beginning of this, in the winter or whenever the temperature was sufficiently low, it is undoubtedly true that these cryolaccoliths on Nevado de Colima were used by the local inhabitants to store snow and ice when covered with hay. When convenient, the snow and ice were placed in a type of cyst made of stone slabs compressed into blocks, and then transported to the neighbouring towns to be sold. In fact, a natural ice factory! Indeed, one such stone cyst was found beside one of the five cryolaccoliths; moreover, in this case, the top of the depression of the cryolaccolith itself had been almost completely squared-off.

The fossil ice wedges and involutions occurring at an elevation of 2,730 m would be the result of a major glaciation, provided that periglacial conditions extended down this far. They would be attributed without hesitation to the Tonicoxco substage at the opening of Wisconsin glaciation, if they occurred on the west or north sides of Iztaccihuatl, since the corresponding till, the Nexcoalango, occurs between 2,750 m and 3,050 m (White 1962, p. 31-4, 41-4). It is not believed that they can reasonably be attributed to the Diamantes substage whose till, the Hueyatlaco, occurs at 3,134 m to 3,650 m, since this is too great a distance away. Since the glacial geology of the east side of Iztaccihuatl, however, has yet to be studied, all this is in the nature of hypothesis.

Although, as must be obvious from this account, some interesting periglacial phenomena have been discovered in Mexico, it will be equally apparent that much more work is necessary before attempting a definitive and exhaustive study of the subject.

REFERENCES CITED

CAILLEUX, ANDRÉ, and TAYLOR, G., 1954, Cryopédologie: Etude des sols gelés: Expéditions polaires françaises, Missions Paul-Emile Victor, v. 4, 218 p.

FOSHAG, W. F., and GONZALEZ, R. JENARO, 1956, Birth and development of Paricutin Volcano: US Geol. Survey Bull., v. 965-D, p. 355-489.

LORENZO, J. L., 1961, Notas sobre geología glacial del Nevado de Colima: Bol. 61, Inst. de Geol. 1-17 Univ. Aut. de México.

————, 1964, Los glaciares de México: Monografs. Inst. de Geofís., no. 1, 123 p.

LLIBOUTRY, LUIS, 1956, Nieves y glaciares de Chile: Fundamentos de Glaciología: Univ. de Chile, 471 p.

————, 1957, Studia Kriopedologiczne w Andach środkowochilipskich: Biul. Peryglac., v. 5, no. 5-10, p. 141-146.

————, 1961, Phénomenes cryonivaux dans les Andes de Santiago: Biul. Peryglac., v. 10, p. 209-224.

MAGNANI, MARIO, 1962, Indagini e ricerche sulle glaciazioni e sulla morfologia periglaciale in Argentina: Ric. Sci., v. 32, no. II-A, p. 297-312.

MOOSER, F., 1963, Historia Tectónica de la Cuenca de México: Bol. 15, Asoc. Mexicana Geol. Petr., v. 11-12, p. 239-245.

ROBLES RAMOS, R., 1944, Algunas ideas sobre la glaciología y morfología del Iztaccihuatl: Rev. Geogr. del Inst. Panamer. de Geog. e Hist., v. 4, no. 10-12, p. 65-75.

SEKYRA, JOSEF., 1960, Pusobení mrazu na pudu: Kryopedologie se zvlástním zřetelem k CSR. Geotechnica, sv. 27, N.C.A.V., 164 p.

————, 1964, Cryological phenomena in the North Pamir (Central Trans-Altai): Biul. Peryglac. 14, p. 311-319.

TRICART, J., 1963, Géomorphologie des régions froides: Coll. "Orbis," Univ. Paris, France, 289 p.

TROLL, CARL, 1955, Forschungen in Zentralmexico 1954: Deutsch Geographentag Hamburg, p. 191-213.

————, 1958, Structure soils, solifluction and frost climates of the Earth: US Army, Snow, Ice, and Permafrost Research Establishment, trans., v. 43, 121 p.

WHITE, SIDNEY E., 1954, The firn field on the Volcano Popocatepetl, México: Jour. Glaciol., v. 2, no. 16, p. 380-392.

————, 1962, El Iztaccíhatl: Acontecimientos volcánicos y geomorfológicos en el lado oeste durante el Pleistoceno superior: Ser. Investigaciones 6, Inst. Nal. Antropol. e Hist., 80 p.

CYCLICAL CHANGE IN
A PATTERNED-GROUND ECOSYSTEM,
THULE, GREENLAND

JOHN W. MARR
Institute of Arctic and Alpine Research, and Department of Biology
University of Colorado, Boulder, Colorado, U.S.A.

ABSTRACT. Areas of fine particles in a bouldery matrix form debris islands along the South River, southeast of Thule, Greenland. Some of these islands are the tops of plugs of fines that rise through the coarse active layer from the permafrost table. The islands vary in size from 0.1 to 80 m², from light sandy colour to almost black, and from slightly convex to concave. The basic unit is never larger than about 5 dm across. Larger debris islands form by aggregations of basic units. Vegetation changes provide a means of arranging islands in a dynamic sequence. The successive building phases are characterized by pioneer moss–lichens (on old moss)–luzula–willow–heather. The mature phase with brownish heather scattered over a convex substratum made dark by lower plants is transitory. In a disintegration sequence, cracks develop in the ground cover, the substratum becomes concave, plant species change, and eventually all plants are blown away. The final product is a concentration of lichen-poor gravel and cobbles in a matrix of lichen-rich boulders. This cyclical process proceeds while the regional environment is relatively stable. It is a product of internal processes of the debris island ecosystem. One possible explanation is that the building processes (the emergence of fines) result from local ice formation in the active layer, and the disintegration processes (the loss of fines and elimination of plants) results from melting of the plug's ice by heat from the dark plants warmed by absorption of solar energy.

RÉSUMÉ. Des zones de fines particules dans une matrice à blocaux forment des îles détritiques le long de la South River, au sud-est de Thulé, Groenland. Certaines de ces îles constituent le sommet de tampons de particules fines qui remontent du pergélisol à travers le mollisol grossier. Ces îles varient en dimensions de 0,1 à 80 m²; leur couleur varie de sable clair à presque noir; leur surface va du légèrement convexe au concave. L'unité de base n'a jamais plus de 5 dm de diamètre: les grandes îles détritiques se constituent par aggrégation de ces unités de base. Les changements de la végétation permettent de classer les îles dans une séquence dynamique. Les stades de construction sont caractérisés successivement par la mousse pionnière, les lichens (sur la vieille mousse, la luzule, le saule et, finalement, la bruyère brunâtre éparpillée sur un substrat convexe assombri par des plantes plus primitives, est transistoire. Dans une séquence de destruction, des fentes se développent dans le revêtement, le substrat devient concave, les espèces changent et les plantes sont éventuellement emportées par le vent. Le résultat final est une concentration de gravier et de cailloux pauvres en lichens dans une matrice à blocaux riches en lichens. Ce processus cyclique est lié à un environnement régional stable: c'est un produit des processus internes de l'écosystème des îles détritiques. Une explication possible serait la suivante: 1) les processus de construction (émergence des particules) résultent de la formation locale de glace dans le mollisol: 2) les processus de destruction (départ des particules et élimination des plantes) résultent de la fonte de la glace du tampon sous l'action des plantes sombres réchauffées par absorption de l'énergie solaire.

CONTENTS

INTRODUCTION

The several hundred square kilometres of landscape inland from Thule, Greenland, between the sea and the ice cap contain many forms of patterned ground. I studied the vegetation and ecology of some of these forms with Arturo Corte in 1957 and found the debris islands and sorted circles (Washburn 1956) to be especially interesting. My attention was drawn to these forms because the vegetation of their relatively fine soil appeared to be uniform on first examination, but under careful analysis was found to be actually complex, consisting of two or more subdivisions that were relatively homogenous. This interesting feature led me to collect data on this phenomenon, and it soon became evident that there were subtle soil and microgeomorphic features associated with the vegetation differences. These characteristics suggested that these units were minute ecosystems (Marr 1961), small pieces of the landscape that were discrete dynamic systems of organisms, soil particles, atmospheric factors, and ecological processes. In time, I came to two intriguing conclusions: the *unit of activity* is never over about 10 dm² in size, and consequently the maximum-sized homogeneous area has the same limits; and the different units have a fixed time relationship to one another and form a cyclical sequence of ecosystem change with a series of building phases followed by a series of disintegration phases. Since all phases were present simultaneously, they could not be products of changes in regional environment; their differences must be related to processes inherent in the individual, minute ecosystems. The present paper will describe the units, relate them to one another, and suggest one possible explanation for some of their dynamics.

LOCALITY AND PROCEDURES

The study area is in northwest Greenland near the point where the road from Thule to Tuto departs from the P Mountain road (Fig. 1). Most observations were made on the north side of the Tuto road towards the South River. The area is part of an immense plain of bouldery glacial till that has been washed and reworked by meltwater from the ice cap and modified further by patterned-ground processes (Fig. 2) (Corte 1962). The general slope of the landscape is to the northwest, and it is made up of broad waves, steps, and low mounds. The riser of each step appears to be flowing over the tread of the next lower step and resembles the forward edge of a solifluction terrace. Excavations by Corte exposed wedges and masses of ground ice mixed through the permafrost. The active layer is about 1 m thick and has a low percentage of fines (sand-silt-clay) and a high percentage of coarse particles up to boulder size; the boulders average 30 cm in diameter, and an occasional one is 4 m in diameter. Fines and gravel at the ground surface are arranged in many different types of patterned-ground

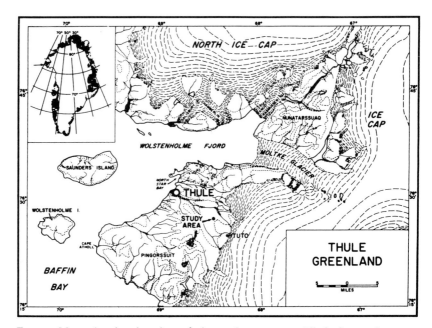

F̲ɪ̲ɢ̲. 1. Maps showing location of the study area near Thule in northwestern Greenland.

forms. Using vegetation as a key, 25 distinct types of patterned-ground ecosystems were identified, ranging in size from 4 m² to 800 m², in two study areas totalling about 10,000 m².

The forms of patterned ground of this study consist of a concentration of fine rock and mineral particles in a matrix of coarse particles and, following Washburn's classification (1956), appear to be debris islands, sorted circles, sorted nets, and sorted polygons (Fig. 3); long troughs over ice wedges form a conspicuous, crudely polygonal pattern.

In several areas, details of the vegetation were recorded by listing the species present or estimating visually the per cent cover of each species contained in a 5 × 2 dm metal frame. Since the tallest plants, heather and luzula, were only a few cm tall, I did not separate the plants into strata. Consequently, many samples produced more than 100 per cent of cover, since some plants overlapped one another. Tables in the following sections are condensations of the original data.

OBSERVATIONS AND DATA ON SELECTED AREAS

Transect

Table 1 summarizes data collected on 15 debris islands encountered on a transect roughly parallel with and north of the Tuto road. These data reveal the following characteristics of the debris islands:

(1) Size: 0.75 to 80 m².

(2) Shape: circular to elongate. Largest circular centres are about 4 m across. Largest elongate centres are 15 × 15 m; most elongate centres are either about 1 or 2 m wide.

(3) Surface form: convex to concave.

(4) Relation to surrounding boulder border: 3 dm above to 4 dm below borders.

(5) Surface character: cracks (contraction?) confined to larger (more than 4 m²) centres.

(6) Soil material: fines with various amounts of gravel (pebbles and cobbles).

(7) Surface: flat to slightly tilted.

(8) Vegetation: lacking to complete cover. Species combinations included the following:

(a) Moss (usually *Polytrichum juniperinum* or *P. commune*) and/or a liverwort (*Gymmomitrium*).

(b) (a) plus crustose lichens. (This ground cover of mosses and lichens will be called the cryptogam carpet hereafter in this paper.)

(c) (b) plus *Luzula spicata* (L.) DC or *L. confusa* Lindeb. (I did not

Fig. 2. View looking eastward across the boulder plain. The left half of the horizon is formed by hills of morainal debris near the margin of the ice cap. The large complex centre is the area of fines in the near centre of the photograph. An army rucksack resting on the centre gives the scale.

Fig. 3. Airphoto of Area Seven with its dark coloured sorted circles in two lines across the right centre. The largest circles are about 4 m across.

differentiate between them consistently.)

(*d*) (*c*) and willow (*Salix artica* Pall.), heather (*Cassiope tetragona* (L.) D. Don) and sometimes foliose and fruticose lichens, *Poa artica* R. Br. and *Luzula nivalis* (Laest.) Beurl.

The following species occurred in low frequency and insignficant cover value: *Potentilla nivea* L., *Cerastium* sp., *Papaver nudicaule* (L.), *Hierochloe alpina* (Sw.) Roem. and Schult. and *Carex nardina* E. Fries. The ground cover of mosses and lichens often had a microhummocky form with the hummocks about 4 cm tall, 4 cm across and several centimetres long. The cover of lichens on rock surfaces ranged from none to 100 per cent. In some centres it appeared that lichen-free boulders were emerging through the ground cover of plants and lichen-covered rocks.

(9) Organization: the area of homogeneous vegetation was rarely more than about 0.4 m², but some was about 1 m² in some areas.

(10) Contact with boulder border: from bare fines overflowing into boulders, to moss-lichen-covered fines, to sharp contact of organic soil-supporting heather.

The information on the transect suggested that there was a dynamic relationship between the different types of debris islands, that they formed a dynamic building sequence similar to the arrangement under (8) above.

Large complex debris island

A large debris island (Fig. 2) occurred at the end of the above transect about 100 m north of the Tuto road. It was about 5 $\times$ 15 m in size, rose somewhat above the general bouldery surroundings, and its surface was tilted to the west. The lower side had a more complete plant cover and appeared to be relatively stable, while the higher side had few plants, and there was evidence of current movement in the active layer.

This debris island was perplexing on first examination because, although it was an obvious unit distinct from its surroundings in terms of surface materials, its surface was complex; it appeared to be a confused jumble in terms of microtopography, vegetation, and amount of fines at the surface. Detailed study, however, revealed a pattern of organization. The large debris island was divided by microtopography into many units about 1 m² in area which were in turn broken into units of about 12 dm² surface area. Since these smallest units (12 dm²) were relatively homogeneous in vegetation, surface material, and microtopography, I concluded that they must be the structural and functional units of debris islands (Figs. 4 and 10) and could properly be termed microstands, a stand being the basic ecosystem unit in the terminology

TABLE 1

THULE FINE CENTER ECOSYSTEMS

Stand Number	Size dm²	Number 10dm² samples	Bare Rock	Rock Lichens	Poly-trichum	Live Poly. & Lichens	Dead Poly. & Lichens	Fol. & Frut. Lichens	Luzula confusa	Luzula nivalis	Potentilla	Poa artica	Salix	Cassiope
5XA	10	1	18	18	18	5	18		18					
5XB	8	1	20	20	43	8			8					
5XC	6	1		38	1	1	15		38					
5XD	14	1		25		10	50		15					
5XH	8	1			10	30	60		15					
5XXXIIIJ	100	10	2	4	1	2	76	1	1	1	1	1	5	1
5XXXIIIK	100	10	8	8		20	36	1	1		1	1	8	16
5XG	10	1	3	15	1	5	15		63					5
5XE	25	2		35		5	50							15
5XF	8	1		25		5	25	10	25					25
5XI	14	10	8	26	1	3	26	10	17	10		2	1	2
5XXXV	100+	5	5	45		20	10	10	10			1		20
5XXXVIA	1000+	10	10	30	10	5	20	10	20					
5XXXVIC	140+	10	2	5		+	42	2					30	40
5XXXVIF	2000	13	0	11			47	8	2				13	36

Plants (per cent cover)

Notes:

5XXXIIIJ: No bare soil; microhummocks of lichens; rich in humus; 45 willow seedlings.

5XXXIIIK: Also present: Hierochloe (2%), Dryas (1%), Papaver (1%).

5XF: Cassiope young & vigorous.

5XI: Clumps of vigorous Polytrichum at margin; Poa artica and Cassiope confined to margins and central crack; some Papaver.

5XXXV: Cassiope (2 seedl.)

5XXXVIF: Cassiope (3 seedl.)

employed in this report. As an aid to analysis and communication, the three different microstands were termed rank I, II, and III.

Data on rank II microstands 5XXIIIJ and 5XXIIIK are in Table 1. Figure 4 illustrates an active rank II microstand.

The information collected on this complex area can be summarized as follows:

(1) The active microstands are domed, contain a relatively high percentage of fines, lack plants, and rise above the borders.

(2) Relatively stable microstands are flat or concave, contain less fine soil, have a complete plant cover on both soil and rocks, and are lower than the bouldery borders.

(3) Some of the rank II microstands are made up of an active rank I microstand in the centre surrounded by several other rank I microstands that have different percentages of their surface covered with plants.

(4) There was often a depressed area between adjacent rank II microstands, and *Rhacomitrium* moss and willow were common in these slightly protected microsites.

(5) Study of the relationship between microstands revealed a probable successional sequence similar to that outlined above under (8) on the transect. In addition, the complex centre produced the key to the solution of a puzzling feature.

The data collected up to this point appeared to indicate that willow was present in several different successional stages. This was strange, because it seemed likely that a relatively large woody plant such as the willow would have a rather narrow ecological amplitude in the severe high arctic environment. It was finally noted that there were differences in the vigour of the willow in the different microstands, and, furthermore, that the differences were related to other ecosystem features as follows:

(*a*) Vigorous willows occur in two different types of microstands: (*i*) microstands that are convex have continuous moss and lichen cover on both ground and rock and no heather; and (*ii*) microstands that are concave have cracks and lichen-free cobbles breaking the plant cover and have old heather. In this second type, the willow is rooted in the fines exposed by cracks in the plant ground cover.

(*b*) Senescent willows, often minute and very slow growing, occur in microstands that are concave or flat, have continuous lichen cover, and old heather.

Analysis and observations up to this point now suggested the following hypothesis: Microstands follow one another in a sequence of building phases up to a highly developed system dominated by lichens and heather. This highest unit persists for a period of many tens of years, but eventually begins to break up and disintegrate; that is, the entire process is cyclical, having a building sequence and a disintegration sequence.

It appears that willow is a component of units in both the building and the disintegration sequence of the cycle. It is apparently unable to become established on a continuous moss or lichen ground cover. Consequently, it develops only in stands of the building sequence that do not yet have a complete cover, or those in the disintegration sequence that have cracks and other breaks in the ground cover that produce exposure of fines where a seedling can get started.

The inability of willow to compete with other species in the mature heather stand is dramatically demonstrated by the rate of growth in some that have persisted from earlier microstands or germinated in some unusual and favourable microsite. These willows may be only 2 or 3 cm long and 2 mm thick after 10 years of growth!

The juxtaposition of this group of microstands has considerable significance. It indicates that the differences between microstands are related to their differences in age, not to some current change in regional environment. Furthermore, it is apparent that there is a tendency for these dynamic units (the rank II microstands) to be aggregated rather than dispersed through the bouldery ground as discrete units. It would appear that these features may be of some help in working out the geomorphic processes involved in these dynamic ecosystems.

Elongate debris islands

Elongate complex debris islands from a few up to 10 m long (rank III microstands) and 1 to 4 m wide occur in the higher part of the study area. They are found on both gentle slopes and essentially level ground. The latter may have been sloping, however, when the centres were formed. There is evidence of alterations in local topography that may have changed small areas from sloping to horizontal positions in the landscape.

It is possible that these microstands do not develop in precisely the same manner as the others studied, but they definitely go through the same general patterns of cyclical development.

Rank III microstand XXXVIF had the following characteristics:

(1) Elongate, 10 × 2 m, domed.

(2) Long crack down middle of long axis (Fig. 5); no other cracks. Each half, on either side of the crack, consists of a series of low domed rank II microstands, averaging 1 m² in area.

(3) Sand under the plant cover is dark brown. Data on vegetation

FIG. 4. Active centre in large complex centre. Note sedges on soil and lichens on rocks, indicating long stability of surrounding soil around active unit.

FIG. 5. Surface of elongate complex centre. Note dark colour of all surfaces, the long crack marked by the knife, willow leaves, and clumps of heather.

are in Table 1. *Rhacomitrium* and *Cetraria* spp. are common along the mid-line crack.

(4) Heather is abundant, even along the edges adjacent to the boulders. Since heather only occurs in the last stage of the building sequence and this sequence occurs only on relatively stable soil, the soil of this complex must have been stable for many tens of years.

The ground surface of this stand exhibited one of the striking features of these ecosystems: the relationship of lichen-covered cobbles to the cryptogam carpet (Fig. 5) was similar to the effect achieved when cherries are dropped with some force onto a thick layer of fresh cake icing. The cryptogam carpet appears to be bulging up all around the cobbles. This is another of those features that is probably related to the fundamental processes generating these systems. When we can explain this form, we will be closer to an understanding of the dynamics of the system.

One end of stand XXXVIF had all the characteristics of mature and stable microstands. At the other end, however, microstands that had once been mature were in several stages of disintegration. Lichen-free cobbles were emerging through the cryptogam carpet and the microstand surface was collapsing. There was much less fine material between the cobbles in these collapsing units than in the mature microstands. Adjacent to the complex stand there were centres of pebbles and cobbles, and it appeared possible that these coarse centres were end products of the disintegration sequence of the cycle of development.

Luzula nivalis *debris island*

An elongate centre about 4.5 m in diameter, located near the transect, illustrated differences that had been observed throughout the area in the ecology of the two most common species of *Luzula*. *Luzula spicata* is present only in the building sequence while *Luzula nivalis* is present only in the mature and disintegrating microstands.

Area Seven

Area Seven, located just north of the large complex centre, is distinguished by two lines of rank III microstands (Figs. 3 and 6). This area has an almost imperceptible slope from south to north, and the lines of microstands are parallel to the contours. In part of the area the microstands are so close together that the borders of boulders are only a few decimetres wide. The boulders on the south or upslope side of the strip of centres have less complete lichen covers than the boulders on the other side. Many of the microstands appeared at first to be similar to one another, but the only feature they actually had in common was that they contain finer particles than their borders. Table 2 gives data on representative microstands. The characteristics of the microstands can be summarized in the following manner:

(1) They range in size from approximately 0.1 m² to 10 m².

(2) The larger microstands are divided into a few to several smaller microstands.

(3) Surfaces vary from convex to concave, from rising above the general level of surrounding boulders to depressed below them, and from horizontal to slightly tipped.

(4) Centres may lack boulders or have a few among the fines (Fig. 7).

(5) The plant cover ranges from none to 100 per cent over both soil and rocks. Some cryptogam carpets that had once been complete were now broken by cracks or by emerging lichen-free boulders.

(6) The following combinations of plant species were common on individual rank 1 microstands: (a) *Polytrichum* moss, sometimes with *Luzula spicata* or *Luzula confusa*; (b) crustose and foliose lichens on dead *Polytrichum* substratum and rocks; (c) crustose and foliose lichens on dead *Polytrichum* substratum and rocks, plus *Luzula spicata* and *Luzula confusa*; (d) same as (c) above plus willow; (e) lichens and willow; (f) lichens, *Luzula nivalis*, and heather; (g) lichens and heather.

(7) There was a gradation of microstands in relation to activity. The most plant-free and smaller microstands were at the west end, and there was a progressive increase in the size and degree of plant cover towards the east. The south line of microstands probably began development before the north line.

Considering all the features of Area Seven, it appears that the microstands did not develop simultaneously or, if they did come to the surface at the same time, they ceased activity at different times. The surface form and plant cover show that the easternmost microstands stabilized first, and there was a progression in stabilization from east to west. Consequently, there is a gradient from west to east of the phases (microstands) of the cycle of development. The first phase of the building sequence is found only at the west end; increasingly more mature building phases occur eastward until the most mature heather is reached. Still farther to the east there are early phases of the disintegration sequence, but there are no late phases in this immediate area.

Collapsing heather debris island

About 200 m southeast of Area Seven occurs a rank 111 microstand that appears to be a mature heather stand in several stages of disintegra-

FIG. 6. Area Seven sorted circles. Largest centre is about 4 m across.

FIG. 7. Area Seven young building centre. Note domed surface, absence of lichens, and clumps of *Luzula*.

TABLE 2
AREA SEVEN MICROSTANDS

Stand Number	Size dm²	Surface	Relation to Boulder Border	Number of Samples	Bare Rock	Bare Soil	Rock Lichens	Polytrichum	Live Polytrichum + lichens	Lichens on Dead Polytrichum	Foliose and Fruticose Lichens	Luzula spicata	Luzula nivalis	Carex nardina	Papaver	Poa artica	Potentilla	Willow	Heather
7A	100	convex	above	5	20	10	30	10	15	10		2	1	1	1				1 (seedlings)
7B	100	flat	above	4	8	8	35	4		34		5			1				1
7C	20	convex	even	2	12	15	26	2		38		3							1
7D	12	convex	below	1		64		15				15							
7E	180	flat, tipped	below	8	4	2	2	2	2	78		8	5		2		1		2 (seedlings)
7F	144	convex	level	(Four cells of activity)															
a				2		98 (combined)	1			1									
b				1	2	44	10	10	10	15						63			
c				2	4	48	15	10	15	10						1			
d				1			15		25	15									
7G	10	convex	level	1						25	10	25	10		5				50
7H	20	flat	depressed	2				8	10	35	5	10	10	5					
7I	900	flat	above	9	20	5	20	5	5	40		5	5	5	5				10 (seedlings)
7L	1000+	concave	depressed	13	4		9	2	2	82	2	10	3			3		4 (seed-lings or dwarfs)	7 (seedlings) / 2 (seedlings)
7M	1000+	flat	depressed	9	2		8	2	2	50	2	4	3			7	2		12 / 3 (seedlings)

7L — Elliptical complex of activity cells. Some active areas. *Luzula* spp. and *Poa* more abundant at borders.

7M — Hummock, many cracks. Some active units

tion. The collapsing heather stand was elongate dome-shaped and its sides were breaking up into lumps of the cryptogam carpet on which some old and senescent heather was rooted (Fig. 8). Lichen-free boulders were emerging through the cryptogam carpet. There was evidence of some wind erosion of the west end of the stand.

The west end of the area showed remnants of cryptogam carpet with a few old and senescent heather plants (Fig. 9). These chunks of vegetation appeared to rest unconformably on the pebbles and boulders underneath in a relationship often seen along a river cutbank where chunks of sod have been eroded from the bank, carried some distance, and deposited on a cobble bar. Neither the sod nor the cryptogam carpet could have developed on the substratum on which they now rest.

The following hypothesis for the history of the microstand is proposed: It once had features similar to either Area Seven or the elongate microstands. At least parts of the complex developed to the mature heather microstand of the building sequence and then the entire complex began disintegrating. The central part of the complex broke up more rapidly than the ends. The two areas at the ends are less advanced stages in the disintegration process, but their days are numbered because they are actively breaking up today. The end product of the cycle will be an area of finer material and flatter surface than the adjacent parts of the landscape that have not undergone the cyclical development.

Miscellaneous stands

Many additional centres were observed and described. Information on a few of them follows:

(1) Area Six, 30 m south of Tuto road opposite the transect: Heather stand developed on overflowing plug of sand. Emergence process has been inactive so long that a thick organic soil horizon has formed.

A solifluction terrace is moving over this stand along its upslope margin; therefore, stability of the heather stand is long in comparison to the rate of solifluction movement.

(2) East of Area Five: (a) *Carex nardina* may be an indicator of a collapsing phase; (b) lichen-covered rocks plus *Polytrichum* and lichens at periphery indicate building sequence; fewer rock lichens (because fresh rock surfaces are emerging through the cryptogam carpet) and no *Polytrichum* or vigorous lichens indicate disintegration sequence; (c) microhummocks in the cryptogam carpet might be produced by the fact that *Polytrichum* starts on sand between pebbles; extrusion pressure is stronger in sand and therefore the *Polytrichum* wells up around pebbles.

Fig. 8. Collapsing mature heather stand in late disintegration stage of the cycle.

Fig. 9. Late disintegration stage. Note paucity of rock lichens, remnants of cryptogam carpet, and dwarfed heather.

(3) Stand 5XXXVI D: Centre of pebbles; 10 dm²; uniform stippling of lichens of species not present on the older rock surfaces. Surrounded by the following low domes: (*a*) cryptogam carpet and willow; (*b*) cryptogam carpet, willow, and heather; (*c*) cryptogam carpet and heather; (*d*) cryptogam carpet, willow, and heather; (*e*) cryptogam carpet and heather; (*f*) cryptogam carpet, willow, and heather; (*g*) cryptogam carpet and *Luzula nivalis*. Parts of this complex are obviously disintegrating. Abundance of heather and *Luzula nivalis* and absence of *Polytrichum* indicate a long period of the building sequence. The pebble centre could be a late disintegration phase. Some of the microstands with both willow and heather may be in the building sequence and others in the disintegration sequence. There are many relatively young pebble centres in a line parallel with this stand. They could be end products of the cycle of development.

(4) Stand 5XXXVI E: Sandy centre; flat top. Shoulders have *Polytrichum*, lichens, heather, and small willow. Middle and higher part is being eroded by wind; both lichens and sand are being removed.

(5) Stand XXXVII: Three hundred metres east of Stand XXXVI in similar microtopography setting. Heather centres in all stages of disintegration. Covering an area of 16 × 1.25 m. Boulders adjacent to the stand have very few lichens and are, therefore, lighter in colour than those a few metres away. Characteristics of the microstands are listed in Table 3.

TABLE 3

STAND XXXVII MICROSTANDS

Microstand	Size dm²	Surface	Cryptogam carpet		Luzula confusa	Luzula nivalis	Cassiope
			young	old			
B	50	Domed	80% (10% sand being eroded by wind)	0	0	5%	0
A	50	Domed	0 (wind eroded)	50%	0	0	25% (90% dead)
C	50	Flat	70 (10% bare soil)		1	1	20
D	150	Flat	80		1	1	20

Cryptogam remnant area

An area between the Tuto road and Area Seven has several features that contrast sharply with the surrounding bouldery ground surface. This conspicuous area is flat, covered with gravel and pebbles instead of boulders, and the rock surfaces are lichen-free. In addition, there are some small lumps of the cryptogam carpet resting unconformably on the gravel substratum. This area is similar to heather remnants described above, but it either never achieved the mature phase or it has gone farther in disintegration. The cryptogam carpet fragments could be remnants of any phase of the late building sequence.

DISCUSSION AND SUMMARY

Many debris islands in a predominantly bouldery ground surface occur in the Thule area. Two hypotheses for origin, from the many considered, have survived intensive testing in the field and subsequent analysis of data and notes: (1) the unit of origin of the islands has a maximum size of approximately 0.2 m² (Fig. 10), and (2) these activity units are minute ecosystems (microstands) with internal processes that result in a cycle of development made up of a building and a disintegration sequence (Fig. 11). Analysis of these hypotheses in association with various data and observations produced the following summary of information on ecosystem processes in the Thule region:

(1) The Thule regional environment has been relatively stable for many tens of years; any climatic fluctuations that have occurred were of a magnitude less than the ecological amplitude of the local ecosystem species and processes. This conclusion is based on the following evidence. There has been adequate time for soil processes to stain pebbles a dark brown and to produce an organic surface soil layer 2.5 to 5.0 cm thick. The moss, *Rhacomitrium canescens*, in the boulder borders has grown upward in the spaces between boulders for more than 30 cm. I have no data on annual growth rates, but I suspect that they are only one or a few centimetres. Many willows in the area are 60 to 100 years old, as indicated by the growth rings in their stems.

(2) Under certain local conditions today, and for at least the past 100 years or so, a patterned-ground process has been active under which fines rise up through the bouldery active layer as plugs which may emerge on the surface to produce debris islands with surfaces rising slightly above their borders. Pebbles and boulders are mixed with the fines.

The basic organizational and functional unit of a debris island has a maximum area of fines at the soil surface of about 0.2 m², and it may be only a few square centimetres. These units are minute ecosystems that are termed here rank 1 microstands.

Rank 1 microstands may aggregate; a series of them may develop side by side one after another over a period of time (Fig. 10). They may,

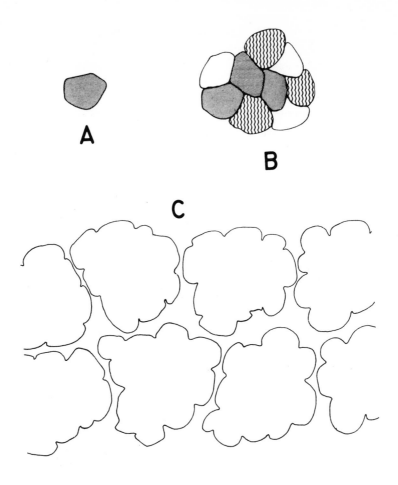

Fig. 10.   The three major types of microstands (debris island ecosystems): (A) Rank I microstand with complete cover of cryptogam carpet. Total surface area approximately 12 dm². (B) Rank II microstand made up of 9 rank I microstands in four different stages of development and, therefore, having different types of vegetation. Total surface area approximately one m². (C) Part of a rank III microstand made up of many rank II's.

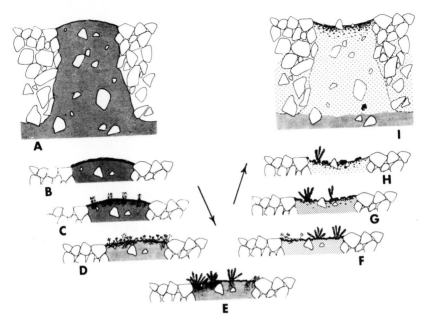

Fig. 11. The hypothetical cycle of microstands. Left series represents the building sequence beginning with stable substratum and a surface that is light in colour, convex, and contains fines. Stage E microstand is the "climax," with all surface components dark in colour. Right series represents disintegration sequence with active substratum, and surface that becomes progressively more concave, cracked, lower in fines, and contains emerged lichen-free stones. Stage I is the final stage in the cycle.

however, "catch up" with one another through ecosystem change processes so that a complex of microstands that are different from one another for an interval, because they differ in age, may eventually get to resemble one another closely. Only slight evidence for this convergence exists.

The aggregations of rank I microstands tend to produce a complex centre with a surface area of about 1 m², referred to as a rank II microstand. These larger units tend in turn to aggregate into still larger complexes, called rank III microstands. The rank III units on flat surfaces are circular in shape with a maximum diameter of about 4 m. On slopes, even on very gentle ones, the rank III microstands are elongate and may reach a length of 6 or 8 m. The elongate rank III's may consist of a single line of rank II's 1 m wide; a double line of rank II's is more common and occasionally there may be four or five lines of rank II's.

In aggregations of microstands, adjacent rank I's may differ greatly in the vigour of current activity or the length of time since activity ceased.

In flat areas, new rank I's tend to develop in a line with the new units always appearing on the same end of the line. On slopes, an elongate rank III grows downslope by the progressive addition of new rank I's.

Corte (1962) states that the units (debris islands of this report) generally occur within bands or "streams" of washed cobbles and boulders. He reports seeing them (personal communication) to be especially common in the vicinity of rivers, particularly near their deltas.

In the same publication, Corte describes the characteristics of the microstands (his "Pattern Type 3") as follows:

(*a*) Surface: uneven, sorted; patterned with centres of fines in coarse, washed material. No primary depositional bedding. Plugs of fine material erupt to surface.

(*b*) Active layer: vertical sorting. Percentage of fines = top — 5 per cent, middle — 11 per cent, bottom — 14 per cent. Accumulation of fines at the permafrost table. No siliceous or calcareous evaporite on undersurface of stones.

(*c*) Ground ice: few or no ice wedges; maximum of a few centimetres wide. Ice masses present.

(3) As activity stops, or possibly just slows down in a microstand, plants become established and they may in time produce a complete vegetation cover. This vegetation development (Fig. 11) is a continuous process, but there is a rather precise sequence of species, and of the percentage of the total area dominated by each species. This appears to be a process of plant succession similar to that which occurs in the

temperate region where changes in the ecosystem result from effects of the plants on the total system.

There is some evidence that this succession may be terminated at any point in its development by a renewal of activity.

The successional development leads to a relatively stable end product that may be a true "climax" in the temperate zone sense of a relatively stable and persistent system. There are other ecosystems in this region that also fit the climax term. The situation with the debris islands is special, however, in that the highest development in the building sequence, the mature heather microstand, is transitory. Some one, or a combination of its features, results in the initiation of ˄ sequence of changes that are destructive to the system and ultimately destroy it completely. Furthermore, there is no evidence to suggest that a new system will develop in the same place. This process differs, therefore, from the cyclical changes described by Watt (1947) for processes within a larger system whose total character remains relatively constant. The cycle at Thule also appears to differ from one described for alpine tundra in Wyoming by Billings and Mooney (1959).

(4) The sequence of microstands (rank 1's) are as follows (Fig. 11):
(a) Building sequence:

(i) Domed, rising above the boulder border; high percentage of fines, and low percentage of pebbles and cobbles in surface; no plants.

(ii) "i" except that moss (usually *Polytrichum*) is present.

(iii) "ii" plus lichens mixed with and growing on the moss, producing a cryptogam carpet.

(iv) "iii" plus *Luzula confusa* or *Luzula spicata*.

(v) "iv" plus vigorous willow.

(vi) Domed surface, somewhat above border; complete cryptogam carpet; most rock surfaces covered with lichens; senescent willow, vigorous heather.

(b) Disintegration sequence:

(i) Cracks in the cryptogam carpet extending down to the mineral substratum (these are different from the contraction cracks common in the mature heather phase in that the latter are old and are faced with lichens while the former are recent and resemble tears in the cryptogam carpet); lichen-free cobbles emerging; surface becoming concave and dropping below the general surface of the boulders.

(ii) Plants and fines being eroded away and more pebbles and cobbles at the surface.

(iii) Finally, a relatively flat area made up of smaller particles than the surrounding area and essentially devoid of plants on soil or rock surfaces.

There are many interesting and puzzling features about these systems that are left unanswered.

The microstands are probably not fundamentally different from those that have been described for other arctic regions. The tantalizing problem of forces and processes that produce these patterns has been explained in many different ways. Troll (1944), Cailleux and Taylor (1954), Washburn (1956), and Drury (1962) have summarized and analysed these theories. The present writer suggests the following hypothesis on processes:

(1) Patterned-ground processes that form the debris islands here studied have precise maximum limits of both the space in which they operate and the length of time in which they function. They may cease to operate at any point in space or time up to that limit.

(2) Some combination of forces maintains many of the ecosystems in a relatively stable condition for tens of years during which time internal ecosystem processes produce changes in characteristics until a mature system is achieved. Some characteristic(s) of this mature system are "out of tune" with the regional environment and consequently they trigger the start of a series of internal changes that result in the disintegration of the system. One possible process involved is that the dark colour of the vegetation of the mature system alters the internal temperature of the system by its absorption of solar radiation, and this temperature change alters the condition of ice in the system in such a way that fine particles descend through the coarse active layer, leaving the vegetation in an alien microenvironment. The plants eventually die, and their remains sift down through the active layer or are blown away. The debris island has now become an area of pebbles or cobbles concentrated at the surface.

One feature of the ecology of these ecosystems is especially interesting. Theoretically, a given combination of ecosystem components (including all factors in the broadest possible sense, organisms, and processes) will produce a single type of mature ecosystem. Consequently, a given debris island, whether it consists of one or many basic microstands, will be identical to all other centres that began with the same components *after time has been adequate* for development of mature ecosystems. Since the microstands of a given complex centre are bound to be of different ages (if the thesis is correct), they will differ from one another for a time. But there is a tendency for convergence to one mature type that should, in time, unify the entire debris island into a mature, homogeneous system. There is field evidence to indicate that these forces are, in reality, operating.

Many complex and almost mature islands can be subdivided into their component microstands on the basis of their vegetation. My data do not prove the existence of a homogeneous large centre that originated from a complex of microstands, and I did not search for such units in the field because the significance of the idea did not occur to me until recently. However, my recollection is that many rank II microstands (1 m^2) are homogeneous, mature centres, but that none of the larger rank III centres are this homogeneous. This could mean either that the largest complexes have not been in existence long enough for ecosystem processes to achieve this homogeneity or that those processes are capable of such achievement only through the rank II level of units. A third possibility is that the microstands of a given island may have started with identical components, but some process, such as the emerging activity, proceeded longer in one than in another and resulted in different combinations of ecosystem components and, consequently, different mature systems. There is a fascinating opportunity here for further study.

ACKNOWLEDGEMENTS. This study was made while the writer was a consultant on ecology to the United States Army Cold Regions Research and Engineering Laboratory, and was working with Arturo Corte. I am grateful to that organization for the opportunity to do the research. I am indebted to Corte for stimulating and helpful discussions and information. I am grateful to William A. Weber for identifying plants, and to James B. Benedict, William A. Bradley, Sidney E. White and Cold Regions Research and Engineering Laboratory staff members for helpful comments on the manuscript.

REFERENCES CITED

BILLINGS, W. D., and MOONEY, H. A., 1959, An apparent frost hummock-sorted polygon cycle in the Alpine Tundra of Wyoming: Ecology, v. 40, p. 16-20.
CAILLEUX, A., and TAYLOR, G., 1954, Cryopédologie, étude des sols gelés, Expéditions polaires françaises 4: Paris, Hermann et Cie., Actualités scientifique et industrielles, p. 1203-1421.
CORTE, ARTURO E., 1962, Relationship between four ground patterns, structure of the active layer, and type and distribution of ice in permafrost: US Army Cold Regions Research and Engineering Laboratory Research Report 88, 79 p.
DRURY, WILLIAM H., JR., 1962, Patterned ground and vegetation on southern Bylot Island, Northwest Territories, Canada: Contribution from the Gray Herbarium of Harvard University, no. CXC, 111 p.
MARR, JOHN W., 1961, Ecosystems of the east slope of the Front Range in Colorado: Univ. of Colorado Stud. Ser. in Biology no. 8, 138 p.
TROLL, VON, CARL, 1944, Strukturboden, solifluktion und frostklimate der erde: Sonderdruck aus der geologischen rundschau, v. 34, p. 545-694.
WASHBURN, A. L., 1956, Classification of patterned ground and review of suggested origins: Bull. Geol. Soc. of Amer., v. 67, p. 823-866.
WATT, A. S., 1947, Pattern and process in the plant community: Jour. Ecology, v. 35, p. 1-22.

EARTH AND ICE MOUNDS:
A TERMINOLOGICAL DISCUSSION

JAN LUNDQVIST
Geological Survey of Sweden
Stockholm, Sweden

ABSTRACT. The following types of mounds related to the processes of freezing and/or thawing in the ground are defined:

(1) PINGOS. The maximum height of pingos is less than 100 m. They consist of the ice and soil of mainly mineral origin. They are formed by transfer of water and are related to freezing. They occur in the zones of continuous and discontinuous permafrost.

(2) PALSAS. The maximum height of palsas is about 10 m. They consist of ice and peat and, rarely, some mineral soil. They are formed by transfer of water and are related to freezing. Their occurrence is in the zone of sporadic permafrost, and the so-called pseudo-palsas occur outside the permafrost zones.

(3) EARTH HUMMOCKS. The maximum height of earth hummocks is about a metre. They consist of mineral and organic soil and are formed by transfer of mineral soil (with water) and related to thawing, and, therefore, only indirectly to freezing. It is possible also that they are directly related to freezing, or irrespective of the freeze-thaw processes. Their occurrence is independent of the permafrost zones.

(4) FROZEN PEAT HUMMOCKS. The maximum height of frozen peat hummocks is about a metre. They consist of ice and peat, and are formed without transfer of water or solid material; they are related to freezing. Their occurrence is within and outside the zone of sporadic permafrost.

It is emphasized that these main types must be kept strictly apart, although it is true that transitions occur, for instance, beween pingos and palsas. In the literature there has been some confusion as to the names and definitions of the types.

RÉSUMÉ. L'auteur définit les types suivants de monticules, liés aux processus de gel et de dégel dans le sol:

(1) PINGOS. La hauteur maximum des pingos est d'une centaine de mètres. Ils sont formés de glace et de sol d'origine surtout minérale. Ils sont construits par le déplacement de l'eau et sont liés au gel. Ils apparaissent dans les zones de pergélisol continu et discontinu.

(2) PALSEN. La hauteur maximum des palsen est de quelques mètres. Ils sont formés de glace et de tourbe avec, rarement, un peu de sol minéral. Ils sont construits par déplacement de l'eau et liés au gel. Ils apparaissent dans la zone de pergélisol sporadique: les soi-disant "pseudo-palsen" apparaissent en dehors des zones de pergélisol.

(3) MAMELONS DE TERRE. Leur hauteur maximum est généralement de moins d'un mètre. Ils sont formés de sol minéral et organique et construits par déplacement de sol minéral (avec de l'eau): ils sont donc liés au dégel et indirectement seulement, au gel. Il est possible aussi qu'ils soient directement liés au gel, ou indépendants des cycles gel-dégel. Leur apparition est indépendante des zones de pergélisol.

(4) MAMELONS DE TOURBE GELÉE. Leur hauteur maximum est d'environ un mètre. Ils sont formés de glace et de tourbe et construits sans déplacement d'eau ou de matériel solide; ils sont liés au gel. Ils apparaîssent à l'intérieur ou à l'extérieur de la zone de pergélisol sporadique.

L'auteur insiste sur la nécessité de distinguer strictement entre ces principaux types, même si des transitions peuvent apparaître, par exemple entre les pingos et les palsen. Dans la littérature, il y a eu un peu de confusion dans la nomenclature et la définition de ces divers types.

ZUSAMMENFASSUNG. Folgende Typen von Hügel, welche mit den Prozessen von Gefrieren und Auftauen im Boden verbunden sind, werden definiert:

(1) PINGOS. Maximalhöhe in Hunderten von Metern. Aus Eis und Mineralerde bestehend. Unter Zufuhr von Wasser gebildt und mit dem Gefrieren verbunden. Vorkommen in den Zonen mit zusammenhägendem und unzusammenhängendem Permafrost.

(2) PALSEN. Maximalhöhe einige Meter. Aus Eis (Segregationseis) und Torf bestehend, ausnahmsweise auch aus Mineralerde. Unter Zufuhr von Wasser gebildet und mit dem Gefriesen verbunden. Vorkommen in der Zone mit sporadischem Permafrost. Pseudo-Palsen kommen ausserhalb den Permafrostzonen vor.

(3) ERDHÜGEL. Maximalhöhe einige Dezimeter. Aus anorganischer und organischer Erde bestehend. Unter Zufuhr von Mineralerde gebildet und mit dem Auftauen verbunden, vielleicht auch unmittelbar mit dem Gefrieren oder ganz unabhängig von diesen Prozessen. Vorkommen unabhängig von den Permafrostzonen.

(4) GEFRORENE TORFHÜGEL. Maximalhöhe einige Dezimeter. Aus Eis und Torf bestehend. Ohne Zufuhr von Wasser oder Erde gebildet. Mit dem Gefrieren verbunden. Vorkommen innerhalb und ausserhalb der Zone mit sporadischem Permafrost.

Es wird betont, dass man unbedingt zwischen diesen Haupttypen unterscheiden muss, trotzden dass Uebergangsformen wahrscheinlich vorkommen, z.B. zwischen Pingos and Palsen. In der Literatur sind früher oft die Namen und Definitionen von den oben erwähnten Hügeltypen vermischt und verwechselt worden.

CONTENTS

FIGURE

The processes related to freeze and thaw affect the relief and structure of the ground in different ways: for instance, through the development of patterned ground. A special effect, which will be the subject of this article, is the generation of a hummocky relief. In some instances this relief should be classified as patterned ground, in others the original definition of "patterned ground" (Washburn 1956) cannot be applied. There has been much confusion in the literature, as well as in verbal discussions, as to the significance of certain terms referring to such phenomena. The relationship between the phenomena, their comparability, and possible transitions to each other have not always been made clear. The purpose of this article is to discuss some of these problems and to define a few phenomena that must be kept apart. The paper only deals with such hummocky features that can be related to freezing and thawing.

Emphasis will be laid on some different types but this does not exclude the possibility of the existence of other types. The "earth hummocks" group, especially, displays numerous other types and variations, which will not be treated here. Müller's (1959, p. 106-111) review of pingo-like phenomena suggests that there are variations within the pingo group, and transitions to palsas.

No effort is made to give the history of the investigations of the different phenomena, nor to collect all synonymous terms that have been used—not even all the instances when these terms have been used erroneously. The purpose is not to determine the origin of the processes resulting in the phenomena described.

PINGOS

The most conspicuous of the phenomena in question are pingos. Pingos are fully described and defined by Müller (1959) and need no further description here. A brief summary of Müller's account will be sufficient.

Pingos reach a maximum height of less than 100 m (Fig. 1). They are more or less cone-shaped and consist mainly of ice, often with a comparatively thin cover of mineral soil. The pingo ice is formed by injection and is a type of permafrost. Climatically, pingos occur in zones of continuous and discontinuous permafrost, especially where the continuous permafrost is thinning out.

Müller distinguished two different main types of pingos: open-system pingos and closed-system pingos. Open-system pingos, which were described from east Greenland, are related to regions with local degrada-

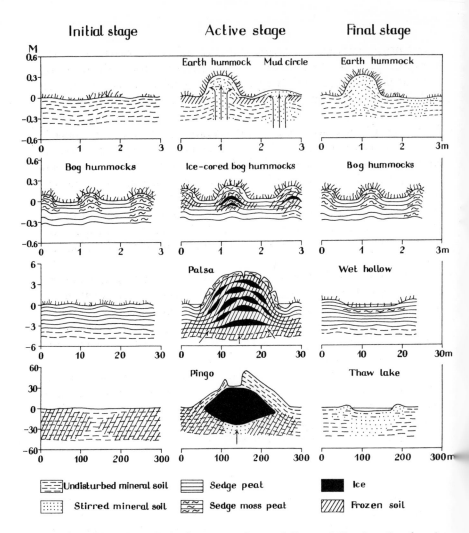

Fig. 1. Sections through the four types of mound discussed. For the sake of readability the thickness of the ice layers in the ice-cored bog hummocks and palsas is somewhat exaggerated. Notice also that there are different height scales used in the different sections.

tion of permafrost. The closed-system type, described from the Mackenzie delta, is on the contrary related to local aggradation of permafrost, normally beneath a lake.

Pingos are formed by injection when water rises through unfrozen gaps in the permafrost. The water can be forced upwards by cryostatic pressure arising when water bodies are trapped beneath a freezing surficial layer. The pressure can also be hydrostatic, that is, the ground water in surrounding, higher country can force the water upwards in the centre of depressions—an artesian phenomenon. In the present connection the origin of the pressure is not so important. The essential fact is that transfer of solid material is unnecessary for the pingo genesis except for the updoming.

Porsild (1938) distinguished two types of mounds similar to the pingos: *Sensu stricto*, which are formed "by local upheaval due to expansion following the progressive downward freezing of a body or lens of water or semi-fluid mud or silt enclosed between bedrock and the frozen surface soil." A smaller type of mound is formed when uplift takes place under the influence of hydraulic pressure. Although deviating from Müller's hypothesis, these types of mound both belong to the pingo group in the present article. The smaller of the two types looks very much like a palsa, but the explanation proposed for its origin is probably not applicable to palsas.

Pingos can be formed in different kinds of overburden. When updoming occurs, all kinds of material, even parts of the bedrock, can be heaved.

The mature pingo stage is represented by the well-known cones. A crater can arise in the pingo top by the melting of the ice in and beneath ruptures originated in the updoming.

When the ice in a pingo melts, the cone disappears. A depression will be left behind, which can be occupied by a thaw lake. After some time, when the fine structure of the superficial soil has been destroyed, the remaining lake is probably an ordinary thaw lake.

PALSAS

"Palsa" is a term that has been frequently misused. This Finnish and Lappish word refers to a very definite phenomenon. Used as a geological term it should be reserved for this phenomenon only. In this connection it may be noted that the plural form of the work in the English language ought to be "palsas." In Swedish geological literature an anglicization of the Swedish word "pals"—English plural, "palses"—is mostly used. This is not to be recommended, and very unfortunate is the German plural form "palsen," adopted even by the *Glossary of Geology and Related Sciences* (1957).

Investigations on palsas have mainly concerned their morphology and distribution, but very seldom their interior structure. This is perhaps because of the great difficulty in making borings and diggings in them. Through G. Lundqvist's (1951) investigation we know the main principles of the stratigraphy of the palsas, but little is known for certain of their genesis.

Palsas are mounds of peat and ice occurring on bogs in the subarctic region. The height of a palsa may be at least some 7 metres. The width of each mound varies from one to another, but is generally of the order of some tens of metres. Very often many palsas combine to form large complexes, which may be several hundreds of metres across. They may also be spread out over a large bog surface.

The surface of the palsas is rather dry and can be covered with a vegetation of low shrubs and lichens, or it can be a barren peat surface. Often it is traversed by open cracks in different directions. Thus the palsas differ clearly from the surrounding bog flat which is mostly very wet and overgrown with sedges, mosses, and other low fen plants. Immediately around a palsa there is often a still wetter zone with free water, the palsa lagg (G. Lundqvist 1951).

A digging in a palsa shows dry peat in the uppermost layers. At a depth of a few dm the peat is frozen with thin layers of clear ice. Still deeper the pure ice occupies a somewhat larger volume, and possibly there is in some cases a small body of clear ice. In general, however, the ice layers are not more than 2 to 3 cm thick. They are formed by segregation. The peat is the same sedge peat as forms the surrounding bog. We know from borings that the palsa body in some instances rests on the substratum of the bog and also that floating ice bodies exist. A simple calculation from the height and weight of the palsas shows that in most cases the palsas must reach down to the substratum. From recent borings (Forsgren 1964) we know that in such instances the substratum can be frozen, but unfrozen substratum has also been described (Hållen 1913).

Topographically, the palsas are generally situated in low parts of the landscape, but this is simply due to the fact that they are almost exclusively bog phenomena, and the bogs are mostly situated in depressions. Within a given depression, however, the palsas are not necessarily concentrated in the lowest part. For instance, G. Lundqvist's (1951, Fig. 3) section through a palsa bog shows them to be situated at and around a local water divide.

In exceptional cases the palsas also consist of mineral soil. G. Lundqvist (1953) mentioned some examples from northern Sweden and others are known from Finland and adjacent regions (Ruuhijärvi 1960, p. 228).

Climatically the palsas belong to the region with sporadic or discontinuous permafrost. J. Lundqvist (1962) showed that in Sweden they occur where the winter season is rather long, that is, where the temperature is below 0°C during more than 200 to 210 days a year. This implies that if the warm season is too long the ice in the palsas will melt, that is, the loss of heat in winter must exceed or counterbalance the heat supply in summer to create and preserve palsas. Where the winter precipitation is too high the snow cover will to some extent protect the ground from freezing. Thus palsas are absent where the precipitation during November–April exceeds 300 mm (J. Lundqvist 1962, p. 93).

In some respects the formation of palsas is very simple (G. Lundqvist 1951, Ruuhijärvi 1960). Their existence entirely depends on the content of ice. There are no signs of a transfer of peat from the surroundings to the palsas. The growth is caused solely by increase of the ice volume. It is not clear what causes this enrichment of ice: whether the capillarity of the peat is sufficient to account for the transfer of water, or if hydrostatic forces are required, as in the case of pingos. Such forces do contribute to the growth in some cases, as is indicated by G. Lundqvist's (1953) observations of mineral soil in the palsas. In general, the ice is separated from the peat only by segregation at the freezing point. This is a process that will create only thin ice layers. It is still not known if these layers in some way can grow thicker, or if injection is necessary for the formation of thicker ice lenses. In any case such lenses seem to occur only exceptionally.

There seems to be a mature stage of the palsas from which they decrease in size by thawing. In some instances this could be the effect of a slight climatic amelioration, but in general the causes are to be found within the palsas themselves. This is demonstrated by the fact that palsas that are apparently thawing, stable, and growing occur side by side, or at least in the same region, as in many large bogs in northernmost Sweden.

From what is known about the interior of the palsas it follows that when a palsa disappears by thawing almost nothing is left in the stratigraphy to demonstrate its former existence. If there has been peat growth on the top of the palsa, this peat will be of a different type from that beneath, and if there has been considerable wind erosion, a hiatus might be found in the stratigraphy. Both these types of "fossil palsas" are insignificant and easily overlooked if the palsa did not exist for a very long time. On the bog surface nothing will be seen of the former palsa except for a wetter part of the surface, comparable with a shallow thaw lake. The longer the palsa exists, the more the peat on the rest of the bog will grow, and the more distinct the pool will be.

It is essential that palsas can be formed without an initial stage in the form of a primary peat hummock or tussock. The bogs where the palsas occur are in general of the fen type, often with a rather smooth surface without distinct hummocks or other large unevennesses. There are, however, phenomena that could be interpreted as transition between palsas and common bog hummocks. These phenomena are more rarely observed. They are azonal features and could be named "pseudopalsas." In these cases ice lenses exist perennially in favourable positions, such as shadowed places far outside the permafrost region (Högbom 1914, p. 307). They give rise to low mounds on the bog surface, invaded by a less hydrophilic flora than on the surrounding bog, a flora that is similar to that of ordinary bog hummocks. The pseudo-palsas are large and flat mounds with a core of perennially frozen peat and ice, which is located entirely in the peat and does not necessarily reach down to the substratum.

From the foregoing, the difference between palsas and pingos is evident: pingos are related to gaps in the permafrost, palsas are formed above a probable permafrost table. Because we know very little about the permafrost conditions beneath the palsa bogs, there is a possibility that some palsas, in fact, are related to gaps in underlying permafrost. In other cases (lower palsas) we know from direct observations (Hållen 1913) that the palsas are formed above a coherent permafrost table by freezing from above, for instance on bog roads, where there are gaps in the winter snow cover. The first palsa type could be considered a type of pingo, as hinted by Müller (1959, p. 111). The second type would be very similar to the above-mentioned pseudo-palsas.

EARTH HUMMOCKS

Earth hummocks of the type to be discussed here belong to the class "non-sorted nets" of Washburn (1956). They are very similar to ordinary peat hummocks in bogs, but they mainly consist of mineral soil. Their height is generally a few dm, but in exceptional cases it can exceed 1 metre. The diameter is of the same magnitude. The hummocks always occur in large groups and mainly on level ground. On slopes they become distorted.

The interior of the earth hummocks often displays a core of fine-grained mineral soil and a rather thick humus mantle. Involutions are typical and the mineral and organic soils are commonly distorted and pressed into each other. The whole structure clearly shows that the mineral soil has been forced upward in and through the humus cover.

Earth hummocks mainly occur on ground rich in vegetation but with low boulder content (G. Lundqvist 1964, 1949). In the Caledonides of Scandinavia they belong to a rather distinct zone of altitude (J. Lundqvist 1962, Fig. 14). The zone rises from 300 to 800 metres above sea level in northern Sweden, to 800 to 1,200 metres in central Sweden. Above this zone the phenomena are absent, but on lower levels they occur at scattered localities, such as old meadows and even down to sea level in central Sweden (Rudberg 1958). The main zone is the area of the tree-line in the mountains and upward as far as coherent vegetation reaches. The distribution indicates that the formation of earth hummocks requires a coherent vegetation which must not, however, be too thick. A cold climate favours the formation, but occurrences, even in a temperate climate, show that earth hummocks can be formed at a mean annual temperature at least as high as $+5\,^{\circ}$C.

The vegetation cover is probably necessary to keep the silty to sandy material collected as mounds. A similar updoming of mineral soil is frequently observed at higher altitudes on barren areas. In these instances the resulting type of patterned ground will not be earth hummocks but more or less dome-shaped mud circles (for this term see Washburn 1947, p. 99). The dome shape seems to be unstable; the phenomena are only raised when newly formed. Their recent character is clearly demonstrated by extremely unstable positions of stones and lumps of earth. Older mud circles are almost flat. Most probably, rain, snow, and other erosive agents destroy the original form quickly if there is no protecting vegetation.

As to the formation of earth hummocks, Beskow (1930, p. 628) proposed the following explanation: "The origin of earth hummocks is local unevenness of the ground and vegetation. A thicker vegetation protects the soil from the frost—the surroundings thus are first frozen. The frost in the ground penetrates under the unfrozen parts, thus pressing soil material upwards. If repeated, the process will result in a hummock. Its growth will stop when it is high enough to allow the frost to penetrate from the sides" (J. Lundqvist 1962, p. 32).

Hopkins and Sigafoos (1954, p. 58) also ascribed importance to hydrostatic pressure in the formation of earth hummocks. Washburn (1956, p. 857) considered this process to have only a local effect, an opinion that the present author shared (J. Lundqvist 1962, p. 32). However, recent observations of involution structures on lake shores, as well as the occurrences of earth hummocks in temperate regions, make it probable that hydrostatic pressure can have a wider importance. The earth hummocks, as well as mud circles, can be explained as quicksand phenomena comparable with frost boils on roads: when a soil, especially if it is rich in silt and supersaturated with water, loses its excess water the discharge generally goes upward where resistance is least. If the soil is semi-liquid, it will be transferred with the water to the surface. Such a discharge commonly takes place when a frozen soil thaws from above, but may also be the effect of, for instance, a change of the water table. The water excess will be removed at random in a homogeneous soil with a uniform vegetation. If there are heterogeneities, such as gaps in the vegetation, the main excess will disappear at such weaker points. When the soil becomes frozen, openings in the frozen layer can theoretically act in the same way. Then the force is cryostatic rather than hydrostatic and the process is, in principle, similar to the formation of closed-system pingos. From this it is evident that the formation of earth hummocks is not yet completely understood and can probably be initiated in different ways. In the present connection it is of essential importance only for earth hummocks to be formed when transfer of solid material takes place by freezing or thawing, and there is no ice content in the mature hummocks. The phenomenon is not related to permafrost; it is known mainly from regions with sporadic or no permafrost.

ICE-CORED BOG HUMMOCKS

During the cold season the hummocks of bogs as well as other ground are frozen in the cold climate regions. If the summer season is warm enough, the ground thaws in the spring. If the loss of heat in the cold season exceeds the heat supply in the following warm season, the ground will persist frozen throughout the whole year. Such conditions are especially favoured in soil, such as peat, with good insulating properties. Therefore, one can often find frozen peat hummocks in bogs at the end of a cool summer, even outside the permafrost regions and when the rest of the ground has thawed. In a wide sense this is also permafrost. In Sweden such frozen hummocks are found within and along the Caledonian mountain range, even south of the zone with sporadic permafrost.

The hummocks of the type mentioned are of the same magnitude as the earth hummocks, but they consist entirely of peat (*Sphagnum* or sedge moss peat) and are located on the bogs. They are not types of patterned ground or permafrost phenomena in the true sense. The hummocks are an entirely biogenic phenomenon because of the differential growth of the vegetation and peat formation. They exist as hummocks regardless of the presence of an ice core. There is no transfer of solid material to the hummocks, nor of water, except from the transfer caused by the capillarity of the peat. The only effect of the freezing is a slight growth of the mound resulting from the volume increase on freezing. When a thaw sets in an ordinary bog hummock will be left behind.

The only reason for referring to this phenomenon, together with the aforementioned one, is the possibility of confusing it with palsas. The existence of a palsa is strictly dependent on the presence of ice: when the ice melts the palsa disappears. Peat hummocks exist whether there is ice or not, and whether there occurs any freezing at all or not.

In some cases, freezing will affect the growth of the hummocks, forming a special type called pounikkos (Ruuhijärvi 1960, p. 158, 220). Pounikkos are perennially frozen and represent a transition type between palsas and common peat hummocks. Probably, they are closely related to the phenomenon named earlier pseudo-palsas, but Ruuhijärvi's description does not fit that of pseudo-palsas. These are much more palsa-like than the pounikkos.

SUMMARY

In the foregoing, the necessity has been emphasized for distinguishing between the following four principal types of mounds related to the processes of freezing and/or thawing in the ground:

(1) PINGOS. The maximum height of pingos is less than 100 m. They consist of injection ice and soil, and are mainly of mineral origin. Formed by transfer of water and related to freezing, they occur in zones with continuous and discontinuous permafrost.

(2) PALSAS. The maximum height of palsas is about 10 m. They consist of segregated ice and peat, and rarely some mineral soil. Formed by transfer of water and related to freezing, they occur in the zone of sporadic permafrost. So-called pseudo-palsas occur azonally outside the permafrost zones.

(3) EARTH HUMMOCKS. The maximum height of the earth hummocks is about a metre. They consist of mineral and organic soil, and are formed by transfer of mineral soil (with water) and related to thawing. It is possible also that they are directly related only to the freezing. They occur independently of the permafrost zones.

(4) ICE-CORED BOG HUMMOCKS. The maximum height of ice-cored bog hummocks is about a metre. They consist of segregated ice and peat, and are formed without transfer of water or solid material, and are related to freezing. They occur within and outside the zone with

sporadic permafrost.

Pingos and palsas seem to be closely related to each other although there are differences. In fact, Müller (1959, p. 111) suggested that there is a third pingo type almost identical with palsas, according to his descriptions. Further study of the substratum of palsas, the type of their ice content, and their surroundings with regard to permafrost conditions would elucidate the similarity to proper pingos.

Earth hummocks have been confused with palsas in the literature but this is due partly to insufficient descriptions and partly to an old idea that there is an upwelling of solid material in palsas (cf. Sharp 1942, p. 420). The difference is clear enough.

Frozen peat hummocks can erroneously be interpreted as palsas and transitions do occur. A close study of the peat and vegetation and sometimes also of climatic conditions will reveal the true nature of the phenomenon.

What is said above does not exclude the existence of more complex phenomena which are formed by more than one process and thus are transitions between the main types. For instance, it is probable that peat or earth hummocks can serve as initial stages of palsas. Also a hummock can be initiated as a pingo by injection, and then develop into a palsa by further segregation of ice and peat. Even in such cases the separation of the processes involved, according to the scheme above, can help to explain the origin.

REFERENCES CITED

AMERICAN GEOLOGICAL INSTITUTE, 1960, Glossary of geology and related sciences, 2nd ed.: Washington, AGI, 325 p.

BESKOW, G., 1930, Erdfliessen und Strukturboden der Hochgebirge im Licht der Frosthebung. Preliminäre Mitteilung: Geol Fören. Förhandl., v. 52, p. 622-638.

FORSGREN, BERNT, 1964, Notes on some methods tried in the study of palsas: Geog. Ann., v. 46, p. 343-344.

HÅLLÉN, K., 1913, Undersökning af en frostknöl (pals) å Kaitajänki myr i Karesuando socken: Geol. Fören. Förhandl., v. 35, p. 81-87.

HÖGBOM, BERTIL, 1914, Über die geologische Bedeutung des Frostes: Bull. Geol. Inst. Uppsala, v. 12, p. 257-389.

HOPKINS, D. M., and SIGAFOOS, R. S., 1954, Discussion: role of frost thrusting in the formation of tussocks: Am. Jour. Sci., v. 252, p. 55-59.

LUNDQVIST, G., 1949, The orientation of the block material in certain species of flow earth: Geog. Ann., v. 31, p. 335-347.

———, 1951, En palsmyr sydost om Kebnekaise: Geol. Fören. Förhandl., v. 73, p. 209-225.

———, 1953, Tillägg till palsfrågan: Geol. Fören. Förhandl., v. 75, p. 149-154.

———, 1964, De svenska fjällens natur STF: s handböcker om det svenska fjället, Stockholm, 440 p.

LUNDQVIST, JAN, 1962, Patterned ground and related frost phenomena in Sweden: Sveriges Geol. Undersökning, ser. c, no. 583, 101 p.

MÜLLER, FRITZ, 1959, Beobachtungen über Pingos: Detailuntersuchungen in Ostgrönland und in der kanadischen Arktis: Medd. om Grönland, v. 153, no. 3, 127 p.

PORSILD, A. E., 1938, Earth mounds in unglaciated arctic Northwestern America: Geog. Rev., v. 28, p. 46-58.

RUDBERG, STEN, 1958, Some observations concerning mass movement on slopes in Sweden: Geol. Fören. Förhandl., v. 80, p. 114-125.

RUUHIJÄRVI, RAUNO, 1960, Über die regionale Einteilung der nord-finnischen Moore: Ann. Botan. Soc. "Vanamo," v. 31, no. 1, 360 p.

SHARP, ROBERT P., 1942, Ground-ice mounds in tundra: Geog. Rev., v. 32, p. 417-423.

WASHBURN, A. L., 1947, Reconnaissance geology of portions of Victoria Island and adjacent regions, arctic Canada: Geol. Soc. America Mem. 22, 142 p.

———, 1956, Classification of patterned ground and review of suggested origins: Geol. Soc. America Bull., v. 67, p. 823-865.

SOIL STRIPES AND POLYGONAL GROUND IN THE SUBANTARCTIC ISLANDS OF CROZET AND KERGUELEN

P. BELLAIR
Laboratoire de Géologie
University of Paris
Paris, France

ABSTRACT. The subantarctic islands of the Indian Ocean—Crozet and Kerguelen—show phenomena associated with permafrost regions: soil stripes, polygonal ground, and large solifluction lobes. Formerly a thick permafrost layer was thought to exist, but this is unlikely because the mean annual temperature is clearly higher than 0°C. These phenomena are perhaps connected with the impermeability of the underlying basalt. Basaltic slabs serve as impermeable layers comparable to permafrost of colder regions. The alternation of wetting and drying is probably the cause of the patterned soils. The soil stripes are not related to the polygonal ground, but form directly on the slopes of the volcanic cones.

CONTENTS

The subantarctic austral islands, Crozet and Kerguelen, exhibit polygonal ground and abundant, well-developed soil stripes (Fig. 1). Very often, because of the very great wetness, the slopes show true slides, unexpected on such inclined soils. The slopes are literally saturated with water, and even during the summer slides occur on the slopes and valley bottoms.

Such a description at first sight might suggest that there is actual or fossil permafrost, or so thought Aubert de la Rüe in 1932. But, after several further field trips, his opinion changed (Aubert de la Rüe 1959). The climate of Kerguelen (49° south latitude) is not, at least at sea

FIG. 1. Soil stripes on an even slope, Possession Island (Crozet).

level, really cold: the temperature ranges from −6°C to +11°C, and the mean annual temperature is above 0°C. But frost days[1] are very numerous and, on account of wetness and lack of large snow cover (owing to very strong winds), gelivation phenomena are very common. Aubert de la Rüe measured, in the eastern coastal plain the weight of matter upheaved by pipekrakes during one frost night (−3°C) at about 9.395 kg for one square metre; another measurement, during winter on moraines, has given 13.5 kg for one square metre.

Soil stripes are exceptionally well developed in Crozet, as well as in Kerguelen. Frequently, a typical selection of tints may be observed: blocktrains are red, while the background is grey.

A change of density is probably the cause of this phenomenon: the larger red stones are composed of very light pumice cinders; the little pebbles are spalls of more dense lava. This shows the consequence of relative density for an heterogeneous soil, but it might be greater for a striped one where gravity plays a more important role.

Philberth (1964) has carefully studied and experimented on polygonal ground, and emphasizes that these soils are motionless during the long time that the soil is snow-covered, but that they are repeatedly revived every summer by imbibition following a dessication. His theory assumes not only quick freeze–thaw cycles, but also quick alternating of wetting and drying. These two phenomena are connected in the subantarctic islands; in Crozet, at 46° south latitude, it often freezes during the night (and it snows), even in summer at 400 m above sea level.

The wetting-drying cycle is also well developed. The country is astonishingly wet, stages of dessication always being very quick. But the surface, owing to the wind, dries, and after a few hours a bare surface becomes dry. So, very distinct lag gravels of deflation are made and *Azorella*, a cushion-like plant, finds difficulty in becoming rooted.

Just above 300 or 400 m above sea level, the vegetation is practically nonexistent. The wealth of soil stripes is probably connected with the deflation over bare grounds.

Polygonal soils, generally atypical, are also known in warm deserts, and especially in playas lakes of Algeria and Tunisia. Their occurrence might be connected with an impermeable underlying layer; here a saline slab corresponds to the permafrost in cold climates.

Perhaps, it is the same at Kerguelen where there are basaltic flows often at a very shallow depth. These lava tables are flat or very gently dipping. Probably, they play the part of an impermeable sub-

[1]A 24-hour period during which the minimum temperature reaches 0°C or colder.

stratum for the typical polygonal soils occurring above unsorted slide rocks. In Possession Islands (Crozet) there are beautiful soil stripes and also gelifluction steps on the slopes of Mount Branca, a cinder cone of a recent volcano.

Indeed, I have not seen that soil stripes originate from stretched polygons as outlined by the orthodox theory. But, the polygons may have disappeared. I think that the striped soils may be shaped by several processes, and it is not necessary to advocate freeze and thaw. The freeze and thaw process is less significant than alternating wetting and surface dessication.

SOLS STRIÉS ET POLYGONAUX AUX ÎLES SUBANTARCTIQUES CROZET, KERGUELEN

Les îles Australes subantarctiques, Crozet et Kerguelen,[1] montrent des sols polygonaux et surtout des sols striés tout à fait remarquables. Très fréquemment, du fait de l'humidité très grande, les versants montrent de véritables marécages qu'on ne s'attendrait pas à trouver sur des sols aussi inclinés. L'ensemble, littéralement gorgé d'eau, montre même en été des marécages de pentes et de fonds de vallées parfois dangereux pour un homme isolé.

Une telle description laisse, de prime abord, penser à l'existence de pergélisols, actuels ou fossiles. Ce fut l'opinion d'Aubert de la Rüe en 1931. Mais les séjours ultérieurs de cet auteur l'ont fait revenir sur cette opinion. Le climat de Kerguelen, la plus haute des îles en latitude (49° latitude sud) n'est pas, au moins au niveau de la mer, franchement froid: la température y oscille de −6°C à +11°C et la température moyenne annuelle est largement au-dessus de 0°C.

Mais les jours de gelée sont extrêmement nombreux et, en raison de l'humidité et de l'absence de couverture nivale continue (phénomène dû aux vents très violents), les phénomènes de gélivation y ont une ampleur exceptionnelle. Aubert de la Rüe a, dans la plaine littorale de l'Est, mesuré le poids de matériaux soulevé par les pipekrakes d'une seule nuit de gel à −3°C: cela fait 9,395 kg. par mètre carré. Une autre mesure en hiver et sur du matériel morainique, a donné 13,5 kg. par m².

Les sols striés atteignent une ampleur exceptionnelle et cela est vrai

[1]Des phenomènes analogues se voient également aux îles Marion et du Prince Edward.

à Crozet comme à Kerguelen. Souvent même, on observe une sélection de coloration très caractéristique: les pierres alignées sont rougeâtres sur fond gris. Ceci est certainement dû à une variation de densité: les pierres rouges, plus grosses, sont formées de scories ponceuses très peu denses; les petits cailloux sont des fragments de lave de densité supérieure. Cela montre l'importance de la densité relative dans le cas de matériel hétérogène, mais ceci doit être plus marqué dans les sols striés où la gravité joue un rôle plus important.

Philberth, qui a étudié avec beaucoup de soin les sols polygonaux et striés pyrénéens et fait des expériences, insiste sur le fait que les sols qu'il a étudiés sont inactifs pendant les longues périodes où le sol est couvert de neige, mais qu'ils sont ranimés plusieurs fois au cours de chaque été par une imbibition après dessication. Sa théorie, qui explique les polygones par un gel plus précoce simultané de la surface et des parois des polygones (par rapport à la masse interne de terre du polygone), suppose non seulement des alternances rapides gel-dégel, mais aussi des alternances rapides imbibition-sécheresse. Or ces deux caractères sont réunis dans les îles subantarctiques. On a vu que l'alternance gel-dégel est constante; même à Crozet, par 46° de latitude, il gèle couramment la nuit (et il neige) en été à 400 mètres d'altitude.

L'alternance imbibition-dessèchement n'est pas moins forte. Le pays est étonnamment humide, les périodes de sécheresse étant toujours très courtes. Mais la surface, sous l'effet du vent, sèche avec une extraordinaire rapidité, et il suffit de quelques heures pour dessécher une surface nue. On a ainsi des *regs* de déflation très marqués où la colonisation végétale par l'*Azorella*, plante en coussinets, se fait difficilement. Dès qu'on a dépassé 300 ou 400 mètres d'altitude, la végétation est quasi inexistante.

C'est certainement au caractère de déflation des sols nus qu'est due l'abondance des sols striés.

On connaît des sols polygonaux, généralement mal constitués, dans les déserts chauds, et particulièrement dans les chotts algéro-tunisiens. Il semble que leur apparition soit liée à un niveau imperméable sous-jacent, représenté par une dalle saline qui correspond à la dalle gelée du pergélisol.

Peut-être en va-t-il de même à Kerguelen où des nappes de basalte existent, souvent à très faible profondeur. Mais ces tables sont horizontales ou très faiblement inclinées. Sans doute jouent-elles ce rôle pour les sols polygonaux francs. Mais il n'en va pas de même pour les sols striés qui se produisent sur des éboulis de granulométrie hétérogène: à l'île de la Possession (Crozet), on en voit de magnifiques sur les pentes du Mont Branca, cône de scories d'un volcan récent, en même temps d'ailleurs que des bourrelets de solifluxion. A la vérité, je n'ai pas observé, suivant la théorie classique, que les sols striés prennent naissance à partir de polygones étirés. Mais ceux-ci peuvent, peut-être, avoir disparu.

Je crois que le phénomène des sols striés peut prendre naissance de plusieurs façons et s'il est, en général, lié à des causes analogues à celles qui donnent naissance aux polygones de pierres, il ne doit pas toujours en être ainsi: le facteur gel-dégel y a moins d'importance que le facteur d'alternance de l'imbibition (et du ruissellement) et de la dessication superficielle.

REFERENCES CITED

Aubert de la Rüe, E., 1932, Etude géologique et géographique de l'Archipel de Kerguelen; Rev. Géog. Phys. Géol. Dynam. et Thèse, 231 p.

——, 1959, Phénomènes périglaciaires et actions éoliennes aux îles de Kerguelen; Mem. Inst. Sc. Madagascar, Série D, t. IX, p. 1-21.

Philberth, K., 1964, Recherches sur les sols polygonaux et striés: Biuletyn peryglacjalny, nr. 13, p. 99-197.

LICHENOMETRIC DATING IN THE CENTRAL ALASKA RANGE

RICHARD D. REGER and TROY L. PÉWÉ
Department of Geology
Arizona State University
Tempe, Arizona, U.S.A.

ABSTRACT. To establish a lichenometric dating scale for the Delta River area of the central Alaska Range, a tentative growth curve for *Rhizocarpon geographicum* was determined based upon lichen diameters on dated Recent moraines of Black Rapids and Canwell glaciers. The ages of these prominent moraines, whose terminal sectors lie below tree-line, were dated by dendrochronology to be 1650(?) and 1830. Maximum-diameter *Rhizocarpon geographicum* on the 1830 terminal moraine of Black Rapids Glacier average 24 mm. Lichens could not be measured on the 1650(?) terminal moraine. A preliminary growth rate curve for *Rhizocarpon geographicum* was constructed in the Canwell Glacier area where maximum-diameter lichens on the 1830 moraine average 30 mm and on the 1650(?) moraine average 144 mm.

The prominent Recent moraines of nearby Gulkana and College glaciers, which lie entirely above tree-line, were dated by comparison of maximum-diameter *Rhizocarpon geographicum* with the preliminary growth curve and were determined to have been formed by advances in 1580(?), 1650(?), 1830, and 1875. Maximum-diameter *Rhizocarpon geographicum* in the Gulkana-College glacier area average 9 mm on 1875 moraines, 31 mm on 1830 moraines, 137 mm on 1650(?) moraines, and 177 mm on 1580(?) moraines.

The growth rate of *Rhizocarpon geographicum* in the central Alaska Range compares favourably with growth rates recorded in the Alps.

RÉSUMÉ. En vue d'établir une échelle de datation lichénométrique pour la région de Delta River dans la chaine centrale de l'Alaska, une courbe expérimentale de croissance du *Rhizocarpon geographicum* a été tracée d'après les diamètres des lichens poussant sur les moraines récentes et datées des glaciers Black Rapids et Canwell. L'âge de ces moraines frontales situées plus bas que la limite des arbres avait été fixé par la dendrochronologie à 1650(?) et 1830. Le diamètre maximum du *Rhizocarpon geographicum* sur la moraine terminale de 1830 du glacier Black Rapids était en moyenne de 24 mm. Les lichens n'ont pu être mesurés sur la moraine terminale de 1650(?). Une première courbe du taux de croissance du *Rhizocarpon geographicum* a été construite dans la zone du glacier Canwell, où le diamètre maximum des lichens atteint une moyenne de 30 mm sur la moraine de 1830 et de 144 mm sur celle de 1650(?).

Les moraines frontales récentes au voisinage des glaciers Gulkana et College, située entièrement au-dessus de la limite des arbres, ont été datées par la comparaison du diamètre maximum du *Rhizocarpon geo-graphicum* avec les courbes de croissance déjà établies: on a pu préciser que ces moraines ont été formées au cours de poussées datant le 1580(?),

1650(?), 1830 et 1875. Le diamètre maximum du *Rhizocarpon geographicum* dans la région du glacier Gulkana-College est en moyenne de 9 mm sur les moraines de 1875, de 31 mm sur celles de 1830, de 137 mm sur celles de 1650(?) et de 177 mm sur celles de 1580(?).

Le taux de croissance du *Rhizocarpon geographicum* dans la chaîne centrale de l'Alaska est tout à fait comparable à celui qui a été observé dans les Alpes.

CONTENTS

FIGURE

INTRODUCTION

To establish a lichenometric dating scale for the Delta River area of the central Alaska Range a tentative growth curve for *Rhizocarpon geographicum* was determined based upon lichen diameters on Recent moraines which have been dated by dendrochronology. The ages of Recent moraines which lie entirely above tree-line were determined by extrapolating the maximum sizes of *Rhizocarpon geographicum* on these moraines to the tentative growth curve.

History of lichenometry

For decades observers in polar and alpine climates have noticed the very slow colonization by lichens on newly-exposed rock surfaces such as are found in front of retreating glaciers or around large melting snow patches. Early investigations were made in the Alps where historic records accurately locate morainal positions (Arnold 1868-98, Klebelsberg 1913, Frey 1922, Faigri 1933, Negri 1934, Friedel 1938a, b, Mattick 1941, and Lüdi 1945). More recent work in the Alps has been done by Beschel (1950, 1957a, 1958a, b) and Heuberger and Beschel (1958); in Sweden by Bergström (1954), Larrson and Logewall (unpublished manuscript), and Stork (1963); in Norway by Bornfeldt and Österborg (1958); in West Greenland by Beschel (1959, 1961b); in the Canadian archipelago by Beschel (1961a, 1963a, b), Ives (1962), and Andrews and Webber (1964); and in central Africa by De Heinzelin (1953), De Heinzelin and Mollaret (1956), and Bergström (1955). Beschel (1957b) suggests a co-operative project to obtain reliable data on lichen diameters and growth rates from definite localities and assembling at the Montreal office of the Arctic Institute a collection of lichen photographs from all over the world.

Principles of lichenometry

Lichenometry is a relatively new method by which one can date recently exposed rock surfaces or recently active geologic processes in treeless areas by measuring the rate of lichen growth. This tool fills the gap in dating between the present and the existing minimum limit of isotope dating. Lichenometry is based on the slow, constant increase of individual plant diameters. Once the growth rate is known the age of a feature or process is determined by measuring the diameters of lichen thalli growing on a critical surface. The length of life of the lichen species used imposes a limit on the ages of exposed surfaces which can be determined by lichenometry.

Growth rates

Crustaceous lichens grow extremely slowly. A freshly-exposed rock surface is sprayed with wind- and water-borne spores and fragments of older lichen stock which become lodged in capillary cracks or small pockets on the surface of the fresh rock face (Beschel 1950, p. 1). Here, if conditions permit, the lichen thalli grow.

Different lichen species grow at very different rates. Some species on a rock surface are microscopic even though they are the same age as the largest visible lichen of a different species on the same exposure. Also, lichens do not grow at constant rates throughout their entire life. During the early stages of growth the thallus is microscopic, and a disproportionally long time interval passes before the individual plant becomes megascopically visible. Then begins a relative acceleration of its increase in size, which ceases at a specific diameter (Beschel 1957a, p. 1). This period of relatively rapid growth ends after a few decades. Following the rapid growth period the increase of diameter per unit of time decreases and gradually approaches a constant rate which continues for many centuries for some species. This uniform growth period produces a straight-line growth curve. Slow-growing lichens have a more constant growth rate compared to lichens which grow rapidly because climatic fluctuations less effectively alter the rate of diameter increase of slow-growing species. Under optimum environmental conditions lichens eventually reach a maximum diameter and the growth rate slows. It is not known how long fully mature lichens will remain in place because they may be removed by weathering, plant competition, human disturbance, sand blasting, and other external processes.

Dating methods

Lichenometric methods are divided into two main types: direct and indirect. Until more is known about the growth rates of the various lichen species in different microenvironments, direct measurement of lichen thalli over long time intervals must remain the basis for any growth analysis (Beschel 1961*b*, p. 1047). Frey (1922, 1959) has photographed and measured lichens for the longest time interval to date—37 years—and has noted little change in some individuals over this period of time. The long life span of lichens and the slow growth rates of these plants prevent direct growth rate determinations by one worker. A simplified lichen growth curve can be indirectly determined by measuring the diameters of the largest lichens growing on several surfaces of different known ages and plotting these sizes against the age of the lichens. The ages of lichens on other surfaces in the same area can then be determined from this curve.

The approach to growth rate curve construction varies considerably. Four different measuring methods are as follows: Beschel (1961*b*, p. 1047) concluded that only the oldest and largest thalli on each surface should be considered because of the large number of uncertainties involved. He considered that the largest lichens will represent individuals growing under optimum local conditions. This conclusion is based on the assumption that the rock surface had no lichens growing on it when the current colonies began to grow. Larrson and Logewall (unpublished manuscript) measured the diameters of at least five of the largest specimens of different lichens and computed the average size within a 25 m^2 area to determine the age of moraines in the Kebnekajse Massif of Sweden. Ives (1962, pp. 200-1) measured between 40 and 100 examples of the largest *Rhizocarpon geographicum* in each locality in north central Baffin Island in an attempt to determine the magnitude of time since the drainage of the former ice-dammed lake of Barnes Ice Cap. In later work around the northwestern margin of the Barnes Ice Cap, Andrews and Webber (1964) marked out 8 × 8 m quadrants at 25 m intervals around the outer moraines of the Ice Cap and recorded the diameters of 50 of the largest thalli in each quadrant.

Limitations of lichenometry

The limitations of lichenometry are due to a lack of information pertaining to: (1) the nature of lichen growth rates, and (2) the effects of varying microenvironments on growth rates. Changes in one or more of the extrinsic factors of lichen growth are thought to cause the rate of diameter increase to vary considerably, but at the present time no quantitative data are available on the parameters of microenvironments. No direct measurements of growth rates have been made for lichens because of the slow growth rates of these plants. Only a few indirect evaluations are available, which are based on the size of lichens found on features of "known" age, and in these cases the varying microenvironments have not been considered. Indirect measurements treat old, large thalli as though they had lived under the same conditions as small thalli on a much more recently exposed rock surface. The growth rates of lichens over the world have not been correlated because of the difficulties of interpreting climatic effects. Geologists and other scientists hoping to use lichenometry are forced to determine growth rates for their respective areas by utilizing other methods, such as dendrochronology and historic records.

The inability to determine the end of active growth also presents a problem in measuring age when growth is slow. Lichens are able to withstand extended periods of desiccation, thereby complicating the problem. Llano (1956, p. 131) stresses that with increasing age lichens lose their individuality when adjacent species coalesce, when the substrata disintegrates, or when the centre of the plant disintegrates. The length of life of lichens varies considerably with relation to climate. Beschel (1961b, p. 1047) states that crustaceous lichens of the genera *Rhizocarpon* and *Lecidea* grow for a period of 600 to 1,300 years in the Alps, 1,000 to 4,000 years in west Greenland, and perhaps longer in higher arctic and antarctic regions.

Dating of glacial movements is based on the assumption that when glaciers move over rock surfaces, these surfaces are scoured clean of any former lichen cover. Thus, one would expect rock surfaces exposed by retreating glaciers and boulders which are released from the ice to have no lichen. This seems to be generally true; however, Goldthwait (1960, p. 95) notes the occurrence of an undamaged lichen cover on a boulder at the bottom of Ice Cliff Glacier in the Nunatarssuaq area of Greenland. These lichens were apparently still alive 30 m behind the ice front and were covered by a thickness of 42.5 m of glacial ice. Beschel (1961b, p. 1050) assumes that this boulder was covered by static ice in a protective pocket and he doubts that the lichens could survive their emergence. Beschel (1961a, p. 196) notes old live lichens and mosses which are partly just emerging from the melting nivation ice sheets on Axel Heiberg Island in arctic Canada. These lichens were permanently frozen and survived, whereas lichens in marginal snow banks did not. Dr. Leslie Viereck (oral communication, 1963) found undamaged large lichens on a very recent moraine of a glacier in the Tonzana River area which definitely had survived emergence from the glacier, but stresses this is a unique occurrence.

LICHENOMETRIC DATING IN THE CENTRAL ALASKA RANGE

To establish a lichen thalli growth rate and set up a lichenometric scale Reger measured in 1962 lichen diameters on the two prominent Recent moraines of Canwell and Black Rapids glaciers, whose termini lie in the Delta River valley (Fig. 1). Dates of the glacial advances which formed these moraines and those of nearby Castner Glacier had been determined by dendrochronology to be about 1650(?) and 1830 (Péwé, unpublished data).

Dating of glacial advances by dendrochronology

BLACK RAPIDS GLACIER. The terminus of Black Rapids Glacier is below tree-line at an elevation of 668 m. At least three prominent arcuate moraines indicate advances in Recent time (Péwé 1951). The oldest end moraine is compound, has low relief and no ice core. It is rather continuous in form and has a dense growth of spruce, willows, alders, and aspen. Boulders in this moraine are only sparsely covered with lichens. In 1951 Péwé noted spruce up to 6.3 cm in diameter and counted 144 annual rings on this moraine. Older trees could not be used because their cores were rotted. He concludes that this moraine was formed by an advance of Black Rapids Glacier in about 1650(?) because he found trees at least 228 years old with rotted cores on the outwash plain just in front of the moraine. It was considered that these trees could have been present on the plain prior to the advance and consequently survived the outwash of sediments from the proglacial streams, but this was not thought likely in view of the number of trees of this age found. A factor of 15 to 20 years was added to the tree ring dates because timberline conditions, severe winds, and shifting of ice-cored moraines prohibit tree growth for at least 15 to 20 years following formation of the moraines. A 4 year old spruce was the first tree found growing (in 1957) on the 1937 moraine of Black Rapids Glacier. The development of an incipient soil on the 1650(?) moraine suggests that the moraine is definitely older than 200 years. This age is also supported by data from Castner and Canwell glaciers. A dense forest with 350 to 500 year old trees lies adjacent to the earliest Recent moraine of Black Rapids Glacier on the west side of the Delta River. This forest is not of first generation trees and is greatly different in maturity from the young forests on the adjacent moraines. The moraine is certainly younger than 400 to 500 years.

The second arcuate terminal moraine of Black Rapids Glacier lies about 0.8 km inside the oldest Recent moraine of the glacier. It is fresh appearing and has no turf cover, but an ice core is present in places. Boulders of this moraine are usually bare of lichens except where there is little or no ice core. Péwé measured spruce trees 4.6 cm in diameter

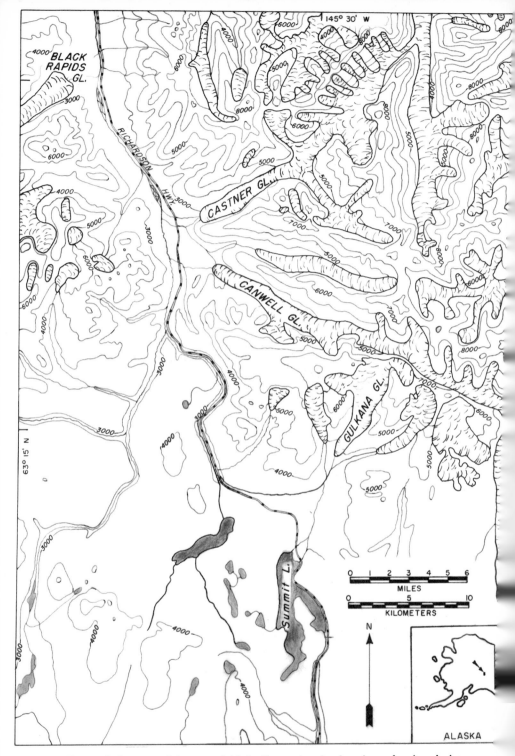

FIG. 1. Index map of the central Alaska Range showing locations of major glaciers. (Base after US Geological Survey Mount Hayes, 1950. 1:250,000).

on this moraine and counted 98 growth rings. Trees growing on a comparable end moraine of Castner Glacier were determined to be 102 years old in 1951. It is concluded that these moraines were the result of an advance of both glaciers in 1830, or about 120 years prior to 1951.

The 1937 advance of Black Rapids Glacier is well documented (Hance 1937, Moffit 1942, and Geist and Péwé 1957). The terminal moraine of this advance is very fresh and has in most areas an actively melting ice core.

CANWELL GLACIER. The terminus of Canwell Glacier is below tree-line at an elevation of 758 m; therefore tree-ring dating could be utilized to determine the ages of the two prominent Recent terminal moraines (Péwé 1957). The outer moraine is fragmentary, rather low in relief, and has no ice core. It is largely forested with primary spruce growth, is covered with a turf cover up to 0.3 m thick, and bears lichen-covered boulders in treeless areas. In 1951 Péwé measured first generation spruce up to 7.5 cm in diameter on this moraine and counted as many as 159 to 165 annual growth rings. A spruce log collected by Péwé in till of this moraine was determined to be less than 200 years old by radio-carbon dating in 1953 (W-268) (Rubin and Suess 1956, p. 442). However, Meyer Rubin (written communication, 1964) stresses that the log could indeed be older than 200 years. The outer moraine is thought to be the result of a Canwell Glacier advance round 1650 (?) because of its forest and soil development and comparable position (relative to the 1830 moraine) with the outer Recent moraine of Black Rapids Glacier.

The inner prominent end moraine of Canwell Glacier lies 0.8 km inside the outer moraine. It is composed of fresh rock and has some ice core remaining. There are few trees, no turf, and lichen-bearing boulders are scant or absent. Péwé measured spruce up to 5.5 cm diameter growing at the base of the moraine and counted 102 annual growth rings. The moraine is thought to correlate with the 1830 moraine of Black Rapids and Castner glaciers.

SUMMARY OF DENDROCHRONOLOGY. The ages of Recent moraines in the central Alaska Range, with the exception of the 1937 terminal moraine of Black Rapids Glacier, are of necessity approximate and are based entirely on tree ring assessments on two prominent terminal moraines of Black Rapids, Castner, and Canwell glaciers by Péwé (1951, 1957, unpublished data). It has been suggested by Viereck (oral communication, 1963) that the 1650(?) date obtained by dendrochro-nology may represent the earliest time at which trees grew in this area because tree-line is rising in parts of the Alaska Range. The 1650(?) moraine thus may be much older. However, Giddings (1941, p. 14) states that standing trees occur near the Recent terminal moraines of Black Rapids Glacier at higher elevations than the moraines. He adds that these trees are more than 500 years old since 3 inches (8 cm) of sound wood out of a possible 10-inch (25 cm) radius yields as many as 350 rings. Péwé also found trees as old as 350 to 500 years just outside the oldest Recent moraines of Castner and Black Rapids glaciers. Therefore, it appears that trees definitely were in the area prior to 1650. The 1650(?) age of the older Recent moraines is supported by the incipient soil and alpine tundra cover developed on these features and the C^{14} date from a log found in till of the 1650(?) Canwell Glacier moraine.

Trees were definitely in this area by 1830, so this date is well established and well correlated between glaciers. Because of the time lapse between morainal formation and the first growth of trees, these advances cannot be dated precisely by the age of trees growing on the various moraines.

Lichen sizes on Recent moraines

The establishment of the relative ages of the Recent moraines of Canwell and Black Rapids glaciers made it possible to determine a standard lichen growth rate for the central Alaska Range. Reger measured lichen diameters on Recent moraines in terminal areas of Canwell and Black Rapids glaciers, but found that results in these areas are misleading because of (1) sandblasting by winds blowing across nearby outwash plains, and (2) the thick growth of moss, willow, alder, aspen, and spruce. This was particularly true on the 1650(?) terminal moraines and true to a lesser degree on the 1830 moraines. Better results were obtained on the south lateral moraines of Canwell Glacier which are above tree-line.

SPECIES AND METHOD. The following lichen species were collected by Reger from Recent moraines in the central Alaska Range and identified by Dr. W. A. Webber.

> *Agyrophora rigida* (Du Rietz) Llano
> *Alectoria pubescens* (L.) Howe
> *Cetraria cucullata* (Bess.) Ach.
> *Cetraria hepatizon* (Ach.) Vain.
> *Cetraria islandica* (L.) Ach.
> *Cetraria nivalis* (L.) Ach.
> *Cetraria tilesii* Ach.
> *Cladonia amaurocraea* (Florke) Schaer.
> *Cladonia coccifera* (L.) Zopf
> *Cladonia deformis* (L.) Hoffm.
> *Cladonia gracilis* (L.) Willd.
> *Cladonia verticillata* (Hoffm.) Schaer
> *Cornicularia aculeata* (Schreb.) Ach.

Dactylina arctica (Richards.) Nyl.
Lecanora sp. (L. *intricata?* (Schrad.) Ach.)
Lobaria linita (Ach.) Rabenh.
Parmelia centrifuga (L.) Ach.
Parmelia stygia (L.) Ach.
Rhizocarpon geographicum (L.) DC.
Solorina crocea (L.) Ach.
Sporostatia testudinea (Ach.) Mass.
Stereocaulon sp. (Schreb.) Hoffm.
Thamnolia vermicularis (Sw.) Ach.
Umbilicaria cylindrica (L.) Del.
Umbilicaria hyperborea (Ach.) Hoffm.
Umbilicaria proboscidea (L.) Schrad.
Umbilicaria torrefacta (Lightf.) Schrad.

Rhizocarpon geographicum (Fig. 2) is utilized for this study because (1) it is abundant in the central Alaska Range and is easily recognized in the field; (2) it has proven reliable in the Alps and provides a basis for comparison of lichen growth rates in the central Alaska Range with rates in other parts of the world; and (3) it shows the most apparent correlation between size and age of all the species present in the central Alaska Range.

Umbilicaria proboscidea, Umbilicaria torrefacta, and *Umbilicaria hyperborea* are abundant, but are not utilized because their size-age ratios do not appear constant in contrast to other areas. Larger individuals are found on 1830 moraines than on 1650(?) moraines, although they are more numerous on 1650(?) moraines. *Umbilicaria cylindrica* is abundant, but time restrictions did not allow a detailed study of this lichen even though its size-age ratio apparently is consistent. *Umbilicaria* spp. were measured at stations where *Rhizocarpon geographicum* are stunted or not present only as a means of correlating moraines.

To determine a lichen growth standard for the central Alaska Range Reger (1964) measured at least 10 of the largest *Rhizocarpon geographicum, Umbilicaria proboscidea,* or *Umbilicaria cylindrica* at each established station when possible. At each station Reger recorded[1] the lichen species measured, diameter in mm, altitude in metres, angle of exposure of the rock face, direction of exposure, estimated mean rock diameter and rock type, whether the habitat is sunny or shady, feet above ground, location and largest diameter of each species measured. Lichens were measured on the largest boulders because these were considered more stable than small boulders. The effect of varying lithology was minimized by measuring lichens on diorite or quartz diorite whenever possible.

[1]All details recorded at each station are listed in Reger (1964), Tables 1, 2, and 3.

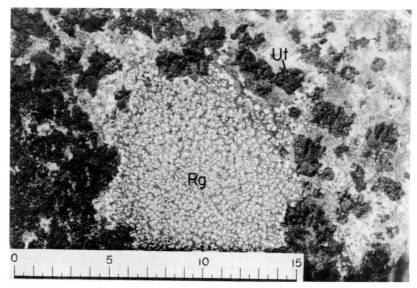

Fig. 2. *Rhizocarpon geographicum* (Rg) and *Umbilicaria torrefacta* (Ut) on quartz diorite boulder of 1650(?) east lateral moraine of Gulkana Glacier, central Alaska Range, Alaska. Scale in centimetres. *Photograph by Troy L. Péwé, August 3, 1962.*

BLACK RAPIDS GLACIER. Results of lichen measurements on the Recent terminal moraines of Black Rapids Glacier are limited (Fig. 3). Unfortunately there was insufficient time available to measure lichens on the lateral moraines of Black Rapids Glacier above tree-line where measurements would provide a much better basis for comparison with other glaciers in the central Alaska Range. The 1650(?) terminal moraine is thickly covered with spruce, aspen, willows, and alders, and lichenometry is not applicable. Dead *Rhizocarpon geographicum* thalli 80 mm in diameter were observed on the east side of Delta River in the well-forested area and widely-scattered live thalli up to 30 mm in diameter were measured. Apparently the encroachment of thick vegetation in approximately 1830 altered the microenvironment to such an extent that pre-existing thalli were killed and the present live lichens represent a secondary colonization. On the 1650(?) terminal moraine west of Delta River, dead thalli up to 75 mm were observed and live thalli up to 40 mm were measured. Here the moraine is partly blanketed with sand, and dead lichen thalli show effects of sandblasting. Apparently lichens which grew on this moraine prior to 1830 were killed during the 1830 advance by windblown sand and picked up from the active outwash plain. Live lichen here are also thought to represent secondary colonization.

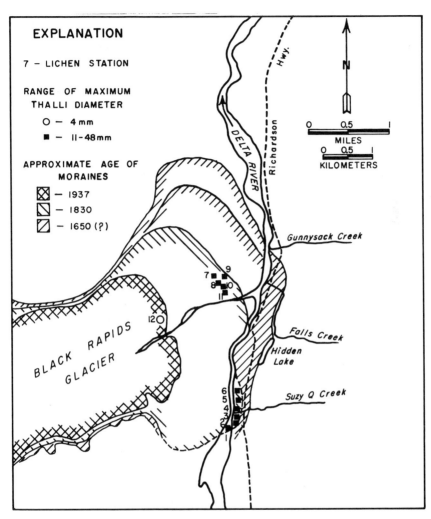

Fig. 3. Relationship of maximum-diameter *Rhizocarpon geographicum* size ranges to Recent moraines of Black Rapids Glacier, central Alaska Range. (Base after US Army Map Service Mount Hayes B-4 and C-4, 1951. 1:50,000).

The largest *Rhizocarpon geographicum* on the 1830 terminal moraine of Black Rapids Glacier range from 11 to 43 mm in diameter and average 24 mm (Fig. 3). Lichens were measured on large boulders on that part of the moraine which was not ice cored wherever possible.

Scattered *Rhizocarpon geographicum* up to 4 mm in diameter were measured on the 1937 terminal moraine, but these are on boulders of the outermost part of this moraine which may not have been ice cored in 1937. No thalli were seen on the ice-cored 1937 terminal moraine in 1962, 25 years after its formation.

The growth rate curve of *Rhizocarpon geographicum* on the Recent moraines of Canwell Glacier was constructed by plotting the average of maximum diameters of thalli on each moraine against time (Fig. 5). This curve may be used to represent the average growth rate of *Rhizocarpon geographicum* in the central Alaska Range. Unfortunately the lack of data from the 1650(?) moraine of Black Rapids Glacier does not permit construction of a growth curve for this glacier or comparison of the growth curves for Canwell and Black Rapids glaciers at the present time. However, the lichen diameters on the 1830 moraines of both Canwell and Black Rapids glaciers are well established and compare favourably (Fig. 5). The average maximum *Rhizocarpon geographicum* diameter on the 1830 terminal moraine of Black Rapids Glacier is only 6 mm less than the average maximum diameter on the 1830 lateral and terminal moraines of Canwell Glacier; the average maximum 1830 lichen diameter on the terminal moraine of Black Rapids Glacier is only 2 mm less than the average maximum diameter of *Rhizocarpon geographicum* on the 1830 terminal moraine of Canwell Glacier.

CANWELL GLACIER. The largest *Rhizocarpon geographicum* on the south 1650(?) lateral moraine range from 132 to 161 mm in diameter and average 144 mm (Fig. 4). The thick moss and spruce cover on the fragment of the 1650(?) terminal moraine remaining is unfavourable for lichen growth and no thalli were observed.

On the 1830 lateral moraine of Canwell Glacier the diameters of the largest *Rhizocarpon geographicum* are 28 to 50 mm, but on the 1830 terminal moraine they are only 18 to 33 mm. The average size for both parts of the 1830 moraine is 30 mm.

GULKANA AND COLLEGE GLACIERS. The determination of the growth rate curve of *Rhizocarpon geographicum* on the moraines of Canwell Glacier provides a scale which aids in dating the Recent moraines of nearby Gulkana and College glaciers, moraines which lie above tree-line. Gulkana Glacier has four Recent moraines and College Glacier has two, of which two of these moraines at each glacier were initially considered

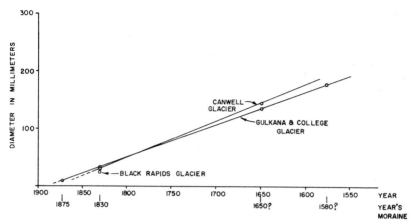

FIG. 4. Comparison of tentative growth rate curves of *Rhizocarpon geographicum* at Canwell, Gulkana, and College glaciers, central Alaska Range, Alaska.

to correlate with the 1650(?) and 1830 moraines, respectively, of Castner, Canwell, and Black Rapids glaciers because of their position and topographic expression. Using these assumed dates and measuring maximum thalli diameters of *Rhizocarpon geographicum* on these prominent moraines a growth rate curve was constructed and compared with the growth rate curve for Canwell Glacier (Fig. 5). The curve for *Rhizocarpon geographicum* in the Gulkana-College glacier area is almost identical with the growth curve of this lichen at Canwell Glacier. This supports our basic assumption that the prominent moraines of Gulkana and College glaciers are equivalent to the 1650(?) and 1830 moraines at Canwell Glacier. Once the growth curve of *Rhizocarpon geographicum* for the Gulkana-College glacier area was established, it was possible to date the two Recent moraines in the Gulkana-College glacier area that apparently have no equivalents at Canwell Glacier. There moraines were determined to date from 1580(?) and 1875 (Fig. 5).

Of the four Recent moraines at Gulkana Glacier, the two oldest moraines form discontinuous ridges which lie just outside younger, continuous moraines. Boulders of the outermost Recent moraine bear anastomosing colonies. Maximum individual *Rhizocarpon geographicum* diameters range from 155 to 198 mm (Fig. 6) and have an average diameter of 177 mm. This moraine has no equivalent at Canwell Glacier, but may represent an advance about 1580.

Inside the 1580(?) moraine is a prominent lateral moraine on which maximum diameters of *Rhizocarpon geographicum* range from 115 to

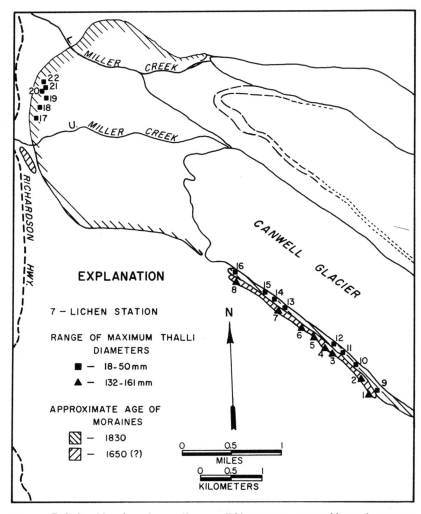

Fɪɢ. 5. Relationship of maximum-diameter *Rhizocarpon geographicum* size ranges to Recent moraines of Canwell Glacier, central Alaska Range. (Base after US Geological Survey Mount Hayes B-4. 1:40,000).

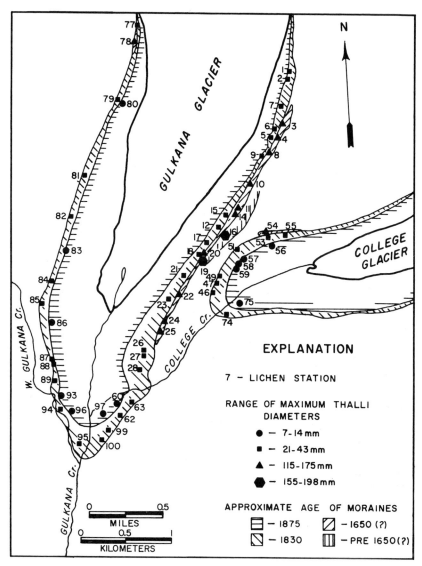

FIG. 6. Relationship of maximum-diameter *Rhizocarpon geographicum* size ranges to Recent moraines of Gulkana and College glaciers, central Alaska Range. (Base after air photograph by US Navy, 9 Aug. 57, identification no. 004 VVAP-61 Det "T" USN 10/c.)

175 mm and average 137 mm. This moraine is thought to be closely equivalent to the 1650(?) moraine of Canwell Glacier where the same lichen averages 144 mm in diameter (Fig. 5).

The 1830 moraines of Canwell and Black Rapids glaciers have a well-defined equivalent at Gulkana Glacier. On this moraine the largest *Rhizocarpon geographicum* range from 21 to 43 mm in diameter with an average maximum diameter of 29 mm, as compared to 30 mm on the 1830 moraine of Canwell Glacier and 24 mm at Black Rapids Glacier (Fig. 5).

The youngest moraine at Gulkana Glacier is much smaller than the other three Recent moraines but is well defined and probably represents a minor advance. The range of maximum *Rhizocarpon geographicum* on this moraine is 7 to 14 mm in diameter and the largest examples of this species average 10 mm in diameter. Gulkana Glacier advanced and formed this moraine in approximately 1875 (Fig. 6).

The equivalency of two Recent moraines of Gulkana Glacier with the moraines of College Glacier has been established by lichen measurements (Fig. 6). The ages of the two oldest Recent moraines at College Glacier are placed at pre-1580(?). Boulders of these moraines are completely, or almost completely, covered by solifluction deposits, and lichen measurements were possible at only one station on the inner moraine. The maximum size of *Rhizocarpon geographicum* at this station is 125 mm. These moraines have no terminal equivalents.

The most conspicuous arcuate moraine of College Glacier dates from about 1830 (Fig. 6). The average maximum diameter of *Rhizocarpon geographicum* on this moraine is 36 mm and maximum diameters of this lichen range from 29 to 50 mm.

The youngest moraine of College Glacier corresponds to the 1875 moraine of Gulkana Glacier. The maximum diameter of *Rhizocarpon geographicum* here is from 6 to 10 mm and averages 8 mm.

Effects of microenvironment on
lichen growth in the central Alaska Range

Apparently the most important decisive factors affecting lichen development in the central Alaska Range are (1) stability of substratum, (2) sunlight, and (3) moisture.

The development of lichen cover on moraines is dependent on the size and rate of ice-core melting in these moraines. Ice cores decrease in volume and rate of melting with increasing age and ice cores melt more rapidly at lower elevations than at higher elevations. No lichens are present on actively moving substrata such as moraines with shallow, rapidly melting ice cores. The 1875 moraines of Gulkana and College glaciers have a scattered and spotty lichen cover which is probably due primarily to a melting ice core. Moraines of 1830 age have smaller ice cores and the lichen cover is better developed. The lichen cover on 1650(?) and 1580(?) moraines is very thick and no ice core is present.

The assumption was made that maximum-diameter lichens are growing in optimum microenvironmental conditions. The dip directions of the rock face hosting the largest thalli in the Gulkana and College glacier areas (Fig. 7 A and 7 B) were plotted and found to have a dominant southwest orientation. These measurements were taken on slopes of widely varying angle and direction, so the results are not weighted by local topography. This dominant orientation may be due to (1) wind direction (Mayo 1963, Fig. 4), (2) differences in temperature on rock faces during morning and afternoon in late winter and early spring, or (3) differences in the length of time that dew remains on southeast and southwest faces during warm seasons. Greater concentrations of small lichens occurred on undersurfaces of boulders where moisture is retained longer than on upper surfaces, but few large lichens are found on undersurfaces which do not receive direct radiation. Lichens in depressions where snow meltwater collects are conspicuously larger than those in drier areas. In depressions where snowbanks remain most of the summer, lichens are absent or stunted and widely scattered.

On the south lateral moraines of Canwell Glacier (Fig. 7 C) maximum-diameter *Rhizocarpon geographicum* tend to grow on southeast faces or in a direction which faces directly up the lateral moraines (Fig. 4). This dominant orientation seems to discount the effect of wind, which blows in the downglacier direction, and may be the result of local topography affecting the amount of direct radiation reaching the area. The effect of sunlight on lichen growth is shown by the rose diagrams of lichens in the Gulkana-College glacier area (Figs. 7A and 7 B) which show most lichen growth to be on south-facing rock faces. In the terminal areas of Canwell and Black Rapids glaciers, which are below tree-line, lichens receive much less direct radiation as previously indicated.

The effects of variations in lithology on lichen growth is not known in detail. This error was minimized by measuring lichens only on rocks of intermediate composition, such as diorite and quartz diorite. In the Gulkana-College glacier area lichens do not grow on limestones or poorly indurated tuff boulders because these rocks spall and disintegrate rapidly in this alpine climate due to the large number of freeze and thaw cycles each year. On the south 1650(?) lateral moraine of Canwell Glacier (Fig. 3) lichens are very stunted or absent on dunite boulders

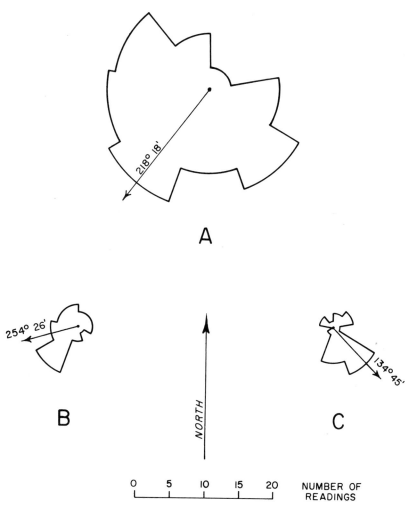

Fig. 7. Frequency distribution of lichen orientations by 40-degree intervals in the central Alaska Range, Alaska:

A = *Rhizocarpon geographicum* in terminal area of Gulkana and College glaciers.

B = *Umbilicaria proboscidea* in terminal area of Gulkana and College glaciers.

C = *Rhizocarpon geographicum* on terminal and south lateral moraines of Canwell Glacier.

which have their source 6.4 to 7.2 km east of the Richardson Highway (Hanson 1963). This stunted growth may be the result of either the basic composition of dunite or the rapid weathering of dunite in the central Alaska Range.

COMPARISON WITH RESULTS ELSEWHERE IN THE WORLD

The diameter of *Rhizocarpon geographicum* in the central Alaska Range increases slightly faster than in parts of the Alps, in Sweden, or in Norway (Fig. 8), although the growth curve nearly parallels that of the Alps. *Rhizocarpon geographicum* apparently requires a longer period of time for initial colonization in the central Alaska Range than in Europe. These lichens on 1830 moraines in the central Alaska Range are approximately 30 mm in diameter but in the Alps they are about 80 mm. On 1650(?) moraines in the central Alaska Range the *Rhizocarpon geographicum* average 140 mm as compared to 174 mm in the Alps. Table 1 shows the comparison between the "lichen factor" for *Rhizocarpon geographicum* in the central Alaska Range and other parts of the world. The average increase of *Rhizocarpon geographicum* on three sets of moraines in the central Alaska Range is about 50 mm/ century for the period of time between 1650(?) and 1830 and compares favourably to the rates measured elsewhere in the world.

The recent advances of Black Rapids, Castner, Canwell, Gulkana, and College glaciers correlate well and apparently occurred about 1580 (Gulkana Glacier), 1650, 1830, and 1875 (Gulkana and College glaciers). Advances by small cirque glaciers in the nearby Amphitheater Mountains appear to be similar in age to the 1650(?) and 1830 advances in the Delta River area (Péwé 1961, p. 201). Wahrhaftig (1958, p. 61-2)

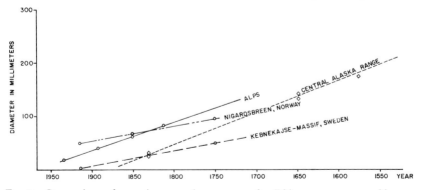

Fig. 8. Comparison of tentative growth rate curve for *Rhizocarpon geographicum* in the central Alaska Range (3 glaciers) with established growth rate curves in Europe (Compiled from Beschel 1957).

describes Recent moraines of Yanert Glacier and other glaciers in the vicinity of the Nenana River valley which probably correlate in part with the 1650(?) and 1830 advances. Hamilton (1965) describes similar advances in the south-central Brooks Range. Lawrence (1950), Ahlmann (1948), and Beschel (1961c) note advances of approximate 1830 age in Southeastern Alaska, Greenland, Europe, and central Africa. The minor 1875 advance of Gulkana Glacier has no known correlative

TABLE 1

COMPARISON OF "LICHEN FACTORS" OF *RHIZOCARPON GEOGRAPH-ICUM* IN VARIOUS PARTS OF THE WORLD

(After Andrews and Webber, 1964, Table 1)

Region	Author	"Lichen factor" (mm per century)
Søndre Størmfiord area of Greenland	Beschel (1961b)	2 to 45
Baffin Island	Andrews and Webber (1964)	5.4
Greenland (Disko area)	Beschel (1963a)	15
Axel Heiberg	Beschel (1963b)	4 to 15
Italy (Gran Paradiso)	Beschel (1958b)	13 to 25
North Sweden	Stork (1963)	20
Austria	Beschel (1957a)	21 to 93
South Norway	Stork (1963)	46
Switzerland (Steingletscher)	Beschel (1957a)	60
Central Alaska Range	this study	50

advances in the central Alaska Range, but Lawrence (1950, p. 219) shows similar advances in Southeastern Alaska. Ahlmann (1948, pp. 72-3) illustrates correlative 1875 advances in Greenland, and according to Beschel (1961b, p. 1059) minor advances occurred in the Alps in the period 1870-80. The periodic glacial advances from 1580 to 1875 in the central Alaska Range correlate well with the worldwide cold epoch following the "climatic optimum" as outlined by Lamb (1964, pp. 334-6).

CONCLUSIONS

Péwé initially dated the prominent 1830 and 1650(?) terminal moraines of Black Rapids, Castner, and Canwell glaciers in areas below tree-line by dendrochronology. In 1962 Reger measured lichen diameters on these moraines. Reliable results at Black Rapids Glacier were obtained only on the 1830 terminal moraine, so no growth curve is at present available for comparison with lichen growth curves from other glaciers in the central Alaska Range. Maximum-diameter *Rhizocarpon geographicum* on the 1830 terminal moraine of Black Rapids Glacier average 24 mm. A preliminary growth rate curve for *Rhizocarpon geographicum* was constructed in the Canwell Glacier area where the best results were obtained. Maximum-diameter *Rhizocarpon geographicum* on the 1830 moraine average 30 mm and on the 1650(?) moraine average 144 mm. The Recent moraines of Gulkana and College glaciers are dated by comparison of maximum-diameter *Rhizocarpon geographicum* and were formed by advances in 1875, 1830, 1650(?), and 1580(?). Maximum-diameter *Rhizocarpon geographicum* in the Gulkana-College glaciers area average 9 mm on 1875 moraines, 31 mm on 1830 moraines, 137 mm on 1650(?) moraines, and 177 mm on 1580(?) moraines.

The growth rates of *Rhizocarpon geographicum* in the central Alaska Range compare favourably with growth rates recorded in the Alps.

ACKNOWLEDGEMENTS. The writers wish to express their sincere thanks to the personnel of the United States Army Cold Weather and Mountain Training School and the U.S. Geological Survey for their aid and assistance in the conduct of this study. Dr. John W. Marr, Director of the Institute of Arctic and Alpine Research, University of Colorado, kindly accompanied us to the study area and offered helpful suggestions concerning field methods and lichen identification. Dr. William A. Weber, Curator of the Herbarium at the University of Colorado, identified the lichen species used in this study. Special gratitude is extended to Mark F. Meier, Lyman W. Taylor, and Gerard C. Bond who provided summer field assistance. Comments and assistance were rendered in the preparation of this manuscript by Dr. Leslie A. Viereck, Research Botanist of the Forestry Science Laboratory, U.S. Forest Service College, Alaska. The fund support for this study was provided by a grant (No. G-22273) to Dr. Troy L. Péwé from the National Science Foundation.

REFERENCES CITED

AHLMANN, H. W., 1948, Glaciological research on the North Atlantic coasts: Royal Geog. Soc., Res. ser. 1, 83 p.
ANDREWS, J. T., and WEBBER, P. J., 1964, A lichenometric study of the northwestern margin of the Barnes Ice Cap: A geomorphological technique: Geogr. Bull., no. 22, p. 80-104.
ARNOLD, R., 1868-1898, Lichenologische Ausfluge in Tirol, XIV, Nachtr, bei XVIII, XV, XVI, XVII, XXIII, XXIV, XXVII: Verh. zool. bot. Ges., Wien.
BERGSTRÖM, E., 1954, Studies of the variations in size of Swedish glaciers in recent centuries: Assoc. Int. d'Hydrologie, Publ. no. 39, p. 356-366.
———, 1955, British Ruwenzori Expedition, 1952, glaciological observations: preliminary report: Jour. Glac., v. 2, p. 468-476.

BESCHEL, R. E., 1950, Flechten aus Altersmasstab rezenter Moränen (Lichens as a yardstick of age of late-glacial moraines): Zeitschrift für Gletscherkunde und glazial Geologie, Band 1, Heft 2, p. 152-161.

———, 1957a, Lichenometrie in Gletschervorfeld (Lichenometry in the glacier foreland): Sonderdruck aus dem Jahrbuch 1957 des Vereins zum Schutze der Alpenflanzen und-Tiere München, Munich 2, Linprimstrasse 50/1Vr. (English translation by Alida W. Herling for the Research Studies Institute, Menell Air Force Base, Alabama.)

———, 1957b, A project to use lichens as indicators of climate and time: Arctic, v. 10, p. 60.

———, 1958a, Flechtenvereine der Städte, Stadtflechten und ihr Wachstum: Naturw. Med. Ver. Innsbruch, Ber. v. 52.

———, 1958b, Ricerche lichenometrich sulle morene del Gruppo del Gran Paradiso: Nuoue Giornale Botanico Italiano, v. 65, p. 538-591.

———, 1959, Lichenometrical studies in West Greenland: Arctic, v. 11, p. 254.

———, 1961a, Botany: and some remarks on the history of vegetation and glacierization, p. 179-199 in Müller, B. S., Editor, Jacobsen-McGill Arctic Research Expedition to Axel Heiberg Island, Preliminary Report 1959-1960: Montreal, McGill Univ., 219 p.

———, 1961b, Dating rock surfaces by lichen growth and its application to glaciology and physiography (Lichenometry): Geol. of the Arctic, v. 11, p. 1044-1062.

———, 1963a, Observations on the time factor in interactions of permafrost and vegetation, p. 43-56 in Brown, R. J. E., Editor, Proceedings of the First Canadian Conference on Permafrost: National Research Council of Canada Associate Committee on Soil and Snow Mechanics, Tech. Memorandum 76.

———, 1963b, Geobotanical studies on Axel Heiberg Island in 1962, p. 199-215 in Müller, F., Editor, Axel Heiberg Island Preliminary Report 1961-1962, Montreal, McGill Univ., 241 p.

BORNFELDT, F., and ÖSTERBORG, M., 1958, Lavarter som Hjaipmedel för datering av ändmoraner vid Norska Glaciärer: Geografiska proseminariet, 50 p.

DE HEINZELIN, J. DE B., 1953, Les Stades de recession du Glacier Stanley occidental (Ruwenzori, Belgian Congo): Expl. Parc. National Albert, ser. 2, fasc. 1.

DE HEINZELIN, J. DE B., and MOLLARET, H., 1956, Biotopes de haute altitude Ruwenzori, 1: Expl. Parc. National Albert, ser. 2, fasc. 3.

FAIGRI, K., 1933, Uber Längenvariationen einiger Gletscher des Jostedalbre und die dadurch bedingten Pflanzensukzessionen: Bergens Mus. Arbok, v. 7, p. 137-142.

FREY, E., 1922, Die Vegetations-verhältnisse der Grimselgegend im Gebiet der zukünftigen Stanssen. Mitt. Naturf.: Ges., Bern, 1921, v. 6, p. 85-281.

———, 1959, Die Flechtenflora und -vegetation des Nationalparks im Unterengadin. II. Die Entwicklung der Flechtenvegetation auf photogrammetrisch kontrollierten Dauerflachen: Schweiz Natlpk., Erg. wiss Unters., N. F., v. 6, p. 239-319.

FRIEDEL, H., 1938a, Boden- und vegetationsentwicklung im Vorfeld des Rhonegletschers: Berg. Geobot. Inst. Rübel., Zürich 1937, p. 65-76.

———, 1938b, Die Pflanzenbesiedlung im Vorfeld des Hintereisferners: Z. F. Gletschekde., v. 26, p. 215-239.

GEIST, O. W., and PÉWÉ, T. L., 1957, Quantitative measurements of the 1937 advance of Black Rapids Glacier, Alaska: Proc. Fifth Alaska Science Conf., p. 51-52.

GIDDINGS, J. L., JR., 1941, Dendrochronology in Northern Alaska: Univ. of Alaska Publ., v. IV, 107 p.

GOLDTHWAIT, R. P., 1960, Study of Ice Cliff Glacier in Nunatarssuaq area, Greenland: US Cold Reg. Res. Eng. Lab., Tech. Rept. 39, 108 p.

HAMILTON, T. D., 1965, Comparative glacier photographs from northern Alaska: Jour. Glac., v. 5, no. 40, p. 479-487.

HANCE, J. H., 1937, The recent advance of Black Rapids Glacier: Jour. Geol., v. 45, p. 775-783.

HANSON, L. G., 1963, Bedrock geology of the Rainbow Mountain area, Alaska Range, Alaska: Unpub. M.Sc. thesis, Univ. of Alaska, 82 p.

HEUBERGER, H., and BESCHEL, R. E., 1958, Beiträge zur Datierung alter Gletscherständae im Hochstubai (Tirol): Schlern. Schr. (Innsbruch), v. 190, p. 73-100.

IVES, J. D., 1962, Indications of recent extensive glacierization in north-central Baffin Island, NWT: Jour. Glac., v. 4, p. 197-205.

KLEBELSBERG, R., 1913, Das Vordringen der Hochgebirgsvegetation in den Tiroler Alpen: Öst. Bot. Z., v. 53.

LAMB, H. H., 1964, The role of atmosphere and oceans in relation to climatic changes and the growth of ice sheets on land, p. 332-348 in Nairns, A. E. M., Editor, Problems in paleoclimatology: Interscience Publishers, 705 p.

LAWRENCE, D. B., 1950, Glacier fluctuation for six centuries in Southeastern Alaska and its relation to solar activity: Geogr. Rev., v. XL, no. 2, p. 191-223.

LLANO, G. A., 1956, Botanical research essential to a knowledge of Antarctica: Amer. Geophys. Union Mon. no. 1, p. 124-133.

LÜDI, W., 1945, Besiedlung und jungen Seitenmoränen des grossen Aletschgletschers: Berlin Geobot. Inst. Rübel, Zürich 1944, p. 35-112.

MATTICK, R., 1941, Die Vegetation frostgeformter Böden der Arktis, der Alpen und des Riesengebirges: Rep. spec. nov. Beih., v. 126, p. 129-183.

MAYO, L. R., 1963, 1961 meteorology and mass balance of Gulkana Glacier, central Alaska Range, Alaska: Unpub. M.Sc. thesis, Univ. of Alaska, 52 p.

MOFFIT, F. H., 1942, Geology of the Gerstle River district, Alaska: with a report on the Black Rapids Glacier: US Geol. Survey Bull. 926-B, p. 107-160.

NEGRI, G., 1934, La vegetation delle morne del ghiacciaio del Lys (Monte Rosa): Boll. Com. Glac. It., v. 14, p. 105-172.

PÉWÉ, T. L., 1951, Recent history of Black Rapids Glacier, Alaska: Geol. Soc. America Bull., v. 62, p. 1558.

———, 1957, Recent history of Canwell and Castner Glaciers, Alaska: Geol. Soc. America Bull., v. 68, p. 1779.

———, 1961, Multiple glaciation in the headwaters area of the Delta River, central Alaska in Short Papers in the geologic and hydrologic sciences: US Geol. Survey Prof. Paper 424-D, p. D 200-201.

REGER, R. D., 1964, Recent glacial history of Gulkana and College Glaciers, central Alaska Range: Unpub. M.Sc. thesis, Univ. of Alaska, 75 p.

RUBIN, M., and SUESS, H. E., 1956, U.S. Geological Survey Radiocarbon Dates III: Science, v. 123, no. 3194, p. 442-448.

STORK, A., 1963, Plant immigration in front of retreating glaciers with examples from Kebnekajse area, Northern Sweden: Geogr. Ann., v. 45, no. 1, pp. 1-22.

WAHRHAFTIG, C., 1958, Quaternary geology of the Nenana River valley and adjacent parts of the Alaska Range: in WAHRHAFTIG, C., and BLACK, R. F., Quaternary and engineering geology in the central part of the Alaska Range: US Geol. Survey Prof. Paper 293, 118 p.

INVESTIGATIONS OF
THE HOLOCENE DEPOSITS
AROUND JAKOBSHAVNS ISBRAE,
WEST GREENLAND

ANKER WEIDICK
Geological Survey of Greenland
Copenhagen, Denmark

ABSTRACT. The fluctuations of Jakobshavns Isbrae during the period from 1850 to 1964 AD have been summarized, and it seems that the altitudinal difference in surface levels of the glacier are in better accordance with the climatic fluctuations than are the frontal fluctuations of the glacier. Fluctuations in the surface level of the Nunatap tasia Lake are treated in conjunction with the fluctuations of the glacier.

Two prehistorical stages of the front of Jakobshavns Isbrae have been found. One has a minimum age of 2,500 years BP and formed at a sea level near the present one. The other stage is represented by marine levels between 35 and 80 m above the present sea level. This stage is considered to have an age of Upper Dryas or Lower Boreal.

RÉSUMÉ. Ce rapport donne les résultats des recherches glaciologiques et géologiques de l'été 1963. On a résumé les fluctuations du Jakobshavns Isbrae pour la période de 1850 à 1965: il semble que les différences d'altitude des niveaux de la surface du glacier sont plus liées aux fluctuations climatiques que les variations de son front. Les fluctuations de niveau du lac Nunatap tasia ont été étudiées en rapport avec les fluctuations du glacier.

On a trouvé deux stades préhistoriques du front du Jakobshavns Isbrae. Le premier a un âge minimum de 2500 ans et s'est formé à un niveau marin égal au niveau actuel. L'autre est représenté par des niveaux marins supérieurs de 35 à 80 m au niveau actuel. On considère que ce stade est du Dryas supérieur ou du Boréal inférieur.

РЕЗЮМЕ. Обобщение колебательных движений Якобсхавнс Исбрэ в течение периода с 1850 по 1964 гг. н.э. показывает, что широтные различия в поверхностных уровнях ледника более соответствуют климатическим колебаниям, чем фронтальные колебания ледника. Колебания поверхностных уровней озера Нунатап тасиа рассматриваются в связи с колебаниями ледника.

Были обнаружены два доисторических яруса фронта Якобсхавнс Исбрэ. Один из них образовался на уровне моря, недалеко от действительного уровня, не позднее 2500 года до н.э. Второй ярус представлен морскими уровнями между 35 и 80 м выше настоящего уровня. Возраст этого яруса относится к верхнему Дриасу или нижнему Ьореалю.

CONTENTS

INTRODUCTION

The area examined is in the interior part of Disko Bugt at approximately 69°10′N and 51°W. Jakobshavns Isfjord forms here a channel about 40 km long and 6 to 7 km wide, connecting Disko Bugt with the lobe of Jakobshavns Isbrae, which drains parts of the central inland ice.

TOPOGRAPHY

Jakobshavns Isfjord is in wintertime a popular fishing ground for halibut for the population of Jakobshavn and Claushavn. The fishermen all give information indicating that the depth of the fiord is 600 to 700 m. According to Bauer and Baussart (1961, p. 18-19) the minimum depth of the fiord near the present glacier front is approximately 550 m. This was concluded from the size of a recently overturned calved part of the front. Icebergs of a similar size as the overturned one described by Bauer and Baussart can be seen at the proximal part of the Isfjaeldsbanken (see below). Hence it must be concluded that the fiord must be at least 550 m deep along its entire length.

At the mouth of the fiord, the great icebergs from Jakobshavns Isbrae become grounded on the Isfjaeldsbanken ("the iceberg bank") (Fig. 3).

On the basis of the size of the icebergs, which are liberated from the bank and drift further to the Davis Strait, Hammer (1883, p. 27) supposed that the sea depth over the bank is at least 130 fathoms (c. 243 m). Possibly this depth must be regarded as a maximum one for submarine channels cutting across the shallow bank. According to the most recent maps of the Royal Danish Hydrographic Office (Chart 1500, 1:400.000, West Coast of Greenland, Rifkol-Hareø), the greater part of the bank is between depths of 50 and 100 m.

Farther away from the bank no continuation of the glacially deepened trough can be traced on the sea charts. A very complex topography of troughs of 500 m depth and small skerries and shoals dominates most of the interior part of Disko Bugt. It is only near the open sea (Davis Strait) that a great submarine valley can be seen on the maps. Its eastern part, between the towns of Godhavn and Egedesminde, has depths up to 900 m, while the western part ends on the continental shelf with depths of 300 to 400 m. It is tempting to associate this overdeepening with glacial action made during the ice ages when great parts of the central Inland ice must have drained this way towards the sea. However, further evidence for such an assumption must be based on a more detailed mapping of the sea floor.

The present glacier lobe of Jakobshavns Isbrae has been well known for two reasons:

(1) Because of relatively easy access to the front, its fluctuations have been described from an early date and have been well known since 1850. Since that time the glacier lobe has retreated so that by 1948 the front was 26 km east of the position of 1850. Summaries of the data concerning fluctuations of the glacier front are given by Meldgaard (Larsen and Meldgaard 1958, p. 24-30) and by Georgi (1959). An advance around 1888 is mentioned by Bauer (1955, p. 55), but Engell (1904, p. 33) questions the determination of the position of the front for that year.

(2) The glacier lobe acts as a drainage channel for much of the central part of the Inland ice (Holtzscherer and Bauer 1954, p. 36) and discharges about 16 km^3 ice to the sea per year (Loewe 1936, p. 327). Estimates of its surface velocity vary. Measurements of the rate of movement at the contemporaneous fronts of the glacier were made in 1880 (Hammer 1883, p. 14-15), 1902 (Engell 1904, p. 43), 1929 (Sorge 1939, p. 361), and in 1963 (Olesen, oral communication, 1963), by intersection from a base-line on the southern side of the glacier. These results are all in accordance with a determined maximum rate of movement of approximately 1 m/hour, while Bauer and Baussart's deter-

minations based on aerial photographs deviate and give greater values (Fig. 1).

FLUCTUATIONS OF JAKOBSHAVNS ISBRAE IN HISTORICAL TIMES

The aforementioned results of the survey of the glacier fluctuations are often cited and are shown in Figure 3. However, fluctuations in the volume of the glacier have attracted little interest in spite of the good historical sources for dating. Additional interest is attached to the fluctuations of the ice-dammed Lake Nunatap tasia, previously described by Hammer (1883) and Engell (1904).

Fluctuations of the ice thickness, based on historical sources

The first data were taken in 1880 by Hammer (1883). These observations include measurements of the height of the ice surface at the front, as well as at the interior nunataks on the north side of the glacier lobe. From the observations, it must be concluded that the glacier surface at its full extent must have been situated close to the highest level of the present trim-line zone, which here, in a terrain of light coloured gneiss, is very easy to distinguish.

At the next visit in 1902 and 1903 (Engell 1904, 1910) a great number of photographs of the glacier lobe and its vicinity were taken. These and the measurements from that date indicate that the glacier had then exposed a trim-line zone of a width of 6 to 35 m. By the following visit by Koch in 1913 (Koch and Wegener 1930, p. 382–391) the trim-line had increased in width to 60 to 90 m near the front.

The area was inspected by Georgi and Sorge (Georgi 1930, p. 158-174) in the summer of 1929. From this trip Georgi has supplied the author with a photograph of the glacier front east of Nunatap tasia. Furthermore, the area was mapped by surveyors of the Geodetic Institute (Geodetic Institute, Map Sheet 1:250,000, 69 V2, Jakobshavn) between 1931 and 1933. The trim-line zone had at that time grown to a size of 120 m near the front.

On aerial photographs from 1948 and 1953 the trim-line zone can be seen to have a width of 220 to 230 m. Nearly the same value was obtained by the investigations of 1963.

Fluctuations of Nunatap tasia Lake

The history of Nunatap tasia is related to the waning of the glacier. Engell (1904, p. 44-50) summarizes its history up to 1902: The water level in Nunatap tasia was at its maximum level in the historic period

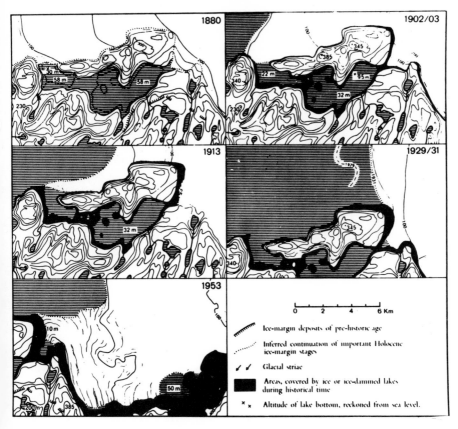

FIG. 1. Extent of Jakobshavns Isbrae and the ice-dammed Lake Nunatap tasia in the years 1880, 1902-03, 1913, 1929-31 and 1953.

in 1880, at 58 m above sea level. Between 1880 and 1892, the water level was sinking slowly, leaving several beach ridges during minor oscillations of the lake level. In 1892 the water dropped suddenly from 40 m above sea level to 22 m above sea level in the western part of the lake, which became separated from the eastern part by a rock threshold up to 32 m above sea level.

During Engell's visit in 1902, the western and eastern parts of the lake still had surface levels of 22 and 32 m. Between 1902 and 1913, in the western part of the lake, the surface dropped to sea level, having, no longer, a glacier barrier between it and Jakobshavns Isfjord. From 1913 onwards, western Nunatap tasia must be considered as only a bay from Jakobshavns Isfjord.

The following changes in the shape of Nunatap tasia took place at the eastern end of the lake. As late as in 1929-33 the drainage of the meltwater from the southernmost parts of Jakobshavns Isbrae took place through Nunatap tasia. This is indicated by Georgi's photograph as well as by the Geodetic Institute's map sheet, which shows, at the glacier margin, a lake with water level of 46 m (corrected by field observations by the author to 43 m). This lake was drained by a river (also described by Georgi 1930, p. 166) to Nunatap tasia.

The rapid lowering of the level of the glacier margin between 1933 and 1948 resulted in the whole of the glacier margin becoming drained towards the present glacier front, and not, in part, via the above-mentioned lake at 43 m above sea level. This lake had in 1963 a height of only 10 m above sea level. The drop in water level of this lake must have occurred mainly between 1933 and 1948 with two short interruptions, represented by terraces at altitudes of 15 and 20 m above sea level. These terraces are continued along the sides of the Jakobshavns Isbrae as minor marginal moraines in the trim-line zone.

Common trends in the fluctuations of Jakobshavns Isbrae

From the above-mentioned data and from the size of lichen colonies, it is evident that only the uppermost 25 m of the trim-line were deglaciated before this century, and that the formation of the trim-line has been isochroneous along a stretch from the glacier front, at least as far as a valley 10 km to the south. This forms a basis for the reconstruction of the phases of the deglaciation of Jakobshavns Isbrae as shown in Figure 2, along a profile through the central parts of the glacier. The profiles are based on the assumption that the shrinkage of the glacier is nearly the same in the central parts as near the margin and that the floor of the fiord is close to a depth of 600 to 700 m below sea level.

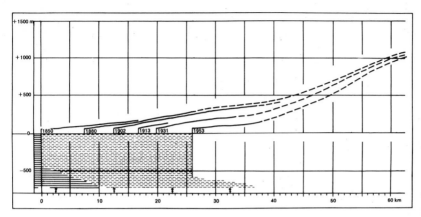

FIG. 2. Profile of Jakobshavns Isbrae along the centre line of the glacier tongue. The position of the centre line of the glacier is marked in Figure 3. Broken horizontal hatching: water body of the fjord, formerly occupied by the glacier lobe.

It is evident that the shrinkage of the glacier was accelerating between 1902 and 1913 and possibly up to 1920, because a halt in the shrinkage is reflected in the lower line of lichen colonies in the trimline zone and by minor moraines at the eastern part of Nunatap tasia. Around 1930 the volume of the glacier was still not very much less than the stage of 1913. Between 1930 and 1948 shrinkage of the glacier increased rapidly. After 1948 and up to 1963 the shrinkage has continued, but possibly not with the same rate as between 1931 and 1948. The fluctuations of the front and of the volume of the glacier are in accord for most of this century, both giving a halt in the glacier's thinning and retreat around 1920. This is also reflected by the temperature observations at Jakobshavn, which show that during the years 1915-22 (as well as in the years 1894-98) the common trend of increasing temperature was interrupted. The total increase in annual temperature between the means of 1882-1911 and 1911-1940 is 2 °C (Lysgaard 1949, p. 19).

In the latter half of the previous century, the increase in temperature scarcely attained the same value as in this century. Nevertheless, half of the frontal retreat of the Jakobshavns Isbrae occurred in this period. It seems here that the slight decrease in the volume of the glacier is a better expression for the climatic alteration than the retreat of the glacier front of 12 km between 1850 and 1902.

The most recent information about the position of the glacier front from 1963 (Olesen, oral communication, 1963) and 1964 (aerial photographs) seem to indicate the beginning of a re-advance of the central parts of the glacier front.

A comparison of the fluctuations of the lobes of the Inland ice in this region shows accordance with those of the glaciers of Pakitsup ilordlia (Beschel and Weidick, in press) and Eqip sermia (Bauer 1955, p. 55) further north. In contradiction to this, the lobes of the Inland ice south of Jakobshavns Isbrae, in the southern branches of Tasiussak, Sarfánguaq and Sarqardleq, seem to have been nearly stationary during the last 100 years. The lobe of Sarfánguaq seems even to be advancing a little over old vegetation. In this glacier lobe marine shells can be seen, transported up from the basement of the glacier.

PRE-HISTORIC STAGES OF THE ICE MARGIN OF JAKOBSHAVNS ISBRAE

Several ice margin deposits have been observed in the area around Jakobshavns Isfjord (Fig. 3). The deposits can be divided, after their occurrence, into two zones, of which the interior one is situated only a few km from the present ice margin, but distal to the trim-line zone of historical time. The outer zone is situated around "Isfjaeldsbanken" in the western part of the fiord.

The inner zone

Moraines from this zone are seen at the southern borders of Nunatap tasia, where they form boulder-gravel ridges. Between these well-defined marginal moraines were observed moraine heaps, similar to

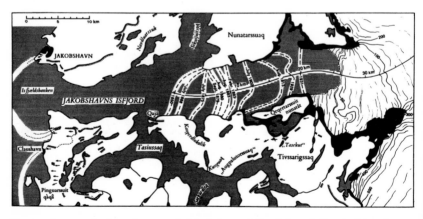

Fig. 3. Ice margin deposits around Jakobshavns Isfjord (comb-lines). Also shown are glacial striae (arrows), the extent of the trim line zone (black areas) and the position of the ice margin at different times in the historical period. The glacier front shown is that of 1953, i.e., at 26 km from the 1850-position of the front.

Andersen's (1960, pp. 64-5) stoss moraines in southern Norway. This development of the moraines must be due to the washboard-like character of the terrain, where northeast-southwest oriented sharp ridges have constituted a major obstruction to the flow of the glacier lobe.

The best development of the moraines of this zone is seen in the Sarfártoq branch of Tasiussak fiord. The moraines are here cut by a terrace washed in the moraines at an altitude of 35 m. No moraine shells were found in connection with these terraces, and it is possible that they have been formed during a period of ice-damming of Tasiussak fiord. With the exception of the gap at Qâja leading to Jakobshavns Isfjord, the Tasiussak Fiord is everywhere barred from the sea by thresholds of at least 40 m above sea level.

Near Qâja, moraines belonging to possibly the same zone are developed along the southern side of Jakobshavns Isfjord. They end abruptly at a bird cliff near Qâja at an altitude of 100 m above sea level. These moraines surround the archeological site of Qâja, which has not been glaciated during the last 2,500 years (Meldgaard and Larsen 1958, p. 28). Consequently the moraines observed here must be older than this date.

An interior zone of similar character as at Jakobshavns Isfjord has been observed further north along the Inland ice margin in Disko Bugt, and around the fiords at Eqe and Torssúkátaq. Its moraines seem not to have been cut by the sea at a level any higher than approximately 5 m above sea level. Even this height could be due to waves from calving icebergs, so that these terraces in reality only mark the present sea level. It is known that in this area the sea level, with the exception of minor fluctuations, has existed at its present level during the last 3,000 to 4,000 years. Hence, at least parts of the inner zone can be supposed to have a maximum age of 3,000 to 4,000 BP. However, it must be stressed that these correlations between the moraines in the interior zone are very tentative and that further investigations are most desirable.

The outer zone

This zone is the continuation of a moraine belt, which can be traced, with a few important interruptions, along the west Greenland coast from at least the southern part of Godthåb district south to the Umanak district north of Disko Bugt. The zone, tentatively called "the fiord stage," is several km wide and has its greater extent in the valleys.

In the area under consideration north of the Jakobshavns Isfjord, it has not been possible to discern more than one phase in the deposition of the ice margin features. This may be due to the lack of time to map this area thoroughly. Access to the deposits is easiest at Sermermiut, immediately south of Jakobshavn (Figs. 3 and 4). At this site, as well as in Jakobshavn, glacial striae indicate that the last glaciation was from the east and not from the southeast, that is, not from Jakobshavns Isfjord. Sometime after this continental glaciation followed the deposition of the oldest member of the sedimentary sequence in the area, a silty "Portlandia clay" mainly characterized by its content of *Macoma calcarea* and *Saxicava arctica*. The occurrence of *Portlandia arctica* also indicates that it belongs to Zones A or D of Laursen (1950, p. 99), which from faunal correlation with Scandinavia are considered by Laursen to be of Older or Younger Dryas age, respectively.

In the cliffs at Sermermiut, a boulder layer lies above the clay, with a sharp boundary between them. This boulder layer can be traced along the rivulet up to the pass at 60 m above sea level, between Jakobshavn and Sermermiut. Here, especially along the sides of the valley, the layer shows transitions to boulder accumulations. The boulder accumulations are continued towards the east by the above-mentioned moraines and by kames terraces, and towards the west by boulder moraines which can be traced to the Isfjaeldsbanken.

It seems very probable that the boulder layer and the moraine have a common origin. In the cliffs of Sermermiut the "Portlandia clay" and the boulder layer are covered by the cultural deposits of the old Eskimo sites of Sermermiut. The dating of the lowermost of these layers to the Sarqaq culture (Larsen and Meldgaard 1958) gives a minimum age of the moraines of 2,500 BP. Weak terrace remnants are found at 30 to 35 m above sea level, but their formation is possibly due to solifluction.

South of Jakobshavns Isfjord the zones become divided, indicating deposition by two lobes of Jakobshavns Isbrae: one through Jakobshavns Isfjord, and another through Tasiussak and over the plains of Pinguarssuit qáqâ. The area situated northeast of Claushavn is a hilly, gneiss terrain with maximum elevations of 400 m above sea level. Because of its hilly nature, small alterations in the volume of the glacier may cause relatively great changes in the extent of the glacier lobes. Accordingly, the history of the changes of the glacier lobes, inferred from their deposits, can be very complicated. However, a first approach has been made in the grouping of these deposits into a "high level phase" and a "low level phase" of deposition.

The "high level phase" is seen in vicinity of Claushavn where it can be traced up to 300 m above sea level towards the east. Towards the sea the ice margin deposits have been cut at several places by continuous beach ridges or terraces at altitudes of 65 to 70 m above sea level. Thus,

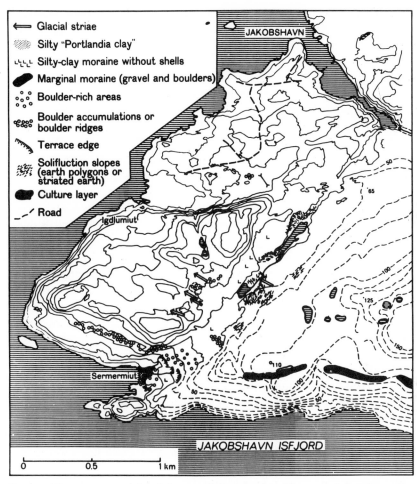

Legend:
- ⟵ Glacial striae
- Silty "Portlandia clay"
- Silty-clay moraine without shells
- Marginal moraine (gravel and boulders)
- Boulder-rich areas
- Boulder accumulations or boulder ridges
- Terrace edge
- Solifluction slopes (earth polygons or striated earth)
- Culture layer
- Road

JAKOBSHAVN

Igdlumiut

Sermermiut

JAKOBSHAVN ISFJORD

0   0.5   1 km

FɪG. 4. The area around Jakobshavn and Sermermiut. The map is based on the Geodetic Institute's map sheet 1:2,000, Jakobshavn and 1:8,000, Sermermiut.

the formation of the moraines from this phase took place at a sea level at least 70 m above the present one. The lack of any marine reworking of these deposits, even in suitable places over 70 to 80 m above sea level, indicates moreover that the sea level during their deposition was scarcely higher than 80 m above sea level.

The great clay plain east of Pinguarssuit qáqâ which forms an isthmus between Tasiussak Fiord and Disko Bugt have heights up to 50 m above sea level. The fauna of the clay in the cliffs of this plain has been described by Laursen (1950), who refers much of the clay to the horizons A and D. Horizon D dominates particularly in the mass of the deposits. A supplementary survey by the author indicates that the "Portlandia clay" at several places reaches altitudes of 50 m above sea level. Overthrust structures were seen in the uppermost clay layers near Pinguarssuit qáqâ and a well-developed dead ice topography is present all over the plain.

It must be concluded that, after the deposition of the "Portlandia clay," the clay plain at Pinguarssuit qáqâ was almost completely overridden by the ice which formed the uppermost "high level phase" of the ice margin deposits, possibly redepositing much of the clay. After a period of thinning out, a re-advance took place, forming the "low level phase."

The "low level phase" must, from the form and size of the marginal moraines, be considered at least partly as a re-advance. Its moraines can be observed towards the east at maximum altitudes of 200 m above sea level. The re-advance has formed or re-formed dead ice topography of the eastern parts of the clay plain, and during its complete melting and recession it must have also made a tunnel-valley in the easternmost part of the terrain, as the great masses of glaciofluviatile gravel cover most of the uppermost metres of the plain. This gravel shows very great variations in thickness. Profiles in valleys (gullies) and cliffs give the impression that the gravel, besides the glacially eroded surface of the clay plain, also has filled former subglacial stream channels in the clay, which possibly may have been formed during the older "high level phase."

On the clay plain at least two morainal ridges were formed during this phase, both situated in the eastern part of the plain. Towards the north the moraines seem to merge in the direction of Jakobshavns Isfjord.

The glaciofluviatile plain on the top of the clay plain at Pinguarssuit qáqâ is very flat and indicates a sandur situated at a sea level between 35 and 45 m above sea level; the higher value is thought to be the most probable one. This glaciofluviatile plain was formed during the last "low level phase." At Isfjeldsbanken the interior moraines were cut by terraces up to 50 m above sea level so the possibility of a correlation of these moraines with the eastern moraines of the plain at Pinguarssuit qáqâ is great.

No absolute date can be given for the two phases of deposition of the outer zone. Laursen's dating based on fauna is tentative and the C^{14} date has so far only demonstrated that no essential change of the sea level has taken place between 3,000 BP and now. However, it is hoped that the study of cores of the organic deposits in the lakes on Pinguarssuit qáqâ plain will furnish a minimum date for the formation of the alluvial plain. The preliminary results of the palynological investigation of the coves (M. Kelly, oral communication, 1964) suggest that the history of the uplift of the area is the same as that determined for other areas in Greenland, that is, the interior parts of Godthåbsfjord (Iversen 1952-53), Northeast Greenland (Davies 1961) and East Greenland (Washburn 1962). If this is correct, the dates of sea levels obtained in the other areas can be accepted here. They suggest the possibility that the deposits of the outer zone were formed between younger Dryas and the oldest parts of the Boreal periods. Such a connection with the Scandinavian Ra-Salpausselkä (youngest phases) or with the North American Valders or Cochrane, *in sensu* Karlström (1956), is very possible.[1]

ACKNOWLEDGEMENTS. With the purpose of dating the fluctuations of the glacier in the historic period as well as in the older Holocene, ice margin deposits of the area were mapped in the summer of 1963 as part of the field investigations of the Geological Survey of Greenland. For good collaboration in the field, the author is indebted to the two other members of the group: Dr. M. Kelly and Mr. O. Olesen.

REFERENCES CITED

ANDERSEN, B., 1960, Sørlandet i Sen-og Postglacial tid (The Late and Postglacial history of Southern Norway between Fevik and Åna-Sira): Norges Geol. Unders., no. 210, 142 p.
BAUER, A., 1955, Le Glacier de l'Eqe: Expéditions polaires françaises 6: Paris, Hermann et Cie, Actualitées scientifiques et industrielles 1225, 118 p.
BAUER, A., and BAUSSART, M., 1961, Photogrammétrie et glaciologie au Groenland: Bull. Société française de Photogrammetrie, no. 3, p. 1-24.
BESCHEL, R., and WEIDICK, A., in press, Geobotanical and geomorphological reconnaissance in West Greenland: Arctic.
DAVIES, W., 1961, Glacial geology of northern Greenland: Polarforschung, bd. 5, Jahrg. 31, Heft 1/2, p. 94-103.

[1] Recent C^{14} datings refer the age of the outer zone to between 7,500 and 9,500 years BP.

Engell, M. C., 1904, Undersøgelser og Opmaalinger ved Jakobshavns Isfjord og i Orpigsuit i Sommeren 1902: Meddel. om Grønland, bd. 26, no. 1, p. 1-70.
——, 1910, Beretning om Undersøgelser af Jakobshavns Isfjord og dens Omgivelser fra Foraaret 1903 til Efteraaret 1904: Meddel. om Grønland, bd. 34, no. 6, p. 155-252.
Georgi, J., 1930, Im Faltboot zum Jakobshavner Eisstrom, p. 158-178 *in* Wegener, A., *et al.*, Mit Motor boot und Schlitten in Grönland.
——, 1959, Der Rückgang des Jakobshavns Isbrae (West-Grönland 69°N): Meddel. om Grønland, bd. 158, no. 5, p. 51-70.
Hammer, R. R. J., 1883, Undersøgelser ved Jakobshavns Isfjord og i naermeste Omegn i Vinteren 1879-80: Meddel. om Grønland, bd. 4, no. 1, p. 1-68.
Holtzscherer, J.-J., and Bauer, A., 1954, Contribution à la connaissance de l'inlandsis du Groenland: Expéditions polaires françaises, no. 37, p. 1-58.
Iversen, Johs., 1952-53, The origin of the flora of western Greenland in the light of pollen analysis: Oikos, 4:2, p. 85-103.
Karlstrom, T., 1956, The problem of Cochrane in late Pleistocene chronology: US Geol. Survey Bull. 1021-J, p. 303-330.
Koch, I. P., and Wegener, A., 1930, Wissenschaftliche Ergebnisse der dänischen Expedition nach Dronning Louises Land und quer über das Inlandseis von Nordgrönland 1912-1913: Meddel. om Grønland, bd. 75, 676 p.
Larsen, H., and Meldgaard, J., 1958, Paleo-Eskimo cultures in Disko Bugt, West Greenland: Meddel. om Grønland, bd. 161, no. 2, 75 p.
Laursen, D., 1950, The stratigraphy of the marine Quaternary deposits in West Greenland: Meddel. om Grønland, bd. 151, no. 1: Also in Bull. Grønlands Geol. Unders., no. 2, 142 p.
Loewe, F., 1936, Höhenverhältnisse und Massenhaushalt des grönländischen Indlandseises: Gerlands Beiträge Geophysik, v. 46, p. 317-330.
Lysgaard, L., 1949, Recent climatic fluctuations: Folia Geog. Danica, v. 5, p. 1-86, 1-94, 1-35.
Sorge, E., 1939, Die Geschwindigkeit und Frontlage des Eisstroms von Jakobshavn: Wissenschaftliche Ergebnisse der Deutschen Grönland-Expedition Alfred Wegener 1929 und 1930-31: bd. 4, no. 2, p. 356-362.
Washburn, A. L., and Stuiver, M., 1962, Radiocarbon-dated postglacial delevelling in northeast Greenland and its implications: Arctic, v. 15, p. 66-73.

THE PLEISTOCENE
HISTORY OF ANTARCTICA

K. K. MARKOV
Moscow State University
Moscow, USSR

ABSTRACT. The Pleistocene history of the Antarctic is extremely peculiar, as is its glacial history.

Data show that glaciation of Antarctica began far before ice appeared in Europe. To the previous indications of Neogene(?) moraine-like formations of Antarctica, it should be added that paleomagnetic investigations have determined pole shifting, which allows the Antarctica glaciation to begin as early as the Paleogene.

The Antarctica glaciation was not interrupted by interglacials, as in continental Europe where the entire ice cover melted. The glaciation of Antarctica existed continuously with only its extent changing. The studies both in the mainland and on the bottom of the ocean adjacent to Antarctica lead to this conclusion. It has been determined through the study of the recent history of the ocean bottom adjacent to the continent that the glacial marine deposits accumulated uninterruptedly during the whole Pleistocene Epoch. Approaching the climate stabilizer—the Antarctic ice shield—the natural conditions of the ocean themselves become more stable.

All ice budgets of the existing Antarctic ice shield are positive, though they refer to the time of warmer climate when the ice diminished in volume in a greater part of the rest of the earth's surface. This supports the hypothesis of Scott, that the Antarctic ice shield, being in the ultracold climate, increased in its volume in the epochs when climate got significantly warmer and decreased when it became colder.

Thus, the Antarctic ice shield is much more viable than the European ice shield. The intensity of the present glaciation of the Antarctic (ice, km^3/glaciation area, km^2) is greater than the intensity of the old mantle glaciation in North America and Eurasia.

RÉSUMÉ. L'histoire pléistocène de l'Antarctique est extrêmement singulière, tout comme son histoire glaciaire.

Les données montrent que la glaciation de l'Antarctique a débuté bien avant que la glace n'apparaîsse en Europe. Aux indications déjà fournies par les formations morainiques néogènes de l'Antarctique, il faut ajouter que des enquêtes de paléomagnétisme ont démontré un déplacement du pôle, ce qui permet de faire débuter la glaciation antarctique dès le Paléogène.

La glaciation antarctique ne fut pas interrompue par des interglaciaires comme en Europe continentale, où toute la calotte glaciaire fondit. La glaciation antarctique a duré de façon continue et seule son extension a varié. Les études, aussi bien de la terre ferme que des fonds de l'océan voisin, amènent à cette conclusion. L'étude de l'histoire récente du fond de l'océan a permis de déterminer que les dépôts glaciaires marins se sont accumulés sans interruption durant tout le Pléistocène. En approchant du stabilisateur climatique—c.à.d. la calotte glaciaire antarctique—les conditions naturelles mêmes de l'océan deviennent plus stables.

Tous les bilans de la calotte glaciaire antarctique actuelle sont positifs, bien qu'ils se rapportent à une époque de climat plus chaud, au moment où la glace diminuait de volume sur la plus grande partie du reste de la surface du globe. Ceci concorde avec l'hypothèse de Scott selon laquelle la calotte glaciaire antarctique, située en climat ultra-froid, a augmenté de volume dans les époques où le climat devenait sensiblement plus chaud et reculé quand il devenait plus froid.

Ainsi, la calotte glaciaire antarctique est beaucoup plus "viable" que la calotte européenne. L'intensité de la glaciation présente (glace en km³/ surface englacée en km²) est plus grande que l'intensité de l'ancienne glaciation de manteau en Amérique du Nord et en Eurasie.

РЕЗЮМЕ. Плейстоценовая история Антарктики исключительно своеобразна, в том числе ее ледниковая история.

Имеются данные, свидетельствующие о том, что история оледенения Антарктики началась ранее, чем в Европе. К прежним указаниям на неогеновые (?) мореноподобные отложения Антарктиды прибавились новые палеомагнитные дзнные свидетельствующие, что перемещение полюсов привело к оледенению Антарктиды уже в палеогене.

Оледенение Антарктиды не прерывалось межледниковьями, как в Европе, когда континентальный лед совершенно растаивал. Оледенение Антарктиды существовало непрерывно, изменялись только его размеры. К этому выводу приводят результаты исследований, как материка, так и дна Южного океана. На дне Южного океана ледниково-морские отложения отлагались непрерывно в течение всего плейстоцена. По мере приближения к Антарктиде — стабилизатору климатических изменений — природные условия самого Южного океана делались более стабильными.

Все результаты определения бюджета оледенения Антарктиды — положительны, хотя они приурочены ко времени потепления климата, когда объем льда уменьшался на большей части остальной поверхности Земли. Еще Р. Скотт высказал эту гипотезу, согласно которой антарктический ледниковый щит, находящийся в ультрахолодном климате увеличивался в объеме, когда климат становился теплее и уменьшался, когда климат становился холоднее. Таким образом, антарктический ледниковый щит гораздо устойчивее, чем европейский. Интенсивность современного оледенения Антарктики (объем льд⁶ км³ площадь льда км²) болнаше интенсивности древнего покровного оледенения С. Америки и Евразии.

CONTENTS

FIGURE

INTRODUCTION

The investigators of a Pleistocene history of Antarctica have tried to find some events analogous to those which took place at the same time in the northern hemisphere. They have established that the same events of the Pleistocene history of the two hemispheres were synchronous. For completely comprehensible reasons the greatest attention was accorded to the former glaciation of the Antarctic and to the comparison of the stages of the glacial history of the Antarctic and North America. I greatly appreciate the results of this research.

But at the same time I shall try to set forth the history of the Pleistocene of Antarctica from a completely different point of view. Antarctica is the most extraordinary of the continents on the earth, and its geological history in the Pleistocene must have been as singular as are its present-day features.

Before reviewing the evidence for this second point of view, I would like to recall to mind also that this point has already been expressed more than once. Even in 1905, Robert Scott proposed the consideration that the Antarctic ice had increased not during the time of cooling as, for example, in Europe, but rather in the periods of the warming of the climate, because the climate of Antarctica has remained extremely cold, but the amount of precipitation in the form of snow has increased. In 1912, the proposal of Robert Scott was supported by the leader of paleoclimatology, E. Brückner, and in 1963 by H. Flöhn. One could cite names of other experts who believed, and who believe today, that during the periods of cooling the glaciers of Antarctica retreated, while during the amelioration of the climate, the glaciers advanced.

I am in agreement with this second point of view, which I formulate in the following manner: the Pleistocene history of Antarctica was in a general way very extraordinary. The following facts support the second point of view.

TERTIARY GLACIATION AND PALEOMAGNETISM

Scientific studies carried out in the Antarctic by the expeditions of Robert Scott and O. Nordenskiold discovered, in sections of the Ross Sea and of the Antarctic Peninsula, some conglomerates of glacial sediments. It was then that the hypothesis about the Tertiary age of the

Antarctic glaciation was advanced. It is obviously only a hypothesis, but at the present time a second supporting factor has been added to this hypothesis. The studies of the paleomagnetism of rocks of different ages in Antarctica have produced the following discoveries: the magnetic and geographic poles of the southern hemisphere which, during Paleozoic and Mesozoic time were far from Antarctica, were already close to Antarctica in the Paleogene period.

Therefore, is it not necessary to believe that the former glaciation of Antarctica started well before that in Europe? But, on the other hand, the ice of Antarctica still exists today. Thus, the entire duration of the Antarctic glaciation is perhaps much greater than that of Europe and North America (with the exception of Greenland).

MARINE GLACIAL DEPOSITS

The existence of the ice sheet of Antarctica was continuous, while in Europe it was interrupted by long interglacial periods. Investigators of Victoria Land in Antarctica (Péwé 1960, Bull, McKelvey, and Webb 1962) have demonstrated that it is necessary to differentiate several stages of advance and retreat of the glaciers; but just stages, and not glacial and interglacial periods in the northern hemisphere sense. One speaks of changes of little importance in the position of the edge of the glacial ice, while the ice cap itself has existed continuously.

The stability of the ice sheet of Antarctica in the Pleistocene is in contrast to the instability of the ice sheets of Eurasia and North America. This conclusion is confirmed by studies in marine geology. Soviet marine geologists have arrived at the conclusion that ice-rafted glacial deposits accumulated continually around Antarctica during the entire Pleistocene Epoch (Licitsine 1960, Fig. 1). The stratigraphy of these deposits in the adjacent ocean, established according to a study of the diatoms (Jouse *et al.* 1963) is even more interesting. The diatoms were changing in time (in proportion to the deposit of sediments) as well as in space (on the meridian) (Fig. 1).

The most important changes were the following: Warm and cold phases succeeded each other several times, and it is for this reason that the position of the geographical limits changed (Fig. 2). In the warm phases the geographical limits were displaced towards the south, in the cold phases, towards the north. But, differently from the northern hemisphere, the position of the limits was changing here on the meridian, not in thousands, but only in hundreds or even tens of kilometres. At the same time, the fluctuations diminished as one approached the boundary of the Antarctic ice cap. Thus, the marine geological studies

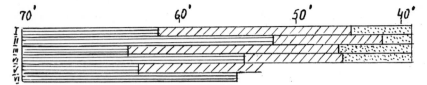

FIG. 1. Climatic zones and stratigraphy of marine Pleistocene deposits in Antarctica (Licitzin 1960). From left to right: (1) ice-rafted deposits, (2) diatomaceous deposits, (3) foraminiferal deposits. I-IV periods of the Pleistocene.

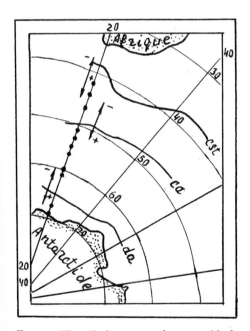

FIG. 2. The displacement of geographical limits during the last periods of the cooling (−) and the warming (+) of the climate (Jouse et al. 1963), current limit, Cst—subtropic convergence; ca—Antarctic convergence; da—Antarctic divergence. Black dots —stratigraphic columns.

have also led to the conclusions of the stability of natural conditions in the Pleistocene, not only for the Antarctic itself, but also for the ocean which surrounds it.

ICE BUDGET

The third group of facts sends us directly back to the idea of Robert Scott and E. Brückner. In reality, on what basis does one acknowledge the synchronous character of the glacial phases for the entire earth? What we know about Antarctica gives more reasons for a contrary conclusion about the non-synchronous character of the phases of glaciation in Antarctica, on one side, and in Europe and North America, on the other.

We know that in the last 10 years glaciers have shrunk over a great part of the world's surface. But not less than ten estimates of the current glacier regimen in Antarctica have given a positive balance sheet. The last estimate of ice balance was made in 1965 by V. I. Bardin and I. A. Souetova, according to the latest data (Table 1).

Logically this balance is probable. The warming of the climate caused a reinforcement of the atmospheric circulation. The Antarctic began to receive more atmospheric precipitation, but as snow. It is for that reason that the volume of the ice increased.

Thus, the history of the Pleistocene of the Antarctic is profoundly extraordinary. It is just this distinctness of the geological history of the Antarctic, which, in my opinion, has the most importance for geological and geographic science.

TABLE 1
BUDGET OF THE ANTARCTIC ICE SHEET
(BARDIN AND SOUETOVA 1965)

Surplus per year (in km³ of water)		Loss per year (in km³ of water)	
Solid atmospheric precipitation (snow, etc.)	2420	Flowing of ice into the ocean (formation of ice bergs)	1180
		Underwater melting of shelf ice	250
		Liquid flowing from the lowest part	20
+2420			−1450
Balance 970 km³ surplus ice per year			

REFERENCES CITED

BARDIN, V., and SOUETOVA, I., 1965, The perimeter and budget of the Antarctical glacial cover: The Antarctic, committee reports, Moscow, p. 67-75.

BRÜCKNER, E., 1912-13, Die Schneegrenze in der Antarktis: Zeitschr. für Gletscherkunde, v. Vii, h. 4, p. 276-279.

BULL, C., McKELVEY, B. C., and WEBB, P. N., 1962, Quaternary glaciations in southern Victoria Land, Antarctica: Jour. Glaciology, v. 4, p. 63-78.

FLÖHN, H., 1963, Zur meteorologischen Interpretation der pelistozanen Klimaschwankungen: Erdgeschichte und Gegenwart, bd. 14, p. 153-160.

JOUSE, A., KOROLEVA, G., and NAGAEVA, G., 1963, Stratigraphical and paleogeographical investigations in the Indian section of the South Ocean: Oceanological Researches, 8, Moscow, p. 137-161.

LISITZIN, A., 1960, Sedimentation in southern parts of the Indian and Pacific Oceans: Internat. Geol. Congr. XXI Session, Reports of Soviet Geologists. Probl. 10, Moscow, p. 86-102.

MEINARDUS, W., 1944, Zum Kanon der Erdbestrahlung: Geol. Rundschau, bd. 34, Klimaheft, h. 7-8, p. 748-762.

NORDENSKIELD, O., 1905, Geographische Untersuchungen aus dem westantarkrischen Gebiete: Bull. Geol. Inst. Uppsala, v. 6, p. 234-246.

PÉWÉ, T. L., 1960, Multiple glaciation in the McMurdo Sound region, Antarctica: A progress report: Jour. Geol., v. 68, p. 498-514.

SCOTT, R., 1905, Results of the national antarctic expedition I: Geographical Journal, v. 25, p. 353-372.

ISOSTATIC RECOVERY NEAR GLACIER-ICE MARGINS:

Some Evidence from Waterloo, Ontario, Canada

STUART A. HARRIS
University of Kansas
Lawrence, Kansas, U.S.A.

ABSTRACT. During the retreat of the Late Wisconsin ice sheets, there was a series of minor re-advances. One of these re-advances deposited the Parkhill till between Guelph and Waterloo and caused a series of local lakes to be formed during the retreat phase. A lobe of ice approached Waterloo from the east-northeast. The lakes were formed initially between the ice front and the Waterloo Sandhills, and as the ice melted lower cols were exposed which caused the formation of a series of overflow channels and erosional terraces at successively lower levels.

The highest lake terrace shows isobases trending at 108° east of true north with an inclination of 4.5 m per km (22 ft per mile) to the south. The direction of the isobases rapidly changed to 92° east of true north at an inclination of 1.4 m/km (8 ft per mile) as the ice melted, possibly because of inequalities in rate of retreat of the ice lobes. Decrease in tilt continued until the end of the retreat phase when Lake Whittlesey was formed south of Galt. The average tilt of the Lake Whittlesey shoreline was 0.8 m per km (4 ft per mile) to the south trending at 110° east of true north. Thereafter the isostatic changes appear to have followed the regional trends.

All these local changes must have taken place very rapidly. Their magnitude strongly suggests that, close to ice margins, the isostatic movements follow the Airy-Heiskanen theory. The effect of these movements is probably superimposed on the effect of the movements suggested in the Vening-Meinesz theory. These results fit in with the evidence of isostatic movements from other sources.

RÉSUMÉ. Pendant le retrait des nappes fini-wisconsiniennes, il se produisit une série de nouvelles avancées mineures. L'une de celles-ci a déposé la tillite de Parkhill entre les villes de Guelph et de Waterloo, Ontario, et a créé une série de petits lacs. Le lobe de glace s'aprochait de Waterloo par le est-nord-est. Les lacs se formèrent d'abord entre le front de glace et le lieu-dit Waterloo Sandhills: à mesure que la glace fondait, elle exposait des cols plus bas, ce qui forma une succession de lits de débordement et de terrasses d'érosion à des niveaux de plus en plus bas. La terrasse lacustre la plus élevée présente des isobases dirigées à 108° à l'est du nord vrai, avec une inclinaison vers le sud de 4,5 m/km (22 pieds au mille). Avec la fonte de la glace, la direction des isobases s'est rapidement orientée à 92° à l'est du nord vrai, avec une inclinaison de 1,4 m/km (8 pieds au mille), peut-être à cause d'inégalités dans le rythme de retrait des deux lobes glaciaires. L'inclinaison continue à diminuer jusqu'à la fin de la phase de retrait, moment où le lac Whittlesey se forma au sud de Galt. La rive de ce lac présentait une inclinaison moyenne vers le sud de 0,8 m par km (4 pieds au mille) et une direction de 110° à l'est du nord vrai. Par la suite, les changements isostatiques semblent avoir suivi les tendances régionales.

Tous ces changements locaux ont dû se produire très rapidement. Leur ampleur suggère nettement qu'au voisinage des limites de la glace, les mouvements isostatiques se conforment à la théorie de Airy-Heiskanen. L'effet de ces mouvements se superpose probablement à l'effet des mouvements suggérés par la théorie de Vening-Meinesz. Ces résultats concordent avec les indices fournis par les mouvements isostatiques d'autres régions.

CONTENTS

FIGURE

TABLE

INTRODUCTION

There are two currently accepted theories as to how isostacy works. One is the Airy-Heiskanen theory which assumes that the adjustments will be located in those areas where the change in loading actually takes place. The other is the Vening-Meinesz theory which assumes that the effect would be spread around the zone of change in load and would not reflect local variations alone.

Isostatic recovery in relation to retreat of ice sheets from glaciated areas has received extensive treatment in the literature. The evidence used is that which can be obtained from well-developed lake or marine terraces occurring over wide areas. In order to prove that isostatic recovery takes place, this evidence is ideal. However, it merely establishes the fact that widespread changes take place slowly and evenly over a fairly long period of time, that is, it proves the operation of the Vening-Meinesz theory.

To the knowledge of the writer, no studies have been carried out to see whether the Airy-Heiskanen theory works in glaciated areas. The following paper describes a test made in the area around Waterloo, Ontario, Canada. The results appear to indicate that the Airy-Heiskanen theory does in fact apply in certain glaciated areas. Where it does, the theory greatly complicates interpretations of directions of drainage, and the validity of the theory must be determined if the history of such an area is to be worked out.

ENVIRONMENTAL CONDITIONS

Southern Ontario consists of a tongue-shaped promontory surrounded on three sides by Lakes Huron (north and west), Erie (south), and Ontario (southeast). It is made up of a dissected fragment of the Niagara Escarpment which has been partially buried beneath glacial drift. Rock outcrops only occur along the escarpment and certain lake shores, while the drift is more than 100 m (330 ft) thick along Lake Erie.

The escarpment runs in a general north-northeast–south-southeast direction across the area, and the highest land is located just behind it. From there occurs a gentle slope towards the southwest. During the Pleistocene, it formed a distinct barrier to ice flow and consequently the peninsula of Ontario lay in an interlobate position in relation to the Late Wisconsin ice sheets (see, for example, Chapman and Putnam 1951, p. 26). At least two lobes of ice were involved, one from Lake Ontario and at least one from Lake Huron. The glacial advances in the two lobes were not coincident.

The Late Wisconsin glacial maximum was marked by the arrival of the ice that deposited the Catfish Creek till in southern Ohio, some 18,000 to 19,000 years BP (Forsyth 1961). In the next 5,000 years the ice retreated in a sporadic fashion and finally left the Waterloo area. The retreat consisted of alternating major retreats and minor re-advances, so that around Waterloo there are three tills on top of the Catfish Creek till in the case of the Ontario lobe. These are the Bamberg till, the Port Stanley till, and the Parkhill till, in order of decreasing age (Harris 1967). The tills of the Huron lobe have yet to be mapped and described. The moraines have usually been interpreted as "push" moraines, except for the so-called "kame-moraines" mapped by Chapman and Putnam (1951), although Karrow (1963, p. 43) notes evidence of ablation deposits indicating stagnation during the melting of the last ice sheet.

Associated with the retreat of the ice are various glacial lakes, both large and small. The classical sequence of major lakes and their relationship to the ice front has been discussed by Hough (1958). The first of these lakes was Lake Whittlesey. Then came a minor ice advance near Hamilton which deposited the Halton till and it was followed by a series of lower lakes of which Lakes Warren and Iroquois are the best known. These were the consequence of the ice retreating and exposing successively lower exits from the Great Lakes basin.

These lakes left well-developed lake shores and associated features which show evidence of tilting or warping. The contours of the warping (isobases) lie roughly parallel to the ice front with the zone of maximum uplift lying in the direction of origin of the ice. The amount of tilting decreases with decreasing age. This represents the main published evidence for isostatic recovery in the area after the melting of the ice sheets. Most authors accept the isostatic origin, although Moore (1948) regarded the warping as largely tectonic, dating from earlier tectonic periods (Hough 1958, p. 137). If it is tectonic, it is tilting rather than localized folding. The underlying rock shows little sign of localized folding, judging by the published borehole data and the evidence from the few exposures available.

LOCAL LAKES

According to Chapman and Putnam (1951), Waterloo and Erbsville lie on the boundary between the area marked as kame-moraine and a large area mapped as a single glacial spillway, several kilometres wide (Fig. 1). The kame-moraine is also known as the Waterloo Sandhills and lies to the west of the line. It consists of hummocky hills rising to more than 400 m (1,300 ft) above sea level, composed mainly of sand and gravel in the general form of a moraine. The spillway area consists of undulating, lower lying land around the Grand River valley. The latter lies at about 320 m (1,000 ft) just north of Waterloo and is the main base level of the surrounding area. Evidence from river profiles indicates that there has been only a limited amount of subsequent stream erosion. Measurements by Packer (1964) suggest that slopes

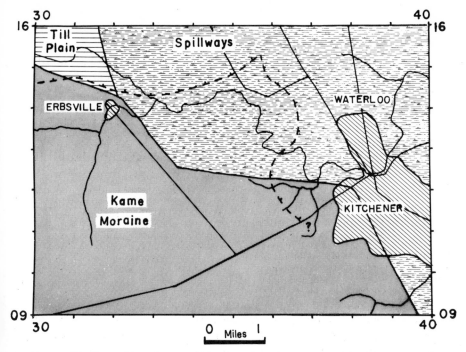

FIG. 1. Physiographic units near Waterloo, Ontario, as mapped by Chapman and Putnam (1951). Also included is the inferred ice front of the Wentworth ice at the time of Lake Erbsville. Note the lowland area lying between the ice margins and the hills of the kame-moraine to the south and west. The grid on this and the other maps is the One Thousand Metre, Universal Mercator Grid, Zone 17. North lies to the top of the maps in all cases.

less than $21°$ are stable under the climatic conditions prevailing since the time of Lake Nipissing.

Two years ago, the writer noticed some erosional terraces in the spillway area between Waterloo and Erbsville. The extent of all flat surfaces found was mapped, and their heights were determined using an aneroid barometer. It soon became clear that the paired surfaces had the form of tilted lake terraces cut into the sides and truncating the tops of the low hills in the area. The consistent slopes ruled out deposition by river action as did the topographic position. Also, they were quite different from subglacial phenomena; two major overflow channels were found. Interpreting these findings as evidence for old lakes, the following sequence of events can be traced.

During the maximum extension of the Parkhill lobe, the ice reached a point just west of Waterloo, while a lobe of ice came east-north-eastwards almost as far as Erbsville (Fig. 2). Meltwater was impounded between the Sandhills and the ice, and this formed a temporary lake (Lake Erbsville, stage 1). Meltwater from the north ice lobe travelled eastwards via a spillway complex to the lake. The lake water cut a good set of terraces across the hills on its shores. Its overflow point has not been located; it probably lay over the ice margin or even through the ice to the south. The ice margin has been drawn where the terracing ceases or where the meltwater channels originate in a series of hummocky hills. One remarkable characteristic is the slope of the shoreline. The effect of the interlobate position is obvious since the isobases trend at $108°$ and have an inclination of 4.5 m/km (22 ft) per mile to the south.

This stage (II) was followed by several more lakes as the ice began to retreat, and new, lower overflow points became uncovered. A second terrace occurs below the first in the same general area. The evidence in the form of terrace remnants is not quite as good as that for Lake Erbsville. It extends appreciably further north so that the north lobe must have retreated by this time. The eastern ice lobe remained almost stationary, and the overflow point may once again have been over or through the glacier. Since it includes the headwaters of the Laurel Creek, it is called the Laurel Lake stage. Stage III was the formation of Lake Westmount. The Ontario ice lobe had retreated so as to open the Maple Hill overflow channel through the area of Westmount Golf Course. This consists of a deep U-shaped valley carved through part of the Waterloo Sandhills near the western boundary of Waterloo and Kitchener. The terrace remnants northwest of Waterloo are shown in Figure 3. It will be seen that both the direction and angle of slope of the terrace had decreased greatly since the Lake Erbsville stage. Mean-

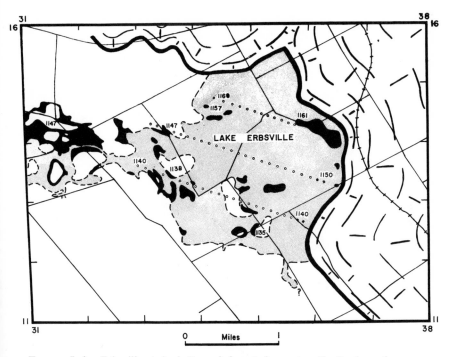

FIG. 2. Lake Erbsville (stippled) as inferred from the distribution of terraces (black) and higher land today (white). The figures refer to height of the terraces above mean sea level in feet. Lines of circles are isobases at a 10 foot (3 m) interval.

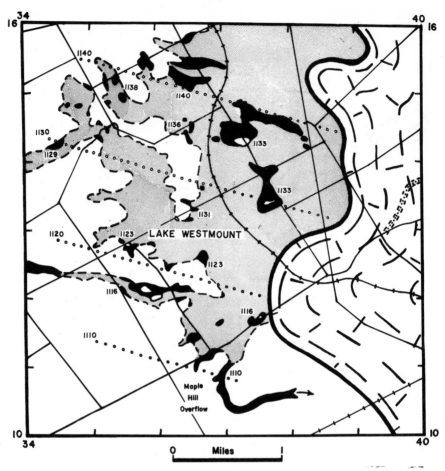

FIG. 3. Position of Lake Westmount northwest of Waterloo. Symbols as in Figure 2

while the ice was decaying, *in situ*, and a subglacial esker was being formed. The latter lay partially beneath the next lake.

Stage IV is represented by a still lower lake (Lake Waterloo), which left extensive terraces across the city of Waterloo (Fig. 4). It has a noticeably lower tilt than Lake Westmount, but appears also to have used the Maple Hill overflow. This suggests that the ice first retreated, draining Lake Westmount and permitting some isostatic recovery. Then the ice must have readvanced, causing Lake Waterloo to come into being. The next lower lake overflow is very large and may owe part of its size to this period of erosion (Fig. 4).

The last two stages are represented by two lakes: Lake Kitchener and Lake Bridgeport. Lake Kitchener was a small lake lying in the valley of the Laurel Creek and overflowing via the main overflow channel to the south. In the middle of the floor of the entrance to this valley is the Carling Brewery, hence the name Carling Overflow Channel. The lake had a small north-south extent because of the shape of the depression occupied by the Laurel Creek, and it is of little use in determining the degree of subsequent tilting. When the ice left the eastern outskirts of Kitchener, a new overflow channel permitted the draining of Lake Kitchener and the formation of a small lake in the valley of the Grand River. This lake remained there for an appreciable period and caused the highest of the flight of terraces above the town of Bridgeport to be eroded. This terrace was more than 1 or 2 km wide and the lake was probably in existence for a considerable period of time until the present Grand River came into being. Its slope appears to be much more gentle than any other lake terrace in the area.

Care must be taken in interpreting the results of these last two terraces since they could be the result of pockets of local ice and morainic debris which remained after the main ice sheet had melted. They are, therefore, best left out of the ensuing discussion.

DISCUSSION AND CONCLUSIONS

Part of the spillway area mapped by Chapman and Putnam is really a complex of local lake terraces cut into the glacial deposits (Fig. 5). The basic data concerning these terraces is summarized in Table 1. It is clear that great depression of the crust occurred when the ice was in the vicinity of Waterloo. The bulk of this depression was quickly compensated for by uplift as soon as the ice melted. Differences in rates of melting of the two ice lobes caused changes in direction of the isobases because of differential uplift. The movements appear to be of an order of magnitude which is too great for a tectonic origin since

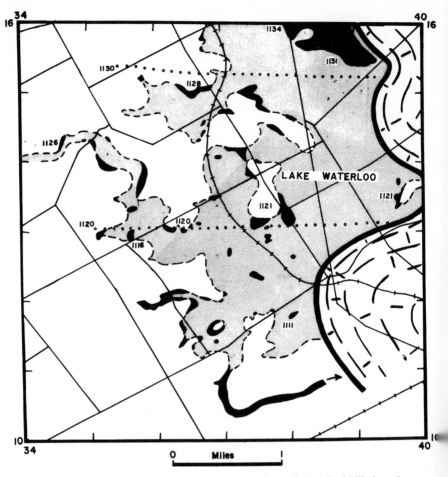

F<small>IG</small>. 4. The Lake Waterloo stage in the melting of the Parkhill ice sheet. Symbols as in Figure 2.

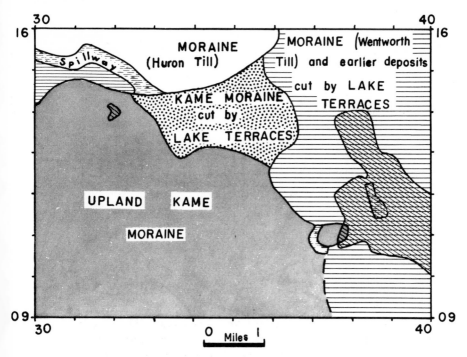

FIG. 5. Physiographic units northwest of Waterloo, based on a differentiation between pre-Wentworth ice advance landscapes and the various post-Wentworth ice advance landscapes. (In the text Wentworth glaciation is now termed Parkhill glaciation; Huron till is now pre-Parkhill till.)

TABLE I
SLOPES AND OUTLETS OF THE SHORELINES OF LOCAL LAKE
TERRACES AROUND WATERLOO COMPARED WITH THE SLOPES
FOR THE MAJOR LAKE TERRACES IN THE GREAT LAKES BASIN

Lake	Height of Outlet Today		Slope of Terrace		Direction of Isobases	Reference
	ft	metres	feet per mile	m/km		
Erbsville	c.1136	345	22	4.5	108°	*Supra*
Laurel	c.1120	340	17	3.2	105°	*Ibid.*
Westmount	1110	333	12	2.3	105°	*Ibid.*
Waterloo	1110	333	8	1.4	92°	*Ibid.*
Kitchener	1078	327				*Ibid.*
Bridgeport	c.1040	315	0	0		*Ibid.*
Whittlesey			4	0.8	110°	Karrow 1963
Warren			2½	0.47	110°	*Ibid.*
Iroquois			2	0.38	110°	Coleman 1937
Algonquin			1	0.19	111°	Goldthwaite 1910

there is no evidence for such folding movements in the underlying rock. According to Karrow (1963, p. 54-55), the entire retreat of the Late Wisconsin ice from the area took 5,000 years. Thus the length of time represented by the Parkhill ice advance and retreat is not likely to be more than 1,000 years. It was followed by the formation of Lake Whittlesey, a lake formed about 13,000 BP. Thus, the time span represented by these local crustal movements is very short. It would be a great coincidence if crustal movements of short duration just happened to occur at this locality when the Parkhill ice sheet was melting.

Also included in Table 1 are the slopes of the terraces for Lake Whittlesey and the later major lakes according to various authorities. The much smaller order movements which have taken place during the whole of the last 13,000 years are readily apparent. It would therefore seem that the bulk of the isostatic movement in the Waterloo area consisted of local rapid crustal movements during the actual local ice retreat, and thus obeyed the concepts of the Airy-Heiskanen theory of isostacy. Only rather slow, small residual adjustments are to be seen in the later broad warping.

This study also raises one other point. A slope of 3.8 m per km (20 ft per mile) is appreciably greater than the gradient of many streams and river valleys in lowland areas. The fact that warping of this order of magnitude may occur along ice margins means that considerable care must be taken in interpreting directions of flow of meltwater as the ice retreated. Present-day slopes in formerly glaciated areas must be treated with caution, and it should be remembered that there is much more rapid warping when the ice front is still close at hand than shortly after the ice has retreated.

ACKNOWLEDGEMENTS. The work was carried out with the aid of a travel grant from the Ontario Research Foundation, which is gratefully acknowledged.

REFERENCES CITED

CHAPMAN, L. J., and PUTNAM, D. F., 1951, The physiography of southern Ontario: University of Toronto Press, 284 p.

COLEMAN, A. P., 1937, Lake Iroquois: Ontario Dept. of Mines, v. 45, p. 1-36.

FORSYTH, J. L., 1961, Dating Ohio's glaciers: Ohio Geol. Survey Information Circular no. 31.

GOLDTHWAITE, J. W., 1910, An instrument survey of the shorelines of the extinct lakes Algonquin and Nipissing in southwestern Ontario: Geol. Surv. Canada, Memoir 10.

HARRIS, S. A., 1964, Origin of part of the Guelph drumlin field and the Galt and Paris Moraines, Ontario: a reinterpretation: Can. Geog., v. 11, p. 16-34.

HOUGH, J. L., 1958, Geology of the Great Lakes: Urbana, Univ. Illinois Press, 313 p.

KARROW, P. F., 1963, Pleistocene geology of the Hamilton-Galt area: Ontario Dept. of Mines Geological Rept. no. 16, 68 p.

MOORE, S., 1948, Crustal movement in the Great Lakes area: Geol. Soc. America Bull., v. 59, p. 697-710.

PACKER, R. W., 1964, Stability slopes in an area of glacial deposition: Can. Geog., v. 8, p. 147-151.

QUATERNARY PERIGLACIAL WIND-WORN SAND GRAINS IN USSR

ANDRÉ CAILLEUX
Geological Institute, University of Paris
Paris, France

ABSTRACT. Beyond the maximum extent of the Würm-Valdai-Wisconsin glaciation, in a belt 500 to 1,000 km wide, there occur many round-dull, wind-shaped grains of quartz which show that during cold Quaternary phases there existed great areas with no vegetation—periglacial deserts. This periglacial northern European belt, formerly known only from Great Britain and France to Poland, is now known to extend farther east, to Moscow and Gorki, and from there to the north to Timan Mountains near the Barents Sea (67°N).

In the heart of northern European glaciated area (Kola Peninsula, Finland, central and northern parts of Sweden), these grains are not found because when the glacier retreated from these countries, the climate quickly ameliorated, the forest and other vegetation took over rapidly, and there was scarcely opportunity for the wind to form round-dull grains.

Strong periglacial wind action also occurred, as far as we can judge from the frequence and beauty of the grains, in Siberia: for instance, in the middle course of the Rivers Ob (about 62°N), Lena (64 to 71°N), and Nertcha, in Transbaikalia (53°N), a more mountainous country where the wind-wearing was, according to the rule, a little less strong. Today, all of these Siberian areas are in the forest zone, but during some Quaternary phases they must have been at least in part desertic and exposed to strong wind action.

In the Soviet sands, as elsewhere, one may find with variable proportions according to the countries other types of grains: unworn, or blunt-shiny (water-worn), or with traces of quartzose, or ferruginous cement rehandled from older sandstones.

RÉSUMÉ. Le long du front glaciaire d'âge Wurm-Valdai-Wisconsin, à son extérieur, sur une largeur de l'ordre de 500 à 1 000 kilomètres, la présence de très nombreux grains de sable quartzeux ronds et mats, façonnés par le vent, indique l'existence, lors des phases froides du Quaternaire, de vastes espaces largement dépourvus de végétation, de déserts périglaciaires. Précédemment connue depuis la Grande-Bretagne et la France jusqu'à la Pologne, cette bordure périglaciaire nord-européenne s'étend bien plus à l'est, jusqu'à Moscou et Gorki, et de là vers le nord, jusqu'aux Monts Timan, au bord de la Mer de Barents (67°N). Dans le cœur de la glaciation nord-européenne (presqu'île de Kola, Finlande, Suède centrale et du nord), on ne trouve pas ces grains, parce que, quand le glacier a quitté ces régions, le climat était fortement réchauffé, la forêt ou d'autre végétation dense prenait pied très vite et ne laissait pas au vent le temps de façonner des grains ronds-mats.

Des actions éoliennes périglaciaires aussi fortes, à en juger par la fréquence de ces grains et leur beauté, se sont exercées aussi en Sibérie, entre autres sur le cours moyen de l'Ob (vers 62°N), de la Léna (64 à 71°N) et enfin de la Nertcha, en Transbaikalie (53°N), région plus montagneuse où elles ont été, suivant l'usage, un peu moins intenses. Aujourd'hui situées dans la zone de la forêt, toutes ces régions de la Sibérie ont été, lors des phases froides du Quaternaire, au moins en partie désertiques et exposées à de fortes actions du vent.

On peut rencontrer aussi dans les sables soviétiques comme ailleurs, en proportions très variables suivant les régions, d'autres types de grains: non-usés, ou émoussés-luisants (usés par l'eau), ou enfin à traces de ciment ferrugineux ou quartzeux (remaniés de grès plus anciens).

ZUSAMMENFASSUNG. Den Glazialrand der Würm-Valdai-Wisconsin, entlang, nach aussen, auf einer Breite von ca 500 to 1,000 km, weist das Auftreten zahlreicher runder und matter windbearbeiteter Quarzkörner auf das Vorhandensein während der kalten Phasen des Quartärs von weitgedehnten, vegetationlosen Bodenflächen, d.h. periglazialen Wüsten. Schon früher von England und Frankreich bis nach Poland gekannt, steeckt sich dieser nord-europäische periglazial Gürtel viel weiter nach Osten aus, bis Moskau und Gorki, und von dort aus nach dem Norden, bis an den Timangebirge am Barentssee (67°N). Im Innersten der nordeuropäischen Vereisung (Kola Halbinsel, Finnland, Zentral- und Nordschweden) findet man solche Körner nicht, denn das Klima war viel wärmer geworden als der Gletscher das Gebiet verliess; Wald und andere dichte Vegetation richtete sich schnell ein und gab dem Wind keine Zeit um rund-matte Körner zu bearbeiten.

Betrachtet man die Häufigkeit solcher Körner und deren Schönheit, so übten sich periglaziale Windwirkungen mit ähnlicher Stärke auch in Siberien, besonders auf dem Mittellauf der Flüsse Ob (62°N), Lena (64 bis 71°N) und auch Nertcha in Transbaïkalien (53°N) welche eine mehr bergige Gegend ist wo solche Wirkungen wie gewöhnlich etwas milder auftreten. Alle diese Gebiete in Siberien die heutzutage in der Waldzone liegen waren während der kalten Phasen des Quartärs, wenigstens zum Teil, öde und an starken Windwirkungen ausgesetzt.

Man kann auch in den Sanden der Soviet Union wie in anderen andere Korntypen treffen, in sehr verschiedenen Verhältnisse je nach der Gegend: unbearbeitete, abgerundet-glänzende vom Wasserabgetragene Körner und auch Körner mit Spuren von Eisen-oder Quarzhaltigenzement (umgearbeitet aus früheren Sandsteinen).

РЕЗЮМЕ. Вдоль внешнего края валдаиского ледника (Wurm-Valda-Wisconsin), в зоне шириной в 500-1000 клм., наличие в песках многочисленных кварцевых матовых круглых зерен, обработанных ветром, указывает на существование обмирных пространств, лишенных растительного покрова-перигляциальных пустынь-во время холодных фаз четвертичного периода. Уже известная от Великобритании и Франции до Польши, эта перигляциальная север но-европейская межа простирается и далее к востоку, до Москвы и Горького, и оттуда к северу, до Тиманьских гор у Баренцева моря (67 сев. шир.). В центре северно-европейского оледенения (Кольский полуостров, Финляндия, центральная и северная Швеция), таковые зёрна не обнаружены, потому что, после исчезновения ледника, при значительном отеплении климата, лес или другая густая растительность очень быстро пускали корни и мешали действию ветра на песок.

Судя по частоте и совершенству форм этих зёрен, перигляциальные действия ветров такой же силы также имели место в Сибири, например в среднем течении Оби (около 62 сев. шир.), Лены (64-71 сев. шир.) и Нерчи, в Забайкальи (53 сев. шир.); в этой горной области, обработка наблюдается в меньшей мере. Хотя они теперь расположены в лесной полосе, все эти районы Сибири были, во время холодных фаз четвертичного периода, пустынями, по меньшей мере частично, и подлежали действию сильных ветров.

В песках Советского Союза как и в других странах встречаются также другие типы зерен: необработанные, окатанные-блестящие (обработанные водой), и со следами железистого или кварцевого цемента (переработанные из более древних песчанников).

CONTENTS

INTRODUCTION

It is well known that, during the cold phases of the Quaternary, the countries lying outside the glaciers in Europe, from England and France to Poland, were subject to very strong wind action; wind-worn sand grains, ventifacts, and true loesses testify to that. The question naturally arises: did this so-called periglacial belt extend further eastward, to Russia and even to Siberia? With the kind help of many Soviet colleagues, I was able to collect some samples in the field and I received from them additional samples. By the study of the shape and aspect of the sand grains, I showed in 1956 that the periglacial wind action extended eastward to the Moscow region, and in 1965 northward to the Timan Mountains, and eastward to the Ob Basin in west Siberia. In this paper I shall report on additional samples. But to be more complete and give a more accurate picture of the present territories of the Soviet Union, I shall treat, together with the new ones, all previous samples mentioned in the quoted papers, and a few others, collected before 1940 in Estonia, Latvia, Lithuania, and the region between Lida and Zdolbunov, which was at that time part of the Polish state. Regions known today to have Quaternary periglacial wind-worn sand grains are shown in Figure 1.

Since this method has not been employed much until now in North America, I shall first give a short account of it.

METHOD AND CRITERIA USED

The sample must weigh 2 to 20 gr. It must be washed, rubbed very strongly in water. The dirty water is decanted, and the sand washed again with clean water until the water stays clear. Brittle grains (mica, etc.) and friable ones (limonite, chalk, etc.) are partly broken or destroyed by rubbing, but neither the quartz nor the feldspars are changed.

If the sample contains limestone, it is washed with cold dilute HCl. If the grains are coated by an iron oxide film or cement, they are treated for 2 minutes with boiling HCl so that their surface becomes whiter and easier to observe. Finally, the sand is rinsed in water several times and left to dry.

Quartz grains 0.2 to 1.5 mm long are studied. For study of wind-wearing, the most interesting are those about 0.7 mm, and the statistics (Tables 1, 2, and 3) are given for that size. The best conditions for observations follow: The grains are observed dry, without Canada balsam, under the binocular microscope, on a black background, by reflection, with a punctual light source, without frosted glass. The beam of light must slope at about 45°. Enlargement is ×40 to ×50 for the 0.7 mm grains, ×80 to ×120 for the smaller ones. Every grain is observed accurately, and the effects of light on it and in it are distinguished thoroughly.

About 4,000 samples—from Precambrian to Recent, collected in all parts of the world, and representing every kind of formation—were observed. Among the quartz grains, four main types (there are transitions between them) and a few other scarcer minor types may be

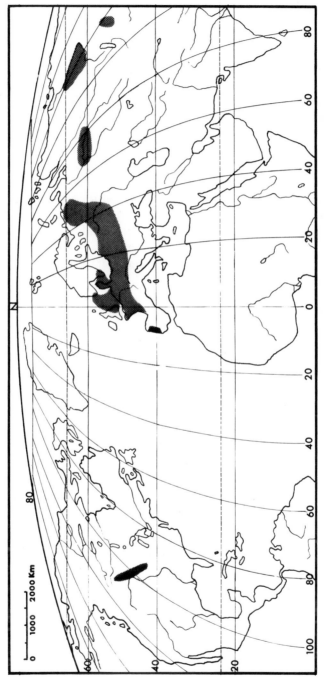

FIG. 1. Shaded areas are regions known to have Quaternary periglacial wind-worn sand grains.

distinguished:

(1) UNWORN GRAINS (NU). Generally, their contour is angular, their edges sharp, their faces either dull or shiny. Such grains are the sign of weak or no mechanical wearing. They are found *in situ* in weathering products, in newly borne sands from mountains, glaciers, small rivers, small beaches or small dunes; they occur when neither water nor wind had time enough to wear distinctly the grains.

(2) BLUNT-SHINY GRAINS (EL) (water-worn). Contour, apices and edges are blunt, their surface is shiny and mostly convex. It is easy to distinguish these grains from shiny unworn ones: the image of the light source can be seen as a shiny point or line beneath the higher part (or parts) of the grains (apices and edges), while on the shiny unworn grains, it is the faces that are shining, and the edges, being too sharp, do not reflect the light. The blunt-shiny grains result from a very long wearing, at least partly mechanical, by rubbing against one another in water. In rivers, only after a 300 km long travel, a few grains 0.7 mm long obtain that aspect, but they keep their general angular shape, and the edges are only slightly smoothed. The case is the same on small or half-closed beaches. On big open beaches, either marine or of very great lakes, the wearing is stronger because of the cumulated effect of the waves, and the grains are much more smoothed and subrounded, though they remain elongated if they were so before.

Experimentally, blunt-shiny grains have been obtained by wearing in water, on limestone particles by Crommelin and Cailleux (1939), and on quartz by Schneider (1964).

(3) ROUND-DULL GRAINS (RM) (wind-worn). On an average, they are more rounded and less elongated than the blunt-shiny ones, and their surface is pitted with microscopic crateriform or nail-stroked shock marks.

They result from a very long wearing by the wind, the grains being knocked against one another. The shocks are much stronger in the air than in the water, for three reasons: (*a*) lesser apparent density (1.65 instead of 2.65); (*b*) greater flow speed; and (*c*) lesser viscosity of the interposed fluid. Round-dull grains predominate in the recent great deserts, for instance, in Mauritania and Libya.

Experimentally, Schneider obtained them, starting from unworn, broken quartz particles, by rotation in a cylinder in dry conditions (without water).

(4) GRAINS WITH TRACES OF QUARTZOSE OR FERRUGINOUS CEMENT. The ferruginous cement is brown or reddish and easy to recognize. In most instances, the quartzose cement is as crystallographically orientated as the quartz grain which it is coating, and it is bound by small planar

facets, parallel to one another. Such grains are easy to differentiate from blunt-shiny ones: if one changes the orientation of the beam of incident light, for a given orientation, all the parallel facets of one shine together at the same time, then a very small change in orientation makes all the facets become extinct. The same result may be obtained with the binocular microscope by closing first one eye, and then the other. In the same conditions, on the face of a blunt-shiny or unworn grain, one sees that the image only changes its place.

The grains with traces of cement may have been primarily wind-worn, water-worn, or unworn. These can be recognized from the less cemented ones. Afterwards, they have been incorporated within a sandstone. Finally, they are rehandled in a younger sediment. It is important to recognize them to avoid misinterpretation and confusion with younger, for example, Quaternary, worn grains. In Tables 1, 2, and 3, such older wind-worn grains (*RS*) have been counted separately from the newer wind-worn ones (*RM*).

HISTORICAL DISCUSSION AND JUSTIFICATION OF THE METHOD

Some of the criteria cited above were described as early as 1880 by the great English geologist, Sorby. The true interpretation of the round-dull grains as wind-worn was established by Cayeux in 1929. The fundamental distinction between the blunt-shiny (water-worn) and round-dull grains was made independently, first by Riess and Conant in 1931, then by the author in 1936. It is a fact and a great pity that the excellent paper by Riess and Conant was overlooked, even in their own country (USA), possibly because it was published in a strictly specialized periodical (*Transactions of American Foundrymen's Association*).

Recently, Kuenen (1961) and his collaborators have opened an interesting discussion. Failing to obtain round-dull grains by experimental wind action, they suggested that such grains might result from dissolution by dew.

We have seen above that Schneider was happier with his own experiments, inasmuch as he obtained round-dull grains. The alleged role of the dew is at most very small, since beautiful round-dull grains were found by Michel (1964) and Cailleux (1962) in the wind-driven sands of the dry valleys of McMurdo Sound (Antarctica), where no dew exists, all atmospheric water condensating there as solid ice.

Nevertheless, Kuenen is correct, and the author agreed in advance with him (Cailleux 1942) when he stresses that some other dulling aspects are not caused by the wind. But they can be distinguished:

(1) By strong and quick dissolution with NaOH, the quartz grains become dull but porous, their surface looking like flour. On natural grains, a silky aspect, resulting from a very shallow and small-sized pitting, seems to be the result of a gentle dissolution by natural water. But both aspects lack the crateriform and nail-stroked shock-marks characteristic of the mechanical wind-wearing. Another difference is that the chemical action usually affects the grains of all sizes, even the smallest ones. Instead, the wind-wearing predominates for the 0.7 mm long ones and is much weaker on the much smaller ones (0.2 mm). Lastly, the chemical action can be seen equally well on unworn angular grains, while wind action tends to round the grains.

(2) With too great enlargements, one can see on quartz, as on any surface, irisated figures in the shape of circles, horseshoes, or points. They are only an optical effect resulting from the fact that their size (about 1 micron) is near the wave-length of the light. This is the reason why one must avoid enlargements greater than × 150.

Surely the observation with the electron microscope which is going on in the United States will give more new information about the surface of the quartz grains. It may allow a distinction between figures of chemical corrosion and hollows resulting from defects of crystallization.

The story of many natural sand grains has been a very long one and includes many reworkings. The observation with the binocular microscope helps to reconstruct this history.

PRE-QUATERNARY SANDSTONES AND SANDS FROM USSR: A SOURCE OF GRAINS FOR THE QUATERNARY DEPOSITS

Since grains of pre-Quaternary age may be incorporated into Quaternary deposits it is absolutely necessary to first examine the pre-Quaternary grains. Especially, old wind-worn grains (RS and RM) must be looked at closely if one wants to distinguish them, in the Quaternary deposits, from the grains resulting from Quaternary periglacial wind action.

Table 1 shows the results. Most values less than 4 per cent are not very significant, and sometimes the corresponding true percentage may be near zero. The round-dull grains with (RS) or without (RM) cement are counted separately, but it is their sum that is characteristic of wind-wearing.

Strong wind action is registered from Cambrian to Permian in the west of the Russian platform. This is frequent, at the same time, in many other areas, such as western Europe, the Sahara, and the conterminous

TABLE 1

PERCENTAGES OF THE DIFFERENT KINDS OF QUARTZ GRAINS 0.7 MM LONG IN PRE-QUATERNARY DEPOSITS OF USSR

	N^1	NU	EL	RM	RS
25 Shilka River, Transbaikalia, Siberia, fluvial Tertiary	1	99	1	0	0
24 Nercha River, Transbaikalia, Siberia, fluvial Tertiary	1	30	70	0	0
23 Azov Sea, east coast, boundary Tertiary-Quaternary	1	22	68	10	0
22 Stantsia morskaya, north of Azov Sea, fluvial Upper Pliocene	1	5	90	5	0
21 Lida, White Russian SSR, fresh-water Miocene	7	28	70	1	1
20 Ukrainian SSR, brackish Miocene, Sarmatian	4	15	37	45	3
19 Poltava, Ukrainian SSR, continental Oligocene	1	44	52	4	0
18 Gaur, Transbaikalia, Siberia, continental Cretaceous-Tertiary	1	99	0	1	0
17 Fergana, Uzbek SSR, lacustrine Trigonoïdes Upper Cretaceous	1	98	1	1	0
16 Near Zhigansk, Lena River basin, Siberia, continental Cretaceous	2	87	10	3	0
15 Zdolbunov, Ukrainian SSR, Cretaceous	1	78	2	0	20
14 Nievirkov, Ukrainian SSR, Lower or Middle Cretaceous	1	18	66	16	0
13 Moscow, marine Aptian	3	13	76	9	2
12 Moscow, marine Upper Neocomian	2	25	66	9	0
11 Near Zhigansk, Lena River basin, Siberia marine Upper Jurassic	1	95	3	1	1
10 Near Moscow, marine Upper Jurassic, Tithonic	2	6	92	2	0
9 Mijatchkova, near Moscow, Middle Jurassic, Continental, Karstic	1	90	7	3	0
8 Nikrace, Latvian SSR, Middle Jurassic, Dogger	1	14	78	0	8
7 Nievirkov and Zdolbunov, Ukrainian SSR, terrestrian Permian	5	48	4	26	22
6 Lenas, Latvian SSR, Upper Old red sandstone, Devonian, with fishes	1	30	16	6	48
5 Sigulda, Rauna, etc., Latvian SSR, Old red sandstone, Devonian	4	43	2	0	55
4 Tartu, Estonian SSR, terrestrian Devonian	2	50	0	0	50
3 Tallinn, Estonian SSR, marine Ordovician	4	15	2	40	43
2 Tosna and Luga rivers, W of Leningrad, Obolus Sand, marine Lower Ordovician	2	8	19	41	30
1 40-50 km south of Leningrad, marine Middle Cambrian	4	8	14	46	32

[1]N = number of samples; NU = unworn; EL = blunt-shiny (water-worn); RM and RS = round-dull (wind-worn); RS are with traces of cement; RM without.

United States. In Poland and western Europe the wind-worn grains are also numerous in the Triassic sandstones. Another but lesser wind action may be noted in the Ukrainian Sarmatian (Miocene) formation.

Strong water-wearing, of the marine type (i.e., with shiny sub-rounded grains), is common in the Jurassic marine sands of Latvia and the Moscow region, in the Cretaceous marine sands of Ukraine and the Moscow region, and in the Tertiary (marine, freshwater, or brackish deposits) of White Russia, Ukraine, and the Southern border of Russia. This is also the case in many other basins in the world at the same time.

In Siberia, the Tertiary fluvial deposits of the Nercha River basin contain a high percentage (70 per cent) of extremely typical subangular blunt-shiny grains, the edges of which are only very slightly, but nevertheless distinctly, smoothed.

Prevailing unworn grains are to be observed in the Jurassic, Cretaceous, or Tertiary of many regions: Shilka River basin and Gaus in Transbaikalia, Zhigansk region near the Verkhoiansk Mountains in Siberia, Fergana, and in one Jurassic karst fill near Moscow. Summing up, we see that some old wind-worn grains are known specially in Paleozoic and Triassic sandstones, and more rarely in younger formations. We shall pay attention to their possible rehandling when studying the Quaternary deposits.

QUATERNARY DEPOSITS OF THE EUROPEAN PART OF USSR

In the USSR, as everywhere, the differences between the glacial, fluvioglacial, fluvial, or lacustrine sands of one given region, so far as the shape of the elements of sand-grain size is concerned, are sometimes small enough to be neglected in a first approximation study. In such cases (Tables 2 and 3), we have treated those deposits altogether. In our tables, most of the sand grains are Pleistocene, a few are Recent, and some have been rehandled from pre-Pleistocene deposits without having been given a different aspect.

Let us begin with the periglacial belt outside the Wisconsin-Würm-Valdai glacial front. The percentage of round-dull, wind-worn grains is known to be very high (sometimes 80 per cent and more) from France to Poland. One can easily follow this belt eastward into Russia: 80 per cent at Pushkine, south of Pskov; about 40 to 50 per cent near Moscow and Vladimir. At Ulovka, near Vladimir, the percentage is about 25 per cent in the till, 40 per cent in the sand above it, and it reaches about 65 per cent in the aeolian sand filling a beautiful contraction wedge (sand-wedge). There we have at the same point the proof (the wedge) of the very cold climate and the strong wind action.

Four hundred km north of Moscow, near Gorki, the percentage of wind-worn quartz grains rises to 75 to 80 per cent and 70 per cent at Iaroslav. Much farther north, it still attains 45 per cent in Cheskskaya Guba and 60 per cent on the northern slopes of the Timan Mountains. The latitude in both places is about 67°N. The periglacial belt extended to there. The wind action is supported not only by sand grains, but also by aeolian deposits.

It is always good to get a counterproof of positive results by negative

TABLE 2

PERCENTAGES OF THE DIFFERENT KINDS OF QUARTZ GRAINS 0.7 MM LONG IN QUATERNARY AND RECENT DEPOSITS OF THE EUROPEAN PART OF USSR

	N^1	NU	EL	RM	RS
Periglacial aeolian belt					
Pushkin, south of Pskov, Recent lake, rehandling Quaternary	1	6	4	80	10
Moscow, 1 Recent and 2 Quaternary fluvial sands	3	16	19	58	7
Moscow, Quaternary, Illinoian-Dniepr till	1	17	40	38	5
Between Vladimir and Moscow, Illinoian-Dniepr and younger glacial, fluvioglacial and fluvial	5	14	23	43	20
Ulovka near Vladimir, Quaternary aeolian filling of a contraction wedge	1	15	16	64	5
Same place, Quaternary sand around the wedge	1	20	30	40	10
Same place, Illinoian-Dniepr red till	1	54	6	26	14
Near Gorki, 400 km east of Moscow, Illinoian fluvioglacial	2	4	11	78	7
Iaroslav, 120 km north of Moscow, Quaternary lake	1	15	10	70	5
Cheshskaya Guba, 67°N, Quaternary fluvial	2	20	17	45	18
North slope of Timan Mountain, 67° north, Quaternary, 1 fluvial and 1 aeolian	2	5	10	60	25
East and south of the aeolian belt					
Junction Kama-Volga, Illinoian-Dniepr fluvial	1	95	0	2	3
Region of Rostov na Donu, Old Quaternary, fluvial	4	3	91	6	0
Stantsia Morskaya, north of Azov Sea, Recent rehandling Pliocene-Quaternary sands	1	5	75	20	0
Northwest of the aeolian belt					
Kandalakshskaya Guba, Recent marine sand	1	98	0	1	1
Kolskiy Peninsula, Quaternary, 2 fluvioglacial and 1 marine	3	88	0	3	9
Latvian SSR, glacial and fluvioglacial, Quaternary	11	48	3	9	40
Kaunas and Siauliai, Lithuanian SSR, glacial and fluvioglacial, Quaternary	3	47	3	18	32
Vilnius and Druskininkai, Lithuanian SSR, aeolian, Quaternary	2	24	4	57	15
Same place, glacial and fluvioglacial Quaternary	4	36	9	21	34
Ostrov, south of Pskov, Quaternary esker	2	15	12	23	50
Nomme near Tallinn, Estonian SSR, dune, Recent	3	23	2	37	38
Pirita near Tallinn, Estonian SSR, Seashore, Recent	1	47	1	13	39
Estonian SSR, glacial and fluvioglacial Quaternary	7	52	0	12	36
20 km east of Leningrad, Quaternary fluvioglacial Kame	1	80	4	7	9

[1]N, NU, EL, RM, RS: see explanations, Table 1

ones. We find some outside the periglacial belt when we go further away from the glacial border. Towards the east, the Middle Quaternary fluvial sands at the junction of the Rivers Kama and Volga contain practically no wind-worn grains (2 per cent) and an extremely large amount of unworn ones (95 per cent); those ones come probably from the Ural Mountains. It is a rule that in all mountainous regions of the

TABLE 3
PERCENTAGES OF THE DIFFERENT KINDS OF QUARTZ GRAINS 0.7 MM LONG IN QUATERNARY AND RECENT DEPOSITS OF SIBERIA AND TURKESTAN

	N^1	NU	EL	RM	RS
Ob Basin					
Soby River, northern Urals, 66°N, Holocene	1	91	3	2	4
Sosva River, northern Urals, 63°N, Quaternary fluvioglacial	2	18	22	25	35
Between Khanty Mansiysk and Surgut, 62°N, Quaternary fluvial	2	5	7	88	0
Yenisei River					
66°N, Turukhansk, Holocene fluvial	1	44	36	18	2
60°N, Recent fluvial	1	34	52	14	0
56°N, Krasnoyarsk, Quaternary Illinoian fluvial	1	90	0	4	6
Yenisei River, 55°N, Quaternary and Recent fluvial	3	94	0	4	2
Lena Basin					
Bychyky River, 71°N, Quaternary aeolian	1	5	20	75	0
67°N, west, Quaternary aeolian, fluvial, and lacustrine	9	3	16	80	1
67°N, centre, Quaternary, 1 eluvial, 2 fluvial	3	3	9	88	0
67°N, east, near Verkhoyanskiy Mountains Quaternary, 1 glacial, 4 fluvioglacial	5	96	0	4	0
64°N, Vilyuy River, Quaternary fluvial	3	38	14	48	0
Transbaikalia					
Nercha River basin, Quaternary, 1 aeolian, 1 fluvial	2	55	1	44	0
Nercha River basin, Recent, fluvial	1	97	2	1	0
Nercha River basin, *in situ* altered crystalline rock	1	100	0	0	0
China (for comparison) Gobi Desert, Etsingol, desert sand, (Sven Hedin expedition)	1	56	3	41	0
Turkestan					
Fergana, Recent, fluvial near high mountains	5	97	0	3	0
Karakum, southwest, near Caspian Sea, dune	1	60	10	30	0
Karakum, west, dune	1	6	56	36	2

^1N, NU, EL, RM, RS: see explanations, Table 1

world—Rocky Mountains, Alps, Karpates, Atlas, etc.—the unworn grains often predominate.

In such regions, and specially in the Kama region, the scarcity of wind-worn grains does not at all mean that the wind did not blow, but that the sands were driven away by the rivers faster than they could be worn and shaped by the wind.

Far again from the glacial border, southward towards the Black Sea near Rostov na Donu there are also very few wind-worn grains (6 per cent). There the most common are the blunt-shiny, water-worn ones (90 per cent), evidently rehandled from the Tertiary deposits where such grains are very abundant and very like the Quaternary ones (Table 1).

Let us now turn back across the periglacial belt and follow the last recession of the glacier towards the north and the northwest. In the Kolskiy Peninsula and the Kandalakshskaya Guba, the fresh wind-worn grains are practically absent (1 to 3 per cent), and the unworn ones greatly predominate (90 to 95 per cent). It is exactly the same picture which is found when following the recession of the Scandinavian Inland ice from Denmark to southern, central, and northern Sweden. The explanation is the same: when the melting glacier left for the last time the more central parts of its territory (Kolskiy Peninsula, central and northern Sweden), the climate was milder, the forest followed almost immediately the departure of the glacier (Swedish pollen-analyses agree with this), the periglacial belt was at that time extremely narrow, and in every place temporary, always shifting towards the north and northwest following the retreat of the ice. Except in local places, the wind had not enough time to wear the sand grains much.

Between the Denmark-Sweden centripetal axis and the northern Russia-Kolskiy Peninsula axis, the Lithuania-Finland axis shows us a similar tendency for the fresh wind-worn grains to diminish. In the south, near the periglacial belt, their percentage attains 20 per cent in glacial and fluvioglacial deposits, reaching 50 to 60 per cent in aeolian ones. Going northwards, near Kaunas and Siauliai, it falls to 15 to 20 per cent, and in Latvia and Estonia to around 10 per cent. An exception is the local dune field of Nomme—a classical place for ventifacts— where it reaches 35 to 40 per cent. But near Leningrad, it falls to 7 per cent and even less further to the northwest in Finland.

The most interesting factor along this Latvia-Finland centripetial axis concerns another type of grains, the old wind-worn ones. Their percentage oscillates around 30 to 40 per cent, and is evidently related to the rehandling of the Cambrian, Ordovician, and Devonian sands or sandstones which crop out in the region forming the sedimentary cover of the Precambrian Shield. This percentage diminishes as one approaches the northern limit of the cover and the outcrop of the shield itself—about 10 per cent near Leningrad, and 0 to 1 per cent in Finland.

The other example of rehandling in the Russian sands is that of former marine subrounded blunt-shiny grains. Maximal, as we have seen, in the south, where they come from the well-known Tertiary deposits of the former big Black Sea basin, they are also present in Poland and in the Moscow region (20 to 40 per cent).

At Moscow, the Illinoian-Dniepr till from Poklonnaya Gora contains the following percentages of grains, at different sizes:

Length mm	0.15	0.30	0.43	0.57	0.85	1.15	1.75
% Not worn	95	55	25	15	20	30	30
% Blunt-shiny	5	35	40	35	45	30	20
% Round-dull (Old + new)		10	35	50	35	40	50

In Poland, the water-worn blunt-shiny grains are rehandled from the marine Oligocene and the lacustrine Miocene. But in Moscow where both those deposits are missing, another source must be found. The question was raised (Cailleux 1965) and is now solved by the new samples: water-worn blunt-shiny grains are present and beautiful, in the marine Jurassic and Cretaceous of the region, as shown above (Table 1).

QUATERNARY DEPOSITS OF SIBERIA AND TURKESTAN

Fresh wind-worn grains are not frequent in the northern Ural Mountains (Soby River basin, 2 per cent; Sosva River basin, 25 per cent), but in the middle course of the River Ob, they appear again beautiful and numerous (85 to 90 per cent). There they are as typical as in the periglacial belt of Europe.

They are much scarcer in the Yenisei River basin (4 to 18 per cent); this agrees with the more mountainous character of the region. But in the flat Lena River basin, they are again extremely typical and common, reaching 75 to 90 per cent, specially in the north (71°N) and the west. The Quaternary wind action is testified also by the aeolian sand covers, discovered by V. V. Kolpakov and N. N. Bobrinskiy (oral communication). Judging from the aspects of sand grains, the wind action here has been as strong as in the periglacial belt of Europe. Here also we get a negative counterproof: towards the east, near the Verkhoyanskiy Mountains, the wind-worn grains are, as is usual in mountainous regions, much scarcer (4 per cent), and the unworn ones prevail (96 per cent).

In the mountainous region of Transbaikalia, we find also the normally prevailing unworn grains (95 to 100 per cent), but two samples contain about 45 per cent wind-worn grains—one of them comes from an aeolian slope-cover, the second from a river eroding such aeolian deposits. Since the present climate of the region is a cold one, it must have been very cold during the Quaternary glacial periods; the wind action was very likely a periglacial one here.

To complete our remarks about wind action, let us mention that the arid desertic type is found in the south, testified to by the round-dull grains found in the Gobi desert (about 40 per cent) and in the Karakum desert sands (about 30 to 35 per cent). The very mountainous region of Fergana shows the usual prevalence of unworn sand grains (95 to 100 per cent).

INTERPRETATIONS AND CONCLUSIONS

With only one exception (Timan and neighbourhood), all the Quaternary periglacial wind effects described here are located in regions where the present natural vegetal formation is the forest. When the wind blew and wore the sand grains during the cold phases of the Quaternary, all those regions (Moscow, Ob, Lena, Transbaikalia) must have been mostly bare, and the northern boundary of the forest must have been much further to the south.

The periglacial aeolian belt, first described from western Europe to Poland, along outside the border of the Wisconsin-Würm-Valdai glaciation, extended itself far away eastward to Moscow and then northward at least to the Timan Mountains. Equally strong wind-wearing existed in several parts of Siberia: Ob region, Lena basin, and, to a lesser degree, Transbaikalia. Very probably, this list does not include all the locations.

Judging from the frequence and beauty of the wind-worn grains in the samples studied until now, the periglacial wind action seems to have been stronger in Europe, and even in Siberia, than in North America (Cailleux 1937). The climates of the New World were different from those of the Old World, in the past as now.

Of course, there are other criteria of wind action, such as wind-worn stones, loesses, or sand-covers. But the shape and aspect of the sand grains, needing a very long time to form, are a very good index. It is the author's hope that this criterion, first discovered in the United States in 1931, might be aplied more extensively in the Soviet Union and in North and South America and other countries in the world.

ACKNOWLEDGEMENTS. I wish to thank Aline Ehrlich, Ruth Fridman, Charles-Laurent Markus, and Jean-Pierre Michel, who helped me with the bibliography and translation.

REFERENCES CITED

CAILLEUX, ANDRÉ, 1936, Les actions éoliennes périglaciaires quaternaires en Europe: Soc. Géol. Fr., Bull., p. 495-505.

CAILLEUX, ANDRÉ, 1937*a*, Traces d'actions éoliennes périglaciaires quaternaires dans l'Amérique du Nord: Soc. Géol. Fr., Comptes-Rendus Somm., p. 28-29.

——, 1937*b*, Traces d'action du vent dans les dépôts du fond de la Mer du Nord: Soc. Géol. Fr., Comptes-Rendus Somm., p. 63-64.

——, 1942, Les actions éoliennes périglaciaires en Europe: Soc. Géol. Fr., Mém., n.s.t. 21, n. 46, 176 p.

——, 1956, Extension des actions éoliennes périglaciaires jusqu'à Moscou: Soc. Géol. Fr., Comptes-Rendus Somm., p. 202-203.

——, (in press), 1967, Etude morphoscopique de quelques sables et grès friables de l'Union Soviétique.

CAYEUX, L., 1929, Les roches sédimentaires de France. Roches siliceuses: Mém. Carte Géol. Fr., 774 p.

CROMMELIN, R. D., and CAILLEUX, ANDRÉ, 1939, Sur les sables calcaires de la côte égyptienne à 50 km à l'Ouest d'Alexandrie: Soc. Géol. Fr., Comptes-Rendus Somm., p. 74-76.

KUNEN, P. H., and PERDOK, W. G., 1961, Frosting of quartz grains: Kon. Nederl. Akad. Wet., Proc. S. B., v. 64, no. 3, p. 343-345.

MICHEL, J. P., 1964, Contribution à l'étude sédimentologique de l'Antarctique: CNFRA (Comité national français des recherches antarctiques), n. 5, p. 1-91.

RIESS, H., and CONANT, G. D., 1931, The character of sand grains: Trans. of Amer. Foundrymen's Assoc., n. 39, p. 353-392.

SCHNEIDER, H. E., 1964, Comment s'usent les grains de sable: Science progrès, la Nature, n. 3345, p. 28-30.

SORBY, H. C., 1880, On the structures and origin of noncalcareous stratified rocks: Quat. Journ. Geol. Soc., p. 46-92.

ADDITIONAL REFERENCES PERTINENT TO WIND-WORN SAND GRAINS

ASENCIO, I., 1960, Genesis y cronologia de los arenas de Torrelodones (Madrid): Madrid, Revista Las Ciencias, v. 25, no. 1, p. 75-84.

ASENCIO, I., and CAILLEUX, ANDRÉ, 1959, Morphoscopie de sables de Madagascar: Tananarive, Mém. Inst. Rech. Madagascar and Le naturaliste malgache, t. 11, no. 1-2, p. 9-17.

BALLAND, R., and CAILLEUX, ANDRÉ, 1946, Etude morphologique de quelques sables de la région bordelaise: Soc. Géol. Fr., Bull., 5 s., t. 16, p. 61-64.

BOUILLET, G., and CAILLEUX, ANDRÉ, 1962, Formes des grains de quartz de sables et grès du Brésil: Soc. Géol. Fr., Bull., 7 s., t. 4, p. 329-335.

BOUT, P., and CAILLEUX, ANDRÉ, 1950, Actions éoliennes au Villafranchien et au Pléistocène ancien en Velay: Soc. Géol. Fr., Comptes-Rendus Somm., p. 268-269.

BRAUN, E. VON, 1953, Geologische und sediment-petrographische Untersuchungen im Hochrheingebiet zwischen Zurzach und Eglisau: Ecl. Geol. Helv., v. 46, p. 143-170.

CAILLEUX, ANDRÉ, 1943, Importance et signification paléobiologique des déserts cambro-siluriens: Acad. Sci. Comptes-Rendus, t. 216, p. 895-896.

——, 1945, Sur quelques sables et grès de la région de Barcelone: Publ. Inst. Geol. Miscel. Almera., p. 65-78.

——, 1948, Lithologie des dépôts émergés actuels de l'embouchure du Var au Cap d'Antibes: Monaco Inst. Océanogr. Bull., no. 940, 11 p.

——, 1949, Morphoscopie de quelques sables de Palestine: Bull. Inst. Egypte., v. 31, p. 177-180.

——, 1962, Aspects mats des grains de quartz: Kon. Nederl. Akad. Wet., Proc., s. b., v. 65, no. 4, p. 393-394.

——, 1962, Sur trois sables actuels de Bulgarie: Soc. Géol. Fr., Comptes-Rendus Somm., p. 300.

CAILLEUX, ANDRÉ, and BOUILLET, G., 1962, Formes des grains de quartz de sables et grès du Brésil: Soc. Géol. Fr., Bull., 7s., t. 4, p. 329-335.

CAILLEUX, ANDRÉ, and TRICART, J., 1950, La surface infratertiaire dans le Bassin de Paris: C. R. 17 Congr. Int. Geogr., p. 651-658.

CAILLEUX, ANDRÉ, and TRICART, J., 1963, Initiation à l'étude des sables et des galets: Paris SEDES, 3 vol., 775 p., 2nd edition.

CAILLEUX, ANDRÉ, and WUTTKE, K., 1964, Morphoscopie des sables quartzeux dans l'Ouest des Etats-Unis d'Amérique du Nord: Curitiba, Bol. Paranaense Geogr., no 10-15, p. 79-87.

CAIRE, A., and CAILLEUX, ANDRÉ, 1957, Morphoscopie des roches gréseuses de la région des Biban (Constantine, Algérie): Soc. Géol. Fr., Bull., p. 819-831.

CARVALHO, S. DE, 1950, Sur les remplissages sableux des fentes de dissolution des calcaires du Portugal: Soc. Géol. Fr., Comptes-Rendus Somm., p. 91-93.

———, 1950, Sur la morphoscopie de quelques grès des dépôts les plus anciens de la bordure méso-cénozoique occidentale du Portugal: Revista da Fac. de Ciencias da Univ. da Coimbra, v. 19, p. 5-10.

———, 1954, Sur les dépôts à galets calcaires du Bassin du Mondego et les sables de la Gandara (Portugal): Rev. Géom. Dyn., t. 5, no. 5, p. 193-203.

CAYEUX, L., 1932, Existence de nombreux grains de quartz d'origine éolienne dans l'Ordovicien des environs de Leningrad: Acad. Sci., Comptes-Rendus, t. 194, p. 1535-1537.

DUPLAIX, S., and CAILLEUX, ANDRÉ, 1950, Sur quelques sables des fonds de 3800 à 7900 m de l'Océan atlantique: Acad. Sci., Comptes-Rendus, t. 230, p. 1964-1966.

MITCHELL, R. C., 1957, A comparison of some arenites of western Irak and northern Saudi Arabia with those of western Sahara: Bull. Fac. Sci. Univ. Baghdad, v. 2, p. 1-10.

MONOD, T., and CAILLEUX, ANDRÉ, 1949, Etude de quelques sables et grès du Sahara occidental: Inst. Fr. Afrique Noire, Bull., no. 104, p. 174-190.

SCHNEIDER, H. E., and CAILLEUX, ANDRÉ, 1959, Signification géomorphologiqus des formes des grains de sable des Etats-Unis: Zeit. Geomorph., v. 3, p. 114-125.

TERS, M., 1953, Existence d'un désert froid en Vendée littorale: Soc. Géol. Fr., Bull., p. 355-368.

———, 1961, La Vendée littorale: Paris Inst. Géogr., 191, rue St. Jacques, 1 vol., 578 p.

WALTER, M., 1951, Nouvelles recherches sur l'influence des facteurs physiques sur la morphologie des sables éoliens et des dunes: Rev. Géom. Dyn., no. 6, p. 242-258.

DISTRIBUTION, SOURCE, AND AGE OF THE LOESS ON THE PLAIN OF CAEN, NORMANDY, FRANCE

A. JOURNAUX, M. HELLUIN, J. P. LAUTRIDOU, J. PELLERIN
University of Caen, Caen, France

ABSTRACT. The loess on the Caen (Normandy, France) plains presents two complexes: calcareous loess in the north and northeast of the region, and non-calcareous loess in the southwest. The non-calcareous loess overlies the calcareous loess where they overlap. The study of many exposures and precise mapping shows that these two loesses have the same composition, except that ankerite is found only in the calcareous loess. The deposits of calcareous loess indicate that the winds blew from northwest to southeast; for the non-calcareous loess the winds blew from southwest to northeast. The two loesses are dated as Würm (Wisconsin) in age by their topographic position and by their mollusc content. The loesses pre-date the formation of fragments of chalk resulting from frost action and post-date the last cold phase.

RÉSUMÉ. Les loess de la plaine de Caen (Normandie, France) présentent deux complexes: des loess calcaires au nord et au nord-est de la région et des loess non calcaires au sud-ouest, ceux-ci recouvrant les premiers. L'étude de nombreuses coupes et la cartographie précise montrent que ces deux loess ont la même composition; seule l'ankérite se trouve uniquement dans les loess calcaires. Les dépôts de loess calcaires indiquent une direction des vents dominants du nord-ouest au sud-est, tandis que pour les loess non calcaires les vents soufflaient du sud-ouest au nord-est. Ces deux loess étant datés par leur position topographique et la faune du Würm, ils sont postérieurs à la formation de grèze et antérieurs à la dernière phase froide.

CONTENTS

FIGURE

INTRODUCTION

A study of the loess on the Caen plains was undertaken by scientists of the *Geomorphological Centre of the National Centre for Scientific Research* at Caen. The mapping was performed following shallow and deep boring, usually 1.2 m (55 in), but as deep as 7 m (25 ft) and spaced every 100 m (310 ft). Two different loess blankets (calcareous and non-calcareous) were identified and mapped (Fig. 1).

PHYSIOGRAPHIC SETTING

The Caen plains stretch from the Armoricain Massif on the west and south to the Dives Valley and the Pays d'Auge plateau to the east, and to the Atlantic on the north. The Orne River and its tributaries, l'Odon being the main one, flow through the plain along with some smaller streams, namely the Seulles which flows directly into the sea. These valleys have three terraces which are easily observed along the Orne Valley in the vicinity of Caen.

The upper terrace, 60 m (225 ft) above sea level, is composed of an old, non-calcareous sediment. All the sediment is weathered and the schist fragments are completely decomposed. Petrographic analysis of the sediments shows that they are similar to the Tertiary deposits

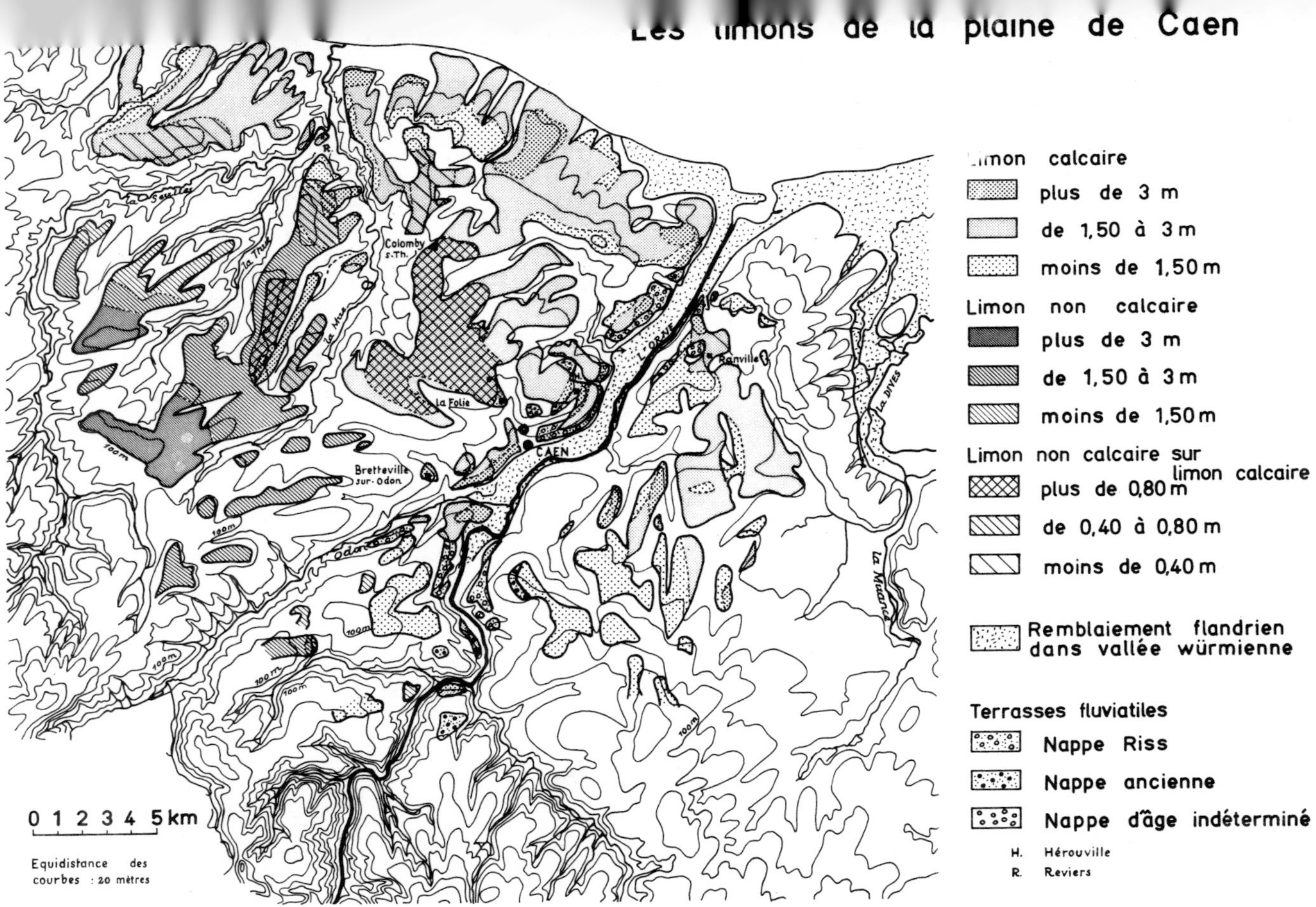
Les limons de la plaine de Caen
Limon calcaire
plus de 3 m
de 1,50 à 3 m
moins de 1,50 m
Limon non calcaire
plus de 3 m
de 1,50 à 3 m
moins de 1,50 m
Limon non calcaire sur limon calcaire
plus de 0,80 m
de 0,40 à 0,80 m
moins de 0,40 m
Remblaiement flandrien dans vallée würmienne
Terrasses fluviatiles
Nappe Riss
Nappe ancienne
Nappe d'âge indéterminé
H. Hérouville
R. Reviers
0 1 2 3 4 5 km
Equidistance des courbes : 20 mètres
Colomby s.-Th.
La Folie
CAEN
Bretteville sur-Odon
Ranville
la Dives
la Muance
Orne
la Mue
la Thue
la Seulles
Odon
100 m

FIG. I. Geologic map of distribution and thickness of calcareous and non-calcareous loess on the Plain of Caen.

characterized particularly by flint found in the clay. This upper terrace contains clay lenses. Sands are poorly sorted, and pebbles are of all sizes. It is of Quaternary age, perhaps Kansan.

The middle terrace, 20 m above sea level (75 ft) is covered by a layer more than 10 m (35 ft) thick. Its petrography is different from sediments of the upper terrace. The granite is always altered, but, on the contrary, the schists are much less so, comprising pebble and sand lenses and some big boulders weighing several tons. The latter were perhaps ice rafted. The terrace dates from the Illinoian (?) Glaciation.

The lower terrace, called Flandrian (post-glacial), is 5 m (16 ft) above sea level at Caen and lies on a rock formation which is 35 m (48 ft) below sea level at the mouth of the Orne River. The terrace is composed of 3 m (15 ft) of gravel at the base (formed of the same sediment as the middle terrace, but unaltered), and is overlain by Flandrian peat and clay which contain fresh water marine molluscs, indicating estuarine conditions.

DISTRIBUTION AND DESCRIPTION

Calcareous loess

The calcareous loess (limon calcaire, Fig. 1) occurs chiefly to the north and northeast of Caen and is not found to the southwest below an elevation of 70 m (250 ft) above sea level. Its thickness is variable—from 1.5 to 5 m (5 to 18 ft)—decreasing towards the south where it is never more than 1.5 m (5 ft) thick.

The loess covers the interfluves, is thicker on the northeastern and eastern slopes, reaching a maximum thickness at the foot of the slopes. The minimum thickness, or a complete lack of it, is in the middle of the slope or at breaks in the slope. The loess does not occur on the south-western and western slopes or in the areas of vales. Perhaps the calcareous loess deposited on the southwestern and western slopes was removed by erosion, but on the eastern slopes the loess was thickened by slope wash.

The calcareous loess shows a typical aeolian size-grade analysis (median approximately 30 microns). From 85 to 95 per cent of the grains are smaller than 100 microns; the clay content is from 10 to 12 per cent. Medium and coarse sands are absent except at the foot of some slopes where the loess is mixed with debris from the middle of the same slope. The loess is yellowish and contains from 14 to 20 per cent calcium carbonate, rising to 26 per cent at the foot of the slopes. Except for concretions, it is without apparent structure. The soil development is approximately 1.2 m (3.5 ft) thick.

Non-calcareous loess

The non-calcareous loess (limon non-calcaire, Fig. 1) is differentiated from the calcareous loess by its yellow-brown hue, by a lack of calcium carbonate, and by its slightly more clayey composition (the clay ranges from 12 to 15 per cent). However, its size-grade analysis also presents a typical aeolian curve.

The non-calcareous loess occurs to the southwest of Caen and overlies the calcareous loess to the west of the Orne River. It reaches its maximum thickness to the southwest (more than 3 m or 12 ft), and decreases from 3 m (12 ft) to 1.5 m (5 ft) towards the northeast, where it rests on the calcareous loess. Here its thickness is always less than 1.5 m (5 ft). It can be pointed out that its deposition does not show the same assymmetry as that of the calcareous loess, and that there is neither evidence of erosion on the slope nor accumulation elsewhere. It is an even blanket deposited over the interfluves. The soil of the non-calcareous loess is less well developed than that of the calcareous one.

STUDY OF SOME PARTICULAR EXPOSURES

La Folie

The exposure is located to the northwest of Caen on a slope facing east southeast (Fig. 2).

Section 1 is on the plateau and exhibits the following succession: (1) limestone at the base (f); (2) clayed sand, likely Tertiary in origin; (3) calcareous loess (d); (4) non-calcareous loess (c); (5) soil (b); and (6) foliated recent colluvium (a).

Section 2 is at the foot of the slopes, and the same succession is found. However, the clayey sand of Tertiary age has very likely been reshaped by mass wasting. A small fissure wedge and cryoturbations at the calcareous level can be observed. There is neither non-calcareous loess nor soil at this exposure. Section 3 is farther down the slope than Section 2. Calcareous loess occurs at the foot of the slope and is covered by non-calcareous colluvial deposits. Figure 3 illustrates size-grade curves of two samples of aeolian loess and one of red sand from the exposure at La Folie.

A study of the heavy minerals (Fig. 4) shows that the calcareous loess and non-calcareous loess have an almost identical composition.

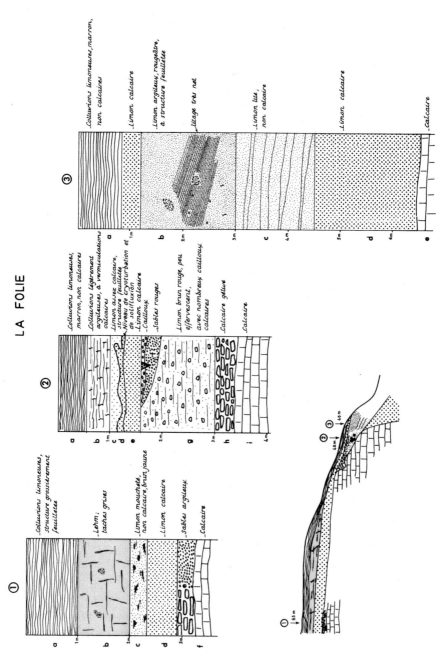

LA FOLIE

①

a ― _Colluvions limoneuses, structure grossièrement feuilletée_
b ― _Lehm; taches grises_
c ― _Limon moucheté, non calcaire, brun jaune_
d ― _Limon calcaire_
e ― _Sables argileux_
f ― _Calcaire_

②

a ― _Colluvions limoneuses, marron, non calcaires_
b ― _Colluvions légèrement argileuses, à vermiculations calcaires_
c ― _Limon assez calcaire, structure feuilletée_
d ― _Niveau de cryoturbation et de solifluxion_
e ― _Limon calcaire_
f ― _Cailloux_
g ― _Sables rouges_
h ― _Limon brun rouge, peu effervescent, avec nombreux cailloux calcaires_
  ― _Calcaire gélian_
i ― _Calcaire_

③

a ― _Colluvions limoneuses, marron, non calcaires_
  ― _Limon calcaire_
b ― _Limon argileux, rougeâtre, à structure feuilletée_
  ― _litage très net_
c ― _Limon lité, non calcaire_
d ― _Limon calcaire_
e ― _calcaire_

Fig. 2. Cross section of Quaternary deposits at La Folie, northwest of Caen.

308

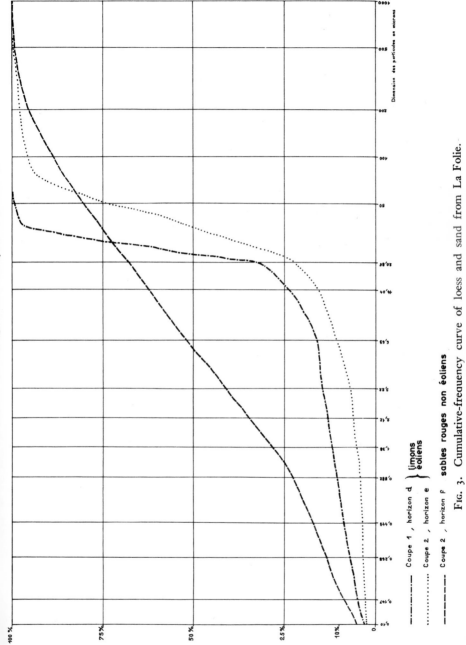

Fig. 3. Cumulative-frequency curve of loess and sand from La Folie.

Coupe 1 , horizon d ⎫ limons
Coupe 2 , horizon e ⎭ éoliens

Coupe 2 , horizon F sables rouges non éoliens

LA FOLIE - Etude des minéraux lourds

Fraction granulométrique comprise entre 50 et 160 microns.

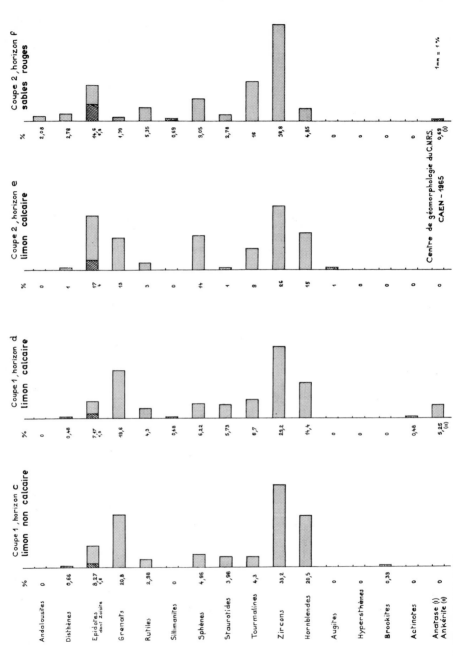

Coupe 1, horizon C — limon non calcaire

Coupe 1, horizon d — limon calcaire

Coupe 2, horizon e — limon calcaire

Coupe 2, horizon F — sables rouges

Centre de géomorphologie du C.N.R.S.
CAEN - 1965

1mm = 1%

However, ankerite appears in the calcareous loess of Section 1. The red sand is different from the rest by the small percentage of garnets and the presence of andalousites and disthenes.

Colomby-sur-Thaon

The exposure of Colomby-sur-Thaon, northwest of Caen (Fig. 5), confirms the succession of the exposure at La Folie. The calcareous and non-calcareous loesses are not very thick. The cryoturbation area is clearly above the non-calcareous loess (d), and the soil layer is altered but not cryoturbated.

Reviers

This exposure occurs on the middle terrace of the Seulles River (Fig. 6). It is a periglacial slope deposit. Calcareous gravel with hardened banks occurs at the foot of the slope showing calcareous loess; the top has a soil development.

Herouville

In a northeastern suburb of Caen, a most interesting complex of loess which is related to the three terraces of the Orne River (Fig. 7) was observed.

The upper terrace is from 65 m (250 ft) to 55 m (200 ft) above sea level. The middle terrace is between 28 and 17 m, (100 and 60 ft), and the lowest terrace is +3 m (10 ft) to −12 m (45 ft). These terraces are separated by slope elements which evolved differently:

(1) The upper terrace shows well developed karst, with pockets going as deep as 10 m (35 ft), filled with red clay (containing a bit of kaolinite). The karst goes progressively towards the middle terrace by a slope covered by fragments of limestone resulting from frost action.

(2) The base of the middle terrace shows a beginning of karstification resulting from the withdrawal of underground waters to the Orne River which is very near. This middle layer is located above the Flandrian terrace and is separated from it by a small escarpment.

On Section 1 (Fig. 8) are shown the three terraces and two barren areas where the rock appears; the whole is covered with calcareous loess not very thick at the top of the slopes (1 m [4 ft]), but thicker at the base or foot of the slopes (3 to 4 m [10 to 12 ft]). Section 2 is a detailed view of the karstified area of the upper terrace. Sections 3a and 3b (Fig. 9) are in the area of the fragments of limestone resulting from frost action at the top of the middle terrace; asymmetric fossil

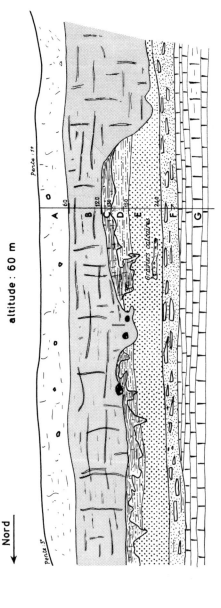

Fɪɢ. 5. Exposure of loess deposits at Colomby-sur-Thaon, northwest of Caen.

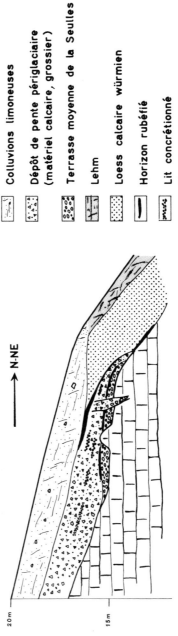

REVIERS

N-NE

20 m

15 m

Colluvions limoneuses

Dépôt de pente périglaciaire (matériel calcaire, grossier)

Terrasse moyenne de la Seulles

Lehm

Loess calcaire würmien

Horizon rubéfié

Lit concrétionné

Fig. 6. Exposure of Quaternary deposits on the middle terrace of Seulles River near Reviers.

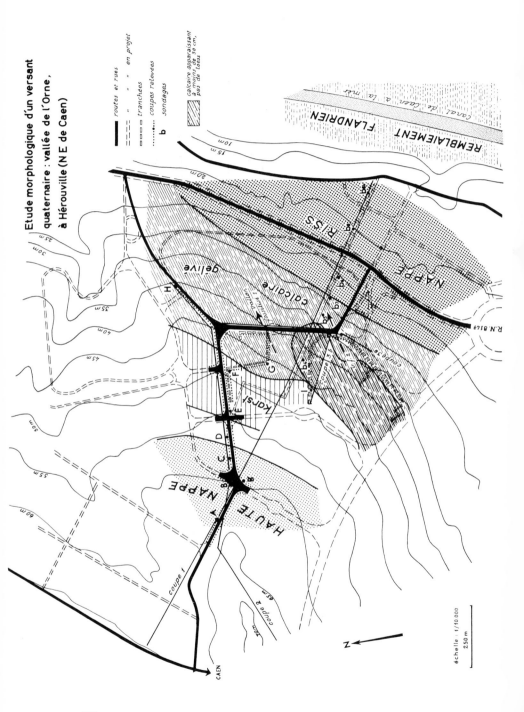

Etude morphologique d'un versant
quaternaire : vallée de l'Orne,
à Hérouville (N E de Caen)

routes et rues
" " " en projet
tranchées
coupes relevées
b   sondages

calcaire apparaissant
à moins de 50 cm,
pas de loess

échelle : 1/10 000

250 m

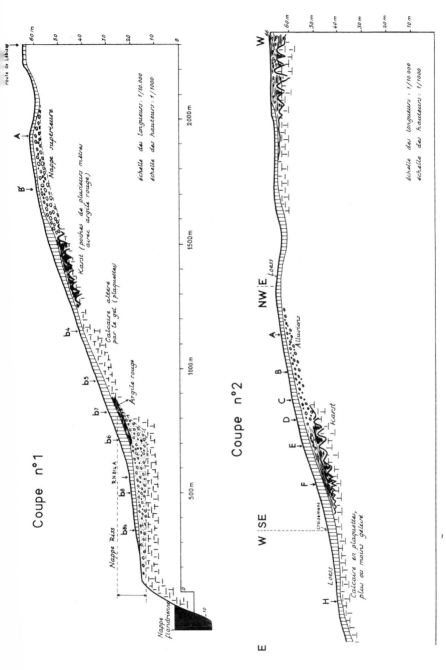

Coupe n°1

route de Lébisey

Nappe supérieure

Karst (poches de plusieurs mètres avec argile rouge)

Calcaire altéré par le gel (plaquettes)

Argile rouge

b4

b5

b7

b6

R.N.814 A

b8

b66

Nappe Riss

Nappe flandrienne

échelle des longueurs : 1/10.000
échelle des hauteurs : 1/1000

Coupe n°2

NW E

W SE

E

Loess

A

B

C

D

E

F

H

Alluvions

Karst

croisement

Calcaire en plaquettes, plus ou moins gélivé

Loess

W

échelle des longueurs : 1/10.000
échelle des hauteurs : 1/1000

FIG. 8. Sections 1 and 2 of Quaternary slope deposits near Herouville.

315

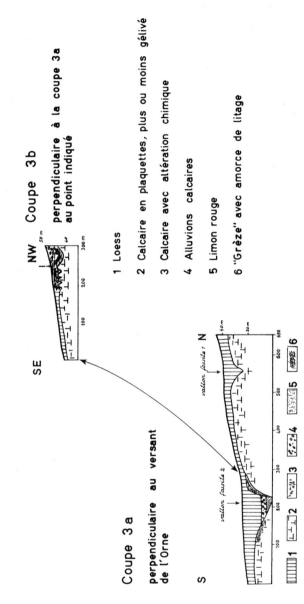

Coupe 3a

perpendiculaire au versant
de l'Orne

S

NW   Coupe   3b

perpendiculaire à la coupe 3a
au point indiqué

SE

1 Loess

2 Calcaire en plaquettes, plus ou moins gélivé

3 Calcaire avec altération chimique

4 Alluvions calcaires

5 Limon rouge

6 "Grèze" avec amorce de litage

Fig. 9. Section 3 of slope deposits near Herouville.

vales were observed, whose upward slopes were facing south when the bottom was filled with calcareous alluvium of the middle terrace. The curves of the size grade analysis show that everywhere the silt is typical loess. However, the heavy minerals differ between the upper and middle terraces: in the upper terrace they are widespread and with predominant resistant minerals, tourmaline and zircon, comprising 80 per cent of the total amount. In the middle terrace there is less zircon and tourmaline (35 per cent) with more of disthene, epidote, garnet, rutile, sphene, staurolite, hornblende, auguite, actinolites, and occasionally ankerite in the calcareous alluvial areas.

RELATIONSHIP BETWEEN THE TWO LOESS DEPOSITS

A great similarity can be observed between the two loesses: the size-grade analysis is similar. Typically aeolian samples are varied, and the same conclusion applies to the samples coming from Sassy, Ernes, Bretteville-sur-Odon, Tournay-sur-Odon (8 km from Caen) (Fig. 10).

The heavy minerals are equally identical (in particular Section 1 of La Folie), although certain elements—weathered—can show differences (La Folie 2 (e) and (f)) (Fig. 11).

However we observe that ankerite in the calcareous loess seems to come from the underlying calcareous layer. This is the conclusion that can be drawn concerning the calcareous loess at Ranville, Sassy, and Bretteville where ankerite is always plentiful.

Between these two loesses there are, however, major differences:

(1) There is no active limestone in the non-calcareous loess, although the pH is very much the same.

(2) The position of these two loesses shows a difference: the non-calcareous loess is above the calcareous loess.

(3) Finally, the non-calcareous loess is located primarily in the southwest of the area under study, is very thick, and lies directly on bedrock.

In conclusion, these two loesses show more similarity than difference. However, is the decalcification of the non-calcareous loess contemporary to the deposition (more humid climate), or do these two forms of loess have different sources or origin?

SOURCE OF THE LOESS

In the north it was observed that the calcareous loess is found on calcareous rocks, and in the south the non-calcareous loess is found on the clay resulting from decalcification, the marnes, and the schists. The

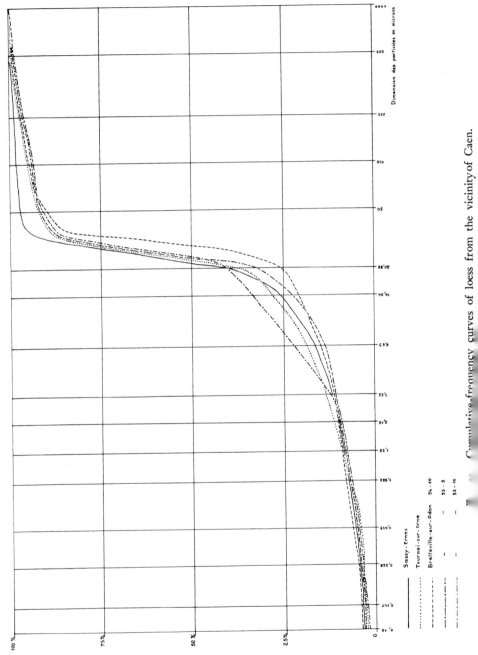

Cumulative-frequency curves of loess from the vicinity of Caen.

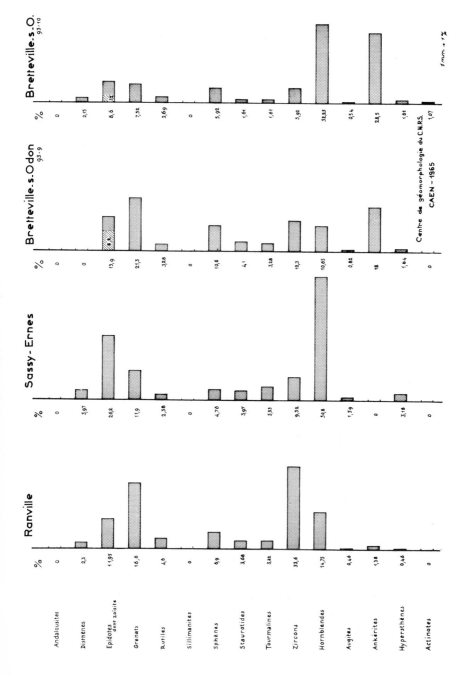

FIG. 11. Distribution of heavy minerals in loess in vicinity of Caen.

possibility of a local amount mixed to a general stock can be translated by an enrichment of the heavy minerals (in particular, the "glauconie," when an ore of this mineral is not very far).

The source of the loess is perhaps responsible for the difference in composition and location. If we admit a change in the orientation of prevailing winds, from the northwest at the time of the deposition of the calcareous loess to the southwest at the time of the deposition of the non-calcareous loess, this would explain:

(1) the more important accumulation to the north of the calcareous loess and to the south for the non-calcareous loess;

(2) that asymmetry is more important for the deposit of calcareous loess, the wind being perpendicular to the axis of the interfluves, when the southwestern winds would have been parallel to these axis; and

(3) moreover, the accumulation of calcareous loess at the foot of the southeastern slopes shows the possibility of a transport via solifluction over the permafrost.

Therefore, the authors concluded that a shift of wind direction is the reason for the observed differences between the calcareous and non-calcareous loess deposits.

AGE OF THE LOESS

The loesses are very likely Wisconsin in age as dated by molluscs (*Pupilla muscorum*, determined by G. Mazenot) and primarily by their topographic location at the foot of the middle terrace. These calcareous and non-calcareous loesses are cryoturbated, therefore they were deposited prior to the last cold phase. The soil is never cryoturbated but is frequently moved by colluvial action. The succession of events seems to be as follows:

(1) Pre-Flandrian downcutting to 35 m (120 ft) below the present sea level at the mouth of the Orne River, and minus 5 m (20 ft) at Caen, with perhaps asymmetry of some small tributary vales;

(2) Formation of fragments of chalk resulting from frost action and filling of the little vales;

(3) Deposition of calcareous loess on fragments of chalk (Bretteville-sur-Oden and Sassy);

(4) Deposition of non-calcareous loess over the calcareous loess;

(5) Final cryoturbation;

(6) Post-glacial soil development.

THE AGE OF
THE PINGOS OF BELGIUM

WILLIAM MULLENDERS and FRANS GULLENTOPS
University of Louvain, Louvain, Belgium

ABSTRACT. In High Belgium many hundreds of pingos (called "viviers" or "mardelles") are known. They are on the high plateaus at an elevation between 500 to 650 m, and most of them are in east Belgium (Baraque Michel). The material filling the collapsed pingos is stratified clay, gyttja-mud, and peat. The oldest pingos date from the end of the Late Glacial (Late Dryas), and most of the gyttja layer belongs to the Preboreal, characterized by a low NAP percentage and the dominance of pine (*Pinus silvestris*) or birch (*Betula pubescens* and *verrucosa*). During this period slight oscillations which may perhaps be synchronous with the Piottino oscillation of the Swiss Alps (8,100 to 7,400 BC, Zoller 1960) occurred regularly. For this purpose, isotope datings will be attempted.

In Low Belgium no pingos are known. However, the origin of the former Lake of Leau (elevation: 30 m), a closed depression of about 100 ha, still remains unexplained, and the pingo hypothesis is considered. The general stratification is: green sand of the Landenian, several gyttja layers, Boreal peat, loam. The Late Glacial and Preboreal diagrams, more or less disturbed by Cenozoic secondary pollen, are very unusual, showing more important oscillations than the pingos of High Belgium, among them the Piottino oscillation (?). It is hoped to separate the secondary pollen by the autofluorescence method of Van Gijzel (1961).

RÉSUMÉ. En Haute Belgique on connait plusieurs centaines de pingos, tous situés entre 500 et 650 m d'altitude. L'analyse pollinique montre que les dépôts de remplissage les plus anciens datent de la fin du Dryas récent ou du début du Préboréal. Une oscillation froide dans le Préboréal est probablement synchrone avec l'oscillation de Piottino (8,100 à 7,400 av. JC, Zoller 1960). L'analyse des minéraux révèle la présence de cendres volcaniques de l'Eifel dans le rempart mais non dans le gyttja ou la tourbe. Ces données indiquent que les pingos de Haute Belgique ont été formés durant le Dryas récent.

En Basse Belgique l'existence d'aucun pingo n'a pu être établie avec certitude. Cependant, la formation de la grande dépression de Leau (Zoutleeuw) ne semble pas pouvoir être expliquée sans recourir à l'hypothèse du pingo. La morphologie de la dépression ainsi que la stratification sont décrites. L'analyse pollinique de la couche de gyttja surmontant le sable landénien montre que les niveaux les plus anciens datent de l'Alleröd. Au cours du Préboréal on observe également une période froide attribuée à l'oscillation de Piottino. Si on observe des pollens secondaires du Landénien, aucun type du Pléistocène antérieur au Würm n'a été décelé. De plus la dépression ne contient guère de loess. Ces faits tendent à montrer que la dépression a été formée au cours du Dryas moyen. Enfin, l'évolution de la dépression est esquissée.

CONTENTS

HIGH BELGIUM

The climates of Low Belgium and of High Belgium are quite different, as shown in Table 2. All the pingos—formerly called "viviers" or "mardelles"—known in High Belgium lie between 500 and 650 m elevation. Most of them, about a thousand, are in east Belgium at the Baraque Michel or Plateau des Hautes Fagnes (Fig. 1). In the central Ardennes at the Plateau des Tailles about 40 pingos are known, while in the west Ardennes (Plateau de Nassogne and Plateau de la Croix Scaille) no pingos so far have been detected. The one exception to this is perhaps in the Forest of St. Hubert (Nassogne) where a probable pingo is completely covered by a peat layer. Their morphology has been described by Pissart (1956, 1963), who was the first in Belgium to recognize the real nature of these depressions: "They are formed in residual clay, covered by aeolian loess, on slopes of less than 5°." Pissart distinguishes two types: closed depressions that are generally circular or oval of about 40 to 50 m diameter (the maximum being 150 m) and of a depth to 8 m maximum, and open depressions that are often elongated with a maximum diameter of 800 m.

It is often said that these pingos are filled only with peat. In fact,

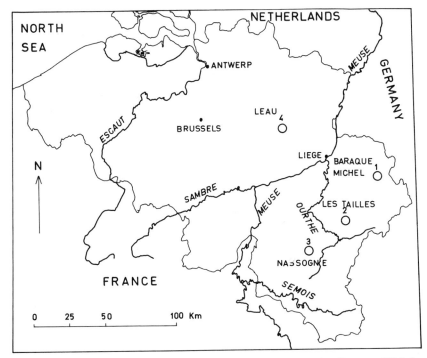

Fig. 1. Map of Belgium showing the location of the pingos: (1) Baraque Michel (Plateau des Hautes Fagnes); (2) Plateau des Tailles; (3) Forest of St. Hubert (Nassogne); (4) Leau (Zoutleeuw).

under the peat—when it still exists, or under the water—one finds a layer of brown-greyish detritus gyttja, often with a silt mixture, and under the gyttja a clay layer with debris of the underlying rocks. The thickness of these layers is variable. The gyttja layer varies between a few cm and 150 cm. Its pH ranges from 5.5 to 7 in contradistinction to the low pH values of all the soil types in the neighbourhood.

The debris-rim around a pingo of Massehottée (Plateau des Tailles) was studied. It is composed of a heterogeneous mixture of loess, clay weathering products of the subsoil, and rock debris in which angular quartzite is predominant. Heavy mineral analysis reveals also the presence of volcanic ash from the Eifel, the most important eruption that is known of Alleröd age (10,000 to 9,000 BC). In the gyttja deposits of the pingo these minerals have not yet been found.

Pollen analysis

The following pollen diagrams of the filling material are so far available:

(1) BARAQUE MICHEL. 5 diagrams of 5 pingos (Florschutz and Van Oye 1939, Vivier Fagnoul-vander Hammen 1953, diagram XIV Belle Croix-Slotboom 1963, Vivier à Botrange-Mullenders and Coremans, 2 pingos sampled by A. Pissart and Fr. Damblon)

(2) PLATEAU DES TAILLES. 5 diagrams of 4 pingos, all at Massehottée (Mullenders and Haesendonck 1963, Coremans, De Ridder)

(3) PLATEAU DE NASSOGNE. 1 diagram (Mullenders and Haesendonck: St. Hubert, Rouge Ponceau I)

The clay layer at the base of the pingo filling contains hardly any pollen. On the other hand, the gyttja layer of all the analysed pingos is fairly rich in pollen. The gyttja layer everywhere shows the same palynological picture: spectra from the Late Dryas and/or the Preboreal (from 8,500 to 6,500 BC), the top of the gyttja layer or the base of the peat layer generally represents the beginning of the Boreal. We shall discuss here only the Dryas and Preboreal diagrams and give as an example the diagram of Massehottée III (Mullenders and Haesendonck 1963). (Location: Plateau des Tailles, elevation 605 m; longitude 1°54′ east of Brussels and latitude 55°81′ north [Fig. 2]).

During the Late Dryas the arboreal pollen (AP) fluctuated between 50 and 60 per cent; it increased during the Preboreal up to 80 to 90 per cent. Generally, *Betula (pubescens* Ehrh. and/or *verrucosa* Ehrh.) dominated with 30 to 60 per cent, followed by *Pinus silvestris* L. (25 per cent), and by *Salix* (5 to 10 per cent). Locally or temporarily, *Pinus* dominated, probably in dryer circumstances.

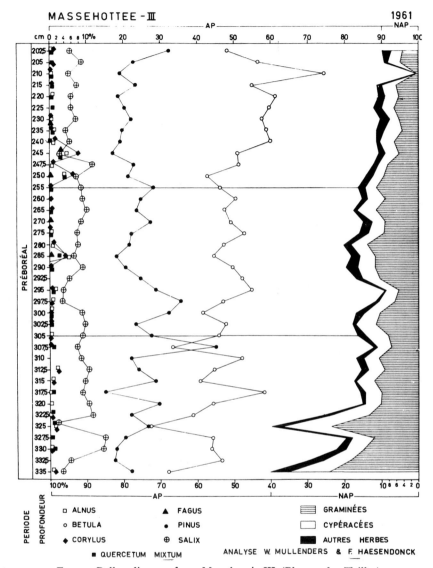

FIG. 2. Pollen diagram from Massehottée III (Plateau des Tailles).

335

The non-arboreal pollen (NAP) species are numerous, as are those in all the Preboreal diagrams of Belgium. Besides the Poaceae and Cyperaceae, the pollen of herbaceous plants and small shrubs (55 taxa), the spores (9 taxa), and the algae (5 taxa) are listed in Table 1. One notices the great number of aquatic and semi-aquatic species: *Pediastrum* (3 species), *Scenedesmus, Equisetum* t. *limosum, Isoetes, Lemna, Littorella, Menyanthes trifoliata, Myriophyllum* (3 species and up to 20 per cent at the base), *Nuphar, Nymphaea, Potamogeton, Batrachium, Sparganium, Typha latifolia;* as well as the open-landscape species: *Artemisia, Centaurea cyanus* and *pratensis, Ephedra, Helianthemum, Hippophae, Plantago, Thalictrum, Sanguisorba minor* and *officinalis, Succisa pratensis.* Few macrofossils have so far been demonstrated: *Sphagnum acutifolium* Ehrh., *Carex inflata* Huds (Slotboom 1963) and the arctic-alpine species *Polytrichum sexangulare* Schwaegr. and *Aulacomnium turgidum* (Florschutz and Van Oye 1939). Many of these species have now disappeared from High Belgium. The diagrams of Massehottée, as well as the diagram of Nassogne, and one diagram of the Baraque Michel (samples Damblon) show slight oscillations occurring regularly at two levels, the higher one being more important. One observes an extension of thermophilous species, namely of *Alnus glutinosa* (L.) Gaertn.,*Corylus avellana* L., *Quercus, Tilia cordata* Mill., and *Ulmus.* This extension is observed in Massehottée at the levels 285 cm and 250 to 245 cm.

A systematic contamination by the peat-sampler can be excluded because three different types have been used: two Hiller and the Danheux-Couteaux samplers. Also, the oscillations occur in different pingos at a different absolute depth.

Accordingly, it is presumed that the period following the mean warm extension recorded at a depth of 250 to 245 cm at Massehottée; thus the 240 to 200 cm layer was deposited during a cooler period indicated merely by the recession of the thermophilous species and a slight extension of *Betula,* but by no extension of NAP. We think this period could be correlated with the Piottino-oscillation which has been demonstrated to us by Zoller (1960) in southeast Switzerland (north Tessin and Misox) between 420 and 1,200 m elevation, and has been dated there by the C[14] method between 8,100 and 7,000 BC. In Belgium, C[14] assays on the gyttja layers of the pingos have been attempted, but so far no definite results can yet be given.

Conclusion

The 11 pingos analysed suggest that the pollen rain in the pingo depressions started at the end of the Late Dryas. The volcanic Laacher

326

TABLE 1
POLLEN, SPORES, AND ALGAE IN PREBOREAL LAYERS OF PINGOS OF HIGH BELGIUM

	1	2	3	4
Pollen				
Apiaceae	x	x	.	x
Apiaceae type Anthriscus	.	.	.	x
Liguliflorae	.	x	.	x
Tubuliflorae	x	x	.	x
Artemisia	x	x	x	x
Centaurea cyanus L.	x	.	.	x
Centaurea type pratensis	.	.	.	x
Brassicaceae	.	x	.	x
Campanulaceae	.	.	x	x
Campanula	x	x	.	x
Jasione	x	.	.	.
Caryophyllaceae	x	x	.	x
Chenopodiaceae	x	x	.	x
Calluna	.	.	.	x
Empetrum	x	.	.	x
Vaccinium	.	.	.	x
Ephedra	.	.	.	x
Epilobium	.	.	.	x
Helianthemum	x	x	.	x
Hippophae	x	.	.	.
Isoetes	x	.	.	.
Lemna	.	.	.	x
Littorella	x	.	.	.
Plantago	.	.	.	x
Menyanthes trifoliata L.	x	x	x	x
Myriophyllum	x	x	.	.
Myriophyllum alterniflorum DC.	.	.	.	x
Myriophyllum spicatum L.	.	.	.	x
Myriophyllum verticillatum L.	.	.	.	x
Nuphar	x	.	.	.
Nymphaea	x	.	.	.
Poaceae type Cerealia	.	.	.	x
Polygonum type aviculare	.	.	.	x
Polygonum bistorta L.	x	.	.	.
Rumex	x	.	.	x
Rumex type acetosella	.	.	x	x
Rumex crispus L.	.	.	.	x
Potamogeton	x	x	.	x
Ranunculaceae	.	x	.	x
Batrachium	x	.	x	x
Thalictrum	x	x	x	x
Rosaceae	.	x	x	x
Filipendula	x	.	x	x
Rubus chamaemorus L.	x	.	.	.
Sanguisorba minor Scop.	.	.	.	x
Sanguisorba officinalis L.	x	.	.	.
Rubiaceae	.	x	.	x
Galium	x	.	x	x
Sparganium type	.	.	.	x
Succisa pratensis Moench.	.	.	x	x
Typha latifolia L.	.	x	.	x
Urtica	x	.	.	x
Valeriana	x	.	.	.
Valeriana officinalis L.	.	.	.	x
Viburnum	.	x	.	.

TABLE 1 continued

	1	2	3	4
Spores				
Sphagnum	x	x	.	x
Equisetum	x	x	.	x
Equisetum type limosum	.	.	.	x
Lycopodium clavatum L.	.	.	.	x
Filices	.	x	.	.
Dryopteris	x	.	.	.
Dryopteris cristata Gray	.	.	x	x
Polypodium vulgare L.	.	x	.	x
Selaginella selaginoides Link.	x	.	.	x
Algae				
Pediastrum	.	x	.	.
Pediastrum boryanum Menegh.	.	.	x	x
Pediastrum duplex Meyen	.	.	x	x
Pediastrum simplex Meyen	.	.	x	x
Scenedesmus bijugatus	.	.	.	x

SOURCE: Col. (1), Vander Hammen 1953, Baraque Michel; Col. (2), Slotboom 1963, Baraque Michel; Col. (3), samples collected by Pissart at Baraque Michel, analysed by Mullenders and Haesendonck; Col. (4), pingos at the Plateau des Tailles analysed by Mullenders and Haesendonck 1963, and Coremans and De Ridder.

See eruption had already taken place. This indicates that the pingos of High Belgium were formed during the Late Dryas. The good morphological preservation of the pingo rims indicates also that no congelifluction took place after their formation; otherwise they would have been levelled. The Late Dryas in Belgium is known as a period when important cryopedologic phenomena took place, so that the pingos must be older or synchronous to it. Pollen and heavy minerals demonstrate that they are synchronous, proving once more that cold conditions in High Belgium during the Late Dryas existed. Of course, conditions for pingo formation have also probably existed before, but the pingos were eventually levelled by congelifluction and covered by loess. Until now, not one of these has been found in High Belgium.

LOW BELGIUM

In Low Belgium no pingos are known with certainty. However, the pingo hypothesis is the only plausible explanation for the huge closed depression of Leau (Zoutleeuw), morphologically studied by Schoeters (1958). This depression, called "Het Vinne," is near Leau between Tirlemont (Tienen) and St. Trond (St. Truiden), 50 km east of Brussels (Fig. 1). The elevation is 30 m, longitude is 0°85′ east of Brussels, and latitude is 56°48′ north. Table 2 gives the climatic conditions. The depression (Fig. 3) lies 1 km east of the Petite Gette River. It has a completely flat bottom at an elevation of 26 m. It is surrounded by a gentle slope to the south and the east, by a rather steep one in the north, and an elongated ridge separates it from the alluvial plain of the Gette which lies at 28 m. Through the western ridge a narrow and steep-sided gully exists, the surface of which lies at 29 m.

In these circumstances a lake should exist in the depression, and indeed historical documents mention a lake since the Middle Ages. It was drained in 1841. Without the active pumping installation it would still be a lake; now it is a prosperous aspen plantation.

The total surface is about 100 ha, the SW-NE diameter is 1,600 m, the SE-NW one is 900 m. There are two remarkable small deltas in the former lake at the altitude of 28 m, one at the east side of the gully, and the other in the south at the mouth of a small brook. Both indicate the altitude of the water surface of the former lake at 28 m. A significant number of springs exists in the east and southeast. The underground of the depression is formed by marine Landenian sands (Lower Eocene), on which in the surrounding slopes exist fluviatile marls and clays of the Landenian formation, while the top of the northern hill is capped by marine Tongrian clayish sands. These Tertiary formations have a very gentle slope to the north (3 to 4°). The complete country-side is covered by a continuous layer of sandy loess of Würm age (Fig. 4).

Borings in the former lake bottom indicate at the surface a thin layer of loamy mud, and an underlying thin layer of peat. Beneath this peat we found a more important deposit of green and then blue lime gyttja rich in diatoms and sponge spicules. Underneath exist the glauconite

TABLE 2

COMPARISON BETWEEN THE CLIMATE OF LOW BELGIUM (LEAU) AND OF HIGH BELGIUM (PONCELET AND MARTIN, 1947)

	Low Belgium	High Belgium
Mean annual temperature (°C)	9.5°	6.5°
Mean maximum temperature	14.0	10.5
Mean minimum temperature	5.5	2.5
Mean temperature, January	3.0	0.0
Mean temperature, July	17.5	14.0
Mean daily maximum temperature, January	5.5	2.5
Mean daily minimum temperature, January	2.5	−3.5
Beginning of mean temperature of 5°C or more	5-10 March	5–15 April
End of mean temperature of 5°C	10-15 Nov.	30 Oct.
Mean number of days with mean temperature of 5°C	250–260	200–210
Mean number of days below 0°C	60–65	110–120
Mean temperature during the growing season	15.5°	12.5°
Annual rainfall	800 mm	1,300-1,400 mm

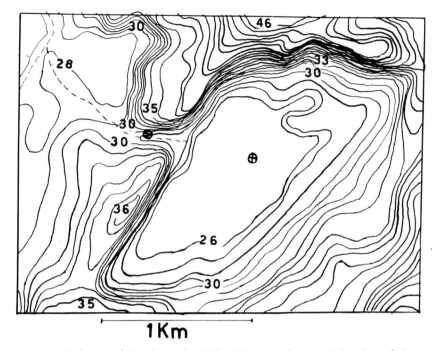

FIG. 3. Relief map of the depression "Het Vinne" at Leau and location of the main borings.

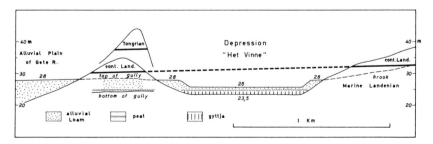

FIG. 4. Geological stratification of the depression "Het Vinne" at Leau.

sands of the marine Landenian formation. In the gully 4.5 m of alluvial loam cover a peat layer. The deltas are also formed by the same loam.

Pollen analysis

Several pollen profiles have been studied from "Het Vinne." The two most important ones are in the outlet and in the middle of the depression (Fig. 3). The pollen data from the profile in the middle of "Het Vinne" are presented in the shortened diagram Leau IV (Fig. 5) as percentages of all the pollen and spores counted at each level. The pollen sum does not include microfossils of algae nor the Cenozoic secondary pollen as far as we could recognize them. The core depth is shown at the left of the diagram. As one might expect, the aquatic and semi-aquatic species are numerous at all levels, but more abundant at the base of the profile. We observed: *Pediastrum boryanum, P. simplex, P. duplex, Desmidiaceae, Diatoms, Lemna, Potamogeton, Spongilla lacustris* L., *Nymphaea, Myriophyllum, Batrachium, Sparganium, Typha latifolia.*

Cenozoic pollen from the Landenian sands are abundant between 250 and 225 cm, but they are observed also higher up in the profile. Different types of the genus *Extratriporopollenites* are observed, one type attaining till 40 per cent. Several types of *Hystrichospheres* and *Dinoflagellates* are noticed up to 200 cm. Other Cenozoic secondary pollens can be expected in this profile, but they can be recognized only by the autofluorescence method (Van Gijzel 1961); such examination will be applied to these sediments.

The following interpretation of the diagram is now possible:

120 cm	beginning of the Boreal
120 to 195 cm	Preboreal
195 to 205 cm	Late Dryas
205 to 250 cm	Alleröd-oscillation.

During the Alleröd-oscillation, AP extends to 75 per cent; *Corylus avellana, Betula, Pinus silvestris* dominate alternatively (30 to 40 per cent). The thermophilous species, *Quercus, Tilia, Ulmus, Alnus glutinosa* reach 5 per cent. Among the NAP we notice: *Epilobium, Galium,* *Aster*-type, *Rumex* type *crispus; Empetrum, Valeriana officinalis, Artemisia, Thalictrum*, etc.

During the Late Dryas, the AP decreases to 30 per cent, *Betula* dominates followed by *Salix*. Among the NAP, the Cyperaceae increase strongly; the following are also noticed: *Sanguisorba minor, Calluna* and other Ericales, *Selaginella elaginoides.*

During the Preboreal, the AP again reaches 70 per cent, with the complete dominance of *Betula*. The thermophilous trees are poorly

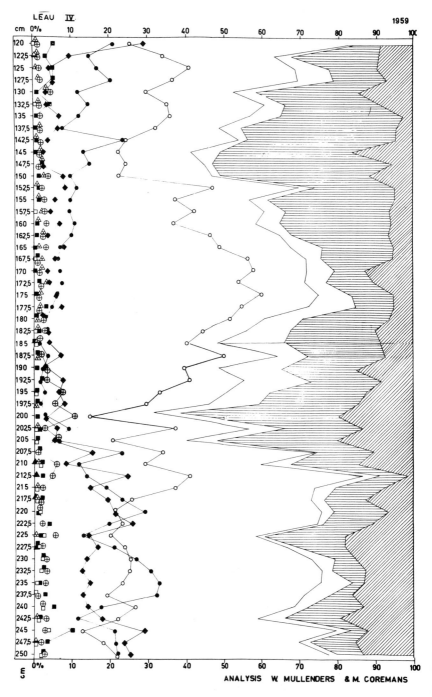

FIG. 5. Pollen diagram of Leau IV.

represented; only *Corylus avellana* reaches 9 per cent. However, at 150 cm, AP recedes again, as well as *Corylus*, the NAP increases to 60 per cent, especially the Cyperaceae. The following are observed: *Empetrum, Botrychium, Lycopodium annotinum* L. and *L. clavatum* and *Ephedra distachya* L. The cold period of the 150 to 130 cm layer may perhaps also correspond with the Piottino-oscillation. The fact that at Leau the NAP extension is well indicated, in contradistinction to the pingo diagrams of High Belgium, may be explained by the presence of a lake and thus of a great space devoid of arboreal vegetation. The general pollen rain of all the surrounding country could thus be easily captured. On the other hand, the ramparts of the little pingos of High Belgium were probably covered by a denser tree and shrub vegetation than the intervening space between them. Here also radiocarbon dates are needed.

Age of the depression

The pollen analysis shows that the oldest sediments of the Leau depression are of Alleröd age, between 10,000 and 9,000 BC. No trace of Eemian pollen has been found (*Picea, Abies, Carpinus*), nor of typical Eemian spectra, nor early Pleistocene pollen.

The depression was formed just before the Alleröd time. The absence in the depression of the Würm loess which is found everywhere around corroborates this conclusion. If the depression had existed during the Würm glaciation, it would have been a very favourable accumulation trap for the loess. The very small deltas are another proof of the recent origin of the depression. The formation of the depression during the Older Dryas can only be explained by the pingo hypothesis. Of course this would mean that we are in the presence of the greatest pingo of this type known until now, and one can question which particular circumstances made it possible. We think that favourable conditions existed in that the underlying Landenian sands are a very important water reservoir, intensely used now by wells and as indicated by the active springs. These sands crop out more than 10 km to the south and must have given an important spring outflow even during the cold Dryas. These springs made the formation of a great pingo or the junction of different small pingos possible.

Evolution of the depression

During the formation of the pingo or pingos, the meltwaters continuously wore away the uplifted sediments, and during the decay of the pingo, meltwaters eroded the gully draining the depression to the Gette River.

After the melting of the pingo, a lake existed in which the gyttja was deposited registering the climatic evolution of the Alleröd, the Late Dryas, and the Preboreal times.

The outflow of the lake eroded the gully continuously and the lake was finally drained; peat growth started at the end of the Boreal and continued during part of the Atlantic. Like all the Middle Belgian valleys (Mullenders and Gullentops 1956), the Gette began alluviating during the Atlantic, an alluviation which was started or accelerated by the Omalian (4,000 BC) and later Neolithic agriculture. By this loamy alluviation, the outlet of the depression became blocked and a new lake came into being. During inundation the loamy water of the Gette even flowed into the lake and the outlet functioned as an inlet, building up the west delta. The finest clay decanted on the lake bottom forming the uppermost loamy mud layer. At the same time, soil erosion along the southern brook occasioned the other small south delta.

Thus, we come to the conclusion that this huge depression has been formed at the end of the Würm glaciation and more precisely, before the Alleröd oscillation, during the Older Dryas, after the Bölling oscillation.

REFERENCES CITED

Florschutz, F., and Van Oye, E., 1939, Recherches analytiques de pollen dans la région des Hautes Fagnes belges: Biologisch Jaarboek, Kon. W. Gen. Dodonaea, p. 227-234.

Mullenders, W., and Gullentops, F., 1956, Evolution de la végétation et de la plaine alluviale de la Dyle à Louvain, depuis le Pléni-Würm: Ac. R. Belgique, Cl. Sc., 5e sér., v. 42, p. 1123-1137.

Mullenders, W., and Haesendonck, Fr., 1963, Note préliminaire sur la palynologie des pingos du Plateau des Tailles (Belgique): Annals of Geomorphology, v. 7, p. 165-168.

Pissart, A., 1956, L'origine périglaciaire des viviers des Hautes Fagnes: Ann. Soc. Géol. de Belgique, v. 74, b., p. 119-131.

———, 1963, Les traces de "pingos" du Pays de Galle (Grande Bretagne) et du Plateau des Hautes Fagnes (Belgique): Annals of Geomorphology, v. 7, p. 147-164.

Poncelet, L., and Martin, H., 1947, Esquisse climatologique de la Belgique: Inst. R. Météor. de Belgique, Mém., v. 27, 265 p.

Schoeters, C., 1958, Regionale studie van de Getestreek in vochtig Haspengouw: Thesis Fac. Sciences, Univ. Louvain, 120 p.

Slotboom, C., 1963, Comparative geomorphological and palynological investigation of the pingos (viviers) in Hautes Fagnes (Belgium) and the Mardellen in the Gutland (Luxemburg), Utrecht, 41 p.

VANDER HAMMEN, TH., 1953, Late glacial flora and periglacial phenomena in the Netherlands: Leidse Geol. Meded., v. 17, p. 73-185.

VAN GIJZEL, P., 1961, Autofluorescence and age of some fossil pollen and spores: Kon. Ned. Akad. Wetensch., Proc. ser. B, v. 64, p. 56-63.

ZOLLER, H., 1960, Pollenanalytische Untersuchungen zur Vegetationsgeschichte der insubrischen Schweiz: Mém. Soc. Helvétique des Sc. nat., v. 83, Mém. 2, p. 45-156.

A PECULIAR TYPE OF
FOSSIL ICE FISSURE

PAUL MACAR
University of Liège
Liège, Belgium

ABSTRACT. Numerous periglacial features of various kinds have been observed in several sand quarries on the plateau near Liège and Namur (Belgium) where ancient deposits of the Meuse River and of its main tributary, the Ourthe, overlie sand of Tertiary age. The most common are thin filled fissures (*fentes à remplissage*). They crosscut the thick gravel beds of the terraces, where present, and terminate in the sand below. They are extremely narrow (only a few cm wide) and extend to a depth of 10 to 12 m. Some have been traced 50 m along the strike. More than 70 of these fissures have been studied. The filling, made up mostly or entirely of clay, is quite different from the enclosing sediments and also is different from the overlying beds. The overlying beds are made of loams of different ages, mostly late Würm (Wisconsin), but some are considered to be at least Mindel (Kansan) in age. In the larger fissures, the filling is very thinly banded parallel to the walls, the banding being due to "interbedded" sandy layers.

Most of the fissures are vertical, but some are inclined from 35° to 55°. Some have an abrupt change in the trend of inclinations, with no change in thickness of the filling. One or two fissures have caused the adjacent gravel layers to be slightly upturned. These filled fissures are thought to be fossil ice wedges, but narrower and deeper than the usual ones. As far as we know, ice fissures of this kind have not been described previously.

RÉSUMÉ. De nombreux phénomènes périglaciaires de types divers ont été découverts dans des carrières de sable sur les plateaux voisins de Liège et de Namur (65 km à l'ouest de Liège). Le sable d'âge tertiaire y est recouvert de graviers de la Meuse et de son affluent principal, l'Ourthe. Les plus abondants parmi ces phénomènes sont des "fentes à remplissage," très étroites et s'effilant vers le bas. Elles traversent les bancs de gravier des terrasses, là où ces bancs sont présents, et se terminent dans le sable sous-jacent. Leur largeur n'est en général que de quelques cm, mais leur profondeur peut atteindre 10 à 12 m. Certaines furent suivies en direction sur une cinquantaine de mètres.

Plus de 70 de ces fentes ont été étudiées. Leur remplissage le plus fréquent est une argile brune, très différente des sédiments des épontes comme de ceux qui surmontent la fente. Ces derniers sont constitués de limons d'âge divers, la plupart datés du Würm, quelques-uns toutefois considérés comme d'âge Mindel. Dans les fentes les plus larges, le remplissage est finement zoné parallèlement aux parois, par suite surtout de la présence de lentilles sableuses interstratifiées.

La plupart des fissures sont verticales, mais certaines ont une forte pente, et quelques-unes, très rares, une pente faible. Plusieurs sont nettement coudées, sans que le remplissage s'en montre affecté. Une ou deux fissures ont provoqué une légère incurvation vers le haut des couches de gravier qu'elles traversent.

Ces fentes à remplissage sont considérées commes des fentes de gel fossiles d'une espèce particulière, plus étroites et plus profondes que les fentes en coin usuelles. A notre connaissance, des fentes de gel de ce type n'avaient pas encore été décrites.

CONTENTS

FIGURE

INTRODUCTION

Narrow fissures a few centimetres in width and up to 13 m in length occur in Oligocene sand outcropping in quarries on the plateau near Liège and Namur (65 km west of Liège) in Belgium. The most common filling is a brown clay that is quite different from the beds that are crosscut by the fissures or from the overlying sediments. In the widest of the fissures the clay filling is distinctly banded parallel to the sides. Most of the fissures are vertical, but some dip steeply, and a very few are slightly inclined. The fissures crosscut, when present, Quaternary gravel of the highest terrace of the Meuse River or of the Ourthe, its main tributary. They are sharply overlain by loess of Würm (Wisconsin) age.

From 1949 to 1963, my colleagues and I observed more than 70 of these thin fissures while studying associated periglacial features (Leckwyjck and Macar 1949, Leckwyjck and Macar 1951, Leckwyjck and Macar 1960, Macar and Leckwyjck 1958, Manil 1959, Manil, Leckwyjck and Macar 1960, Manil 1960, and Pissart and Macar 1963). In addition to these in Belgium, there have been described similar fissures from the southern Netherlands, 50 km north of Liège (Kimpe 1950, and oral communication, G. C. Maarleveld 1965). Fissures of the same kind have been reported from Poland (J. Dylik 1952). The writer recently observed fissures similar to those described in this paper in Quebec, Canada (Macar 1964), and also observed such fissures in Quaternary gravel in the high plateau of Portugal.

Deep, thin, filled fissures of this kind seem more than a mere local phenomenon. Therefore, it is worthwhile presenting a summary of what is known.

PROPERTIES OF THE FISSURES

Dimensions

The fissures are, as a rule, very thin, much more so than typical fossil ice wedges. Only a few are more than 12 cm in width, and the greatest width occurs at one upper end. On the other hand, their depth is greater than most ice wedges, as much as 13 m. They thin very slowly downward, and in some instances the thickness may remain the same for several metres. One small fissure was observed in its entirety and was 13 m long. This fissure thins to a feather edge on each end. It appears in cross section as a very elongated lens.

The fissures are of different sizes: some small ones are very thin and only a metre or so deep, but the greatest number of them extend to depths of several metres. About 10 out of 70 extend downward more than 10 m (Figs. 1 and 2), and the base cannot be seen. Many have their upper parts removed by erosion; therefore, their total depths may be as much as 15m. In plan view a few fissures were traced continuously for a distance of 20 to 30 m. One fissure seen on two opposite quarry faces is certainly more than 50 m long.

Structure

About 75 per cent of the observed fissures are vertical or nearly so. Most of the others are inclined from 35° to 55°, and in some instances have an abrupt change in slope. A few are only slightly inclined, and some are nearly horizontal. The nearly horizontal ones are always small. In quarries where directions of several fissures could be measured, they appear to be about parallel or distributed in two distinct directions.

Several fissures bifurcate downward (Fig. 2) or laterally. A few cross each other, and in many instances the filling or a displacement

Fig. 1. Great fissure with distinctive zoning of the filling. The pick (80 cm long) gives the scale. Quarry of the Roman Shaft, Fontaine, 11 km west of Liège.

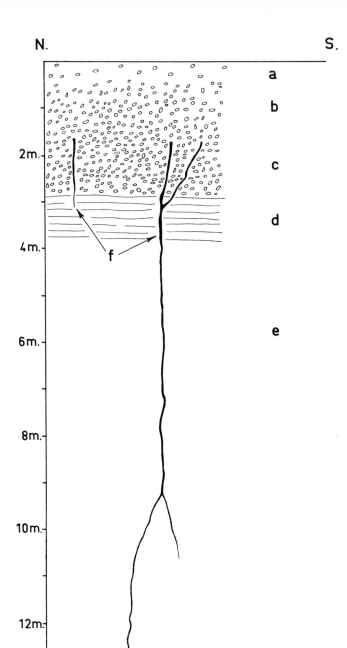

Fig. 2. Two fissures, one large and bifurcated, and the other small, in early Quaternary gravel. (a) Loam with pebbles; (b) fluviatile gravels affected by later solifluction; (c) fluviatile gravel, *in situ*; (d), (e) Tertiary sand, upper part (d) stratified with seams of clay; (f) filled fissures. Quarry of Sart-Haguet, Boncelles, 5 km south of Liège.

shows that one is more recent than the other. The sets of fissures are not evenly distributed; rather abundant at some places, they may be totally lacking in the next hundred metres.

Filling

About 75 per cent of the fissures are filled with a brown plastic clay, very homogeneous in the thin fissures, but "interbedded" with sandier and lighter streaks in the larger ones (Fig. 3). Near the top of the larger fissures the clay sometimes grades into coarser, sandy material, including small pebbles in some instances. The filling is quite distinct from the beds cut by the fissures or the beds overlying the fissures.

Twenty-five per cent of the fissures are filled with a sandier, light grey clay. Both types of filling may have local reddish-brown or red streaks at depth because of limonitic or hematitic material.

Granulometric analyses of the brown clay fillings indicate, in several instances, a peculiar sorting. There is an important and sometimes very high percentage of very pure clay, that is, smaller than two microns in size, practically no particles between 2 and 20 microns, and, for the rest, mostly grains of size between 20 and 200 microns.

The brown and light grey fillings usually occur in separate fissures that in some cases cross and even displace each other. In only a few instances both fillings have been observed in the same fissure. In one case both types of fillings were adjacent, in another case one filling was banded on both sides by the other type, and in a third case one of the fillings replaced the other along the length of the fissure. But, if the two fillings represent quite distinctive types, it has not been possible to ascribe to them a definite relative age.

Two more indications are given by local discoveries: a small pebble occurring at depth of several metres in a thin fissure proves that this fissure has been open at least wide enough to allow the pebble to drop. Elsewhere it was noted that a fissure cut through a line of pebbles, and one of the pebbles extended across the fissure. The fissure, therefore, never reached a width of 5 cm, the width of the pebble. From these two observations it may be concluded that the fissures have certainly been open, but as a rule not widely.

The fissures cut through different materials; they cross boundaries between gravels and sands, go through beds or lenses of gravel in the sands, or in some cases, seams of clay (Fig. 2). Their width does not vary where they cross the boundary between different beds.

Fig. 3. Detail of fissure in Fig. 1. Zoning and overhanging wall with salients and re-entrants, some with straight sides. The rule (50 cm) gives the scale. Quarry of the Roman Shaft, Fontaine, 11 km west of Liège.

In most of the quarries studied, a substratum of chalk or of limestone occurs below the sand in which the fissures are located. One suggestion of the origin is that the fissures are due to solution. This can be ruled out because all the fissures terminate before reaching the soluble substratum. Undisturbed sand is present between the base of the fissure and the underlying chalk limestone. Moreover, the fissures are filled with material foreign to the sediments that they crosscut.

The following peculiarities have convinced us that, despite several features uncommon to fossil ice wedges, these special fissures are a type of fossil ice wedge:

(1) In at least three occurrences, the crosscut thin beds of gravel curve slightly upward on each side of the fissure. The fact that such bending does not occur more frequently is probably due to the thinness of the original ice wedges. Also the majority of fissures cross only homogeneous sand, where no deformation can be seen.

(2) Three of the fissures merge vertically or laterally with typical fossil ice wedges, that are V-shaped and filled with mixed material.

(3) In a quarry near Namur, a large (11 m high) typical ice wedge has a sandy filling with angular lumps of sand in the upper part, and thin zones of differently coloured sands, with clay streaks, below. This filling in the lower part is similar to the filling in the fissures under discussion.

(4) One of the clearest fissures cutting the sand layers shows irregular boundaries, with salients and re-entrants having rectilinear sides (Fig. 3). The zoning of the filling butts against them. Such salients and their straight sides could not stand fast in the sand if this were not frozen at the time the fissure formed.

(5) The homogeneity of the fillings, together with the striking difference between them and the materials of their walls, is further proof that these walls were kept firm by being frozen when the fissures opened. If not, the vertical walls, and above all, the overhanging ones in the inclined fissures, would have given away here and there, bringing some of their wall material into the gap. No wall material occurs in the fissures. On the contrary, in the lower part of the fissures where wall material should chiefly be found, the brown clay fissures as a rule show only quite homogeneous clay.

But could not these fissures, instead of being a special kind of ice wedge, just be remnants of typical ice wedges, that is, just their lower parts? We do not think so because there is no similarity between the light coloured, coarse, heterogeneous filling of the few typical ice wedges occurring in the region and the very fine, homogeneous fillings, either grey or brown, of the fissures. Also, there is no similarity between the quick thinning of the ice wedges with depth and the very slow downward thinning of the fissures.

The ability of the fissures to cut all sediments without changing thickness, and the thinness of the fissures, may suggest earthquake origin. The following do not support the earthquake hypothesis: (*a*) traces of lateral push with subsequent upturning of the adjacent sediments; (*b*) the homogeneity and the fineness of the fillings; and (*c*) their frequent vertical zoning indicating, most probably, numerous reopenings of the fissures. Therefore, the earthquake hypothesis is not considered tenable by the authors.

AGE OF THE FISSURES

All of the fissures that can be followed upward are overlain by loess of Würm age. In several quarries, gravel of the oldest terrace of the Meuse crop out between Würm loess and the Oligocene sands. The fissures cross this gravel and are therefore younger. Above the gravel, the fissures also crosscut sand with typical periglacial involutions. These involutions appear syngenetic, and we consider them to date from the very first glaciation. The fissures are, therefore, ascribed to a glaciation that occurred after the very first one (Günz, or earlier if more than four glaciations occurred) and the last one (Würm).

Other observations indicate a Mindel or ante-Mindel age for at least some of the fissures. In the region of Namur, a red complex composed of sand and gravel occurs either above the highest terrace of the Meuse, or directly above the Tertiary sands where this terrace is lacking. The red colour was formed during the Mindel-Riss interglacial, and the complex is therefore to be considered as having at least that age. Some of the fissures and the large fossil ice wedge mentioned earlier can be traced up to the red complex and butt sharply against it. The fissures in this area, therefore, cannot be younger than Mindel.

CONCLUSIONS

A heretofore unreported special type of fossil ice wedge exists in several areas of Belgium and has been noted elsewhere. The fossil ice wedges appear essentially as thin, filled fissures 1 to 13 m in depth and up to 12 centimetres wide in unconsolidated sediments. The filling is mostly of clay and is quite different from the material of the enclosing walls. It is either homogeneous, or, as in the larger fissures, banded parallel to the walls.

As they are formed in maritime (Belgium) and continental (Poland, Quebec) regions, they seem to have occurred under somewhat diverse climatic conditions. But this needs to be checked by further study.

REFERENCES CITED

DYLIK, JAN, 1952, Peryglacjalne struktury w pleistocenie ś'rodkewej Polski (summary: Periglacial structures in the Pleistocene deposits of middle Poland): Biul. Panstwowy Inst. Geol., v. 66, p. 53-113.

KIMPE, W. F. M., 1950, Kryoturbate verschijnselen in het Mioceen bij Brunssum, Zuid-Limburg: Geol. en Mijnbouw, n.s., v. 12, p. 421-422.

LECKWYJK, WILLIAM, VAN, et MACAR, PAUL, 1949, Phémonènes pseudo-tectoniques, la plupart d'origine périglaciaire, dans les dépôts sablo-graveleux dits "Onx" et les terrasses fluviales de la région liégeoise: Soc. Géol. Belgique Ann., v. 73, p. M 3-78.

——, 1951, Nouvelles observations sur des phénomènes périglaciaires dans la région de Liège: Soc. Géol. Belgique Ann., v. 75, p. B 49-72.

——, 1960, Les structures périglaciaires antérieures au Würm en Belgique: Biul. Peryglacjalny, nr. 9, p. 47-59.

MACAR, PAUL, 1964, Observations sur les dépôts quaternaires de la région Beaupré— St-Ferréol (Province de Québec): Cahiers de Géogr. de Québec, Québec, v. 15, p. 95-98.

MACAR, PAUL, et LECKWYJCK, WILLIAM, VAN, 1958, Les fentes à remplissage de la région liégeoise: Soc. Geol. Belgique Ann., v. 81, p. B 359-407.

MANIL, GEORGES, 1959, Observations macromorphologiques, microscopiques et analytiques sur le remplissage des fentes de gel: Soc. Géol. Belgique Ann., v. 81, B 409-421.

MANIL, GEORGES, LECKWYJCK, WILLIAM, VAN, et MACAR, PAUL, 1960, Compte rendu de l'excursion du 10 juin 1959 à Namur et à Liège: Biul. Peryglacjalny, nr. 9, p. 177-185.

——, 1960, Observations sur le remplissage des fentes de gel: Biul. Peryglacjalny, nr. 9, p. 127-134.

PISSART, ALBERT, et MACAR, PAUL, 1963, Fentes à remplissage, poches d'effondrement et variations de faciès dans la sablière du Sart-Haguet (Boncelles): Soc. Géol. Belgique Ann., v. 85, p. B 329-345.

PERIGLACIAL PHENOMENA RECENTLY OBSERVED IN THE TERRACES OF THE SEINE SOUTHEAST OF BONNIÈRES, FRANCE

ELAINE BASSE DE MÉNORVAL
The National Center of Scientific Research
Paris, France

ABSTRACT. Along the south bank of the Seine River, 70 km west of Paris, near Bonnières, new excavations have revealed an old terrace of the Seine, as yet unreported, overlaying Senonian chalk.

This terrace, Riss in age, shows cryoturbations and some single or composite fossil ice wedges filled with loessoid clay-with-flints.

RÉSUMÉ. Des tranchées pratiquées dans la colline de Galicet (région parisienne) m'ont récemment montré l'existence d'une terrasse ancienne de la Seine couvrant la Craie sénonienne et affectée de cryoturbation (involutians de la presle superficielle immiscée *per ascensum* dans la terrasse); des fentes simples ou complexes de glace s'y remarquent, remplies de limon loessoide à silex.

CONTENTS

FIGURE

INTRODUCTION

The slopes of the Galicet hill have remained until today completely sealed off to the investigations of Quaternary scientists. The demands of new construction, however, have necessitated excavations that provide the remarkable exposure mentioned in the discussion which follows.

In this region the lower terrace, which is Würm in age, is well developed and is approximately 20 m above river level. On the north side of the Galicet hill a higher terrace exists, about 55 to 60 m above river level. This higher terrace is Riss in age.

The upper terrace is capped with 1 m of loess. Under the loess is 2.5 m of bright yellow sand and gravel mixed with flint fragments, probably fractured by frost action. These terrace deposits lie on chalk (Senonian C⁷).

The three or four pits excavated towards the top of the slope show some interesting effects of solifluction. The solifluction deposits are modified by the impermeable, marly-chalk substratum and of the effects of cryoturbation, the action which has stirred the sediments of the terrace. The upper layer of the Senonian chalk, probably already stirred before the deposits of the fluvial deposits, has become, under a periglacial climate, a moist, cold, and pasty material which then penetrates *per ascensum* throughout the thickness of the sand and gravel of the terrace. The sand and gravel also become involuted (Fig. 1).

In addition to the involutions many fossil ice wedges exist. The wedges are simple, only rarely complex, composites, with several parallel points as is the case here; their filling is of the subjacent loess-like silt, in which no stratification can be distinguished. The proximity of the most beautiful of these composite ice wedges with the effects of cryoturbation in the mass of the subjacent terrace is spectacular (Fig. 1). Towards the top of the slope these phenomena are more numerous and the best developed. These fossil ice wedges are similar to existing ice wedges in Alaska (Leffingwell 1919). Péwé (1966) shows that ice wedges are actively growing in northern Alaska today where the mean annual temperature is −6° to −8°C, and the snow cover thin.

Involutions are less common in sediments in the Würm terrace in this area. However, in deposits on the Würm terrace of the Seine River, near the village of Moisson and in the village of Bonnières, there are well-marked scallops of cryoturbation and also some fossil ice wedges, although the latter are not very common.

Fig. 1. Exposure of deposits of Riss age on the high terrace of the Seine near Bonnières, France, showing a broad complex fossil ice wedge filled with loess-like silt. Note the involutions of the white chalk into the sands and gravels of the Riss terrace overlying the santonian chalk.

REERENCES CITED

LEFFINGWELL, E. DE K., 1919, The Canning River region, northern Alaska: US Geol. Survey Prof. Paper 109, 251 p.

PÉWÉ, T. L., 1966, Ice wedges in Alaska: Classification, distribution, and climatic significance: Proc. Intern. Permafrost Conf., Nat. Acad. Sci.—Nat. Research Council Pub. No. 1287, p. 76-81.

FOSSIL ICE WEDGE POLYGONS IN SOUTHEAST ESSEX, ENGLAND

RUTH GRUHN and ALAN LYLE BRYAN
Dept. of Anthropology
University of Alberta
Edmonton, Alberta, Canada

ABSTRACT. Striking frost structures formed in permafrost near the glacial margins in Essex, southeastern England, in Pleistocene time. Fossil ice wedge polygons in old river terraces are visible in aerial photographs. The fossil ice wedges and other periglacial features are exposed in commercial gravel pits. Downwarping of the gravel adjacent to the wedges occurs. Study of the local geochronology in order to date a Lower Paleolithic site at one gravel pit revealed an interglacial soil formed in the upper part of the fill of one fossil ice wedge. The soil is overlain by loess. It is suggested that the ice wedge polygons most probably formed during the Penultimate (Riss) glaciation when the ice sheet halted about 10 miles farther north in Essex.

RÉSUMÉ. A l'époque pléistocène, des structures de gel se sont formées dans le pergélisol voisin des marges glaciaires, dans l'Essex, au sud-est de l'Angleterre. On peut apercevoir des polygones à coin de glace fossiles sur des photographies aériennes d'anciennes terrasses fluviatiles. On découvre les coins de glace fossiles et d'autres traits périglaciaires dans des carrières commerciales. Au voisinage d'un coin, les graviers sont gauchis vers le bas. Une étude de chronologie locale destinée à dater un site du Paléolithique inférieur découvert dans une carrière a révélé un sol interglaciaire formé dans la partie supérieure d'une fente en coin fossile. Ce sol avait été recouvert de loess. Les auteurs supposent que ces polygones à coin de glace se sont tout probablement formés durant l'avant-dernière glaciation (Riss), au moment où la calotte glaciaire s'arrêtait à environ dix milles (16 km) plus au nord.

ZUSAMMENFASSUNG. Während des Pleistozäns enstanden im Permafrost unweit des Gletscherrandes in Essex im Südosten von England merkwürdige Eisstrukturen. Auf Flugaufnahmen alter Flussterrassen sind diluviale Frostspalten als polygonförmige Gebilde erkennbar. Frostspalten und andere periglaziale Gebilde werden auch in Kiesgruben aufgedeckt. Das den Frostspalten angrenzende Geröl ist abwärts verlagert. Geochronologische Untersuchungen, die zur Datierung einer frühpaläolithischen Fundstätte angestellt wurden, erwiesen im oberen Teil der Ausfüllung solcher fossilen Frostspalten einen während einer Zwischeneiszeit entstandenen Boden. Dieser Boden ist von Löss überlagert. Man nimmt an, dass die Frostspaltenpolygone wahrscheinlich während des vorletzten Glazials (Riss) entstanden sind, und zwar zu einer Zeit, da der Rand der Eisdecke sich etwa 10 Meilen weiter nördlich in Essex befand.

CONTENTS

FIGURE

INTRODUCTION

This paper presents a detailed description of the most striking fossil frost structures in the Pleistocene deposits of southeast Essex in the region north and northeast of Southend-on-Sea, between the Thames and the Blackwater estuaries (Fig. 1). The structures were studied as a part of a geochronology project to date an archaeological site.

Most of the region studied is relatively low-lying coastal plain. In the area between the Thames and the Crouch rivers, high land is limited on the west to the Rayleigh Hills, extending above 200 feet OD (Ordnance Datum); and on the south to the ridge on which the city of Southend is situated, extending more than 100 feet OD in the western part. To the north and east of these landmarks the level of the land decreases gradually to 10 feet OD or less, on the large alluvial islands of the North Sea coast. Between the Crouch and the Blackwater rivers the relief is greater, and most of the land is higher than 50 feet OD except within a few miles of the coast where the surface drops off steeply into low marshy country at about 10 feet OD or less. In this region Pleistocene gravels are widely distributed (Fig. 1). There are some patches of gravel on the Rayleigh Hills at more than 200 feet OD, and much of the city of Southend is situated on a thick (up to 40 feet) deposit of gravel with surface level at 90 to 80 feet OD. Elsewhere, gravel deposits are generally about 10 to 20 feet in thickness, while their surfaces vary in a regular manner between 70 feet above OD and 50 feet below OD. A series of river terraces have been postulated in a separate study of the geochronology of the region. Throughout much of the

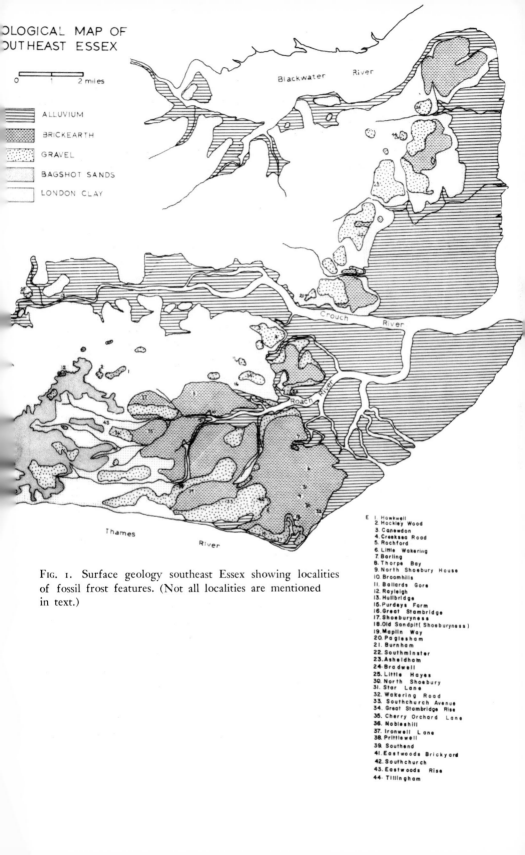

GEOLOGICAL MAP OF
SOUTHEAST ESSEX

0   1   2 miles

ALLUVIUM
BRICKEARTH
GRAVEL
BAGSHOT SANDS
LONDON CLAY

Blackwater   River

Crouch   River

Roach   RIVER

Thames   River

FIG. 1. Surface geology southeast Essex showing localities
of fossil frost features. (Not all localities are mentioned
in text.)

E 1. Hawkwell
2. Hockley Wood
3. Canewdon
4. Creeksea Road
5. Rochford
6. Little Wakering
7. Barling
8. Thorpe Bay
9. North Shoebury House
10. Broomhills
11. Ballards Gore
12. Rayleigh
13. Hullbridge
15. Purdeys Farm
16. Great Stambridge
17. Shoeburyness
18. Old Sandpit (Shoeburyness)
19. Maplin Way
20. Paglesham
21. Burnham
22. Southminster
23. Asheldham
24. Bradwell
25. Little Hayes
30. North Shoebury
31. Star Lane
32. Wakering Road
33. Southchurch Avenue
34. Great Stambridge Rise
35. Cherry Orchard Lane
36. Nobleshill
37. Ironwell Lane
38. Prittlewell
39. Southend
41. Eastwoods Brickyard
42. Southchurch
43. Eastwoods Rise
44. Tillingham

region east and north of Southend the gravels are covered by 10 feet or more of brickearth. In two areas, one west of the Southend airport (Localities 35, 41, 43) and another extending north and west of Shoebury (Localities 8, 31, 42), analysis of the brickearth has shown that it is graded like loess. The fossil ice wedge polygons and the loess are evidence for periglacial conditions in the region during the past.

DESCRIPTION OF ICE WEDGE POLYGONS

The locations of identifiable fossil ice wedge polygons in the region of southeast Essex are shown in Figure 1. Figure 2 presents scale drawings of patterned ground traced from aerial photographs which were available only for the area between the Thames and the Crouch rivers. Fossil ice wedges were sectioned in the Creeksea Road gravel pits near Canewdon (Locality 4, Creeksea Road in Fig. 1), Barling (Locality 7), Asheldham (Locality 23), and Tillingham (Locality 44); reportedly at Purdey's Farm (Locality 15); and identifiable at north Shoebury (Locality 30), Rochford (Locality 5), and Southminster (Locality 22). The clearest features will be described.

Ice wedge polygons were widespread in the Creeksea Sand and Ballast Company gravel pit along Creeksea Road in the east part of Canewdon parish. These gravels appear to be a remnant of a broad 40 foot terrace north of the Roach River. The surface level of the gravel at the site is about 40 feet OD, sloping slightly down to the southeast. The lower 10 feet of gravel is finer in grade, more sandy, and a paler colour than the upper few feet of gravel, occurring in a matrix of somewhat loamy sand slightly cemented by iron oxide. The gravel is locally overlain by up to 4 feet of flood loam.

The pattern of fossil ice wedge polygons revealed by crop marks in the field adjacent to the gravel pit is shown in Figure 3, drawn from an enlarged aerial photograph. The pattern is suborthogonal. Most of the individual polygons are tetragonal; diameters are between 25 and 50 feet. It may be seen that the fossil ice wedges vary in width; the widest may have been enlarged by run-off during the thaw (Hopkins et al. 1955, Church, Péwé, and Andresen 1965).

Within the gravel pit fossil ice wedges were sectioned transversely and longitudinally. Figures 4 and 5 illustrate a cross section of a fossil ice wedge exposed on the northwest side of the area shown in Figure 3. Because of slump on this face of the pit, the wedge could not be cleared to its base; 12 feet of the wedge was exposed. In cross section the wedge is funnel-shaped, with a long narrow stem or neck that may extend into the London Clay bedrock, the surface of which is about

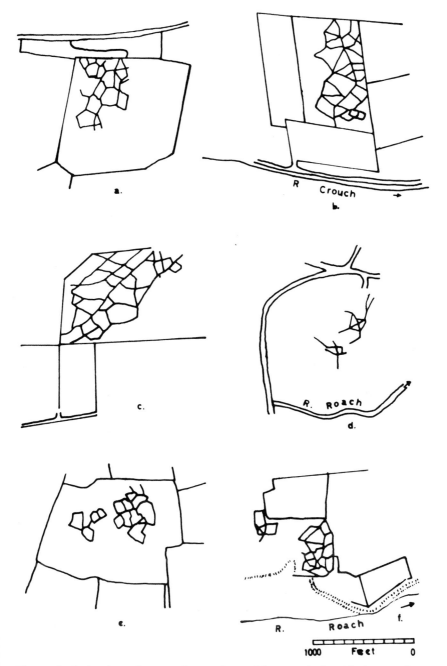

FIG. 2. Scale drawings of patterned ground traced from vertical aerial photographs.

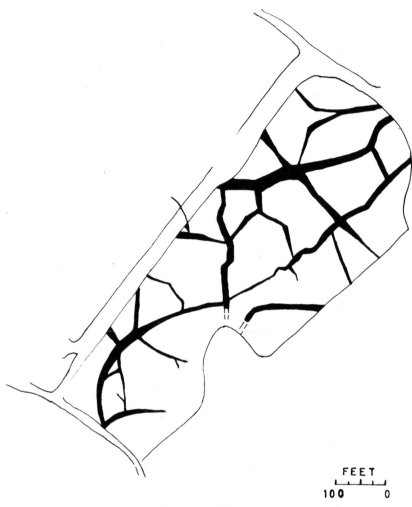

FEET

100   0

Fɪɢ. 3. Scale drawing from enlarged aerial photograph of patterned ground at locality 4 (Creeksea Road pit near Canewdon). Arrow is location of Figures 4 and 5.

FIG. 4. Close-up of fossil ice wedge at Creeksea Road pit. Scale is in inches.

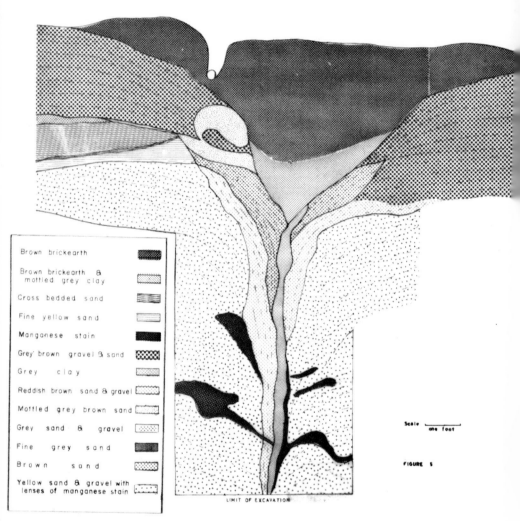

Brown brickearth

Brown brickearth &
mottled grey clay

Cross bedded sand

Fine yellow sand

Manganese stain

Grey brown gravel & sand

Grey clay

Reddish brown sand & gravel

Mottled grey brown sand

Grey sand & gravel

Fine grey sand

Brown sand

Yellow sand & gravel with
lenses of manganese stain

Scale one foot

FIGURE 5

LIMIT OF EXCAVATION

FIG. 5. Cross section to scale of fossil ice wedge at Creeksea Road pit. Arrow on Figure 3 indicates approximate location of cross section.

6 feet below the limit of excavation. The maximum width of this wedge is about 6 feet at the top.

The gravel strata adjacent and within a foot or so of this wedge (Fig. 5) are warped downward and steeply inclined to become almost parallel to the wedge border. The matrix of the border zone within the fossil wedge is a mixture of sand and clay, mottled grey, yellow-brown, or reddish-brown in colour, which appears to have been derived from the upper part of the reddish gravel.

The fill within the fossil ice wedges in the Creeksea Road pit consisted mainly of clay mixed with sand. This material is largely derived from the superficial clayey loam which must have washed in after the ice had disappeared. The colour of the fill—grey in the lowermost part, becoming a dark brown at the top of the wedge—suggests gleying and subsequent oxidation of the upper part of the fill. A study of samples in thin section showed that the fill is indeed a mixture of materials, both fine-grained and coarse-grained materials occurring in juxtaposition in the matrix. The upper part of the deposit is much weathered, and weathered material mixed with unweathered material occurs deep within the wedge. This mixture of materials probably occurred when the ground was still partially frozen.

Far down into the wedge (Fig. 5) in the narrow "stem," the grey sandy clay contained numerous fragmentary remains of plants. Mr. Alan Eddy of the Department of Botany of the British Museum (Natural History) was able to identify three species of mosses: *Bryum pseudotriquetrum*, *Depanocladus* sp.? *aduncus*? and *Cratoneuran filicinum*. He informed us that these species are not in themselves indicative of arctic conditions, but may occur in either arctic or temperate climates under wet conditions. With the description of peat or turf growing on mud above the ice mass in the wedges in mind (Leffingwell 1915, Paterson 1940), one may envisage such plant material slipping down into this wedge upon thawing of the ice mass. Samples of the clay were examined for pollen grains, but none were found.

About 1 mile south of Barling Church, on Baldwin's Farm, is a large gravel pit. The gravels are part of a broad 25-foot terrace extending north from Shoebury through Paglesham to the Crouch River. At Baldwin's Farm these gravels have yielded an Acheulian industry with faunal remains, and a full report on the geochronology of the site has been prepared. The surface of the gravel deposit is about 16 feet OD, sloping down towards the sea wall to the east; the bench of London Clay is about 0 to −5 feet OD, also sloping down towards the east. The lower 5 to 10 feet of the gravel, yellow-grey and very sandy, with frequent large lenses of sand, shows finely laminated crossbedding resulting from cut and fill action of shifting channels. The upper part of the gravel is coarser grained, and is slightly cemented in a matrix of reddish-brown loamy sand. The gravels are covered by 2 to 4 feet of loess, which our studies indicate pertains to the Last Glaciation.

The available aerial photograph of Baldwin's Farm reveals no indication of the fossil ice wedge polygon pattern which has been exposed by the operations in the gravel pit. The manager of the pit, however, commented that he had noticed that crop marks in the cultivated field to the south at the beginning of a new crop traced out the pattern of thick clay seams orientated in various directions.

In 1962 a fossil ice wedge trending in a northeast direction had been left standing by the excavators as a series of ridges and "islands," giving both longitudinal and cross-sectional views of the wedge. The total length of this wedge as exposed, and including the collapsed and missing portions, measured about 160 feet. The maximum exposed depth of the wedge was about 12 feet; the maximum width, near the top, was about 6 feet. The form of this wedge is similar to that described from near Canewdon: in cross section, funnel-shaped, with long narrow stem. The wedge was flanked by a layer of gravel and reddish sand, about 6 feet to 12 inches in width, the pebbles maintaining an orientation parallel to the sides of the wedge. Evidence of small-scale faulting can be seen adjacent to the neck of the wedge. The fill within the wedge consisted of a mixture of sand and clay, grey in the lower part of the stem, a mottled grey and reddish-brown in the lower part of the wedge, and a reddish brown in the upper part of the wedge. These colour changes appeared to be horizons of a soil and suggested that weathering of the upper part of the fill had occurred subsequent to the thawing and filling of the wedge by a sandy clay flood loam-like deposit which must have overlain the gravel at the time of thawing, although no remnant of it is now found outside the fossil ice wedge cavities in this pit. Thin section analysis of a sample from the upper part of the wedge indicated that the weathering had proceeded to the stage of a parabraunerde verging on a braunlehm, a type of soil which forms under very warm humid conditions (Cornwall 1958, p. 103), perhaps during an interglacial period.

Along the south face of the pit, about 10 feet east of this large wedge, a deep vertical line of up-ended pebbles was observed in the gravel. Several smaller examples of this type of frost crack feature were noted in this pit; they may be remnants of incipient ice wedges.

In the east end of the pit, where the thickness of the gravel is about 10 feet and the deposit consists mostly of sand and fine gravel, there is considerable distortion and festooning by frost action. Several small wedge-shaped features were observed in this zone, and it was noted that the mixture of sand and clay filling the wedges was also contorted. In this section the distorted laminations of pebbles, sand, and clay were highly coloured by the stains of manganese and iron oxides.

DISCUSSION

Ice wedge polygons are now widely distributed in regions of permafrost, and many studies of these features have been made (Leffingwell 1915, Paterson 1940, Black 1954, Hopkins *et al.* 1955, Washburn 1956, Drew and Tedrow 1962, Lachenbruch 1962).

The phenomenon of fossil ice wedges is reliable evidence for permafrost, which in arctic regions at present has a distribution mainly north of $0°C$ mean annual temperature isotherm. Péwé (1966) notes that ice wedges are actively growing only when the mean annual temperature is colder than $-6°$ to $-8°C$. Conditions for permafrost and active ice wedges could occur in Britain only during a period of major glaciation. We must therefore envisage a periglacial environment for the lowlands of southeast Essex during a glacial stage of the Pleistocene, when the North Sea bed was dry land and Britain was connected to the Continent. Fossil ice wedge polygons have been reported elsewhere in Britain. Shotton (1962) describes such patterned ground revealed in aerial photographs of crop marks in East Anglia and the Midlands. Dimbleby (1952) found similar features in Yorkshire which he dated to some glaciation earlier than the Last Glacial. Fossil ice wedges were exposed in the gravel at the Travellers Rest Pit near Cambridge (Paterson 1940). As in the southeast Essex examples, the gravel layers adjacent to the wedge cavities are distorted downward. These wedges have been dated to a pre-Würm glaciation (Dimbleby 1952, p. 5). Fossil ice wedge polygons are known from the lower Thames valley. Dewey (1936, p. 44-6) unknowingly described fossil ice wedges in Rickson's Pit, near Swanscombe.

Paterson (1940) describes the phenomenon of downwarping pebble beds adjacent to the walls of fossil ice wedges in the Travellers Rest Pit near Cambridge, and attributes it to slumping of the gravel adjacent to the walls of the wedge as the ice mass thawed and retracted from the walls. D. M. Hopkins, T. L. Péwé, and A. L. Washburn (personal communications 1965) all agree with this interpretation from their observations on collapsing ice wedges, and believe that both downwarping strata and microfaulting adjacent to wedge necks can be explained by slow slumping (Péwé *et al.* 1965, p. 32) during and after thawing, without the involvement of lateral pressures (Church, Péwé, and An-

361

dresen 1965).

Dating of the fossil ice wedges exposed in southeast Essex must be based upon analysis of their stratigraphic position. The flood loam in the wedge fill at Barling was weathered, apparently in place, to a para-braunerde soil. This evidence reveals an important paleoclimatological sequence subsequent to redeposition of the fossiliferous artifact-bearing gravels: (*a*) periglacial conditions with ice wedge formation, (*b*) filling with the flood loam after the ice wedges melted, (*c*) interglacial or very warm interstadial weathering when the climate was much warmer than now, and (*d*) arctic conditions with loess deposition.

Also, at Purdey's Farm and North Shoebury, the fossil ice wedges are overlain unconformably by loess of the Last Glacial, and it is apparent that the ice wedges pertain to an earlier cold phase separated from the later period of loess deposition. Late Middle Acheulian hand axes and the fauna in the Barling gravels suggested that occupation by man occurred during the final part of the Great Interglacial or possibly an interstadial of the Penultimate Glacial. The Barling wedges must therefore be dated to the Penultimate (Riss, Saale, Gipping) Glacial, and as the other two localities pertain to the same terrace they most likely formed at the same time. At Canewdon, Asheldham, Tillingham, and Rochford, the fossil ice wedges were filled with material of the present superficial deposit and no overlying loess has been identified; these wedges could pertain to a later major period of glaciation than the others, but their similarity in size and form argues for con-temporaneity with the others.

REFERENCES CITED

BLACK, R. F., 1954, Permafrost: A review: Geol. Soc. America Bull., v. 65, p. 839-956.
CHURCH, R. E., PÉWÉ, T. L., and ANDRESEN, M. J., 1965, Origin and environmental significance of large-scale patterned ground, Donnelly Dome area, Alaska: US Army Cold Regions Res. and Eng. Lab. Res. Rept. 159, 71 p.
CORNWALL, IAN, 1958, Soils for the archaeologist: New York, Macmillan, 230 p.
DEWEY, HENRY, 1936, The Palaeolithic deposits of the Lower Thames Valley: Geol. Soc. London Quart. Jour., v. 88, p. 35-56.
DIMBLEBY, G. W., 1952, Pleistocene ice wedges in northeast Yorkshire: Jour. Soil Sci., v. 3, p. 1-19.
DREW, J. V., and TEDROW, J. C. F., 1962, Arctic soil classification and patterned ground: Arctic, v. 15, p. 109-116.
HOPKINS, D. M., KARLSTROM, T. N. V., et al., 1955, Permafrost and ground water in Alaska: US Geol. Survey Prof. Paper 264-F, p. 113-146.
LACHENBRUCH, A. H., 1962, Mechanics of thermal contraction cracks and ice wedge polygons in permafrost: Geol. Soc. America Spec. Paper 70, 65 p.
LEFFINGWELL, E. DE K., 1915, Ground-ice wedges, the dominant form of ground ice on the north coast of Alaska: Jour. Geol., v. 23, p. 635-654.

PATERSON, T. T., 1940, The effects of frost action and solifluction around Baffin Bay and in the Cambridge district: Geol. Soc. London Quart. Jour., v. 96, p. 99-130.

PÉWÉ, T. L., 1966, Ice-wedges in Alaska: Classification, distribution, and climatic significance: Proc. Intern. Permafrost Conf., Nat. Acad. Sci.—Nat. Res. Council Pub. No. 1287, p. 76-81.

PÉWÉ, T. L., NICHOLS, D. R., FERRIANS, O. V., and KARLSTROM, T. N. V., 1965, Guide book for central and south central Alaska: INQUA (VII Int. Assoc. Quat. Res.), 141 p.

SHOTTON, F. W., 1962, The physical background of Britain in the Pleistocene: Advanc. of Sci., v. 21, p. 193-206.

WASHBURN, A. L., 1956, Classification of patterned ground and a review of suggested origins: Geol. Soc. America Bull., v. 67, p. 823-866.

SLOPE DEVELOPMENT
AFFECTED BY FROST FISSURES
AND THERMAL EROSION

JAN DYLIK
Institute of Geography
University of Łódź
Łódź, Poland

ABSTRACT. A valley slope of Würm age, composed mainly of the rhythmically bedded slope deposits, exhibits in its vertical profile two fossil slopes. At the bottom of the younger one a block, 10 m or so in length, was exhumed. The block is composed of the rhythmically bedded deposits and broke off from a steep periglacial valley slope by undercutting by a channel of the braided river. On the surface of permafrost existing at that time in the described area a net of polygonal frost fissures developed. As a result of the thermal erosion occurring in the places where river waters came into contact with the slope cut in permafrost, thermoerosional niches were formed. Development of the niches contributed greatly to the undercutting of the river bank. Thus, when the thermoerosional niches approached the fissure parallel to the bank, the block broke off along it. Subsequent vigorous processes buried the block under a cover of slope deposits, which in turn were overlain by river sediments. This explains the preservation of the permafrost block. Recent occurrences of the described phenomenon are rather common in Alaska and Siberia, but this is the first recognition of the phenomenon in Pleistocene time.

RÉSUMÉ. Dans la vallée de la Mroga en Pologne centrale, près du village de Walewice, on a étudié un glacis d'accumulation formé pendant la phase froide du dernier Würm. Le glacis, composé de sable et de limons lités d'une façon périodique, a été formé par la congélifluxion et surtout le ruissellement diffus. La surface du glacis, recouverte de dépôts postérieurs, descend très doucement vers l'axe de la vallée. Sur une distance qui varie de quelques dizaines de mètres à 100 m et davantage, la surface fossile du glacis plonge brusquement sous les dépôts fluviatiles. Au-dessous de la limite entre les dépôts de versant et la nappe fluviatile, on retrouve le versant fossile abrupt et presque vertical. On a trouvé au pied du versant des blocs de matériel lité semblable à celui qui compose le glacis. Les blocs, de quelques mètres de longueur et de quelques décimètres jusqu'à un mètre environ de largeur et d'épaisseur, sont ensevelis sous les dépôts de versant qui ont la forme de coulées de boue.

Tous les processus se sont déroulés en milieu de pergélisol. Les blocs se sont détachés et sont descendu le long des fentes de gel disposées en polygones. L'érosion thermique par les eaux de la rivière et les eaux de ruissellement sur la surface des fentes a facilité aussi bien le sapement des versants que les mouvements de descente des blocs de pergélisol compris êntre la surface du versant et les fentes. La formation de ces blocs de pergélisol tombés est fonction de la distance, car dans le cas où la distance entre le versant et les fentes a été trop grande, les blocs détachés n'ont été que gauchis.

En même temps, les anciennes fentes de gel ont été conservées par moulage. La gravité a déformé et orienté les structures de moulage vers le sens de l'axe de la vallée.

Les processus de formation des phénomènes présentés ici étaient connus dans les régions de pergélisol actuel, mais jusqu'à présent, on n'avait pas encore observé leurs traces fossilisées dans les dépôts pléistocènes.

РЕЗЮМЕ. В продольном профиле пологого склона долины реки Мроги, сложенного ритмично слоистыми образованиями, зафиксированы два ископаемые склона.

Более древний из них разрезает террасовые осадки и покрыт конгелифлюкционной глиной. Он погребен под ритмично слоистыми склоновыми отложениями времени максимума последнего холодного периода. Более молодой ископаемый склон срезает ритмично слоистые образования и покрыт более поздними склоновыми отложениями, а также речным песком и гравием.

У подножия более молодого ископаемого склона была обнаружена и раскопана глыба, состоящая из ритмично слоистых отложений длиной около 10 м. Эта глыба оторвалась от крутого склона перигляциальной долины в результате подмыва водами одного из блуждающих русел древней гидрографической сети реки Мроги. Поверхность вечной мерзлоты в то время была разбита полигональной системой морозобойных трещин. Термическая эрозия, развивающаяся на контакте текучих вод со склоном, врезанным в вечномерзлые породы, привела к образованию у подножия склона ниши. Откалывание глыбы вечномерзлых пород произошло вдоль морозобойных трещин в тех местах, где упомянутые выше термоэрозионные ними разрастаясь приблизились к простирающимся параллельно склону морозобойным трещинам, заполненным льдом. Дальнейшие процессы содействовали захоронению оторванной глыбы под речными и склоновыми отложениями. Благодаря этому глыба вечномерзлых пород не была размыта и сохранилась до наших дней.

Образовывание таким же путем подобных глыб происходит в настоящее время на территории Аляски и Сибири. Ископаемые же следы этого явления в плейстоценовых отложениях обнаружены у нас впервые.

ZARYS TREŚCI. W profilu podłużnym łagodnego stoku doliny Mrogi zbudowanego z osadów rytmicznie warstwowanych widoczne są dwa stoki kopalne. Starszy z nich wycięty w osadach terasowych i powleczony gliną kongeliflukcyjną jest pogrzebany przez osady stokowe rytmicznie warstwowane wytworzone w czasie pełni ostatniego piętra zimnego. Młodszy stok kopalny ścina osady rytmicznie warstwowane, a przykrywają go późniejsze osady stokowe oraz piaski i żwiry rzeczne. U stóp młodszego stoku kopalnego odsłonięto i wypreparowano blok o długości około 10 m zbudowany z osadów rytmicznie warstwowanych. Został on oderwany od stromego stoku doliny peryglacjalnej wskutek podcięcia przez wody płynące jednym z koryt błądzącego systemu odpływu ówczesnej Mrogi. Na powierzchni wiecznej zmarzliny istniała wtedy sieć wieloboków szczelin mrozowych. Erozja termiczna działająca w kontakcie wody płynącej ze stokiem wyciętym w wiecznej zmarzlinie doprowadziła do wytworzenia niszy u podstawy stoku. Oderwanie się bloku zmarzlinowego dokonało się wzdłuż szczelin mrozowych w miejscach, gdzie owe nisze termo-erozyjne rozwijając się osiągały bliskie sąsiedztwo szczelin lodowych równoległych do krawędzi stoku. Późniejsze procesy spowodowały pogrzebanie bloku przez osady stokowe i rzeczne. Dzięki temu blok zmarzlinowy nie uległ zniszczeniu i zachował się. Tworzenie się podobnych bloków dokonuje się współcześnie na Alasce i na Syberii w sposób analogiczny do opisanego. Natomiast kopalne ślady tego zjawiska w osadach plejstoceńskich stwierdzono tu po raz pierwszy.

CONTENTS

FIGURE

INTRODUCTION

In 1963 and 1964 the author carried out investigations in the area of Walewice, situated almost in the heart of Poland, 20 km west of Łowicz. The area under investigation lies on a long and gentle slope of the 10 to 20 metre terrace of the Warsaw-Berlin Pradolina (Fig. 1). A rich series of periglacial phenomena of different origin and age were noted in the many intersecting trenches dug during this investigation. Field work at Walewice has not been completed as yet; however, some results are interesting and important for the better understanding of

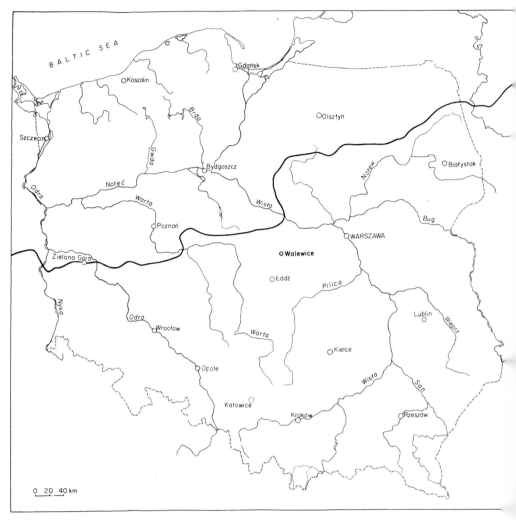

Fig. 1.   Geographic position of Walewice, Poland. Heavy line represents southern extent of Würm glaciation.

periglacial environment and associated processes.

A section, 184 m long, perpendicular to the edge of the present terrace slope was made. It reached the bottom of the valley, thus permitting a study of the structure of the terrace, the slope, as well as the bottom of the valley. The section (Fig. 2) shows in detail the structure of the slope and enables the study of its complicated history.

The top of the terrace consists of boulder clay derived from the Middle Polish (Riss) glaciation. The last glaciation did not reach this area; its maximal extent is some 50 km away (Fig. 1). The boulder clay cover is thin, rarely measuring 1 m in thickness, and is not continuous. This is due to subsequent processes, for example, weathering which took place mainly during the Eem interglacial and under conditions of the last cold stage of Würm.

The boulder clay is underlain by river sand showing ripple marks with numerous lenses of brown silt usually less than 50 cm in thickness. Towards the valley axis, the slope sediments are cut along a steep slope covered with subsequent sediments. There are chiefly slope deposits of different type. They represent, roughly speaking, two periglacial facies formed by various processes which were dependent on the climatic changes through time.

OLDER FOSSIL SLOPE

The immediate layer covering the slope is of boulder clay. It is rather thin, but increases in thickness downward (Fig. 2). There are two different possible explanations for the origin of the boulder clay cover: origin by erosion, if the boulder clay on the slope represents the remains of the till filling the lower part of the valley below the terrace; or origin by secondary accumulation, if the boulder clay cover is slope sediment accumulated as a result of congelifluction.

The second explanation is more plausible, because it is supported by the fabric and structure of the mantle. The shape of the slope covered by the boulder clay gives additional support for this theory. Its contour is sharp without bendings and squeezings which should have occurred as the result of ice-sheet pressure bringing the boulder clay. In another section of the fossil slope, made several metres from the main section, a typical congelifluction lobe has been observed. The lobe has changed its original position, because it was affected by action of a later process, probably congelistatic pressure that took place during the same cold period. The analysis of fabric features provides equally convincing evidence for the congelifluction origin of the boulder clay pavement. The boulder clay cover contains all components of the terrace: charac-

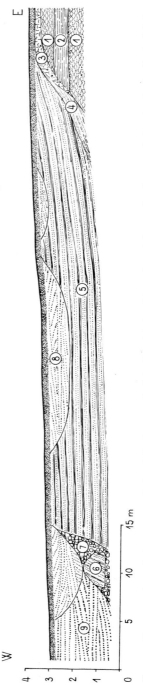

Fig. 2. Cross section of the terrace slope: (1) river sand, (2) silt, (3) boulder clay, (4) proximal part of the rhythmically bedded slope deposits, (5) distal part of the rhythmically bedded slope deposits, (6) block, (7) congelifluction deposits, (8), (9) river sediments.

teristic river sand and silt. Finally, the measurements of the longer axes of stones usually show an orientation in the direction parallel to the inclination of the slope, but with the characteristic upturn.

The cover of congelifluction boulder clay is overlain by a series of rhythmically bedded slope deposits, which measure more than 10 m in thickness in the lower part of the slope. Layers of sand and silt alternate. In the series we distinguished two parts: small proximal part adjacent to the slope, and a much larger, distal part extending in the direction of the valley centre (Figs. 2 and 3).

Difference of particles is immediately observable. The proximal part shows predominance of silt and fine sand grains. At the same time small lumps of boulder clay appear which formed the terrace, together with sand and silt. In the distal part sand dominates over small layers of silt.

Stratification is not very distinct in the proximal part, because the layers are very thin, short, and discontinuous. Also quite uniform small-sized material makes observation of the stratification difficult. The inclination of the layers is parallel to the slope and reaches about 30°. The stratification of the distal part presents a different picture. The layers are more continuous and their length measurable in metres rather than in centimetres, such as in the proximal part. The thickness of layers measures several centimetres, while in the proximal part only a few millimetres. The difference is apparent between thicker sand and silt layers. The inclination of the layers is smaller than in the proximal part and decreases as it approaches the valley axis from about 20° to about 5°.

There is no doubt that sediments originated from the slope processes. This is shown by the origin of the material derived from the components of the terrace and by inclination of layers originally parallel to the slope. It is also supported by the nature of transport, which led to the sedimentation: slope processes and mainly congelifluction and downwash, active under periglacial conditions and, in all probability, over frozen ground.

The role of congelifluction and downwash in the sedimentation of rhythmically bedded deposits varied. This is clearly shown by analysis of deposits in their proximal and distal parts. The variety of material, the dominance of fine particles, the thinness of layers, their limited continuity, and considerable inclination show that congelifluction was the dominant process in the sedimentation of the proximal part of the deposits. However, the structure and fabric of the distal part point to the dominance of downwash. This occurred because of better segregation and greater continuity of the layers characterized by increased thickness, especially as to the sand layers. Probably the finest particles were removed to the bottom of the valley. Sheet wash predominated. Sometimes, however, there was turbulent flow, as indicated by fossil grooves frequently observed in the entire area of distal sediments. These grooves are seen in vertical profiles as pockets varying in size and deepness. The grooves occurring in the periods of turbulent flow were later filled in. Sometimes traces of inversion of the relief in miniature were observed. The discussed slope sediments form a continuous cover, consisting of coalescent alluvial fans. Thus, the entire slope is to be considered as the slightly inclined *glacis d'accumulation*.

Rhythmically bedded slope deposits occurring in central Poland were described several years ago (Dylik 1955, 1960). They should be assigned to the deposits made during the climax of the last cold stage because of their stratigraphical position and the contents of periglacial structures, both contemporaneous with the deposits, and epigenic (Dylik, 1968).

On the described slope deposits lie river sediments: sand, gravel, and pebbles. River sediments taper off in the direction of the terrace edge and they grow thicker in the opposite direction, that is, in the direction of the valley axis. A section through the sediments shows a series of filled troughs and channels from which it can be concluded that the Pleistocene Mroga River had a system of braided water (Figs. 2 and 4). It is known that such a system is characteristic of periglacial rivers, especially those draining glacier areas. Numerous examples of braided rivers in Siberia (Lavrushin 1961, 1964), Alaska, and arctic Canada are described. Undoubtedly rivers in periglacial areas during the Pleistocene were braided. Except for a few cases, as, for example, the Netherlands (Zonnenveld 1956, Edelman and Maarleveld 1958), the problem of periglacial rivers has not yet been studied.

YOUNGER FOSSIL SLOPE

Rhythmically bedded slope deposits plunge under the river sediments and are cut abruptly along the line of a steep slope shown on Figure 4. This is the second, younger fossil slope buried under a new series of slope and river sediments.

In the vertical section at the base of the younger slope an unusual feature appears. To explain its origin by two-dimensional investigations proved to be very difficult. In the vertical section the feature has the shape of an irregular rectangle, inside of which vertical stratification is to be seen. The assumption that this represents traces of glacial tectonics

Fig. 3.   Rhythmically bedded slope deposits covering the older slope. *Photograph by J. Dylik.*

Fig. 4.   Cross section of the younger fossil slope. *Photograph by J. Dylik.*

is not feasible, since the material in the feature is identical with rhythmically bedded deposits. As shown by investigations carried out in several places around Lódz, these deposits date from Würm, when the ice sheet stopped far north of Walewice.

The study of structural features of the deposits lying between the described structure and the younger slope was the starting point. It appeared that there were the slope deposits with packets and blocks which broke off from the slope (Fig. 4). From this it can be inferred that the puzzling feature differed from the mentioned packets only quantitatively. To test this hypothesis the excavation was deepened, taking advantage of a seasonal lowering of ground water level. It appeared that the structure is closed below. The entire vertically stratified deposits lie discordantly on a series of different formations. Further excavation revealed a large block situated parallel to the slope (Fig. 5). The exhumed part of the block measured about 5 m in length. The test trenches indicated that it was about 10 m long. Other dimensions of the uncovered part ranged from 40 cm to 1 m.

The material and position of the block show that it broke off from a steep slope. The compactness of the block and its well-preserved state indicate that it was perennially frozen when it broke off from the slope. Other data also point to the existence of permafrost during the formation of rhythmically bedded deposits and during the development of present fossil slope.

YOUNGER GENERATION OF FROST FISSURE POLYGONS

It is possible that the sediments of rhythmically bedded slope deposits occurred under specific conditions of permafrost and were connected with the thawing of active layer and aggradation of permafrost (Dylik 1963). The strongest argument is provided by fossil ice wedges and frost fissure polygons. At Walewice a series of frost fissures was found in several vertical sections. A whole polygon with parts of a more extensive polygon net were also uncovered (Fig. 6). The polygon measured about 18 m in diameter. This size is most frequent in Pleistocene polygons and in present day permafrost as well (Gozdzik 1964).

The described frost fissure polygons point to the existence of permafrost in the investigated area and support the hypothesis that the block was formed under permafrost conditions. However, it is not possible to connect directly the frost fissures with the process that accompanied the formation of the block. It appears that the generation of the frost fissure polygons is younger than the block. A fissure that may be linked with the polygonal system intersects the deposits covering the block

Fig. 5. Exhumed block and ice wedge cast in the sediments overlying the block. *Photograph by J. Dylik.*

Fig. 6. Fragment of a net of frost fissure polygons. *Photograph by L. Jedrasik.*

(Fig. 5). The sequence of the process is clear: the block broke off, then it was covered with a new series of slope deposits, then covered by river sediments, and finally there developed the ice wedge polygons.

In order to understand how the block was formed, and, in particular, to explain why the frozen ground broke off almost along a straight line of considerable length, a detailed examination was carried out along the edge of the block in the transitional zone between the slope deposits and river sediments. As a result, a series of various structures of slope deposits were found, which points to a variety of processes that occurred on the slope, and traces of second, older formations of frost fissure polygons were found.

OLDER GENERATION OF FROST FISSURE POLYGONS

Traces of earlier frost fissures were preserved in two ways. One is represented by a fissure which intersects rhythmically bedded deposits and is filled with sand and silt and with small lumps of the same material (Fig. 7). The fissure was uncovered in several vertical sections and observed in a plan several metres long. The fissure is bent in the direction of the valley axis. Rhythmically bedded deposits lying on the same side and separated by the fissures from the main deposits show in vertical section a different dipping of inclined layers than the dipping in the main mass of deposits on the other side of the fissure. It is clear that a part of the deposit is separated by the fissure and shifted in the direction of the river. In this case, the block was not formed. The mass probably was too large and the undercutting too small. Probably the slope was not steep enough. Nevertheless, the observation throws light on the mechanics of the formation of blocks connected with frost fissure polygons.

The second type of evidence of frost fissure polygons is represented by small furrows (gullies) made in rhythmically bedded deposits, mostly filled with sand (Fig. 8). The furrows form polygons, although their dominant direction is perpendicular to the slope edge. It is known that not every type of waning development of fissure-ice polygons leads to the formation of features called ice wedge casts. Disappearance of fissure ice on the curved surface was under certain conditions caused by the melting of the ice in polygonal furrows through which the water flowed. Thus, instead of filling the "wedges," channels were formed not only in the place of earlier fissure ice, but also on the eroded walls of the fissure. Examples of such development are mentioned in the papers by Gusiev (1958) and by Frost (1952). It is highly probable that at Walewice this type of waning development of fissure ice occurred only

Fɪɢ. 7.   Fissure interpreted as a fragment of the older generation of frost fissure polygons. *Photograph by J. Dylik.*

Fɪɢ. 8.   Fossilized furrow interpreted as the result of melting of fissure ice. *Photograph by J. Dylik.*

377

in the direction of slope inclination. The sides of polygons parallel to the slope edge developed in the way which led to the formation of ice wedge casts. One proof of such differentiation of the waning development of polygons occurs in the area of the described block. Exactly in the place where the block ends the furrow structures which descend to the valley and intersect the slope appear.

Polygons with fissure ice played an important role in the formation of the frozen block. They were places of weakness where the present fossil slope was cut. They represented points for potential breaking off of blocks as shown in the area of the curved fissure (Fig. 7). Nevertheless, the polygons and the earlier fissure ice mass played only a passive role, because the breaking off of the block was not caused by the fissure alone.

THERMAL EROSION

In search of the main process which directly caused the collapse of the block we should pay more attention to the structure of the slope deposits that underlie and overlie the block, and to the structure of the same type of deposits in the vicinity where no block was formed. The analysis of the profile shape of the slope was also necessary.

Three profiles normal to the edge were made at the distance of 1 to 2 m from the end of the block. In these places the slope was steep and even overhung. On the other hand, the lower part of the profile showed niche-like curve of the slope directed to the terrace edge. The main mass of slope deposits shows a very characteristic structure which may be defined as a small slide structure. In the niche itself and in its immediate vicinity the structure is not clear (Fig. 9). This contrasts on the one hand with distinct original structure of rhythmically bedded slope deposits and, on the other hand, with distinct slide structure. It is better to define the random arrangement of the materials in the niche as a fabric that lacks stratification and shows random arrangement of very small lumps of sand and single grains of sand. This arrangement of mineral material may have been caused by melting of ground ice—probably of segregation ice—from the permafrost exposed on the surface of the slope. The melting occurred in the contact zone of river water and the bank cut in permafrost, and as a result of thermal capacity of running water which was by far greater than it was in the case of the mineral mass. This process is called thermal erosion. The formation of the so-called thermoerosional niches has been described in the literature (Walker and Morgan 1964, Walker and Arnborg 1966). In the frozen areas of Siberia and Alaska thermoerosional niches are observable in the contact of rivers' surfaces with permafrost of the slope. At Walewice the forms have been found by analysis of the shape of the slope and slope sediments' structure.

The structure of the river sediments at Walewice points to the existence of a braided river at the bottom of the Mroga River valley during the formation of rhythmically bedded deposits. When the younger slope was formed, one channel of the system shifted to the edge of the valley, undercutting and eroding the slope of *glacis*. Thermal and mechanical erosion contributed greatly to the recession of the *glacis*, and left particular traces in the area of the present fossil slope. It formed and preserved the steepness of the slope and produced the overhang. Permafrost, polygons with fissure ice (ice wedge polygons), and thermal erosion caused the specific development of the valley slope.

The thermal erosion by the stream water which undercut the *glacis* was most important. The formation of thermoerosional niches by undercutting at the base of the slope caused the collapse of the bank. Because of this, the slope continuously remained steep.

When the surface of the *glacis* near the edge showed roughly parallel fissure, the breaking-up of frozen masses became more intensive, causing the formation of specific forms. If the thermoerosional niche reached the fissure ice or approached the lower part of the fissure, the entire mass lying between the fissure and the edge of the slope would have broken off, and a block would have been formed at the foot of the slope, roughly parallel to its edge. However, the thermoerosional niche was not always close enough to the fissure to cause the collapse of the entire mass which would form the block. Figure 7 shows that the frozen mass lying between the fissure and the slope did not collapse, but merely shifted. This was caused by the loss of balance by the frozen mass and the separation of the mass from the compact frozen ground of the rhythmically bedded deposits. This fact is important to understand in the dynamics of the block formation.

The formation of similar blocks in present areas of permafrost is well understood. Perhaps the most interesting and similar case is described by Walker and Morgan (1964) and by Walker and Arnborg (1966) from the area of Colville River in northern Alaska. The photograph (Fig. 10) shows similarity to the block at Walewice. Above the block we see ice wedges, the formation of which was of such importance. Figure 11 shows the undercutting of a bank by the development of thermoerosional niche on the lower Yukon River in Alaska. The niche

FIG. 9. Vertical section of slope deposits showing the slide structure in miniature and the particular fabric of thermoerosional niche. *Photograph by J. Dylik.*

FIG. 10. Colville River delta. Blocks and the ice wedges along which fracture occurred. From Walker and Arnborg, 1966.

Fig. 11. North bank of lower Yukon River near Galena, Alaska. Vegetal mat is overhanging bank of perennially frozen silt (permafrost). River has cut well-developed thermoniche in frozen silt at water level. *Photograph by Troy L. Péwé* (US Geological Survey), August 5, 1946. (From Péwé, 1948).

is also comparable with the niche at Walewice which was reconstructed by analysis of the slope's shape and deposits (Fig. 9).

Frozen blocks and associated thermoerosional niches are quite common in present periglacial areas (Péwé 1948), but their fossil counterparts have not been recognized as yet. Thus far, Walewice is the first place where Pleistocene traces of the described phenomena have been recognized.

PRESERVATION OF THE BLOCK

Although the explanation of the origin of the block at Walewice and the reconstruction of the conditions and processes responsible for its formation are known, the whole problem is not yet resolved. The next question is how the block was preserved when so many processes, such as the melting of ground ice and the action of flowing water, could destroy it completely.

To answer the question there was necessity of analysing certain deposits in the slope section. The deposits underlying the block, similar deposits covering it, and river sediments were distinguished. The fossil block lies in the transitional zone where the predominance of slope and river processes alternated. Ephemeric nature of the stream bed and its short lapse of activity time were essential for the preservation of the block. Therefore, we should keep in mind that the Mroga River valley had a braided water system.

Figure 12 represents an extremely interesting structure. It shows minute layers which are almost vertically inclined downslope. The structure is the result of sloughing of mud, caused by slow thawing of small particles of ground ice on the frozen surface of the steep slope. The participants of the Field Conference of the VIIth INQUA Congress in Alaska have observed a similar process on the permafrost bank at Ready Bullion Creek near Fairbanks (Péwé et al. 1965). The block is underlain by slope deposits which were formed by sloughing and by other processes when mud flow was more intensive. This explains the compactness of the block. It did not crack or break to pieces, because it probably did not fall, but slid and settled on a soft congelifluction ground.

Once the block broke off, intensive slope processes occurred which buried it and pushed the braided river bed in the direction of the valley axis. The following phase or phases of the expansion of the stream failed to destroy the protecting cover of slope deposits above the block. On the contrary, the aggradating river sediments led to the growth of the protecting cover. As a result, the block and the covering slope deposits

Fig. 12. Sloughing structure in the deposits covering the younger slope. *Photograph by J. Dylik.*

were preserved.

The discovery of the so far unknown fossil structures at Walewice, and the explanation of their origin and of several processes have been made possible by the adoption of certain methods of investigation which are worth describing.

The investigation was very detailed and intensive. This is shown by comparing the size of the area examined and the time spent. The field works performed by four persons on the area of 3.2 km² took about 200 days. The area of vertical sections measured 1,262 m², and the horizontal exposures measured 800 m². All sections were carefully cleaned. The surface of the stone pavement and the frozen block were exhumed by archaeological method with small shovels, spoons, and brushes. To recognize the sedimentary environments and the processes involved, each structure was studied in detail. The structure was analysed by means of three-dimensional observations. Finally, comparable data from the present area of permafrost were obtained, if possible. Examples are provided by the blocks and thermoerosional niches from Colville River delta and the sloughing phenomena from Ready Bullion Creek.

CHRONOLOGICAL SEQUENCE OF THE PROCESSES

Unfortunately no organic deposits or fossil soils were found at Walewice. Therefore, the dating of the described phenomena can be based only on the known stratigraphy of Łódz area, and on the analysis of structural features of mineral deposits formed in colder periods or stadials after the glacial terminology.

Rhythmically bedded slope deposits are helpful in this respect. Stratigraphical position, determined in several places of Łódz region, and the type of periglacial structure found in these deposits indicate that they originated during the climax of the last cold stage. This supposition is supported by polygons with fissure ice and by the block at Walewice.

The older fossil slope (Fig. 2) was cut during the Eem interglacial or during one of the older Würm interstadials. Manikowska (1966) thinks that the stadial following the Brörup interstadial was marked by intensive erosion. This would put the formation of congelifluction cover, built mainly by boulder clay and covering the older slope, after the Brörup interstadial. It is quite possible that while the boulder clay was forming, permafrost already existed. The data from Józefów indicate that in central Poland permafrost began to form after Amersfoort interstadial (Dylik 1965). This is also suggested by the preservation of congelifluction sediments that cover the older slope at Walewice. It seems that there was no distinct break between the settling of the cover and the beginning of the sedimentation of rhythmically bedded deposits. The type of the deposits, and particularly the proximal part, suggest that their sedimentation was caused by congelifluction. This occurred in permafrost and in connection with its aggradation.

The collapse of the block also occurred during the climax of the last cold stage. This is shown by further sedimentation by rhythmically bedded deposits that continued long after the block collapsed. More evidence for the climax is provided by frost fissure polygons which developed in sediments covering the block.

Perhaps during the formation of the block, the climate became warmer and more humid. Such conditions might also provoke that type of waning development of fissure ice polygons which resulted in the formation of erosional furrows replacing former fissures with the ground ice. The sudden development of slope deposits with a slide structure indicates that there was a mobile mineral mass ready to flow down the slope. Probably this resulted from deep thawing and the considerable thickness in the active layer. Perhaps this indicates an interstadial interrupting the uniformity of the climax phase. For lack of more exact data, however, it is only a supposition.

In the upper part of the *glacis d'accumulation* near the terrace edge lies a stone pavement. The author interprets it as remains of a once thicker congelifluction cover. It covered the surface of the *glacis* where polygons with fissure ice developed earlier. Numerous wind-worn stones found in the pavement were formed at another place and then transported by congelifluction. Aeolian erosion probably occurred during the formation of fissure polygons. Fissure ice was buried by congelifluction cover and did not melt until much later. Then the **ice** wedge cast was formed and on the surface of the pavement appeared furrows which show the position of the former fissure ice. Intensive congelifluction, reflected in the flow of mud with stones on a gently inclined surface of the pavement, indicates a humid climate. Therefore, the appearance of the congelifluction mantle seems to mark the beginning of the waning phase of the last cold stage.

River sediments indicate the same process. Some ice fissures of the younger polygons occurred in the bottom part of river sediments. Therefore, the beginning of the more vigorous river accumulation seems to have taken place during the climax. Further accumulation of sediments, however, occurred during the waning phase. This conclusion rests on the fact that river sediments lie high, near the edge of the terrace (Fig. 2). Such a high water level is only explainable by the change in climate which was marked by considerable precipitation.

This agrees with observations made in several places of central Poland. Field work at Walewice is not sufficient to show the processes that occurred during the waning phase, which in other places are not adequately understood either. Perhaps further investigations at Walewice will provide new and more complete data.

REFERENCES CITED

DYLIK, JAN, 1955, Rhythmically stratified periglacial slope deposits: Biul. Peryglacjalny, nr 2, p. 15-33.
————, 1960, Rhythmically stratified slope waste deposits: Biul. Peryglacjalny, nr 8, p. 31-43.
————, 1963, Problèmes périglaciaires de La Hongrie: Biul. Peryglacjalny, nr 12, p. 91-111.
————, 1965, L'étude de la dynamique d'évolution des dépressions fermées aux environs de Łódź: Rev. d. Géomorphol. Dyn., XVe Année, p. 158-178.
————, 1968, The main elements of Upper Pleistocene paleogeography in central Poland: Biul. Peryglacjalny, nr 16, p. 85-116.
EDELMAN, C. H., MAARLEVELD, G. C., 1958, Pleistozängeologische Ergebnisse der Bodenkartienung in den Niederlanden: Geol. Jb. Bd. 73, p. 639-684.
FROST, R. E., 1952, Interpretation of permafrost features from airphotos in Frost action in soils, a symposium, Natl. Acad. Sci., Spec. Rept. 2, p. 223-246.
GOŹDZIK, J., 1964, L'étude de la répartition topographique des structures périglaciaires: Biul. Peryglacjalny, nr 14, p. 217-251.
GUSIEV, A. I., 1958, Ob iskopaiemykh "sledakh" mierzloty i "liedanykh" klinakh v chetviertichnykh otlozheniakh (Fossil "traces" of permafrost and "ice wedges" in Quaternary deposits): Geol. Sb. Lvovkogo Geol. Obshch.
LAVRUSHIN, J. A., 1961, Tipy chetviertichnogo aluvia nizhnego Yenisieya (Types of Quaternary river deposits in lower Yenisiey): Geol. Inst. Aka. Nauk, SSSR, v. 47, 92 p.
————, 1964, Principal features of the alluvium of plain rivers in the subarctic belt and the periglacial regions of continental glaciations: Report VIth INQUA Congress, Warsaw, 1961, v. IV, p. 111-120.
MANIKOWSKA, B., 1966, Gleby młodszego plejstocenu w okolicach Łodzi (Résumé: Les sols du Pléistocène supérieur aux environs de Łódź): Acta Geogr. Łodz., nr 22.
PÉWÉ, T. L., 1948, Terrain and permafrost, Galena area, Alaska: Permafrost program, Rept. no. 7, US Geol. Survey, Eng. Intel. Div. Office, Chief of Engineers, 52 p.
PÉWÉ, T. L., FERRIANS, OSCAR, NICHOLS, O. R., and KARLSTROM, T. N. V., 1965, Guidebook, Field Conference F., Alaska, VIIth Inter. Cong. INQUA, 141 p.
WALKER, H. J., and MORGAN, H. M., 1964, Unusual weather and river bank erosion in the delta of the Colville River, Alaska: Arctic 17, p. 41-48.
WALKER, H. J., and ARNBORG, 1966, Permafrost ice-wedge effect on riverbank erosion: Proc. Intern. Permafrost Conf., Nat. Acad. Sci. — Nat. Res. Council Pub. No. 1287, p. 164-171.
ZONNENVELD, J. I. S., 1956, Fluvial deposits Tubantian: in PANNEKOEK, A. J., Geological History of the Netherlands, S-Gravenhage. Staatsdrukkerijen Uitgeverijbedrijf, 1956, p. 103-107.

DOLOMITE TORS AND SANDFILLED SINK HOLES IN THE CARBONIFEROUS LIMESTONE OF DERBYSHIRE, ENGLAND

TREVOR D. FORD
University of Leicester
Leicester, England

ABSTRACT. Permo-Triassic dolomitization of a part of the limestone massif was followed by hydrothermal mineral deposition in solution cavities at the dolomite-limestone contact. Subsequent ground-water solution at the same contact initiated collapse of the overlying dolomite. In Tertiary times the collapse caused sink holes to develop, letting down the cover of siliceous sands and clays. Intervening areas of dolomite were decalcified around their bases and disaggregated to a loose crystal "sand." During the Pleistocene, intermittent mass wastage repeatedly exposed the unweathered dolomite as tors, but these in turn were broken down and removed by glacier action. Present-day tors are thought to be the result of weathering during the Last Interglacial interval, followed by removal of the debris and exposure of the tors. Fossil tors still remain buried in their own breakdown "sand."

RÉSUMÉ. La dolomitisation permo-triassique d'une partie du massif calcaire a été suivie par la déposition hydrothermale de minéraux dans les cavités de solution au contact de la dolomite et du calcaire. Au Tertiaire, la mise en solution de ces minéraux par les eaux souterraines a provoqué un début d'effondrement de la dolomite. Cet effondrement a entraîné la formation de dolines et la chûte de la couverture d'argiles et de sables siliceux. Les aires intermédiaires de dolomite ont été décalcifiées autour de leur base et désagrégées en un "sable" de cristaux détachés. Au Pléistocène, l'affouillement intermittent a exposé à plusieurs reprises la dolomite non-altérée, sous forme de "tors" (pics coniques), mais ceux-ci ont été démolis et emportés par l'action glaciaire. On croit que les tors actuels résultent de l'altération subie au cours du dernier interglaciaire (Riss-Würm), suivie par l'érosion des débris et donc, le dégagement des tors. Les tors fossiles demeurent enfouis sous leur propre "sable" de désagrégation.

CONTENTS

387

INTRODUCTION

The Peak District of Derbyshire lies at the southern end of the Pennine Mountains in north-central England. The district is commonly and erroneously referred to as a dome, but is more accurately a series of flexures with undulating crest lines of Lower Carboniferous limestone, flanked on three sides by cuestas of Upper Carboniferous sandstones and shales, locally known as the Millstone Grit Series, and, on the south, unconformably, by Triassic sedimentary rocks. The limestone area is roughly 25 miles north-south and 15 miles east-west and rises to an altitude of about 1500 feet above sea level. Whereas much of the limestone area is a gently undulating plateau with a relict soil on till or loess, along with deeply incised late Pleistocene river valleys, about 10 square miles presents a topography of dolomite tors and sink holes filled with silica sand, with only scattered patches of chert gravel and soils on till and loess. Because these areas are surrounded by the normal glacio-karst topography of the limestone at the same altitude, it is evident that the geological history is reflected in the present morphology. This short paper summarizes the geological history leading to this present-day morphology, as an example of the way in which the events that took place in remote geological times affect much more recent denudational processes. It also emphasizes the fact that subterranean processes and their results may affect the surface. Furthermore, it shows how land forms, generally characteristic of warm, moist climates, may occur in association with glacial deposits.

THE DOLOMITE TORS

The tors vary from isolated stacks and pinnacles, perhaps 50 feet high, to castellated escarpments 200 feet or more in height, and one-half mile in length. The more typical tors consist of masses of incompletely dolomitized limestone often 100 feet high and wide. All have their tops formed of large blocks separated by wide, open joints, with tree roots actively wedging. Heaps of dislodged blocks lie round the bases of most tors, forming slopes at the angle of rest. These slopes rest at their foot on almost level ground, with few blocks showing through the turf. The block slopes are commonly covered with scrub bushes rooted deep below the blocks. Preparations for quarrying showed temporary exposures of part of a block pile almost burying the parent tor, with the underlying dolomite broken down into dolomite crystal "sand." The bushes and moss testify to the continuing dampness of the ground at such levels, whereas the upper parts of the tors are dry and highly porous. At the bases of the tors, percolating rain not only maintains the dampness for plant growth, but also decalcifies (i.e., removes the residual calcite) the dolomitized limestone, leaving disaggregated dolomite "sand."

The present tors are thus undergoing slow breakdown, but no surface streams remove the debris, and slopes are usually too gentle for hill-creep, so ultimately a nearly flat featureless landscape must result. A similar process has presumably operated in the past, but the presence of the existing tors indicates other processes at intervening times.

The tors almost all occur between 900 and 1,100 feet above sea level but not necessarily at the highest points of the hills bearing them. They are also in areas where the dip of the strata varies from horizontal to about 25°. They are in three separate areas, corresponding with the distribution of the dolomitized limestone (Fig. 1). The surrounding limestone does not carry tors, so the nature of the dolomite is an important factor.

THE DOLOMITIZED LIMESTONE

The distribution of dolomitized limestone in Derbyshire was mapped by Parsons (1922), slightly revised by Shirley (1958), Ford (1963), and herein. The dolomitization is secondary after bioclastic limestones of Lower Carboniferous age. The dolomitized limestone invariably overlies unaltered limestone with an irregular, undulating, but generally sharp contact. The base of dolomitization often projects down major joints. The undulation crosses palaeontological zonal boundaries, and the depth of dolomitization is known to penetrate as much as 500 feet below the present surface. Parsons (1922) described the chemical composition of the dolomitized limestones, showing that the proportion of $MgCO_3$ ranged up to about 43 per cent, with an average of about

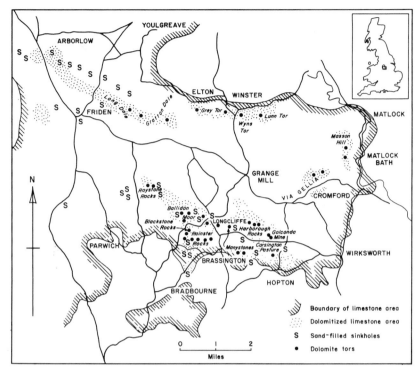

Fig. 1. Map to show the distribution of dolomite tors, sink holes, and dolomitized limestone within the Carboniferous Limestone massif of Derbyshire. Inset: location of area within Britain.

33 per cent, thus leaving considerable residual calcite which could be attacked by chemical weathering or by ground water. Parsons (1922) also noted that the porosity of the dolomite increased in proportion to the $MgCO_3$ content; it averaged about 5 per cent and reached a maximum of 14 per cent. In contrast, the porosity of the unaltered limestone is negligible. Parsons (1922) also noted that the intensity of dolomitization was highly variable in a short distance, being stronger along joints.

Dolomitization probably took place during or following the denudation of the limestone, after the Armorican folding had uplifted the Upper Carboniferous sandstones and shales. Magnesium-bearing fluids may have invaded as an early phase of the introduction of lead-fluorite-baryte mineral deposits, probably during the Permo-Triassic; or subsurface waters beneath the Permian seas or Triassic playas may have brought the magnesium downward. In either case, the restricted distribution of dolomitized limestone is as yet unexplained. Dolomitization clearly took place before the introduction of the lead-fluorite-baryte mineral veins which cut limestone and dolomite alike. These are either vertical fissure fillings or nearly horizontal replacements and solution-cavity fillings. Both of these had and still have unfilled cavities, with some degree of interconnection providing routes for underground water, with resultant cave formation and sink hole development.

THE SINK HOLES

About 60 known sink holes filled with silica sand and clay are scattered along a belt about 12 miles long and 2 miles wide, roughly coinciding with the main dolomitized areas. The sands and clays have been worked for refractory brick manufacture. They are known as "Pocket Deposits," under which title they have been described by Yorke (1954-61). As seen in the workings, the sink holes range up to one-half mile in length and one-quarter mile across, though more or less circular sink holes about 100 yards in diameter are more common. The removal of the sand and clay shows walls of weathered dolomite, with occasional detached pinnacles surrounded by sand. No debris slopes of dolomite have been seen, and no sink hole has ever been excavated to rock bottom; in fact only one borehole has touched rock at a depth of 250 feet. A few sink holes are in unaltered limestone with dolomitized joints only, and these sink holes are always close to the dolomite outcrops.

The sink holes commonly occur between dolomite tors; many are covered by till to a depth of 10 feet or so. They are also, sometimes, clearly cut across by dry valleys. Thus, the sink holes and their fills are clearly preglacial in origin. The nature of their formation is controversial. Subsurface collapse beneath Millstone Grit, or Triassic, or Tertiary cover has been proposed, as well as open doline formation with infillings washed in (Kent 1957). The sand fills contain pebbles undoubtedly originating in the Bunter Pebble Beds of Triassic age, which still outcrop about 10 miles to the south. But redistribution of these prior to the mid-Tertiary uplift of the Pennines seems a better possibility for explaining the distribution of sink holes and fills.

Until recently, no hydrological explanation of the sink holes had been put forward, but recent discoveries in a disused mine beneath the dolomite sink hole area have shown that the explanation is closely linked to the mode of mineral deposition and to the hydrology of the mineralizing solutions (Ford and King, in press).

The only evidence of age of the sand fills is that fossil pollen and wood were found in the highest subtill clay of one sink. They suggested a Tertiary age to Challinor (1961) and a late Pliocene or early Pleistocene age to Shotton (*in litt.*). Scattered patches of sand and pebbles over much of the limestone plateau suggest that the cover was once much more widespread, though glacial redistribution confuses the picture.

MINERALIZATION AND THE SINK HOLES

The traditional view of the introduction of the lead-fluorite-baryte veins of Derbyshire is that they originated as hydrothermal solutions rising up fault fractures, some of which continued to move during and after mineral emplacement. Barriers to upward migration through the limestone are present in the form of interbedded basaltic lava flows and the cover of impervious shales of the Millstone Grit Series. In some cases migration was lateral, and deposits rest on the lava flows, indicating hydrological gradients through what is now limestone of negligible porosity. Recent exploration of the ramifying workings of the Golconda Mine at Brassington has shown that the mineral solutions there travelled laterally and initially dissolved out cavities at the base of the porous dolomite before refilling them with layers of galena and baryte. Repeated subsequent phases of solution were accompanied by collapse and brecciation of the mineral deposits and, later on, the roof of dolomite. Some of these collapses have worked their way through to the surface 350 to 500 feet above to cause sink holes. The sand fills have been washed down through some of the collapse breccias into the partly block-filled caverns below, where redistribution by slowly running ground water has given irregularly bedded gravel, sand, silt, and clay.

Old mining records suggest that a similar condition of mineral deposition with solution cavities and collapse structures is widespread beneath the dolomite outcrop. It is thus probably present also beneath many of the sink holes, though this is yet to be tested by drilling.

Because the main phases of mineral emplacement are thought to have taken place beneath the impervious shale member of the Millstone Grit, an outlet for the demineralized waters must have existed. This outlet was probably along the highs of the fold crests where denudation had broken the shale cover, but no direct evidence of the sites is known today.

THE RELATIONSHIP OF THE TORS TO THE SINK HOLES

Because the removal of the silica sands exposes walls of blocky dolomite, it might be argued that all the tors were once covered with sand, but this would only put the formation of the tors back a stage. None of the sink holes has ever been demonstrated to contain the break-down products of the tors, and the bedding in the sands implies that they were let down or washed into sink holes rather than deposited as an unconformable cover on the upstanding tors. Therefore, it appears that the tor-like appearance of the sink hole walls may be misleading. However, early coalescence of sink holes may have left dolomite pinnacles standing in preglacial times. Some of the present tors may be rejuvenated equivalents of such early tors.

THE RELATIONSHIP OF THE TORS AND SINK HOLES TO GLACIAL DEPOSITS

The glacial deposits of the Derbyshire limestone plateau have not yet been investigated in detail. Jowett and Charlesworth (1929) mapped their general distribution, showing patches of thin drift only. Yorke (1954–61) described the till over the sand pockets as usually not more than 10 feet thick, but with downward "intrusions" of till into the underlying sand. The till contains many limestone and dolomite boulders, patches of chert gravel (presumably transported as frozen masses from surrounding areas of insoluble residue lying on the limestone), blocks of Millstone Grit and black shale, and occasional erratics derived from mineral-vein outcrops or from farther afield, for example, the Lake District. Pigott (1962) noted wide occurrence of loessic soils lying on limestone, dolomite, lava, and silica-sand fills.

No tor of dolomite has yet been found buried in till. On the contrary, block fields near some tors have spread by hill creep over the till on the sand fills. Large blocks of dolomite, up to 10 feet long, are included in the till.

Several sink holes and their fills have been truncated by now-dry valleys during phases of stream erosion on frozen ground, and valley-bottom alluvium lies above the sand. Other sink holes are in hillsides, where they may be covered by scree of limestone and dolomite. The screes in places also cover till.

CHRONOLOGY

The Carboniferous limestone, with its scattered interbedded lavas, was covered by Upper Carboniferous (Millstone Grit) deltaic shales and sandstones and probably by Coal Measures also.

During the Permo-Carboniferous Armorican orogeny, gentle folding and some faulting took place, followed by denudation.

Late Permian and/or Triassic subsurface waters caused dolomitization, possibly only of those areas directly exposed to the floors of Permian or Triassic seas or lagoons.

Mineralization followed closely, probably during Triassic times (Moorbath 1962), with attendant hydrological phases of repeated solution, infilling (Fig. 2.1), and collapse.

The rest of the Mesozoic was a time of low-lying static ground-waters, probably beneath shallow transgressive Jurassic and Cretaceous seas.

The early Tertiary saw a cover of sands derived from surrounding Triassic Millstone Grit and Coal Measures (Fig. 2.2).

Miocene uplift brought a renewal of solution and collapse, resulting in sink holes, some with foundered sand fills, others with a fill of inwashed sand and clay (Fig. 2.3). The uplift carried the limestone plateau to over 1,000 feet above present sea level; the lack of major incised valleys kept the hydrological gradients low, and slow solution and collapse continued into the Pleistocene. Hills of dolomite were encased in dolomite sand produced by solutional decalcification, and, although the sand was washed into adjacent sink holes, further solution prevented its preservation.

The onset of Pleistocene glaciation allowed removal of the dolomite sand by solifluction, leaving tors upstanding, but the advance of ice tongues destroyed these, and the derived blocks were deposited in the till. The cutting of now dry valleys during periglacial retreat phases provided new hills of dolomite for solutional decalcification during the ensuing interglacial. Reappearance of colder, wetter conditions allowed the uncovering of new tors, but the sink holes remained covered in

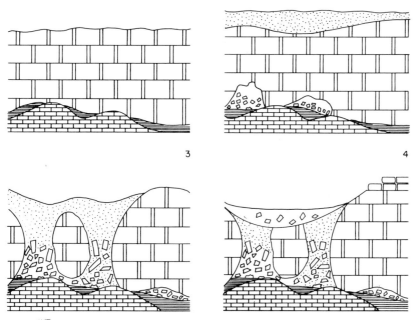

Fig. 2. Diagrammatic sketches to show the evolution of the dolomite tors and sink holes:

(1) Layered galena-baryte mineral deposits lie in solution cavities developed at the dolomite-limestone contact.

(2) A cover of sands of probable Tertiary age lies on the dolomite, whilst solution, collapse, and brecciation of the dolomite above the mineral deposits is in progress.

(3) Further solution and collapse allows the sand cover to sag into sink holes.

(4) Following glacial truncation of the sink holes and their sand fills, till is left lying in hollows, but weathering of the intervening dolomite hills initiates tor formation and periglacial wastage of decalcified dolomite "sand" exposes the blocky tors.

glacial till (Fig. 2.4). How many times this cycle was repeated is not known, for the entire Pleistocene chronology of Derbyshire is still to be worked out. The frozen ground prevented solution and collapse at depth, and no erratics are found in the sand fills. The Derbyshire limestone plateau was not covered by ice during the Last Glaciation (Würm), so the present tors represent the deep weathering of the Last Interglacial (Riss-Würm), followed by removal of the dolomite sand under periglacial conditions. Post-glacial weathering today tends to break down the tors by tree-root wedging. The valleys are deeply incised by streams, at least some of which were probably fed from the overflow of preglacial lakes in Cheshire. The water table under much of the dolomite country has thus been lowered, and its tors and sand-filled sink holes are to a large extent now high and dry, so that further solutional collapse is unlikely.

CONCLUSION

The present unusual karst topography of dolomite tors and sand-filled sink holes is shown to have resulted first from phases of Carboniferous to Triassic geological history, then exposed by a complex interplay of Tertiary denudation and sedimentation, and further modified by Pleistocene glacial and periglacial erosion.

ACKNOWLEDGEMENTS. Acknowledgement is due for useful discussion and correspondence on various aspects of this work to Dr. T. Deans, Dr. P. E. Kent, and Professor F. W. Shotton. Dr. Gary Stewart critically read the manuscript.

REFERENCES CITED

CHALLINOR, W. G., 1961, Summary of Progress of the Geological Survey of G.B. for 1960: *in* Palaeontology Dept. Report, p. 52.

FORD, T. D., 1963, The dolomite tors of Derbyshire: East Midland Geogr., v. 3, p. 148-153.

FORD, T. D., and KING, R. J., 1965, Epigenetic bedded Galena-Baryte deposits in the Golconda Mine, Brassington, Derbyshire: Economic Geology, v. 60, p. 1686-1702.

—— and ——, in press, The origin of the pocket deposits of the Derbyshire limestone: International Jour. Speleology.

JOWETT, A., and CHARLESWORTH, J. K., 1929, The glacial geology of the Derbyshire dome and the Southwest Pennines: Quar. Jour. Geol. Soc. London, v. 85, p. 307-334.

KENT, P. E., 1957, Triassic relics and the 1000 foot surface in the Southern Pennines: East Midland Geogr., v. 1, no. 8, p. 3-10.

MOORBATH, S., 1962, Lead isotope abundance studies: Phil. Trans. Roy. Soc., ser. A, v. 254, p. 295-360.

PARSONS, L. M., 1922, Dolomitization in the Carboniferous Limestone of the Midlands: Geol. Mag., v. 59, p. 51-53, 104-117.

PIGOTT, C. D., 1962, Soil formation and development on the Carboniferous Limestone of Derbyshire. I. Parent Materials: Jour. Ecology, v. 50, p. 145-156.

SHIRLEY, J., 1958, The Carboniferous Limestone of the Monyash-Wirksworth area, Derbyshire: Quar. Jour. Geol. Soc. London, v. 114, p. 411-430.

YORKE, COURTENAY, 1954-61, The pocket deposits of Derbyshire: Birkenhead, private publications.

PERMAFROST AND TEMPERATURE CONDITIONS IN ENGLAND DURING THE LAST GLACIAL PERIOD

R. B. G. WILLIAMS
Department of Geography
University of Cambridge, England

ABSTRACT. The extent of former permafrost in southern England is indicated by various types of patterned ground. Southwestern England seems to have been relatively free from permafrost in the lowlands. Very few permafrost structures have been found, and most of these may be relics of the Saale glacial period. Permafrost, however, occurred widely on the higher ground, descending to 900 feet on Dartmoor.

In central and eastern England permafrost features are much more abundant. In East Anglia, involutions and ice wedges can be found in half the gravel pits, and involutions in two-thirds of the chalk pits. In certain districts (e.g., southwest Norfolk) half the area is estimated to be underlain by patterned ground. This contrasts with the lowlands of Dorset and Devon, where the number of permafrost structures is so small it is difficult to set a figure for their frequency.

It is suggested that extensive permafrost occurred in the lowlands approximately as far west as a line from Southampton to central Somerset and on high ground further southwest. The mean annual isotherm of —6°C to —8°C must have lain across southern England during the coldest part of the last glacial period.

RÉSUMÉ. Divers types de sols géométriques indiquent l'extension du pergélisol ancien dans le sud de l'Angleterre. Les basses-terres du sud-ouest de l'Angleterre semblent être restées relativement libres de pergélisol. On y a trouvé très peu de structures de pergélisol et la plupart de celles-ci seraient des reliques de la période glaciaire de Saale. Cependant, le pergélisol est apparu largement sur les hautes-terres, descendant jusqu'à 900 pieds (274,5 m) sur le Dartmoor.

Dans le centre et l'est de l'Angleterre, les traits de pergélisol sont beaucoup plus abondants. On trouve en East Anglia des involutions et des coins de glace dans la moitié des carrières de gravier et des involutions dans les deux tiers des carrières de craie. Dans certains districts (p.ex. le sud-ouest du Norfolk), on estime que la moitié de la surface est constituée de sol polygonal. Ceci contraste avec les basses-terres du Dorset et du Devon, où le nombre de traits de pergélisol est si minime qu'il est difficile de chiffrer leur fréquence.

L'auteur suppose que le pergélisol a couvert les basses-terres vers l'ouest, jusqu'à une ligne qui va de Southampton jusqu'au centre du Somerset et plus loin vers le sud-ouest sur les hautes-terres. L'isotherme annuel moyen de —6°C à —8°C devait traverser le sud de l'Angleterre durant la période la plus froide de la dernière glaciation.

ZUSAMMENFASSUNG. Auf die Ausdehnung des vorherigen Dauerfrostbodens in Südengland weisen die verschiedenen Arten des Struktur-
bodens hin. Südwestengland scheint verhältnismässig frei vom Dauerfrostboden gewesen zu sein. Nur wenige Strukturen des Dauerfrostbodens
sind gefunden worden, und die meisten darunter mögen Überreste der
Saaleneiszeit sein. Der Dauerfrostboden aber kam weitreichend auf dem
Hochboden vor, bis zu einer Höhe von 900 Fuss herab.
Mittel- und Südengland sind viel reicher an Dauerfrostboden kennzei-
chnenden Zügen. In Ostengland (East Anglia) kann man Würfe oder
Taschenboden und Eiskeile in fast der Hälfte der Kiesgruben, und
Eiskeile in zwei Drittel der Kreidegruben finden. Es ist berechnet worden,
dass in gewissen Gebieten (z.b. Südwest Norfolk) die Hälfte der Grund-
fläche mit Strukturboden unterlegt ist. Das bietet einen Gegensatz zum
Tiefland von Dorset und Devon an, wo die Anzahl von Dauerfrost-
bodenenstrukturen so klein ist, dass es schwer ist, ihre Häufigkeit mit
Bestimmtheit festzustellen.
Es wird vorgeschlagen, dass ausgedehnter Dauerfrostboden im Tiefland bis zu einer Linie im Westen ungefähr von Southampton zu Mittel-
Somerset vorkam, und im Hochland noch weiter zum Südwesten. Die
durchschnittliche jährliche Isotherme von —6°C bis —8°C muss über
Südengland während der kältesten Periode der letzten Eiszeit gelegen
haben.

CONTENTS

During the last glacial period in Britain much of central and eastern
England, as well as the south, was unglaciated. Numerous discoveries of
fossil ice wedges have shown that permafrost existed in many parts of
this area. Less certain indications of former permafrost are given by
giant stone polygons and stripes, the trough patterns of the chalkland
(Williams 1964), and involutions (Fig. 1).

It has proved difficult to determine the extent and continuity of the
permafrost. Manley (1951, 1953) considered that there was almost no

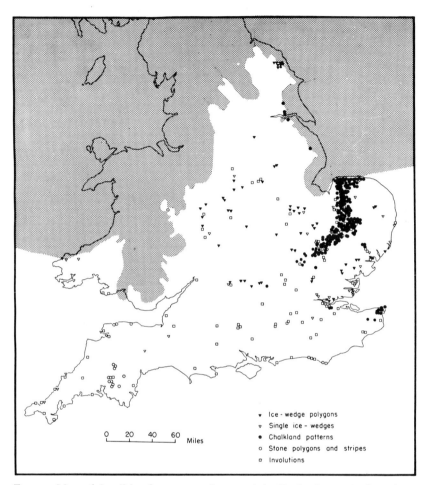

Fig. 1. Map of localities for patterned ground in England presumed to have formed during the Last Glaciation (Wisconsin). The stippled area shows the maximum extent of ice during the last glacial period. Only patterns that may belong to this period are indicated. As some areas have been investigated more than others, the map is only partly a guide to the frequency of permafrost structures.

SOURCES: The map is based upon field work, Geological Survey photographs, and the following published data: Avery 1964, Bridges 1964, Curtis and James 1959, Dimbleby 1952, Fitzpatrick 1956, Gruhn and Bryan 1968, Kerney 1965, Shotton 1960, 1962, Stephens and Synge 1966, Te Punga 1957, Trist 1952, Waters 1961, Williams 1964. Certain unpublished information was supplied by the following: Mr. F. Nicholson, Mr. N. Stephens, Dr. R. G. West, Miss F. Bell, Mr. B. John, and Mr. R. Randall. The interpretations embodied in the map and in this article do not always follow these sources.

perennially frozen ground in southwest England in the lowlands, and this view has become widely accepted by geomorphologists. It is chiefly based on evidence of the former position of the snow-line and the displacement of plant zones. In particular, Manley pointed out that no high ground in the southwest was glaciated, even though Dartmoor rises to more than 2,000 feet above sea level. He suggested that mean annual temperatures were high compared with the glaciated part of England and were above freezing.

However, in recent years a number of fossil permafrost structures have been found in the southwest, notably by Te Punga (1957), Waters (1961), and Stephens and Synge (1966). Many areas of giant stone stripes and polygons have been found on Dartmoor. Their presence suggests that mean annual temperatures were subfreezing, necessitating a reconsideration of why the area was not glaciated. Palaeoclimatic maps constructed by many European writers show the southern boundary of the permafrost lying well south of the British Isles during the last glacial period (Poser 1948, Klute 1951, Tricart 1956, Kaiser 1960, Wright 1961).

How many periglacial structures belong to the last glacial period and how many to previous glacial advances is in many cases uncertain. The main periods of periglacial activity in eastern England have been outlined by West (1966), but the firm dating of individual structures is largely impossible at present, particularly in the south and west. The next to the last glaciation (Gipping) extended further than its successor and left only the southernmost parts of the country uncovered by ice. In the absence of detailed evidence the most reasonable possibility is that permafrost at this period was widespread throughout the un-glaciated area in the south because of the nearness of the ice margin. Nevertheless, it is doubtful if many structures of Gipping age have been preserved. The majority of patterned-ground sites in the Midlands and eastern England probably belong to the Weichsel. Some sites can be directly dated by associated last glacial deposits; others conform so closely to the present land surface that, as Shotton (1962) noted, an age earlier than the last glacial period can be excluded. Even during the late glacial (zone III) the climate in northern and western areas was still sufficiently cold for the widespread development of involutions and wedges (Galloway 1961a, b, Watson 1965). In southern England, too, a few involutions are known to have formed (Kerney 1963).

The frequency of permafrost structures in England varies greatly between different areas and also according to geological materials (Table 1). In the southwest there are very few indications of perma-frost except on high ground. Permafrost structures are much more

TABLE 1
PERCENTAGE OF EXPOSURES WITH CERTAIN TYPES OF
PERIGLACIAL FEATURES

		Wedges only, or wedges and involutions	Involutions Only	No Structures	
EAST ANGLIA (western part)	Sand and gravel	32	20	48	⎱ 15 to 20 ⎰ miles of ⎱ face ⎰ examined
	Chalk	0	62	38	
S. DORSET	Sand and gravel	0	8	92	⎱ 10 to 15 ⎰ miles of ⎱ face ⎰ examined
S. HANTS	Chalk	0	7	93	

frequent in eastern England. For example, in East Anglia involutions or fossil ice wedges are found in half the sand and gravel pits, and involutions in two out of three chalk pits. In Dorset, by contrast, several miles of suitable face have been examined in many places on the Tertiary gravels and the chalk, yet only a few involutions have been found.

These two areas are chosen as examples because they are closely comparable in terrain and geology. The frequency of structures varies within any particular area so much, according to geological material, that to make any regional comparisons similar deposits must be selected. The frequency also seems to depend on the wetness of the materials, especially in the case of sands and gravels. The drier that such deposits are at the present day the less frequently do they show periglacial structures. It is a general rule that pits more than 20 feet deep which have no water on their floors and show no signs of seepage seldom have any involutions or wedges. The many dry pits in the Folkestone Beds of Surrey, for instance, lack structures for presumably this reason. The obvious inference is that most deposits which are dry now were also dry under periglacial conditions and were so poor in ground ice that they were relatively immune from the frost heaving or cracking which would have formed structures. Many wet pits are so full of water that they cannot be investigated for structures and do not enter into the table. There are more wet pits in East Anglia in proportion to dry pits than there are in Dorset. If the frequency of structures increases with the wetness of the materials, the table may underemphasize the difference between the two areas.

The high frequency of involutions in the Chalk has several causes.

Chalk is very susceptible to frost action. The silt-size particles are ideal for growth of Taber ice, a term suggested by Péwé in 1963 (Péwé, 1966b). A large amount of water is contained in the pores and water is brought in during the freezing process. The poor bonding breaks down rapidly under the action of freeze–thaw. However, involutions can only be recognized in the Chalk where shallow thicknesses of superficial deposits are present. They cannot be found either where the Chalk is completely bare, or where it is thickly covered. Dorset and East Anglia are roughly comparable in the amount and thickness of the superficial cover on the Chalk. The nature of the superficial deposits does not seem to be important because involutions occur in Chalk with all kinds of overlying material—sands, gravels, chalky sands and sludges, loess, and even clay-with-flints. The depth of the superficial material however may well be significant. As might be expected involutions seem able to form under greater thicknesses of sands and gravels than of clays.

A major difference between eastern England and Dorset is the greater number of chalk pits located on steep hillsides in the southwest. Involutions do not seem to occur on slopes of greater than 6°, and for this reason exposures in both areas on slopes greater than this angle have been excluded from the table. It is not possible to exclude pits in bare Chalk from the percentages, because the fact that an area of the Chalk is without superficial deposits now is no proof that it was without cover during periglacial times. Superficial deposits may be preserved in involutions after they have been eroded from the surrounding area.

It will be seen from the map that the majority of features in southwestern and south-central England are involutions. If the view is taken that these are not permafrost features, the area in which permafrost structures are scarce is greatly extended. The majority of involutions seem to be periglacial. They frequently occur in the same exposure as other periglacial structures such as wedges. Involution-like structures very rarely occur in post-glacial sediments. As has frequently been noted, the structure of most involutions suggests permafrost. The upper parts are usually very irregular, yet at any one site the involutions all reach approximately the same depth. This lower limit would seem to represent the top of the permafrost in late summer with the active layer above containing the involutions.

The rarity of periglacial features in the southwest suggests two possible explanations. The simplest is that mean annual temperatures were too high for the formation of permafrost. Alternatively, a deep snow cover persisting until summer might have prevented the development of permafrost by protecting the ground during the cold part of the year.

It is an implied condition of the second explanation that precipitation was higher in the southwest of Britain than in the east. This seems to have been the case. All the evidence points to the conclusion that precipitation in Britain was similar in distribution to the present day, but markedly less in total amount. The centres of ice accumulation during the last glaciation were where the highest rainfall occurs now (Manley 1951). The distribution of corries in Scotland demonstrates a snow-line which was much lower in the west than in the east as present altitudinal zones are (Linton 1957). The distribution of aeolian features also agrees with an increase in wetness or vegetational cover in a westerly direction across England (Fig. 2). Loess, wind-blown sand, and ventifacts are largely restricted to the eastern part of the country, and in the Midlands to a zone immediately to the south of the ice sheet. Even in these areas aeolian action was far less intense than in neighbouring parts of the Continent, such as Holland. In southwestern and south-central England no traces of major aeolian action have been found, apart from a few exceptional sites such as the loess of the Lizard (Coombe and Frost, 1956), despite the occurrence of large areas of sand and gravel.

The low amounts of precipitation in southern England can best be judged from the fact that Dartmoor and other high ground were never glaciated. The reason does not seem to have been hot summers. As Manley held, the lack of forest in southern England indicates that the mean temperature of the warmest month was less than 10°C. Cool conditions are also indicated by involutions and other structures which show that only relatively shallow depths of ground thawed in summer (Williams, unpublished). It has frequently been stated that summers in periglacial Europe must have been warmer than present day arctic areas with the same mean annual temperatures because the sun would have risen higher in the sky on account of the latitude. Such reasoning ignores the effect of the different lengths of day. In fact, on a clear summer day in the Arctic the amount of the sun's heat received on the ground approaches that measured in Europe. In periglacial Europe, daily maxima may have been higher than present arctic areas with the same mean annual temperatures. However, daily or monthly averages could not have been higher without winters having been correspondingly colder. This is hardly likely as periglacial Europe must have received some solar radiation even in mid-winter, whilst arctic areas have 24 hours of darkness.

The lack of glaciation on Dartmoor seems to have been due to low precipitation. With mean annual temperatures as low as those indicated

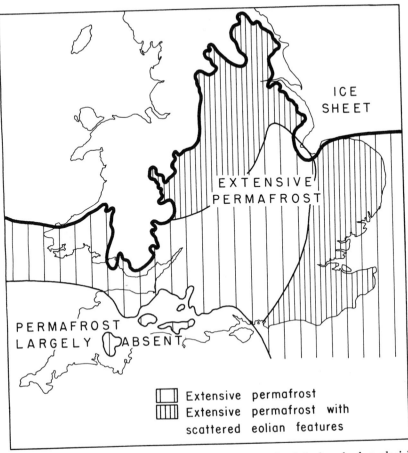

ICE
SHEET

EXTENSIVE
PERMAFROST

PERMAFROST
LARGELY ABSENT

⊞ Extensive permafrost
⊞ Extensive permafrost with
scattered eolian features

FIG. 2. Conjectural distribution of permafrost in England during the last glacial period (Wisconsin). Aeolian features recognized are loess, sand dunes, and venti-facts.

by the polygons, glaciation would have been inevitable if precipitation had been at present values. It is difficult to imagine precipitation could have been more than one-third of what it is at present (for a contrary view see Manley 1951). There must have been many relatively snow-free sites on the Moor. On lower ground in the southwest precipitation would have been lower and summer temperatures somewhat higher than on Dartmoor. Snow would have lasted on the ground for presumably an even shorter period.

Even if a deep blanket of snow existed, it fails to provide a satisfactory explanation why permafrost structures are so rare. First, if it is correct that structures are not found because of snow, it follows that those structures which are found ought to show a preference for the more snow-free sites. This is not the case, even in the southwest. For instance, stone stripes occur on the lower slopes of several deep valleys on Dartmoor. In present winters these valleys become deeply filled with snow swept off the higher parts of the moor by the wind. Presumably snow also collected in these valleys in periglacial times, yet this did not prevent the development of patterns. In fact, a snow cover aids rather than inhibits pattern formation, by keeping the soil saturated. For instance, some giant stone polygons in the Rocky Mountains are currently forming on ill-drained ground in the front of large snow drifts in the absence of permafrost (Benedict 1965). Such polygons are usually thought to require permafrost for their formation. In the Rockies they are forming at temperatures slightly above those necessary for permafrost, though still below freezing point.

The best explanation for the scarcity of permafrost structures in the southwest is that mean annual temperatures were too high. Invasions of Atlantic air moderated the climate sufficiently to prevent extreme winter cold. However, the mild maritime air does not seem to have extended its influence far across the country. Extensive permafrost seems to have occurred as far west as west Sussex and Salisbury Plain (Williams 1965) (Fig. 2). Preliminary results from these districts show that the frequency of structures is not markedly less than in the Midlands and eastern England. Further west, in east Devon and west Dorset, permafrost seems to have been largely absent from Chalk and gravels on low ground. Stone stripes and other structures suggest that permafrost, or at least subfreezing mean annual temperatures, extended down to about 900 feet on Dartmoor.

It is difficult to relate the British permafrost to the zones of continuous and discontinuous permafrost recognized in present periglacial regions (Péwé 1969, Brown 1968). The map probably shows the transition from restricted to extensive permafrost more abruptly than it actually was, quite apart from the cartographic fiction of showing it as a line. South-central England may have represented the discontinuous zone, but this is tentative. The southwest may have been the equivalent to the southern part of the discontinuous zone.

In eastern England and the Midlands the abundance of structures suggests that continuous permafrost must have existed in certain districts. Permafrost structures underlie an estimated 50 per cent of the land surface in such areas as the lower Thames valley and the Breckland of western Norfolk and Suffolk. Permafrost was probably continuous, since not every place where it occurred would be occupied by structures, and not all structures would be preserved. The structures show no preference for slopes facing northeast or damp valley floors to which permafrost would tend to be restricted if it were discontinuous. Additional evidence is provided by fossil ice wedges. These occur in Britain mainly in sands and gravels. In the discontinuous zone in Alaska, wedges in silts and clays contain inactive foliated ice wedges; those in sands and gravels are represented by casts (Péwé 1966*b*, Church, Péwé, Andresen 1965, Péwé 1966*a*). Only in the zone of continuous permafrost are wedges actively forming in all materials. The critical mean annual temperature necessary for continuous permafrost is accepted as about $-6°$ C to $-8°$ C (Péwé 1969) if the snow cover is thin. This isotherm must have lain to the southwest of the Midlands and eastern districts during the height of the last glacial period if continuous permafrost existed in these areas. The position deduced for this isotherm depends on the interpretation which is placed on the margin of extensive permafrost. If the margin represents the edge of the continuous zone, it must also correspond to the $-6°$ C to $-8°$ C isotherm. If as seems more likely the margin marks the edge of the discontinuous zone, the $-6°$ C to $-8°$ C isotherm would have lain across southern England a little further to the northeast. The difference between the two cases amounts to less than 100 miles. Further north, in the Midlands, the average temperature could have been more than $15°$ C lower than today during the coldest part of the last glacial period.

REFERENCES CITED

AVERY, B. W., 1964, The soils and land use of the district around Aylesbury and Hemel Hempstead: Mem. of the Soil Survey of Great Britain, London, HMSO, 216 p.

BENEDICT, J., 1965, Patterned ground on Niwot Ridge, Boulder County, Colorado: *In* Guidebook for Boulder area, Colorado: INQUA (VII International Assoc. Quat. Res.), p. 23-26.

BRIDGES, E. M., 1964, Examples of periglacial phenomena in Derbyshire: East Midland Geogr., v. 3, p. 262-266.

Brown, R. J. E., 1969, Factors influencing discontinuous permafrost in Canada: p. 11-53 *in* Péwé, T. L., *Editor*, The periglacial environment: past and present: Montreal, McGill Univ. Press, 488 p.

Church, R. E., Péwé, T. L., and Andresen, M. J., 1965, Origin and environmental significance of large-scale pattern ground in the Donnelly Dome area, Alaska: Research Dept. no. 159, US Army, Cold Region Research & Engineering Laboratory, 71 p.

Coombe, D. E., and Frost, L. C., 1956, The nature and origin of the soils over the Cornish serpentine: Jour. of Ecol., v. 44, p. 605-615.

Curtis, L. F. and James, J. H., 1959, Frost-heaved soils of Barrow, Rutland: Proc. Geol. Assoc., v. 70, p. 310-314.

Dimbleby, G. W., 1952, Pleistocene ice wedges in north-east Yorkshire: Jour. Soil Sci., v. 3, p. 1-19.

Fitzpatrick, E. A., 1956, Progress report on the observation of periglacial phenomena in the British Isles: Biul. Peryglacjalny, nr. 4, p. 99-115.

Galloway, R. W., 1961a, Ice wedges and involutions in Scotland: Biul. Peryglacjalny, nr. 10, p. 169-193.

———, 1961b, Periglacial phenomena in Scotland: Geog. Ann., v. 43, p. 348-353.

Gruhn, Ruth, and Bryan, A. L., 1969, Fossil ice wedge polygons in southeast Essex, England, p. 351-363 *in* Péwé, T. L., *Editor*, The periglacial environment: past and present: Montreal, McGill Univ. Press, 488 p.

Kaiser, K. K., 1960, Klimazeugen des periglazialen Dauerfrostbodens in Mittel-und Westeuropa: Eiszeitalter u. Gegenwart, v. 11, p. 121-141.

Kerney, M. P., 1963, Late-glacial deposits on the Chalk of south-east England: Phil. Trans. Roy. Soc., v. 246, p. 203-254.

———, 1965, Weischselian deposits in the Isle of Thanet, East Kent: Proc. Geol. Assoc., v. 76, p. 269-274.

Klute, F., 1951, Das Klima Europas während des Maximums der Weischel-Würm Eiszeit und die Änderungen bis zur Jetztzeit. Erdkunde, v. 5, p. 273-283.

Linton, D. L., 1957, Radiating valleys in glaciated lands: Tijdschr. Kon. Ned. Aadr. Gen., v. 74, p. 297-312.

Manley, G., 1951, The range of variation of the British climate: Geog. Jour., v. 117, p. 43-68.

———, 1953, Reviews of modern meteorology—climatic variation: Quat. Jour. Roy. Met. Soc., v. 79, p. 185-209.

Péwé, T. L., 1966a, Paleoclimatic significance of fossil ice wedges: Biul. Peryglacjalny, nr. 15, p. 65-73.

———, 1966b, Ice-wedges in Alaska: Classification, distribution, and climatic significance: Proc. Intern. Permafrost Conf., Nat. Acad. Sci.—Nat. Res. Council Pub. No. 1287, p. 76-81.

———, 1969, The periglacial environment: p. 1-9 *in* Péwé, T. L., *Editor*, The periglacial environment: past and present: Montreal, McGill Univ. Press, 488 p.

Poser, H., 1948, Boden—und Klimaverhältnisse in Mittel—und West-europa während der Würmeiszeit: Erdkunde, v. 2, p. 53-68.

Shotton, F. W., 1960, Large scale patterned ground in the valley of the Worcestershire Avon: Geol. Mag., v. 97, p. 404-408.

———, 1962, The physical background of Britain in the Pleistocene: Advanc. Sci., v. 19, p. 193-206.

Stephens, N., and Synge, F. M., 1966, Pleistocene Shorelines, *in* Dury, G. H., Essays in Geomorphology, London, Heinemann, 51 p.

Te Punga, M. T., 1957, Periglaciation in southern England: Tijdschr. Kon. Ned. Aardr. Gen., v. 74, p. 400-412.

Tricart, J., 1956, Cartes des phénomènes périglaciaires quaternaires en France: Carte Geol. de France, Mem. Paris, Imprimerie nationale, 40 p.

Trist, P. J. O., 1952, Frost cracks: Trans. Suffolk Nat. Soc., v. 8, p. 26-30.

WATERS, R. S., 1961, Involutions and ice-wedges in Devon: Nature, v. 189, p. 389-390.

WATSON, E., 1965, Periglacial structures in the Aberystwyth region of central Wales: Proc. Geol. Assoc., v. 76, p. 443-462.

WEST, R. G., 1969, Stratigraphy of periglacial features in East Anglia and adjacent areas, England, p. 411-415 *in* Péwé, T. L., *Editor*, The periglacial environment: past and present: Montreal, McGill Univ. Press, 488 p.

WILLIAMS, R. B. G., 1964, Fossil patterned ground in eastern England: Biul. Peryglacjalny, nr. 14, p. 337-349.

———, 1965, Permafrost in England during the last glacial period: Nature, v. 205, p. 1304-1305.

WRIGHT, H. E., 1961, Late Pleistocene climate of Europe: a review: Geol. Soc. America Bull., v. 72, p. 933-984.

STRATIGRAPHY OF PERIGLACIAL FEATURES IN EAST ANGLIA AND ADJACENT AREAS

R. G. WEST
Sub-department of Quaternary Research
Botany School, University of Cambridge
Cambridge, England

ABSTRACT. A table is given showing the stratigraphical relations of various horizons of periglacial activity in East Anglia and southeast England during the Pleistocene. Permafrost periods are known from four cold stages, and involutions or solifluction deposits from five. The horizons are dated by C14 and by reference to tills and temperate organic deposits.

RÉSUMÉ. L'auteur dresse un tableau montrant les relations stratigraphiques entre les divers horizons d'activité périglaciaire dans l'East Anglia et le sud-est de l'Angleterre durant le Pléistocène. On a reconnu des périodes de pergélisol pour quatre stades glaciaires et des involutions ou des dépôts de solifluxion pour cinq stades. Grâce au C14, on a pu dater les horizons par rapport aux tills et aux dépôts organiques de climat tempéré.

ZUSAMMENFASSUNG. Eine Tabelle zeigt stratigraphische Lage von Brodelböden, Fliesserden, Eiskeilen und von äolischen Bildungen im Pleistozän von East Anglia und angrenzenden Gebieten. Zeugnisse von Dauerfrostboden (Eiskeile) werden von vier Kaltzeiten und Brodelböden oder Fliesserden von fünf Kaltzeiten erkannt. Das Alter dieser Bildungen wird entweder durch C14 oder durch ihre stratigraphische Lage in Beziehung zu Grundmoränen und warmzeitlichen organischen Ablagerungen bestimmt.

CONTENTS

Climatic changes in the Pleistocene of Britain have been adduced mainly from studies of till, faunal, and vegetational sequences. But sequences of periglacial features also give valuable information on

TABLE I
THE STRATIGRAPHY OF IMPORTANT HORIZONS OF PERIGLACIAL ACTIVITY IN EAST ANGLIA AND THE ADJACENT AREA TO THE SOUTH

Locality	Feature	Periods of freeze/thaw (F/T), permafrost (P), aeolian activity (A)	Outline of Stratigraphy Proving Age	Age (non-periglacial intervals in brackets)	Tentative correlation with North American sequence	Reference (if none given, author's unpublished observations)
Isle of Thanet, Folkestone, Medway Valley, Kent	chalk detritus (snow or thaw meltwater deposits), combe cutting	F/T	overlies C14 dated soil (Q463 11,944 ±210 BP)	Late Weichselian Zone III (Allerød)	Wisconsin	Kerney 1963
	chalk detritus (snow or thaw meltwater deposits)	F/T	overlies C14 dated soil (Q473 13,190 ±230 BP)	Late Weichselian Zone Ic (Bølling)		Kerney 1965
	loess	A	underly C14 dated soil	Middle Weichselian		Kerney, Brown and Chandler 1964
	snow meltwater deposits, involutions, solifluction (coombe rock)	F/T				
Wretton, Norfolk	ice wedge casts	P	overly organic deposits of probable Chelford age	Middle Weichselian		
	penetrate involutions	F/T				
				(Ipswichian)	Sangamon	
Beetley, Norfolk	ice wedge cast	P	underlies Ipswichian, penetrates valley outwash	Late Gippingian		
Ebbsfleet, Kent	Solifluction (coombe rock)	F/T	on Chalk, below Ipswichian	Gippingian	Illinoian	Burchell in Zeuner, 1959; West, Lambert and

				(Cromerian)	Aftonian
West Runton, Mundesley, Beeston, Norfolk	ice wedge casts, involutions	P F/T	underly Cromerian, penetrate Pastonian, associated with arctic plant beds	Beestonian	Nebraskan West & Wilson, 1966
				(Pastonian)	
Covehithe, Suffolk	involutions	F/T	disturb upper Baventian silts	Late Baventian	
Beeston, Norfolk	solifluction (coombe rock)	F/T	on Chalk, below Pastonian	Baventian	

environmental conditions. Thus, the development of ice wedges indicates permafrost, of involutions and solifluction the presence of freeze-thaw zones near the surface, and of loess, the prevalence of wind deposition.

Periglacial features occur in many different stratigraphical positions in East Anglia and the adjacent area to the south, and it is now possible to give the relative age of several important horizons exhibiting involutions, solifluction, ice wedge casts, and loess formation. Most detail is known of the sequences of the Weichselian (Last) glacial stage, as might be expected, but there are also horizons related to the older cold stages of the Pleistocene, both those cold stages showing till formation and those yet earlier ones with which no tills have yet been associated.

Table 1 summarizes the stratigraphy of important horizons of periglacial activity in East Anglia and the adjacent area to the south. The succession of cold stages to which the horizons of periglacial activity are referred, are those given by West (1963) and West and Wilson (1966).

There are permafrost periods associated with the Beestonian cold stage, with an early pre-till part of the Lowestoftian glacial stage, with a post-outwash part of the Gippingian glacial stage, and with the middle Weichselian. As with the Weichselian, it is evident that climatic changes resulting in the formation of periglacial features and sequences are important in the older cold stages. It will be of great interest to relate the actual ice advances responsible for till formation to the climatic sequence within each glaciation. This is not yet possible, even with the Weichselian in England, where it seems clear that in the east and southeast middle Weichselian phases of solifluction and involution were followed by drier conditions when aeolian deposition became important and ice wedge formation occurred. And in the late Weichselian, freeze-thaw activity again became prevalent in the southeast.

Much further work is required for the building-up of these periglacial successions and their relation to the glacial deposits, but at least we now have an outline of the stratigraphical relations of important horizons of periglacial activity through a large part of the Pleistocene.

REFERENCES CITED

DONNER, J. J., and WEST, R. G., 1958, A note on Pleistocene frost structures on the Cliff Section at Bacton, Norfolk: Norfolk and Norwich Nat. Soc., v. 18, p. 8-9.
KERNEY, M. P., 1963, Late-glacial deposits on the Chalk of south-east England: Royal Soc. London Philos. Trans., ser. B, v. 246, p. 203-254.

KERNEY, M. P., 1965, Weichselian deposits in the Isle of Thanet, East Kent: Geol. Assoc. London, Proc., v. 76, p. 269-274.

KERNEY, M. P., BROWN, E. H., and CHANDLER, T. J., 1964, The Late-glacial and Post-glacial history of the Chalk escarpment near Brook, Kent: Royal Soc. London Philos. Trans., ser. B, v. 248, p. 135-204.

WEST, R. G., 1963, Problems of the British Quaternary: Geol. Assoc. London, Proc., v. 74, p. 147-186.

WEST, R. G., LAMBERT, C. A., and SPARKS, B. W., 1964, Interglacial deposits at Ilford, Essex: Royal Soc. London Philos. Trans., ser. B, v. 247, p. 185-212.

WEST, R. G., and WILSON, D. G., 1966, Cromer Forest Bed Series: Nature, v. 209, p. 497-498.

ZEUNER, F. E., 1959, The Pleistocene Period: London, Hutchinson, 447 p.

PROCESSES AND ENVIRONMENTS
OF THE BRAZILIAN QUATERNARY

JOÃO JOSÉ BIGARELLA, MARIA REGINA MOUSINHO,
JORGE XAVIER DA SILVA
University of Paraná, Curitiba, Brazil

ABSTRACT. Study of the processes and environments of the southeastern and southern Brazilian Pleistocene cold phases brings up many questions about geomorphology, sedimentation, paleoclimates, and weathering.

The sedimentary textures indicate different processes of weathering in which mechanical disintegration was dominant and therefore extremely different from those acting nowadays in the humid tropical or subtropical areas. Sedimentary structures allow the recognition of processes involved in the transport of debris into the basins, as well as in the mechanism of sedimentation.

Through the geomorphological survey of the area, pediplane, pediments, *glacis* of colluvium, and river terraces have been identified. In the river valleys most of the shoulders, formerly considered as river terraces, are actually remnants of pediments.

Study of the basins (*cuvette, alveolos*) in very different geographical areas, close to the sea or in the high mountains, has shown equal numbers of erosion levels (pediment remnants), as well as the same characteristic *glacis* of colluvium and the lower terrace.

Two different sets of processes have been visualized. One operated during the Pleistocene semi-arid climatic phases (= glacial time) producing lateral degradation (parallel retreat of slopes) forming pediments. The other acted during Pleistocene humid climatic phases (= interglacial time) promoting linear erosion causing dissection.

In the semi-arid phase the local base levels were better preserved, and when lowered the planated erosion surface (pediment) was constantly regraded. In the humid phase the local base levels dropped down causing deep incision with dissection of topography.

The erosion levels have an alternating climatic control caused mainly by extreme climatic changes. This would be the reason why the same geomorphic picture is found in different basins (*cuvette*) at very different geographical sites, regardless of uplift implications.

RÉSUMÉ. L'étude des processus et des milieux durant les périodes froides du Pléistocène dans le sud-est et le sud du Brésil amène à poser de nombreuses questions sur la géomorphologie, la sédimentation, les paléoclimats et l'altération.

Les textures sédimentaires révèlent différents processus d'altération, parmi lesquels la désintégration mécanique a été dominante; ces processus étaient donc extrêmement différents de ceux qui agissent actuellement dans les régions tropicales humides ou subtropicales. Les structures sédimentaires permettent de reconnaître les processus impliqués dans le transport des débris vers les bassins, ainsi que le mécanisme de la sédimentation.

Par l'étude géomorphologique de la région, on a pu identifier une pédi-plaine, des pédiments, des glacis "colluviaux" et des terrasses fluviatiles. Dans les vallées fluviales, la plupart des épaulements autrefois considérés comme des terrasses fluviatiles sont en fait des restes de pédiments.

L'étude des bassins (*cuvette, alveolos*) dans des régions géographiques très différentes, près de la mer comme en haute montagne, a montré un nombre égal de niveaux d'érosion (restes de pédiments), ainsi que le même glacis "colluvial" caractéristique et la même terrasse inférieure.

Les auteurs ont imaginés deux ensembles de processus différents. L'un fonctionnait durant les périodes semi-arides du Pléistocène (= périodes glaciaires), produisant une dégradation latérale (recul parallèle des pentes) formatrice de pédiments. L'autre fonctionnait durant les phases clima-tiques humides (= périodes interglaciaires), favorisant l'érosion linéaire et donc la dissection.

Dans la phase semi-aride, les niveaux de base locaux étaient mieux con-servés; lorsqu'ils étaient abaissés, la surface d'érosion (pédiment) était constamment renivelée. Dans la phase humide, les niveaux de base s'abais-saient, provoquant une profonde incision, avec dissection du relief.

Les niveaux d'érosion possèdent un contrôle climatique alternant, dû principalement à des changements extrêmes du climat. C'est ce qui ex-pliquerait que l'on retrouve la même image "géomorphique" dans des bassins différents, en des sites géographiques très différents, sans égard aux implications isostatiques.

ZUSAMMENFASSUNG. Die Untersuchung der Vorgaenge und des Mileus in Suedost-und Suedbrasilien waehrend der kalten Epochen des Pleistozaens stellt die Forschung vor viele Fragen hinsichtlich der Geo-morphologie, der Sedimentation, des Palaeoklimas und der Verwitterung.

Die Texturen der Sedimente weisen auf verschiedene Vorgaenge der Verwitterung hin, wobei der mechanische Zerfall vorherrschend war und damit aeusserst verschieden von denjenigen, die heute in den feuchten subtropischen Gebieten wirksam sind.

Ablagerungs Strukturen erlaubten die Vorgaenge zu erkennen, die waehrend des Transports der Gestein-Fragmente in das Becken wirksam waren, ebenso wie den Mechanismus der Sedimentation.

Durch die geomorphologische Untersuchung der Abtragungs-Niveaus und der Pedimente wurden kolluviale Glacis und Fluss-Terrassen identi-fiziert. Die meisten Gelaendestufen in den Flusstaelern, frueher als Fluss-Terrassen bezeichnet, sind jetzt als Reliktenformen von Pedimenten (Ueberschuettungs-Fussflaechen) erkannt.

Die Untersuchung der Sedimentations-Becken (Cuvette, alveolos) in den verschiedensten geographischen Gebieten, in der Naehe der Meeres oder in den Hoehen der Gebirge, hat die gleiche Anzahl von Erosions-Niveaus (Pediment-Reste) erwiesen, wie auch die gleichen charakteri-stichen Glacis des Kolluviums und die tiefere Terrasse.

Zwei verschiedene Folgen von Vergaengen wurden erkannt. Ein Vor-gang Wirkte waehrend semiarider Epochen des Pleistozaens (= quartaere Eiszeit) die seitliche Erniedrigung (Zurueckverlegung des Hanges, *paral-lel retreat of slopes*), verursachte und Pedimente formte. Der andere Vorgang wirkte waehrend der humiden Epochen des Pleistozaens (= entsprechend den Interglazialzeiten), und foerderte lineare Erosion die Zerschneidung verursachte.

In der semiariden Epoche wurde das likale Basis-Niveau besser erhalten und wenn vertieft die verebnete Abtragungs-Oberflaeche (das Pediment) staendig zurueckverlegt. Mittlerweile in der humiden Epoche, war das lokale Basis-Niveau tiefer gelegt und das feuchte Klima verursachte tiefe

Zerschneidung mit Zergliederung der Topographie. Die Erosions-Niveaus zeigen wechselnde klimatische Einfluesse, die hauptsaechlich durch extreme Klimaaenderungen verursacht wurden. Das wird auch der Grund sein, dass das gleiche geomorphologische Bild in den verschiedensten Becken (*Cuvettes*) und geographischen Lagen gefunden wurde, unbeschadet epirogenetischer Hebungen.

RESUMEN. El estudio de los procesos y locales del sudeste y sur brasileño durante las fases frias del Pleistoceno llevanta muchas questiones sobre geomorfologia, sedimentacion, paleoclimas y intemperización.

Las texturas sedimentares muestran la operación de diferentes procesos de ación del intemperisimo en que la desintegración mecánica fué dominante y por lo tanto muy dèstincta de lo que se pasa hoydia em las areas tropicales o subtropicales.

Las estruturas sedimentarias permiten reconocer los procesos concernientes en el transporte de detritus para las bacias, asi como em el mecanismo de sedimentación.

Por medio de una investigación geomorfologica de la región, se pudo identificar los pedimentos, glacis de coluvio y terrazos de rios. En los valles de rios muchas de las encuestras, anteriormente consideradas como terrazos, son en realidad remanentes de pedimentos.

El estudio de una bacia (*cuvette, alveolos*) en muchas regiones geograficas diferentes, junto al mar e en las altas montanas, ha puesto de manifesto numero igual de niveles de erosión (*pediment remnants*), asi como las mismas caracteristicas glacis de coluvios y terrazas bajas.

Dos diferentes grupos de procesos han sido vizualizados. Uno operó durante las fases climáticas semiaridas del Pleistoceno (= estagio glacial) produciendo degradación lateral (*parallel retreat of slopes*) formando pedimentos. El otro tuvo logar durante las fases climaticas humidas del Pleistoceno (= estagio interglacial) causando erosión linear y la resultante disección.

En la fase semiarid los niveles de la base local no fueron preservados y quando rebajados, la superfície aplanada de erosion (*pediment*) seria constantemente regradada. Por otro lado, en la fase humida, los niveles locales de la base caieron causando incisiones profundas con la disección de la topografia.

Los niveles de erosion tienen un control climatico alternado causado principalmente por los cambios extremos de clima. Estos serian la razon porque el mismo aspecto geomorfico es hallado en diferente bacias (*cuvettes*) en los mas diversos sitios geográficos a pesar de implicaciones de llevantamiento.

CONTENTS

FIGURE

INTRODUCTION

Deep climatic changes and smaller climatic variations played an important role in the morphological development of the eastern and central parts of Brazil. Recent studies have shown great climatic instability during the Pleistocene in many different parts of the earth. Initially, the tendency was to correlate the glacial periods of high latitudes to pluvial phases in the tropical and subtropical belt. Up to now, many authors maintained this point of view. Others believed that a displacement of the climatic zones took place during the glacial phases.

However, lately, it has been generally accepted that during the Quaternarian cold phases in most of the tropical and subtropical regions an outstanding decrease of the pluviosity occurred, together with a change in the rainfall distribution. These modifications originated a generalized aridity or semi-aridity, and the humid phases should correspond to the interglacial times.

Studies of some Brazilian landscapes reinforce this last hypothesis. Sedimentary formations indicating semi-arid continental environments are presently below sea level (Alexandra and Graxaim formations). They were deposited when sea level was glacioeustatically lowered. The contemporaneity between dry climatic phases and marine regressions was also suggested by the observations of Cailleux and Tricart (1959, p. 14) in Cubatão (State of São Paulo), where can be found deposits related to a dryer climate, apparently dipping under coastal plain formations considered Flandrian in age by the mentioned authors. On the other hand, Ewing (personal communication) mentioned the work of L. J. Groot and C. R. Groot in which pollen analysis of deep cores from the south Atlantic Argentine basin revealed a sequence of alternating layers, from which conclusions on alternation of paleoclimates could be deduced. The layer with pollen from *Ephedra* and *Chenopodiacea* corresponds to a semi-arid plant assemblage on the continent where it existed at the time of lower sea level (glacial Pleistocene times), while the layers bearing arboreal pollen would correspond to the interglacials.

During the Pleistocene, in large areas of the Brazilian territory, two

421

alternate and different groups of processes submitted the landscape to lateral degradation during the semi-arid climates (glacial epochs) and to dissection during the humid climates (interglacial epochs). Such correlation was previously suggested by Bigarella and Ab'Sáber (1964) and Bigarella and Andrade (1965). The erosive activity would have been very effective in the periods of transition from one type of climate to the other.

A brief analysis of the results of climatic changes on the landscape development is made here.

We believe that, at the present stage of geomorphology, it is essential to establish not only a better qualitative, but also a quantitative knowledge of the processes operating upon slopes under the present climatic conditions. Based on these observations, it is possible to deduce to some extent the trend of the actual evolution of the morphologic features. On the other hand, the paleoclimatic influences upon the topography may be deduced, although we recognize that in the past there might have occurred special climatic conditions and morphoclimatic processes which are not observed today.

The mechanism of slope development consists basically of the subtle interaction of climatic changes, local base level displacements, and uplift. The landscape of southeastern and southern Brazil results from a periodic alternation of two different sets of processes. One set, operating during semi-arid climate, was represented by processes of mechanical morphogenesis, promoting lateral degradation of the topography answering for the development of pedimentary surfaces. The other set, acting during humid climatic conditions, caused chemical weathering with linear erosion and deep dissection of the terrain. The combination of these two different sets of processes is used in this paper as a clue to the interpretation of the landscapes.

The climatic control of the landscape evolution does not exclude the effect of tectonic or eustatic movements. However, uplift is not considered to be absent or underestimated in its relation to the landscape development. On the contrary, whenever present it would have accentuated the differences in level between the shoulders, promoting a deeper dissection of the relief during the humid epochs. Nevertheless, uplift plays a secondary role in the sculpturing of the landscape in which the cyclicity of the erosion levels (shoulders, etc.) is due mainly to a "climatic change" control. Furthermore, the cyclic features are related to local base levels rather than to the sea level.

There is opposition to this proposed approach from Davis (1954), Penck (1953), and Hack (1960). The study of the erosive forms and their related deposits in the eastern part of Brazil provided data concerning the interpretation of the climatic conditions existing at the time of their formation; it enabled a correlation between levels of pediment remnants and their actual detrital deposits, either in the pedimentation area or in the complete drainage area (fluvial terraces with gravel deposits). A cyclic repetition in the landscape was noticed. Genetically similar levels are found in most varied areas of the country. Such levels could have been formed contemporaneously at different elevations, either on the coast, on the plateau, or in the high mountains, for development of pedimentation processes was tied to the local base levels of the drainage.

If one compares basins, (*alveolo*, Port.; *cuvette*, Fr.), geographically distant and of varied altimetric position, the repetition of the same basic scheme of distribution of the various erosion levels calls attention to the fact that there ought to be, besides the movements of the crust, another far more important control that would be able to sculpture the same erosive patterns in the most varied basins independently in this aspect of the epeirogenic movements.

Studying the processes which worked in the elaboration of the bevelled erosion surfaces of the past, represented today by shoulders, it became possible to create a new hypothesis to explain the cyclicity of erosion, based chiefly on the climatic changes and, consequently, the change in the morphoclimatic processes acting on the slopes.

Morphological evolution under humid conditions

WEATHERING. It is known that the interpretation of the type of weathering in one area depends not only on the geological and topographical situation, but also, and mainly, on the climatic conditions. Therefore, the detrital material has many features which can help the interpretation of paleoclimates and processes effecting the removal of the weathering products.

The weathering mantle, formed under humid climatic conditions in the forested crystalline regions of southeastern and southern Brazil, gives a measure of the great importance of chemical decomposition in the development of the local landforms. The weathered zone normally reaches 10 to 15 m thickness. The depth reached by chemical decomposition depends on the type of rock and on its system of fractures. The less fractured zones, having rocks of uniform and fine texture (granitic types of rock) and a system of concentric joints, may become the topographically higher ones. Weathering reduces at a higher rate the areas around this nucleus which tend to be accentuated, originating the forms that under successive climatic changes evolve into the "sugar loaf" type of landform. Areas with rocks either less fractured or less susceptible to decomposition because of their own mineralogical constitution and textural characteristics appear as hills in the landscape. Those more deeply fractured suffer a more intense chemical decomposition, being the areas where valleys and depressions are developed by differential erosion.

Weathering of the bedrock, progressing from the joints, can isolate blocks that become inlaid in a mantle weathered *in situ*. Usually the regolithic profile comprises: (*a*) a completely weathered zone; (*b*) a weathered zone with fresh rock blocks of various sizes; (*c*) a zone of decomposition showing the joint system and the beginning of the isolation of blocks; and (*d*) a joint zone in fresh rock. If the environmental conditions remain constant and the regolith does not suffer mobilization, there would be a tendency to total chemical decomposition of all the blocks originating a homogeneous weathered mantle. However, climatic variations causing semi-aridity and a change in the vegetation allow mobilization of inclined slopes through mass movements (solifluction or landslides) of the heterogeneous weathered mantle.

In the area studied, the tops of the hills and shoulders have usually a more developed eluvial profile covered by a thin mantle of colluvium. The latter has a greater development in the lower part of the slopes, reaching greater thickness in the depressions where solifluction processes are or were important.

REGOLITH DISPLACEMENT ON THE SLOPES. In the tropical and subtropical regions of Brazil, in the areas densely covered with forest, there is a relative stability of the weathered material. Compared with other processes, rain wash seems to be of low efficiency in the areas covered with forests, be they temperate, subtropical, or tropical. The creep, understood as the individual movement of the particles, is also not very efficient in displacing the waste material. The soil of the forest areas is generally protected against erosion by a thick layer of vegetal remains. The falling of trees or the action of animals seem to be insignificant in relation to the importance of the displacement suffered by the weathered mantle. Nevertheless, the removal of material in solution is important (leaching). However, under dryer climatic conditions within the humid epoch, with a sparser vegetal cover such processes could have acted more efficiently, the slopes thus being submitted to the action of rain wash. This contributed to a partial removal of the weathering mantle and caused incipient gullying.

It must be pointed out that during these short climatic fluctuations, mass movements and rain wash must have acted together, although it is difficult at the present stage of research to establish clearly the limiting action of these two processes. The study of the slope deposits (colluvium) shows undeniably, however, that most of the mass movements occurred as morphological agents.

When a small creek starts to cut into the undisturbed regolith, a disequilibrium is initiated. According to the topography, density of vegetation, and climate, the unbalanced material may evolve differently. On very steep forested slopes (with declivity greater than 40°), after a long period of heavy rainfall violent landslides in which the sliding plane is usually the limit between the weathered mantle and the fresh rock may occur. This phenomenon caused many scars in the steep slopes of the Serra do Mar. Its occurrence is not very frequent and is restricted to exceptionally humid years and very steep slopes. Landslides may also occur after the anthropologically originated removal of the forest on slopes of smaller gradient, being in this case a mere reactivation of the mass movement. An inspection of the present-day landscape shows that visible landsliding in small slope declines is not an active process promoting the degradation of the topography; it is restricted to areas in which man disturbed the hill slope equilibrium (highway cuts). This, however, is a local process, and cannot be considered active in the general lowering of the topography.

Solifluction occurs not only in areas where an impermeable layer is formed by frozen ground (periglacial), but also under the most variable climatic conditions (Birot 1960, p. 34, Baulig 1956, p. 23). It is only necessary that an impermeable layer exist, which would not allow the infiltration of the waters and would therefore cause the soaking of the upper layers, thus providing their loss of stability. Slower movements such as solifluction occur usually where the slopes are much steeper, these movements being recognized by the slanting of the trees.

In the crystalline tropical and subtropical regions, the talus deposits have their origin related to landslides in the regolith of very steep slopes, and to rockfalls from exfoliated bare slopes. Once deposited in the talus, the fragments tend to be weathered and covered by vegetation.

Observations made in many talus deposits show blocks and fine material forming a mass of great thickness, testifying to a hastened denudation of the slopes under rougher climatic conditions which were able to furnish the heterogeneous material.

Mass movement processes have been studied in some detail at the mountainous area of the Serra do Mar in Paraná. Deep chemical weathering is conspicuous all over the area originating a regolith cover more than 15 m thick. The area has a humid climate. Rainfall in the Serra do Mar may reach over 3,000 mm per year. The weathered material was formed *in situ*, and the original structures of the rock are still preserved. In many places a downslope movement occurred, destroying all the original structures. The result is a structureless mass (colluvium) of fine-grained matrix, having enclosed coarser material of pebble to boulder size. The coarser material tends to be concentrated at the bottom of the sliding mass as well as in its edges. Nevertheless, the greatest rudaceous material concentration is located where the running water flows. The lithologic composition of the slide varies according to the parent rock. The material does not present any sorting.

The inspection of the structure of numerous road cuts in southeastern and southern Brazil indicates that solifluction processes in subactual or more remote epochs were of great importance in the development of many characteristics found in the present-day landscape morphology. However, in most of the cuts, it was noticed that the process was practically halted some time ago. This seems to be a conspicuous feature all over the researched area, from Santa Catarina up to Rio de Janeiro (Figs. 1–5). Its generalized occurrence is linked to past, more drastic climatic conditions within the present humid epoch. Nowadays the displacement caused by gravity action is extremely slow and frequently unnoticed.

Many times the composite slopes of variable declivities covered with weathered material present basin-shaped inclined scars which stretch and narrow themselves downward. These scars end with a local break of gradient when inlaid high in the slope, or when situated at the base of the slope, by a fan-like, slightly inclined *glacis* of colluvium material.

Studying these erosive forms of varied amplitude and the corresponding depositional cones, we came to the following conclusion: These forms result from a loss of stability from part of the regolith which slid down during phases of dryer climatic conditions, different, therefore, from the present ones. The scars do occur, generally, where the rock is more susceptible to weathering and presents a thicker regolith. On the other hand, they are placed laterally to the thinner and more stable portions of the regolith, generally found on the eluvium, at the expense of which they progressively tend to expand themselves.

Once mobilized the regolith loses consistency, thus facilitating the infiltration of rain waters and the subsequent mass displacements. At the same time, erosion is accomplished by rain wash which, being concentrated in some places, promotes the removal of the fine matrix and accumulates blocks in the drainage channels. The texture and lack

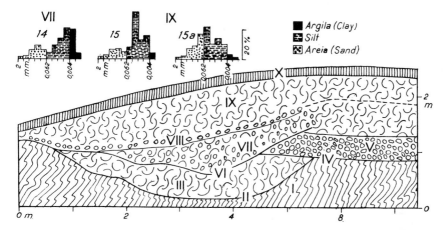

Fig. 1. Structure of a remnant of the pediment P_2 surface. Sequence of several colluvium layers and paleopavements. Cut in the road Curitiba-Ressaca-Colombo, 200 m before the Atuba River. I—Weathered gneiss (eluvium); II—erosive unconformity; III—red colluvium, rich in angular and subangular quartz pebbles (6 cm of maximum size) imbedded in a silty-clayey sandy matrix; IV—erosive unconformity; V—thick gravel accumulation of subangular to subrounded quartz pebbles, generally small (2-3 cm) with some larger up to 8 cm diameter; VI—erosive unconformity; VII—reddish colluvium rich in small angular to subangular quartz pebbles sparsely imbedded in a sandy-silty-clayey matrix (Sample 14 of the illustration). Occasionally rounded diabase cobbles measuring up to 20 cm occur; VIII—detrital paleopavement formed by angular to subangular granules and small pebbles of quartz; IX—brown colluvium. A silty-sandy matrix with granules and small angular quartz pebbles (Samples 15 and 15a); X—humic zone.

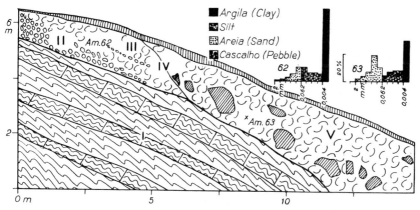

Fig. 2. Road cut 3.5 km from Itapema in the direction to Florianopolis (State of Santa Catarina). I—crystalline basement; II, III—reddish colluvial material encompassing blocks and pebbles from the local bedrock; IV—erosive unconformity; V—brownish colluvial layer with pebbles and large generally angular blocks.

427

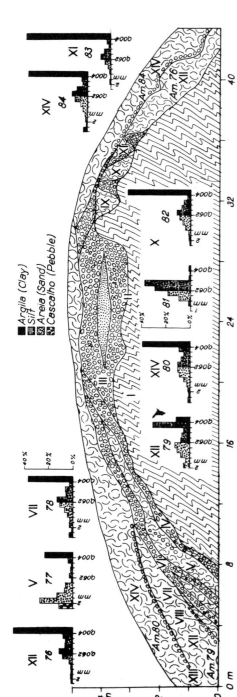

Argila (Clay)
Silt
Areia (Sand)
Cascalho (Pebble)

Fig. 3. Road cut between Brusque and Gaspar (State of Santa Catarina), 2.5 km from Brusque. I—weathered phyllite (Sample 81); II—erosive unconformity; III—gravel deposit. Angular to subrounded quartz and quartzite pebbles reaching 10 cm in maximum size; IV—paleopavement of angular to subangular quartz and quartzitic pebbles (smaller than 10 cm) lying on an irregular erosion surface (erosive unconformity). At the contact with the phyllite quartz and quartzite blocks (30 cm of maximum size), subrounded and imbedded in a fine matrix can be seen; V—sandy colluvium, mottled red (Sample 77); VI—paleopavement of angular to subrounded quartz and quartzite pebbles of varied size (maximum 15 cm); VII—silty-sandy reddish-brown colluvium, having sparse quartz pebbles (3 cm of maximum size)—Sample 78. This colluvium is crossed by a line of small size quartz pebbles; VIII—thin and discontinuous pebble line; IX—reddish-brown colluvium unconformably deposited on the phyllites; X—reddish-brown colluvium unconformably deposited on the phyllites (Sample 82); XI—reddish-brown colluvium (Sample 83) separated from the anterior colluvium (X) by a thin pebble line; XII—silty-sandy reddish-brown colluvium, containing angular and subangular quartz subangular quartz pebbles reaching 2 cm maximum size. This paleopavement becomes thicker in the higher part of the exposed section (centre); XIV—brown colluvium having small quartz granules (Samples 80 and 84).

This section consists of dissected remnants of a terrace. The pebble layer (III) was extensively deposited in the past drainage trough of the Itajaí-Mirim River, during the semi-arid epoch relative to the development of the pediment P_1.

In a subsequent humid climate epoch the terrace was dissected; thereafter came the re-covering of the slopes and lateral depressions by a sequence of paleopavements and reddish-brown colluvia.

In the left side of the exposure of the post gravel III initial fill (IV to VIII) was partially preserved, while in the right side of the exposure those deposits were entirely removed by a new dissection. Other reddish-brown colluvia (IX to XI) occurred again whose remnants are found in small depressions in the right side of the road cut.

A new intense colluviation re-covered both slopes. Finally a very recent paleopavement approximately follows the present

XIII—discontinuous and thin paleopavement with angular and

428

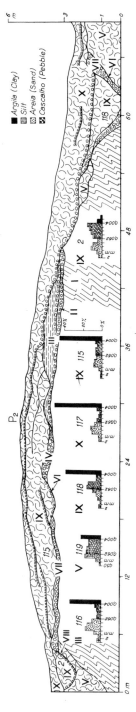

Legend:
- ■ Argila (Clay)
- ▦ Silt
- ▨ Areia (Sand)
- ▩ Cascalho (Pebble)

Fig. 4. Road cut at 640 m from Santa Candida in the road Curitiba-Colombo. The exposure corresponds to the P_2 level. I—weathered gneiss rich in quartz veins; II—erosive unconformity; III—grey sediments from the Guabirotuba Formation reworked during the pedimentation phase P_2. The lower part of this layer is more sandy and very rich in pebbles smaller than 8 cm, generally angular to subangular. The higher part consists of unstratified silty-clayey material (Sample 116); IV—detrital paleopavement formed generally by angular and subangular quartz pebbles reaching 8 cm of maximum size; V—lilac-red colluvium spotted with lighter colour. Silty-clayey texture.

Contains angular granules and small pebbles of quartz and less frequently of feldspar (Sample 119); VI—erosive unconformity; VII—detrital paleopavement. Angular to subangular quartz pebbles smaller than 8 cm; VIII—erosive unconformity; IX— dark red colluvium consisting of silty-sandy matrix containing abundantly angular quartz granules and less frequently feldspar granules (Sample 115, 118 and 2). Thereafter a detrital paleopavement occurs; X—brown colluvium containing many granules and small pebbles of quartz in a silty-sandy matrix (Sample 117). It has also a discontinuous line of granules and small angular pebbles of quartz.

429

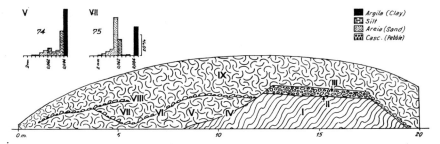

Fig. 5. Exposure of a slope structure 22.8 km from Brusque on the road to São João Batista (State of Santa Catarina). I—weathered phyllites, rich in quartz veins; II—erosive unconformity; III—detrital paleopavement formed by angular quartz pebbles smaller than 8 cm; IV—erosive unconformity; V—reddish colluvium with abundant angular quartz pebbles smaller than 8 cm imbedded in a silty-clayey matrix (Sample 74); VI—small erosive scars indicated by a discontinuous line of angular quartz pebbles smaller than 8 cm; VII—brownish colluvium consisting of a clayey-sandy matrix containing granules and small pebbles of quartz (Sample 75); VIII—discontinuous pebble line; IX—yellowish-brown colluvium.

of stratification of the debris concentrated at the bottom of the landslide deposits demonstrate the important role played by mass movement in the genesis of the described basin-like scars.

Solifluction phenomena or other waste displacements verified through the examination of the regional morphology and road cuts are characteristic of a humid climate having fluctuations towards dryness. This relative climatic instability resulted in the formation of two types of regolith, one retaining the rocks' former structure (eluvium), and the other with evident signs of movement (colluvium). Under the present climate the displacements and slidings have not been as effective as in the past, bringing up the problem of what might have been the conditions that formerly favoured them.

To explain the epochs of extensive solifluction we have to consider the controlling climatic conditions, or more precisely, the fluctuations which caused a pluvial cycle responsible for the soaking of the weathered mantle. These conditions could be propitiated by a climate more humid than the present one or by a dryer climate with concentrated rainfalls. The first hypothesis does not seem very probable, although possible. The second one has some evidence in the nature of the flood plain deposits. The end of the last fluctuation towards dryness occurred about 2,400 years BP (Bigarella 1964, p. 219). At that time the vegetation was not so dense, leaving the soils less protected against erosion, and the rainfalls were unevenly distributed. The regolith formed under full humid conditions might have lost its stability during the fluctuations towards dryness and concentrated rainfall, and having become soaked, started a mass movement even on low-angle slopes.

The end of the last extensive solifluction and landslide movements seems to have occurred about 2,400 years ago. However, this was not the only period of mass movement. Some of the road cuts present evidence that landslide phenomena had a cyclic recurrence. Therefore, it may be possible to document older fluctuations towards dryness, still inside the present humid climatic phase. This type of phenomenon, successively repeated, seems to be one of the most important features in the development of the slopes under humid climate.

Field observations suggest that each period of mechanical morphogenesis was followed by a phase of extensive colluviation. A similar occurrence is found after the episodes of detrital pavementation of rudaceous material. An alternation of colluvia with paleosoils was also observed.

Frequently one colluvium is separated from the other by a pebbly horizon representative of one paleopavement. Generally there is a sequence of two or three colluvia (Figs. 1 and 3). As at the south of

Lajes (SC), at km 386 of the highway Br-2, are found seven colluvia separated by detrital pavementation.

A paleopavement upon a colluvium indicates a former greater thickness of the latter. Paleopavementation is generally the product of a dryer climatic phase resulting in a much scarcer vegetation. In this phase, rain wash removes the finer debris, concentrating the coarser ones on the surface. Afterwards, a new colluvium is deposited upon the former, creating a sharp separation between them. When the colluvial mass is poor in coarse detrital material, no pebble line is formed between the two successive colluvia, making the separation between them somewhat difficult and unclear.

Sometimes paleosoils are found inside a sequence of colluvia. Their age, specific relation with the colluvium sequence, and the climatic conditions under which they developed are still unknown.

The identification of various paleopavementation episodes associated with subsequent colluviation allowed the organization of a stratigraphy for the colluvial sequence. The determination of the age of paleopavements is, therefore, of great importance for dating the colluvial phases (Fig. 3).

The paleopavement was considered by Bigarella and Ab'Sáber (1964, p. 303) as formed in the Lower Holocene or in the limit between this Epoch and the Pleistocene. However, Bigarella and Andrade (1965) support a greater age for them, the oldest one possibly contemporaneous to the last glaciation (Wisconsin). They refer to the necessity of considering, in the development of the paleopavements, the recurrence of dry phases from which results successive reworking not distinguishable stratigraphically. The authors also point out that the pebble horizon may have different ages, depending upon the area researched.

With some caution one may correlate a determined colluvium to a pediment level or terrace. Thus, for example, on the surface of the pediplane Pd_1 there are places where a reddish colluvium is preserved. Reddish to brown-reddish colluvium can be ascribed to post-pediment P_2 episodes, while brown-yellow colluvia are posterior to the pediment P_1.

Generally, the colluvium formed immediately after the epochs of bevelling are poorly preserved because they suffered successive reworking in later climatic phases. However, some of the road cuts studied permitted one to see the structural and stratigraphic complexity of the colluvium. In the study of the Quaternary sedimentary stratigraphy (Guabirotuba, Riacho Môrno, and Pariquera-Açu formations), several lithological units are formed by old colluvia. Sometimes, they are intercalated between defined pebbly horizons representing terraces and are therefore datable to a certain degree.

SLOPE EVOLUTION. During the humid climatic periods, the degradation of the land by linear erosion and chemical weathering would have a differential erosive effect. More resistant rocks would be selected and knickpoints formed. Still, the drainage's main lines would be oriented by zones of structural weakness of the local rock basement. With a complete development of the forest covering, the disposal of detritus from the slopes for the fluvial transport decreases considerably. The streams become unable to promote a great downcutting of their knickpoints.

The valleys would be V-shaped and eventually, according to their position towards the base level, have or not have a flood plain. During the floods the material to be disposed of is composed mainly of silts and clays which can accumulate partly in the flood plain.

Chemical weathering progresses rapidly in zones of greater fracturing or less resistant lithology. This initiates an irregular weathering mantle of variable thickness. In the most deeply weathered areas the regolith is thicker and acquires the form of a lens or a basin. There will occur a stronger infiltration of the pluvial waters in these places, which causes, when excessive, solifluction and landslides in the chemically developed weathering mantle. We attribute great importance to the episodic climatic fluctuations within the humid epochs. They would promote an acceleration of the regolith removal, colluviation, and dissection of the landscape itself.

The processes acting during humid epochs promoted differential erosion of the slopes. The retreat of the slopes was accomplished by a progressive decrease of its decline, through the formation of a convexity in the upper part and an increase of a concave lower part, resulting from the migration downslope of the colluvium material.

The diminution of the slope angle by colluviation depends on the efficiency of the weathering processes which act upon the slope. However, it is to be noted that very steep slopes tend to be preserved, protected by their own decline against a more accentuated chemical alteration (Figs. 6, 7, 8, and 9).

Morphological evolution under semi-arid conditions

PROCESSES ACTING ON THE SLOPES. In the semi-arid areas, like the tropical and subtropical regions of southern and southeastern Brazil, the effect of chemical weathering is strongly noticeable in the evolution of the landscape. The humid phases prepare a thick regolith, facilitating a posterior opening of wide basins by processes of mechanical morpho-

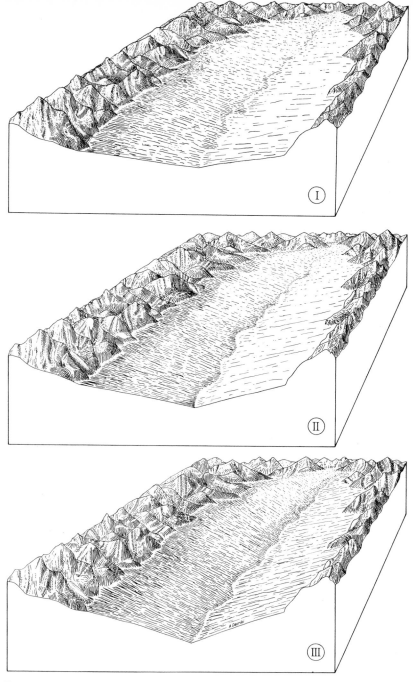

Figures 6, 7, and 8. Basic scheme of slope evolution. I—extensive intermontaine surface formed by pediplanation under semi-arid climate; II, III—regrading of the planated surface caused by a slight lowering of the local erosion base level in consequence of small climatic fluctuations toward humid conditions during the semi-arid epoch; IV—generalized dissection of the planated surface resulting from

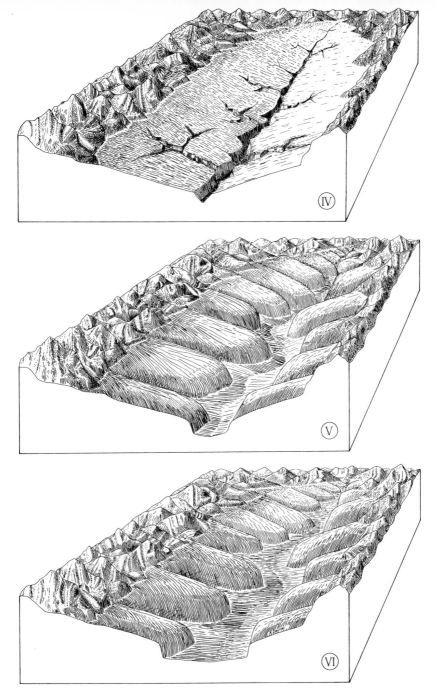

a climatic change toward humid conditions; V—valley widening, alluviation, and colluviation accelerated by fluctuations toward semi-aridity during the humid epoch; VI—lateral degradation and formation of a pedimentary surface under semi-arid climatic conditions; VII—regrading of the pedimentary surface caused by a slight lowering of the local base level in consequence of small climatic

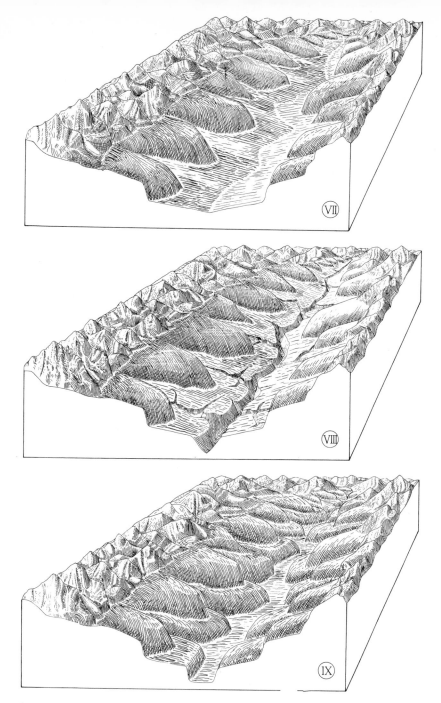

fluctuations toward humidity during the semi-arid epoch; VIII—generalized dissection resulting from the installation of a new humid epoch; IX—widening and
filling of the valleys during the humid epoch; essentially caused by episodic
climatic fluctuations toward drier conditions.

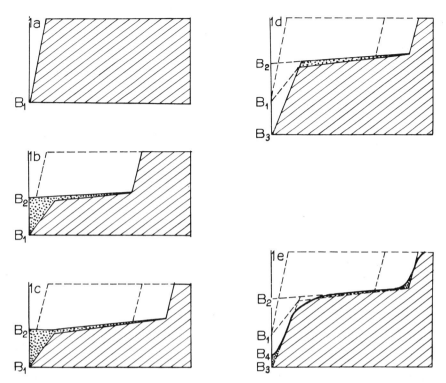

Fig. 9. Basic scheme of slope evolution (lateral view). (1a) humid climate. Dissection. Base level at B_1; (1b) semi-aridity. Parallel slope retreat. Rocky and detrital pediments. Base level raised by aggradation; (1c) continuous lateral degradation. Fixed base level. Equilibrium between arrival and outgo of debris; (1d) new humid phase. Dissection. Base level at B_3; (1e) fluctuations toward dryer conditions inside a humid epoch. Talus formation. Rounded higher section of slopes.

genesis, resulting in lateral degradation of the topography.

Under severe semi-arid conditions on the mountain slopes or in the escarpments, weathering processes elaborate successive layers of material to be removed. The slope is principally submitted to processes of mechanical disintegration. The chemical decomposition seems to have acted with greater efficiency only during the short climatic fluctuations towards humidity within the severe semi-arid epoch. Thermic variations act chiefly upon the surficial part of the rocks. The chemical decomposition along the joints facilitates the liberation of blocks. The general lowering of the earth's average temperature during the glaciations seems to have permitted, in the studied area, the occurrence of cryoturbation. The loosened material on the steep slopes could be initially accumulated as talus deposits until other removal processes would come into play. Rain wash, either as stream flood, rill wash, or sheet wash, plays an active role in the removal of the waste from the slopes.

During the semi-arid phases, small climatic fluctuations could have occurred, promoting an increase of humidity and appearance of a denser vegetal cover. Some importance is attributed to these fluctuations in that they may have helped the thickening of the weathered mantle. Later on, this thickened regolith would be more easily removed by the agents of denudation. Particularly the grus formation (arenization) from crystalline rocks might have benefited from these climatic fluctuations. These frequent fluctuations contributed to reduce the size of the pebbles and blocks of the crystalline rocks allowing only the more resistant ones to subsist. They facilitated also the mass movement mechanism which originated high density sandflows or mudflows.

SLOPE EVOLUTION. We call the process of pediment formation by parallel slope retreat "lateral degradation."

In southeastern and southern Brazil during semi-arid climatic periods, the lateral degradation inside the basins (*cuvette*), had a tendency to cut all rocks and structures forming a slightly dipping planated surface. The pedimentation processes in every basin were controlled by local base levels. The sequence of knickpoints inside the basins was eliminated upstream from the local base level up to the next basin.

However, principal knickpoints in the drainage net, inherited from the anterior humid phase, tend to subsist during the pedimentation processes. They act as local base levels for the isolated basins of different elevations, thus, somehow, controlling their development. Nevertheless, the disappearance of these local base levels eventually would happen through the coalescence of the basins consequent to a greater advance of the lateral degradation processes.

Under semi-arid conditions, the slopes would suffer initially the removal of the weathering mantle elaborated during the former humid climatic phase. The regolith would be quickly transported to the depressions of the terrain and there deposited through the various mass wasting processes, especially those related to high-density fluids. In this way, the upper parts of the slopes would be exposed to agents of mechanical morphogenesis, while their base would have its development altered and retarded because it has been re-covered. From then on, the slopes would retreat parallel to themselves, a planated surface (rocky pediment) being formed, slightly inclined towards the centre of the valley or intermontane depression. In this way, the valleys would present steep walls and an almost flat bottom, resulting from the hillslopes' parallel retreat. The material originating from the retreating slope tends to re-cover the lower section of the rocky pediment while filling the depression. The material is transported especially through rain wash which can develop itself as mass movements in high density fluids, whether in sheets or channelled (sheet floods, mudflows, sandflows, stream floods, etc.). The coarser detrital material is transported towards the central portion of the basin by *arroyos* that remove also the fine vehicle which contains it. Consequently, in such areas, submitted to deep climatic changes from humid to semi-arid conditions and deeply dissected by linear erosion, the usually thin veneer that re-covers the pediment may gain in thickness locally for it has to fill the irregularities of the pre-existing topography before an almost levelled surface is attained. Before the planated surface reaches the *bajada* environment it shows an important detrital phase, represented by a quite thick sequence of rudaceous material (detrital pediment). There is no break of the gradient between the rocky and detrital pediments. When the sub-surficial structure cannot be examined, it is impossible to determine the exact contact between the two features.

Small fluctuations towards humidity within the semi-arid epoch caused a lowering of the basin local base level in the mountainous areas. From this resulted a constant regrading of the bevelled surface expressed by an increase of its dipping angle, which attains a much higher value than the usual $1°$ to $4°$ found in the classical descriptions of such morphological features.

Many of the extensive erosion surfaces in Brazil can be associated with their correlative deposits. This correlation allows their genetic interpretation. In the tropics they were elaborated through processes operating during long-lasting, severe semi-arid conditions. The coalescence of pediments originated this surface of erosion—the pediplanes. A pediplane consists of rocky portions covered by a thin veneer of clastics and has, in some places, a detrital portion where its correlative sediments are more thickly accumulated (bolson plain environment). The Brazilian morphology presents great bevelled surfaces, normally much dissected. The older ones are usually documented by dispersed remnants preserved in rocks which resist erosion under more humid climatic conditions. In certain areas, deposits correlative to the formation of erosion surfaces have already been studied and stratigraphically characterized as having originated under semi-arid conditions. In other regions, where the deposition of a thicker sequence was not favoured, preservation and mapping becomes more difficult (Figs. 6, 7, 8, and 9).

Climatic transitions

The temperature and rainfall distribution (amount and concentration) of the past are not well known. These conditions and their related phenomena were guessed from relatively scarce evidence and therefore, frequently are questionable. What has been done up to now to explain the landscape is mostly connected with the present-day climate. The climatic conditions of the Pleistocene cold phases probably were so different and extreme when compared with the present climates that they cannot be conceived from present patterns. Although details of the Pleistocene climate itself are not known, we can be reasonably sure that two different climates were prevailing alternately over the whole studied area. These conclusions came out of the study of sediment textures and structures, as well as from observations about remnants of erosive levels.

Conditioned by the climatic changes, two different sets of processes operating alternately subjected the landscape to lateral degradation (semi-arid climate) and dissection (humid climate). Erosive action would be very effective during the transition from one type of climate to the other. The consequences of climatic change in the landscape development will be briefly analysed here.

In the transition from one climatic epoch into the other, not only an important change in the vegetation cover, but also a great change in the several processes involved should be taken into account. From the analysis of the landscape, it seems probable that knickpoints in the longitudinal profile of the rivers have resulted from two different causes. Knickpoints originated by uplift seem to migrate constantly upstream. Associated with this migration, narrow canyons may be formed. Knickpoints may also be originated where rocks of greater resistance to linear erosion occur. This type of erosion becomes progressively predominant when humid climatic conditions start to prevail.

Since the climatic changes had a cyclic character, most of these knickpoints were created and eradicated according to the mentioned climatic alternation. Consequently, most of them had periodic disappearances (semi-arid epochs) and reappearances (humid epochs) more or less in the same locale but always at lower elevation. Nevertheless, the climatically controlled knickpoints represent a diversified manifestation of previous crustal movements.

The transition from a humid to a semi-arid climate seems to have caused only a small lowering of the local base levels. On the other hand, during the transition from semi-arid to humid climatic conditions, the greatest lowering of the local base levels occurred.

There may be a difference between the facts occurring in intermontane basins and the occurrences in those areas situated at the coast. In the latter, the maximum incision may correspond to the maximum lowering of former sea level. This is indicated by river canyons presently found submerged in the continental shelf.

The regolith can partially, or as whole, move downslope with variable rapidity according to the type of transporting agent. This movement occurs mainly during climatic modifications from which alterations in the vegetation result.

In the transition from a humid to a dryer climate the forest would retreat, being substituted by a thinner plant cover of the *cerrado* or *caatinga* type. With the forest cover, the soils were protected against fast erosion. This is no longer true under the new type of vegetation. Conditioned by a regimen of concentrated rainfall, the rivers tend to be intermittent, having therefore great changes in the discharge. There is also a progressive increase in the solid load of the rivers, which is accounted for by the fast erosion of the unprotected slopes.

The change to dryer climate means the dominance of processes that are much more active in the removal of the slope waste, thus accelerating the slope evolution. Mass transport would be effective at this time. The thick chemically developed regolith would be removed rapidly from the slopes exposing the rocks to a new weathering process in which mechanical disintegration dominates.

The transition to a dryer climate could be to a new climatic epoch (semi-arid) or just a fluctuation towards dryness inside the humid epoch. In the first case the mechanism of slope development would change radically with the installation of lateral degradation processes. The removal of the weathered upper part of the terrain would bring to the surface the jointed and partially weathered parent rock which usually is fractured in blocks of various sizes. In pedimentation processes, for example, a great quantity of coarse waste of varied size and angularity would easily be removed. The waste might have been partly evacuated throughout the local base level, but a large amount of it tends to be accumulated in the valley floor, aggrading it. Mass movements, however, would have the tendency to clog the basin outlet with sediments, thus decreasing the downcutting capability of the river. In this way, the base level tends to be raised.

The transition from semi-aridity towards humid conditions could be either to a new and long humid epoch or just a fluctuation towards humidity inside a semi-arid climatic epoch. In the first case there is a radical change in the development of the landscape, with the operation of chemical weathering processes and the installation of linear erosion resulting in dissection of the land. Concerning the second case, the consequences can only be deduced, for there is no clear evidence of these fluctuations in the landscape.

The climatic change towards humid conditions favours the development of soils upon which is installed a new type of vegetation. The semi-arid vegetal association is progressively replaced by forest. The chemical weathering reaches greater depth, and the superficial portion of the terrain becomes more protected against the action of rain wash. The mass movements are more effective where there are high pluviosity and steep declivities.

In this climatic transition the river regimen changes from intermittent to permanent. It follows a progressive increase of the river discharges, as well as a decrease of the solid load. At the beginning of the transition, with increasing discharges, the rivers were able to remobilize the detrital material accumulated as valley fill, realizing a downcutting of their beds and an accentuated lowering of the local base level.

A subject deserving special attention within southeastern Brazil is the *felsenmeer* existing at more than 2,000 m of elevation in the Itatiaia massif. Such blocks, *in situ* or slightly displaced, were by many authors related to strong cryoturbation processes or even local glaciation (De Martonne 1943, 1944, Rich 1953, King 1956, Ruellan 1944). In our view, adopting some ideas of Odman (1955) and Dresch (1957, p. 289), they would be produced by an interaction of Quaternarian climatic fluctuations. The blocks would have been individualized in depth by chemical weathering acting on the joint system. Later on, dryer climatic conditions (corresponding to the last glacial epoch) would have promoted the removal of the waste material from the jointed zones.

Displacement of blocks may have occurred when a thicker regolith existed. In the upper portion of the weathered mantle, richer in fine clastics, solifluction would displace blocks downslope. The blocks situated at greater depths remained in place or suffered only small displacement. The removal of the fine waste material from the joints by rain wash contributed to the isolation of individual blocks.

We do not deny the possible occurrence of frost action in the area during the cold and dry Pleistocene epochs. Frost splitting may have accelerated the formation of blocks and angular pebbles that are found embedded in solifluction masses (not necessarily of periglacial origin). Thus, we have in this area a convergence of effects represented by the action of mechanical morphogenesis with cryoturbation in the sculpturing of this Brazilian landscape during the cold epochs of the Quaternary.

Erosive morphology of southern and southeastern Brazil in the Cenozoic

The discovery of the occurrence of great cyclic climatic changes during the Cenozoic at the Serra do Mar and at the coastal area of Santa Catarina and Paraná made possible a new approach to the geomorphological problems of the region.

From Garuva (Santa Catarina), at the foot of the Serra do Iquererim (local name of the Serra do Mar), Bigarella, Marques, and Ab'Sáber (1961) described remnants of pediments, as well as the character of the detrital material, named by them, Iquererim Formation. Based on sedimentological studies, they concluded that the rocky and the detrital pediments were not forms of the present day climate, having instead been developed under harsh semi-arid conditions. Pediments at three different levels were found, meaning that, at least on three occasions, semi-arid climatic conditions persisted during the Quaternary, with parallel retreat of the slopes alternating with humid climatic conditions, resulting in linear erosion and deep dissection of the terrain. These three main erosion levels (pediplane and pediments) in our field work were designated pediplane, Pd_1, and pediments, P_2 and P_1, the latter being the youngest. Pd_1 was proved to have originated through the coalescence of multiple P_3 pediments. This pediplane is considered to be the youngest among the extensive planated erosion surfaces of the Brazilian plateau. Two older pediplanes, occurring at higher elevations, are designated as Pd_2 and Pd_3 as their ages increase (Bigarella and Ab'Sáber, 1964). Tentatively, Bigarella and Ab'Sáber (1964) considered the events here described as having taken place during the Cenozoic. The pediments were related to the glacial stages and the vertical downcutting (humid climate) to the interglacial stages. Bigarella and Andrade (1965) suggested that the sequence of events from Brazil could be correlated with those from Colorado whose age was established by Scott (1960). This correlation is made based on world-wide cyclic climatic changes probably controlled by changes in radiation of cosmic origin. The development of pediplane Pd_1 occurred during Nebraskan time, while the pediments P_2 and P_1 were formed during the Kansan and Illinoian ice ages, respectively.

Evidences of lateral degradation in the surveyed area are very frequent. Remnants of pediments appear today as shoulders in the slopes. They are conspicuous features of the dryer *caatinga* areas (semi-arid zone presently) of Bahia and northeastern Brazil, as well as of the humid southern and southeastern Brazilian regions. Moreover, remnants of pediments have been found as a general feature all over the surveyed area, from the La Plata River to northeastern Brazil.

The pediments were more easily recognized and correlated with past semi-arid processes in the coastal zone, especially at the foot of the Serra do Mar (Fig. 10). Their remnants are also well identified elsewhere, in places which have been deeply dissected by humid climate linear erosion. Without considering in detail the processes involved in their formation, we believe that they represent semi-arid climatic conditions which operated in the whole area during the Quaternary. In these areas they remain as shoulders. We believe and can prove that many shoulders inset in the present topography are actually remnants of pediments. This is a basic point in our hypothesis of slope development. To be sure that the shoulders would correspond to remnants of pediments, we traced them into areas where the pediment features are typical and unquestioned, that is, into areas where the lateral degradation processes could be identified and demonstrated through their correlative sediments.

The correlative deposits of the different pedimentation phases enable us to interpret the environmental conditions and the nature of the processes involved. The texture, mineral composition, and primary structures of the sediments are explained by semi-arid conditions, effective dominance of mechanical disintegration of the rocks (several processes), heavy concentrated rainfalls, and consequent occurrence of sheet floods, sheet wash, stream floods, and other processes of denudation. Such deposits, filling previous depressions, frequently reach great thickness and can be considered true detrital pediments.

Basing his assumptions on base level variations, Davis (1954) postulated that an erosive wave would migrate upstream. We can deduce, however, that since the change to more humid climatic conditions occurs over the whole drainage net, vertical erosion would occur in all the area affected by the mentioned climatic change. On the other hand, in spite of cutting the knickpoints, the drainage net does not have the capability to make all of them disappear completely during the humid epoch. Consequently, the subsequent climatic epoch of lateral degradation will act at the same time upon the basins maintained at varied elevations by their corresponding knickpoints. Only with effective and continuous action of the process of lateral degradation was it possible to reach in some long-lasting semi-arid epochs the coalescence of the basins.

Based on these considerations we can affirm that the forms of the slopes can be correlated over long distances from one basin to the other and are datable through the age of their corresponding pedimentation or dissection epochs.

The oldest pediplane (Pd_3) was sculptured in early Tertiary. In some places it can be recognized by summit concordance. In Paraná this erosion surface is represented by the summits of the old plateaus. It has also reworked remnants in some high massifs of the Serra do Mar's interior slopes and on the reverse slope of the Devonian escarpment. In São Paulo it has the local name of Cristas Medias or Japi surface.

The Cenozoic of the studied area was characterized by intensive erosive activity with which started the dissection of the pediplane Pd_3. This pediplane was deformed by deep-seated folding which was responsible for faulting in the eastern part of Brazil and for an eastward reversal of part of the drainage system.

By semi-arid pedimentation processes, new interplateau and peripherical surfaces were developed. Before the succeeding pediplane (Pd_2) had reached its complete development, there occurred an alternation of dry and humid phases which was mainly responsible for the levels inlaid between the two extensive erosion surfaces, pediplanes Pd_3 and Pd_2.

The pediplane Pd_2, elaborated during the middle Tertiary, very seldom represents a summit surface. It is found generally inlaid in mountainous areas, constituting great and dissected old basins. They correspond to the oldest phase of basin sculpturing in the uplifted areas of southeastern and southern Brazil.

During the Quaternary, the climate had many cyclic changes. The origin of successive cyclic features is related to palaeoclimates. These forms are clearly noticeable in the topography because of their recency. The semi-arid epochs were interrupted by humid phases, when different morphogenetic processes were in action. Mechanical morphogenesis and lateral degradation, typical of semi-aridity, were able only to sculpture pediments which, especially in middle and late Quaternary, did not coalesce in large scale. Only the oldest of the Quaternarian surfaces (pediplane Pd_1), probably concluded during the Nebraskan, reached a larger extension, suggesting a more effective and prolonged prevalence of mechanical morphogenesis. The pedimentation processes acted inside several of the main valleys, opening large inclined basins, and were, therefore, controlled by different regional base levels situated at different elevations.

Humid fluctuations must have also occurred within this extensive semi-arid epoch, but their influence was insufficient to break the monotony of the surface. Only less intense dissection, caused by fluctuations towards humidity, could be almost completely erased from the topography by the morphogenetic processes acting during the predominant semi-arid climate. However, a progressive regrading of the bevelled surface occurred, tending to smooth out the small irregularities and to increase the general declivity of the transverse profile. The final result at Serra do Mar in Santa Catarina was a tilted plane beginning at the edge of the plateau and dipping towards the regional base level, and limited upward by escarpments. Consequently, the remnants of this surface inset in the block mountain system dip between 10° and 20°. Meanwhile, the former erosion surfaces, pediplanes Pd_2 and Pd_3, were slightly reworked (Fig. 10).

Among the extensive Brazilian erosion surfaces (pediplanes) Pd_1 is the most recent one. In the interior it forms interplateau depressions along the main lines of drainage, being slightly inclined downstream. In Curitiba and São Paulo regions this erosion surface is slightly inset in the next older erosion surface (pediplane Pd_2), and from all directions it has a composite low angle dip towards the central part of the depression and also towards the outlet of the depression's drainage system. For the Curitiba area regional base level was formed by the Furnas Sandstone at the narrow canyon entering the Paleozoic plateau. On the coastal zone the Pd_1 was slightly inclined towards the ocean and its base level was probably the ocean itself. The remnants of this pediplane can be observed from Rio Grande do Sul to Amazonas. This surface has received many names: "surface of the Chãs and Tabuleiros" in Pernambuco, "Neógena" in São Paulo, "Curitiba" in Paraná, "Campanha" in Rio Grande do Sul, and "Montevideo" in Uruguay.

A humid climatic epoch followed the semi-arid one and was responsible for the dissection of the pediplane Pd_1. The land was dissected, and the drainage system was in part superimposed on the structure. In the area of the former pediplane basin, numerous knickpoints developed, some of them controlling the more important tributaries thus subdividing the original basin into others of smaller size. In these basins a next pedimentation phase promoted lateral degradation and formation of pediment P_2. Only the controlling knickpoints (local base levels) remained. The knickpoints inside the basins were eliminated by the lateral degradation processes.

After pediment P_2 was formed, a new humid climatic epoch brought dissection of the land. The remnants of pediment P_2 were preserved in several places, usually as shoulders. Knickpoints developed all over the area. Many of them during the next semi-arid epoch became local base levels for the pedimentation phase that originated pediment P_1.

The P_2 basin had been divided into several other smaller basins. In P_1 time, the number of compartments in which pedimentation phenomena took place increased very much. The development of each one of these compartments was controlled by the most important or resistant knickpoint of the stream's longitudinal profile.

A new humid climatic epoch succeeded the semi-arid one in which pediment P_1 was formed. This new cycle caused pediment dissection. The remnants are usually found as shoulders. Later on, other climatic changes occurred, but no longer produced pediments. The morphogenic processes formed paleopavements, *glacis* of colluvium, and low terraces, all of them under climatic control.

Two levels of low gravel terraces found in the bottom of valleys are connected to two definite occurrences of semi-arid conditions during the Wisconsin glaciation; separated by a more humid period when dissection occurred. The relatively short or mild conditions of semi-aridity did not allow the formation of typical pediments at that time, resulting only in an accelerated slope denudation and the accumulation of waste in the valley bottom through mass movements. Removal of the finer material caused a concentration of the rudaceous material which comprises a great part of the debris.

After the last glaciation, predominant humid conditions have promoted a general dissection of the landscape. Fluctuations towards dryness brought to the landscape extensive colluviation and formation of detrital paleopavement on the slopes, as well as deposition of sands by braided streams in the valley flat. The colluvial material interfingered with the alluvial material of the flood plain, originating slightly inclined forms (*glacis* of colluvium), which contrast with the horizontally disposed deposits of the present flood plain.

The conclusions obtained until now through the analysis of sediments, the attitude of pediment remnants, the amount of downcutting in valleys, and much other evidence permits only a qualitative appreciation of the regional geomorphological evolution. A quantitative determination concerning hydrological and climatic conditions is still impossible. Up to now we have not had an appropriate methodology for this type of study.

We conclude that the slopes of southeastern and southern Brazil suffered two distinct types of evolution which were repeated cyclically and which basically result from great climatic changes.

CORRELATIVE DEPOSITS

Introduction

A stratigraphical revision of the Brazilian Cenozoic deposits cannot be realized successfully by using the classical methods of stratigraphy. Because of the peculiar nature of the deposits, usually non-fossiliferous, as well as the lack of guide layers, the adoption of an appropriate methodology becomes necessary. The new methods should allow a reasonable correlation among the sedimentation basins and enable the dating of the depositional sequences. For this purpose, the introduction of geomorphological methods based mainly on the interpretation of degradational and aggradational surfaces which become guide elements for correlations and make possible the elaboration of a chronology (Fig. 11) is needed.

Sedimentary sequences resulting from aggradational processes and occurring simultaneously with degradation phenomena in their source area constitute the correlative deposits. Concerning southern Brazil, the correlative deposits of pedimentation processes were described by Bigarella, Marques, and Ab'Sáber (1961) and Bigarella and Salamuni (1961). The problem of paleogeography and paleoclimatology of the Cenozoic of southern Brazil was summarized by Bigarella and Ab'Sáber (1964) when they correlated depositional processes of numerous small basins with erosive phenomena acting in their source area during a semi-arid climate. The study of the problem was done for the Quaternary by Bigarella and Andrade (1965).

The correlation of deposits from the different pedimentation phases enables us to interpret the environmental conditions and the nature of the processes involved. The sediments are composed usually of several textural classes which are, therefore, poorly sorted. The degree of roundness is generally low. The mineral composition of the arenaceous material has a high content of feldspar. Caliche is present. The gravels, normally subangular to subrounded, are composed mostly of quartz and quartzite; less frequently of granite, gneiss, phyllites, and other metamorphics. Stratification is rare. The deposits sometimes present cut-and-fill structures. Intraformational erosional features are rather frequent. An incipient stratification is many times due to successive deposition of mudflow sequences. These characteristics are explained

Fig. 10. Remnants of pediplanes Pd₂ and Pd₁. Eastern front of the Serra do Mar. Florianopolis-Lajes road, State of Santa Catarina.

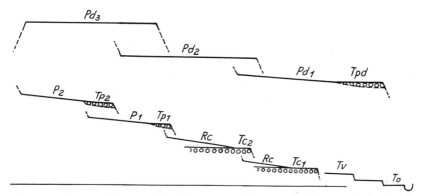

Fig. 11. Scheme of the spatial relationship existing among the aggradational and degradational surfaces. *Pd*—pediplane; *Tpd*—terrace corresponding to a pediplane; *P*—pediment; *Tp*—terrace corresponding to a pediment; *Rc*—glacis of colluvium; *Tc*—low terrace with gravel; *Tv*—flood plain terrace and *To*—present flood plain.

by semi-arid conditions, with a dominance of mechanical disintegration of rocks (several processes) and heavy concentrated rainfalls, and with mass movements (sheetflood and mudflows, among other processes). Generally, these correlative formations show the influence of various pedimentation phases. The sedimentation occurs normally during periods of pediplanation and pedimentation active during the semi-arid climatic epochs. Between these epochs, humid climatic conditions were interposed, with dominance of dissection, resulting in erosive unconformities in the sedimentary sequences. Deposition in humid phases would eventually occur in some basins forming lacustrine deposits, as well as part of valley flat and deltaic depositional sequences.

The correlation between sedimentary sequences and degradational surfaces presents a series of difficulties chiefly if we consider the older pediplanes. The discontinuity verified between the degradation and aggradation areas most of the time does not allow us to set up safe correlations. This situation is aggravated by the occurrence of deep-seated folding.

Part of the rudaceous material mixed with finer clastics may be deposited as detrital pediment in depressions of the pedimentation area, while the other part may be evacuated throughout the local base level and be deposited farther down. This first deposition is characterized by angularity and lithological heterogeneity of the phenoclasts (quartz, quartzite, and different types of metastable rocks). The sediments constitute a conglomeratic mud and, when lithified, could be called paraconglomerate or conglomeratic mudstone, according to Pettijohn's classification (1957, p. 261). If the area under mechanical morphogenesis is sufficiently close to the sea the subaerial mass transported material may enter the water body and develop a subaquatic flow originating turbidity currents. Therefore, continental rudaceous deposits may be associated with marine sediments. Also the extensive sand accumulations in the platform and littoral zone may have an immediate and compatible origin in semi-arid morphogenetic processes acting over the continent during the glaciations.

Considerations about rudaceous deposits

The lithologic assemblage which makes up the rudaceous deposits depends not only on the rock types occurring in the source area and on the distance of transportation, but especially on the climatic and geomorphic processes operating at the source area.

In regions where rough climatic conditions favour mechanical disintegration of the rocks, heterogeneous waste accumulations may be produced, with pebbles proceeding from all the regional rocks. This may occur in low relief areas, but happens mostly in rugged terrain.

The talus formed at the foot of a disintegrating slope rockwall or the solifluction deposits would be a first stage in the evolution of a rudaceous deposit. Thereafter, the different transporting agents, the distance of transportation, and the climatic conditions modify the original character of the pebbly association affording for the next stage of deposition a different degree of maturity. The mature stage is quickly attained through sorting of the more resistant pebbles.

Low-relief regions under humid climate have the tendency to produce small and lithologically homogeneous pebbles. They constitute the chemically inert residue of the humid climate weathering. Gravel deposits formed by them are said to be mature. They may be concentrated in different ways. If a dryer period occurs in a humid forested area long enough to cause a retreat of the forest, the ground will be exposed and submitted to several processes of removal. Its heavier fragments tend to concentrate on the surface, forming a kind of pavement, while the finer material is carried downslope. Usually a thin pebbly layer is formed, which in some cases may reach up to 1 metre in thickness. This feature occurred over great areas of the presently forested region. The small and homogeneous pebbles may also form gravel deposits in depressions of the terrain, or they may be deposited downstream along the valley floors.

The areas with high relief would produce, under humid climate chemical weathering, not only chemically inert coarse fragments (quartz pebbles), but would also form, by solifluction and especially by landslides, a talus of heterogeneous character with phenoclasts of the parent rocks. However, under humid conditions the coarser fragments do not have a chance to be moved away and deposited further down as a stratigraphic unit. The blocks and pebbles usually rest on the creek or stream valley bottom and are not transported by the present stream. They concentrate in the drainage channel by downslope movement of the regolith and subsequent removal of the finer material by the stream. The downslope mass movements seem to have been much more important sometime in the past. Inspection of the present landscape shows only occasional and localized landslides, solifluction being restricted to much steeper slopes.

Pebbles originating under humid climate can also be concentrated as gravel accumulations during the following dryer climates. Coarser fragments would be easily moved under semi-arid conditions by high density fluids, like sheetfloods or mudflows, giving rise to immature rudaceous deposits of polymictic character. It seems, however, that in the surveyed area, the most effective processes of coarse fragment production were those operating under the rough semi-arid climate. Also the effective removal of the waste material from the talus or from the slopes seems to have been achieved mainly under semi-arid conditions by rain wash and sheetflood, among other processes.

Caution must be exercised in the interpretation of older conglomerates. They testify to some extent to the occurrence of crustal movements. Nevertheless, their origin is related to changes in the morphogenetic processes operating in their source area. These changes are due particularly to climatic modifications.

In the stratigraphic literature is found the assertion that granite-bearing conglomerates and arkoses represent a fast erosion of the crystalline basement resulting from a major uplift of the source area. On the other hand, conglomerates devoid of granitic debris may record only a minor interlude in the sedimentary history of a basin (Pettijohn 1957, p. 257). However, according to our observations, the presence of granitic debris is not necessarily connected with major uplift displacements. These debris may have another completely different origin; for example, they may be the result of deep climatic changes in their source area.

One of the most impressive granite-bearing conglomerates validating the hypothesis is near Cabo (Pernambuco) and belongs to the Tertiary Cabo Formation. The conglomerate is 60 m to 80 m thick and is made up of granitic and other crystalline phenoclasts.

This conglomerate has an intact framework in which the phenoclasts are in direct contact with each other and the voids are filled with an arkosic matrix. Pettijohn (1957, p. 254) states that in conglomerates presenting intact framework (orthoconglomerates) the gravels were collected by ordinary water currents. This may be true for many conglomerates, especially the finer ones, but it is not true for the coarse Cabo Formation conglomerate and for some other sediments like the Iquererim Formation rudaceous deposits.

Several origins have been attributed to the Cabo Formation conglomerate (Andrade and Lins 1961). Bigarella and Andrade (1964) have found, intercalated in the conglomerate, lenses of arkose with scattered polymictic phenoclasts, actually a paraconglomerate according to Pettijohn's 1957 classification. East of the conglomerate outcrop, but still associated with it, occur sequences of structureless, medium-to-coarse-grained arkose with scattered pebbles.The arkosic matrix, the intercalated arkose-pebbly lenses, and the associated arkose sequences afford a clue to the interpretation of the orthopolymictic Cabo Formation conglomerate. The processes operating in the source area were those of rough semi-arid environment. Under these conditions mass movement filled a long and relatively narrow subsiding basin whose origin is possibly related to deep-seated folding. The phenoclasts were transported in a high density fluid, such as mudflow, and subsequently the arkosic vehicle was washed away. The source area might have been uplifted, but the uplift itself did not create the conglomerate. If in this region a humid climate was then prevailing, possibly the Cabo Formation conglomerate would not have been formed. Its origin was actually subordinated to semi-arid climatic conditions.

The literature provides several explanations for conglomeratic mudstones. Pettijohn (1957, p. 265) notes that "these rocks have been attributed to catastrophic flash floods of the arid regions, to deposition from glacial ice, to rafting and deposition from icebergs, to landslides and mud flows, to solifluction, and to subaqueous mudstreams and turbidity flows." Although not denying the several possibilities, he emphasizes that these deposits are the product of subaqueous mudstreams related to turbidity flows, precluding, therefore, a terrestrial origin. We believe that some conglomeratic mudstones may be easily explained in this way. To others, however, this explanation presents many handicaps.

The tilloids may be formed either in subaquatic or subaerial conditions. The turbidity flow, with its clay content, has a lubricating property and is, therefore, unable to realize the large-scale submarine mechanical disintegration necessary to produce the pebbly assemblage that makes up many of the known tilloids.

This statement is made after a preliminary study of the Camarinha Formation paraconglomerate, probably of Precambrian age (Muratori 1965). This conglomerate (more than 100 m thick) is made up of a disrupted but concentrated framework of lithologically heterogeneous angular to subrounded phenoclasts (mainly phyllites, granite, dolomite, among other rocks). The matrix has a lithic character, being made up mainly of fine-grained metamorphic rock fragments of sand to granule size. The elaboration of this type of material would require a continental environment in which climatic conditions would induce a very effective mechanical disintegration of the parent rocks.

Part of the Camarinha Formation paraconglomerate seems to be subaerial, while the other part associated with phyllites has a subaqueous origin. We explain the latter one in the following way: The pebbles and matrix have possibly been previously originated in an uplifted area where rough semi-arid conditions prevailed. Mass movements started over the land and continued downward into the sea. Entering the water body, the high density subaerial flow changed and moved as a subaqueous mudstream. This explains the texture of the deposit which otherwise would be difficult to understand. Thus, it is possible that many of the paraconglomerates, mentioned by Pettijohn as being almost exclusively related to turbidity flows, may have had the mixed origin explained above.

During the Pleistocene semi-arid epochs, or even during smaller climatic variations from humid to semi-arid, conglomeratic muds of the tilloid type (according to Pettijohn's classification 1957, p. 255) were formed in the studied area. When a thick chemically weathered regolith loses its forest cover and is exposed to heavy concentrated rainfall, it turns into mudflow which on its way down collects every pebble on the way. When deposited, the material transported by the mudflow constitutes a siltic clayey sediment containing scattered pebbles. A good example of this feature is furnished by the pre-Canhanduva layers (Bigarella and Salamuni 1961, p. 181).

The deep climatic changes of the Quaternary seem to have affected the whole earth. During the glaciations, processes of mechanical morphogenesis were important not only in periglacial areas, but also in lower latitudes. Conditions of climatic severity allowed an almost universal formation of planated surfaces and characteristic correlative deposits. This correlation between climate and morphogenesis can be projected further into the geologic past. During various geologic periods or epochs, sequences of continental sediments were deposited under severe climatic conditions in many parts of the world. These sediments seem to have been synchronistically deposited, indicating a simultaneous presence of mechanical morphogenesis over distant geographic areas.

The great climatic changes affecting large areas of the earth's surface have a cyclic character. Although it is still too early to speculate about a cyclicity of world-wide character of the alternations between conditions of semi-aridity and humidity, there are many evidences making this hypothesis very attractive. The mechanism of these alternations seems to be connected to the degree of radiation received by the earth's atmosphere, having, therefore, a cosmic or astronomic origin.

A tentative correlation is made here between the processes which operate in the evacuation trough and those which act in the pedimentation areas. The former were responsible for the elaboration of terraces with gravels, while the latter originated the pediments situated in the periphery of evacuation troughs or around a local massif.

When the Pd_1 pediplanation started, the landscape was already deeply dissected as a result of the anterior humid epoch. With the climatic change towards semi-aridity, the regolith was moved in disorder to depressions of the terrain by processes of mass movement clogging the evacuation trough. The continuous aggradation elevated by sedimentation the local base level, which started to control the processes of mechanical morphogenesis. These were responsible for the elaboration of pediplane Pd_1, and for the filling of the dissected part of the valley by a detrital sequence reaching up to the Pd_1 level. Eventually a balance will be established between the arrival of waste from the slopes and the debris removal by the evacuation trough.

Remnants of this former evacuation trough remain as high terraces near the basin's edge, which laterally correspond to the level of pediplane Pd_1. The terraces are maintained by gravel deposits made up of rounded to subrounded pebbles showing noticeable transport. They were rounded by successive reworking through different basins or were reworked from terrace levels corresponding to older pedimentation epochs. This fact contrasts strongly with the gravel deposits from the detrital pediplane that are made up of angular to subangular pebbles.

Along the evacuation trough, braided streams would have channels whose remnants disappear with the posterior removal of the largest part of the deposits of the basin's central portion.

Inset in the above-mentioned level exist two more pedimentation levels, P_2 and P_1. Similar relation to the one existing between the pediplane Pd_1 and the gravelly high terrace (here called Tpd_1) occurs between the pediments (P_2 and P_1) and two terrace levels with gravels (Tp_2 and Tp_1) (Figs. 12, 13, and 14).

After the elaboration of the Tp_1 corresponding to the pediment P_1 came a new humid climatic epoch with dissection of the landscape and development of a forest cover. The drainage became entrenched below the present valley flat level.

Later, semi-aridity returned, now perhaps with a more moderate character or smaller duration. The processes of mechanical morphogenesis were re-established in two distinct phases, intercalated by a dissection phase in humid climate. There are no signs of pedimentation, but two levels of low terraces with gravel were formed then.

The gravel deposits of Tc_2 and Tc_1, about 1 metre thick in the peripheral area, are made up of pebbles of quartz and quartzite, smaller than 8 cm, subrounded to rounded, and successively reworked from the upper levels. The voids are normally filled with arenaceous material. Sandy or silty-clayey layers are sometimes found intercalated.

In the periphery of the Itajai-Mirim evacuation trough, remnants of the Tc_2 and Tc_1 were found at various places. The rudaceous deposits remain over Precambrian basement rocks (phyllites of the Brusque Group) or, more frequently, cover an arenaceous sedimentary sequence.

455

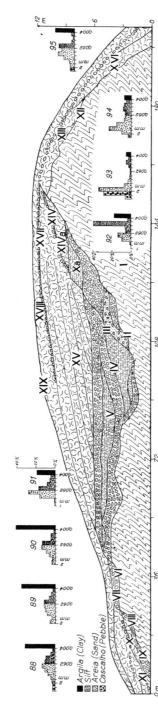

FIG. 12. Exposure in the Brusque-Gaspar road (State of Catarina), 5.2 km before Brusque. It corresponds to the Tp_2 terrace, contemporaneous to the formation of pediment P_2 in the Itajaí-Mirim River valley. I—weathered phyllites; II—erosive unconformity represented by a fluvial channel; III—sequence of layers of subangular to subrounded quartz pebbles having 5 cm of maximum size. Above the pebbles occur a non-stratified sandy layer with abundant subangular to subrounded quartz pebbles. Inside the cut-and-fill structure occurs a grey clayey-silty deposit showing trough cross-bedding (Sample 92) and having in its basal part a very sandy layer (Sample 93), in its top appears another sandy layer (Sample 94); IV—erosive unconformity; V—sequence of layers of subangular to subrounded pebbles about 5 cm in diameter. Between the pebble layers well stratified sandy-silty-clayey deposits (Sample 91) occur; VI—erosive unconformity; VII—gravel deposit similar to V; VIII—erosive unconformity; IX—gravel layer formed reworking of higher gravel deposits; X—mottled colluvium consisting of sandy-silty-clayey material (Sample 88) containing small subrounded pebbles. Over the colluvium occurs a detrital paleopavement; Xa—stratified clayey-sandy material; XI—reddish-brown colluvium with abundant granules and small quartz pebbles, including an incipient paleopavement (Sample 89); XII—erosive unconformity at the right side of the road cut; XIII—reddish colluvium: XIV—reddish and mottled colluvium: $XIVa$—detrital paleopavement; XV—sequence of red-brown colluvia (Sample 95). Texture sandy-silty-clayey, with abundant granules and small pebbles. Crossed by small and discontinuous pebble lines; XVI—reddish colluvium; XVII—discontinuous detrital paleopavement, with angular to subangular granules and small quartz pebbles, following approximately the present topography; XVIII—sandy-silty-clayey brown colluvium (Sample 90) containing very sparse quartz granules; XIX —humic zone.

Argila (Clay)
Silt
Areia (Sand)
Cascalho (Pebble)

The formation of the Tc_2 (upper low terrace with gravel) can be explained as follows: the valley, then topographically situated on a lower level, suffered an aggradation; consequently the valley flat was raised to the level of the Tc_2. The aggradation, caused by a change to conditions of semi-aridity, filled the valley to the level corresponding to the Tc_2. The terrace was apparently developed during an epoch of equilibrium between the income and outgo of debris from the basin. The structure of the valley fill deposits shows that the aggradation of the valley bottom was made by successive accumulation of pebble and sand sheets. Deposits of silty-clayey sediments are less frequent, having been possibly restricted to places of quieter waters.

After the deposition of the Tc_2 sediments, a new humid phase conditioned a new drainage entrenchment accomplished through the removal of part of the sediments deposited at the elaboration of Tc_2. A new climatic change to the semi-arid, still in the Wisconsin, repeated the process, causing the valley to aggrade up to the Tc_1 level. At the advent of the present humid epoch, a new drainage entrenchment happened. Afterwards, the valley flat was filled by flood plain deposits.

In most of the researched valleys, the dissection subsequent to the formation of the low terraces with gravel removed mostly or all the correlative deposits of previous semi-arid phases. Another possibility, although hypothetical, to explain the absence of these morphological features in certain valleys would be that the remains of the terraces would have been covered by later aggradation of the valley flat.

The low terraces with gravels Tc_2 and Tc_1 are mostly covered by a colluvial mantle inclined towards the centre of the valley. This slightly inclined topographic feature is here referred to as *glacis* (Rc—*rampa de coluvio*, Port.). These features mask the original form of the terraces, and safe identification is possible only if their structure is examined. The *glacis* of colluvium were essentially originated by solifluction and rain wash processes. Their nature depends fundamentally on the lithology of the source area. The colluvia lack structure and have a low sorting coefficient. Each terrace (Tc_1 and Tc_2) has a *glacis* of colluvium re-covering it. These are dissected. There is still another one partially re-covering the flood plain deposits, and apparently showing no dissection. The *glacis* are not genetically related to the terraces. They result from colluviation phases, and their stratigraphical and environmental implications still need more detailed studies.

Correlative formations

In this section a revision is made concerning different sediments which are correlative to the several erosion surfaces of the Brazilian Cenozoic.

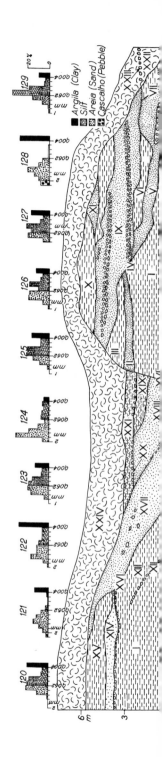

to Tres Rios, State of Rio de Janeiro). It shows the Tp_2 level at the Paraiba Valley. The structure shown comprises deposits relative to Tp_2 (I to XV), to Tp_1 (XVII to XXI) and to colluviation (XXII to XXIV).

Older sequence (right side of the road cut).

I—banded, red sandy-silty-clayey material (Sample 123); II—light purple silty sand (Sample 126); III—banded, red sandy-silty-clayey material; IV—erosive unconformity; V—yellow feldspathic sand having sparse granules and small pebbles (maximum size 5 cm) of quartz (Sample 122). It includes gravel lenses containing angular and subangular quartz and feldspar pebbles (5 cm maximum size); VI—purplish-red sandy-silty-clayey material (Sample 125); VII—erosive unconformity; VIII—unstratified sandy-silty-clayey material having small ferruginous granules (Sample 120); IX—yellow arkosic sands with abundant quartz pebbles. The pebbles form lines intercalated with more sandy bands (Sample 125). The quartz pebbles are subangular to subrounded, with 3 to 10 cm sizes; X—reddish colluvial material apparently without pebbles; XI—sandy material.

Same older sequence (left side of the road cut).

XII—pebble line (erosive unconformity); XIII—silty sand: partly arkosic, with pinkish-red colour (Sample 129); XIV—reddish sand lying upon a gravel pavement; XV—reddish colluvial material, apparently without pebbles (similar to X).

Younger sequence (centre of the road cut).

XVI—great erosive unconformity separating the younger from the older sequence; XVII—arkosic sand containing pebbles of variable size, angular, subangular and subrounded, and showing a slight tendency to orientation; XVIII—brown-yellow arkosic sand, with small quartz pebbles lying on a sub-sandy-silty-clayey material 'Sample 127); XX—gravel layer 20 cm thick. Quartz pebbles subangular to subrounded about 5 cm in diameter. Some pebbles 15 cm in diameter; XXI—light yellow colluvial material, with abundant small angular quartz pebbles (Sample 128); XXII—brown colluvium with sparse quartz pebbles, subangular to subrounded (8 cm maximum size) (Sample 121); XXIII—local detrital paleopavement; XXIV—brown colluvium apparently without granules.

In this outcrop two distinguishable depositional sequences are shown which are separated by a clear erosive unconformity (XVI). The older sequence is represented in both sides of the road cut. It consists of silty-clayey, sandy and rudaceous layers deposited in the evacuation trough during the elaboration of the pediment P_2. It corresponds therefore to the terrace (Tp_2) relative to the mentioned pedimentation phase. The lack of stratification, the arkosic sands and the abundance of rudaceous material showing some rounding, indicate a semi-arid environment and transportation through high density fluids. The filling of the old evacuation trough was completed by an episode of colluviation (X and XV). Afterwards the dissection and consequently the formation of the older terrace (humid climate) occurred.

Deposition over this dissected surface occurred again indicating semi-arid conditions (elaboration of the pediment P_1). As in the previous sequence, a colluvial layer re-covers this sedimentary sequence related to P_1. A posterior dissection turned these deposits to the evacuation through of P_1 times into another terrace (Tp_1). Episodes of colluviation succeeded (XXII, XXIII and XXIV) which progressively masked the original forms of the terraces, that presently can be recognized only through the examination of their structures.

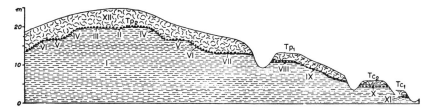

FIG. 14. Road cut between Lorena and Piquette (State of São Paulo), 10 km from the crossing with the Rio-São Paulo highway. Represents a sequence of many of the terrace levels found in the Paraiba Valley. I—Tertiary sandy-clayey sediments; II—erosive unconformity; III—gravel layer 30 to 50 cm thick, formed by subangular to subrounded quartz pebbles. Corresponds to the local Tp_2 level; IV—erosive unconformity followed by a detrital paleopavement with quartz pebbles reworked from the gravel layer III; V—level re-covered by subangular to subrounded pebbles; VI—erosive unconformity followed by a detrital paleopavement with quartz pebbles reworked from the higher gravel layers; VII—level re-covered by a gravel accumulation similar to V; VIII—another gravel accumulation at a level slightly lower than VII, demonstrating the existence of small erosive unconformity between the two levels. The gravels VII and VIII seem to represent, as a unit, the local Tp_1 terrace; IX—erosive unconformity; X—level of gravel accumulation, similar to the previous ones, and representing the upper low terrace with pebbles of the Paraiba valley (Tc_2); XI—another level with gravel similar to the previously described. It is the most recent level of low terrace with pebbles of the Paraiba valley (Tc_1); XII—colluvial re-covering of several ages.

This is a relatively extensive section in which a clearly defined sequence of upper Pleistocene and Holocene events in the Paraiba Valley can be seen. Although the colluviation sequence is not clear (erosive unconformities not clear) the gravel levels, indicating the past topography, make possible the reconstitution of a series of depositional and erosive events.

The textural and structural characteristics of the gravel layers demonstrate that the levels are remnants of old troughs of the Paraiba Valley, being therefore remnants of fluvial terraces. The roundness and the sorting of the quartz pebbles indicate a relatively prolonged transportation, as well as a successive reworking from higher and older terraces. The absence of primary structures demonstrates the transport by non-channelled high density fluids. The rudaceous material was deposited in sheets; the dissection has small amplitude because the Paraiba River, in that area, has a small gradient.

Therefore, it is a return to problems already studied by Bigarella and Ab'Sáber (1964) and Bigarella and Andrade (1965).

Correlative sediments of the pediplane Pd_2 in northeastern Brazil were named Guararapes Formation by Bigarella and Andrade (1964). This formation is the lower stratigraphic unit of the Barreiras Group. It consists of a sequence of unconsolidated clastic deposits of fine- and coarse-grain size. The silty-clays and sands are nearly always poorly sorted, presenting granules and even small pebbles of quartz and feldspar. In some places clear stratification and sometimes cross-bedding can be found. In the deposition of these sediments high-density fluids intervened; for example, mudflows which alternated with sandflows. These flows were able to drag granules and pebbles in suspension. Pebble layers eventually occurred, showing an arrangement in sheets. The Guararapes Formation has its origin related to a wide flexure occurring in the coastal zone in Cenozoic times (Andrade and Lins 1963). This flexure originated conditions in the coastal area for the accumulation of debris brought from the interior by erosive processes. The sediment texture and mineralogical composition suggest the prevalence of severe tropical semi-arid conditions in the source area. The absence of a clear stratification and sorting is due to sheetflows in an environment with a scarce vegetation cover. The frequent layers of arkosic sands were produced by processes of mechanical morphogenesis.

In southern and southeastern Brazil no references are made to Pd_2 correlative deposits. Ab'Sáber and Bigarella (1961) refer to the absence of Pd_2 correlative deposits in the Curitiba Plateau. Later on, Bigarella and Ab'Sáber (1964) considered that this erosion surface originated under subhumid climatic conditions in which the drainage was able to remove material outward from its watershed (*drenagem exorreica*, Port.). Presently we consider that Pd_2 in southern and southeastern Brazil is not different from the other regional erosion surfaces which were elaborated under semi-arid conditions with fluctuations towards humidity. We consider pediplanation processes to be developed fundamentally under such semi-arid conditions which cannot be fully understood through the mere observations of areas presently under semi-arid climates.

Nevertheless, in basins situated along the Paraiba River and in the São Paulo basin, it is possible to correlate, at least partially, some of the sediments with the elaboration of the Paleogenic Surface (name of the Pd_2 in the State of São Paulo).

The drainage then existing in the area under pediplanation was able to evacuate from the area most of the debris shed by the morphogenetic processes. The pediplain remnants are found high in the regional topography and are always situated in zones peripheral to the pediplanated area. This indicates great erosion after the formation of Pd_2. Nevertheless, some sediments must have accumulated somewhere inside the pediplanated area. These deposits may have been later removed by posterior erosive cycles. Preservation of the deposits occurred only in places where faulting allowed the retention of a thicker sediment section which could be preserved from erosion afterwards. Such is the case for the previously mentioned Paraiba Valley and São Paulo Basin.

The pediplane Pd_1 has many correlative deposits spread over several areas of Brazil where the relations between the deposits and the erosive landforms is much clearer than in the Pd_2 case. In northeast and in some other areas of eastern Brazil the transition between the surfaces of aggradation and degradation (surface of the Chãs and Tabuleiros, in the State of Pernambuco) cannot be noticed.

The Riacho Morno Formation (upper part of the Barreiras Group) constitutes the correlative deposit of the pediplane Pd_1 and also of the pediments P_2 and P_1 (Bigarella and Andrade 1964).

Erosive unconformities originated in humid climate and, representing dissection, separate the various sedimentary layers deposited during phases of semi-arid climate.

The correlative deposits of Pd_1 of extensive geographical distribution urgently need a study of their stratigraphic and sedimentological problems (primary structures, textures, and mineralogy). Although the correlative deposits are not known in detail, a series of basic data about the paleoclimatic and paleogeographic interpretation of the lower Pleistocene in Brazil can be obtained. Such deposits occur along the coast from Rio de Janeiro to the north. In the low Ribeira Valley the deposits were described by Bigarella and Mousinho (1965b) as part of the Pariquera-Açu Formation. In Paraná the deposits constitute the deposits of the Alexandra and Guabirotuba formations (Bigarella and Salamuni 1962, Bigarella and Ab'Sáber 1964, p. 291). In Rio Grande do Sul the correlative deposits include parts of the Graxaim Formation (Bigarella and Ab'Sáber 1964, p. 307).

GUABIROTUBA FORMATION. For the origin of the Curitiba Basin we may consider the hypothesis of a tectonic damming, which would answer for the accumulation of sediments inside the basin. However, the importance of climatic changes affecting the removal of detrital material in relationship with the aggradational processes should be considered. The reconstitution of the history of the Curitiba Basin begins with pediplane Pd_2. After this surface was formed, an erosive phase under humid climate began causing a deep dissection in the landscape. In the Alto Iguaçu surface valleys incisions were little more than 100 m.

This phase of degradation originated an irregular hilly surface. In the present topography, many of those hills are found in the subsurface, and when exhumed they appear involved by the sediments of the Guabirotuba Formation.

The erosive phase, realized in humid climate, was suspended by a climatic change. The climate changed to semi-arid with concentrated rainfalls. The vegetation cover became sparse and ineffective in protecting the soil surface against intensive erosion. The rainfall acquired a torrential character. Sheet wash predominated in the removal of waste from the unprotected slopes, carrying sediments down to the valleys and drainage channels. There the laden waters acted like high density mudflows, unable either to select the sediments according to the grain size, or to transport their load very far. Most of this load was deposited in the first break of gradient of the intermittent stream. This process led to the formation of an assemblage of coalescent alluvial fans, which is characteristic of semi-arid climates. When the current in this type of climate loses a first part of its load because of a gradient change, a great part of the silty-clayey particles remain suspended, allowing the transport of coarser grains resulting from the fluid density and torrential character. These sediments are carried to depressions where they are deposited in a playa lake environment. In this way the relatively thick sections of silty-clayey sediments were deposited (Figs. 15 and 16).

During the humid phase, a relatively thick regolith would have been elaborated, and its textural composition should not differ much from the present one. This material should have been the initial source of sediments which filled the basin during the epoch of deposition of the Guabirotuba Formation. The regolith which coated the internal and peripheral surficial rims of the basin, and the one existing in the Alto Iguaçu surface suffered fast erosion and transportation. In this way, a great part of the sediment which constitutes the Guabirotuba Formation was originated when the chemical decomposition of the crystalline Precambrian rocks started under a humid climate. But they were eroded, transported, and deposited in semi-arid climatic conditions. This explains, to a large extent, the textural composition of the sediments. The kaolinitic nature of the clay corroborates the prevalence of humid climatic conditions at the epoch of the regolith elaboration.

ALEXANDRA FORMATION. This stratigraphic designation was given to the continental sediments which occur at the Paraná coast, in the Br-35 highway cuts near Alexandra. They were described in 1959 by Bigarella, Salamuni, and Marques as Tertiary deposits. The sediments lay on an unconformity over gneiss of the Brazilian shield. The lower section of the formation is mainly formed by arkosic sands and rudaceous sedi-

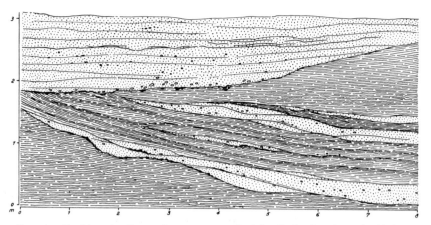

Fig. 15. Guabirotuba Formation structure, Curitiba Basin. Road cut in highway Br-35 (Curitiba-Paranaguá) in the vicinities of Santa Barbara. Alternate arkosic sands and silty-clayey sediments. Environment of semi-arid alluvial cones. Deposition contemporaneous to the elaboration of the pediplane Pd_1 (Curitiba surface).

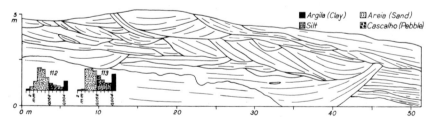

Fig. 16. Guabirotuba Formation structure, Curitiba Basin. Road cut in the Curitiba-São Paulo highway (Br-2), near Quatro Barras. Layers with cross-stratification developed in two kinds of arkosic-sandy sediments, according to the histograms. The coarser type is emphasized by differential erosion. Environment of semi-arid alluvial cones contemporaneous to the elaboration of the pediplane Pd_1.

464

ments, while the remaining part is predominantly of silty-clayey sediments.

Initially a tectonic origin was attributed to this sedimentary basin situated at the foot of the Serra do Mar. It was supposed to be related to faulting at the end of the Serra do Mar development. It was mentioned also that the sediments proceeded from the weathering of crystalline rocks, suffering little transport and fast deposition.

These concepts have been changed since Bigarella and Freire (1960, p. 19), following Dr. Henno Martin's suggestions, interpreted the Alexandra Formation as being formed by sediments of a gradational plain inclined seaward and formed when its level was lower than at present, during the Pleistocene.

The discovery of pediment remnants in the coastal region and on the eastern slopes of the Serra do Mar allowed a revision of the date of the origin and therefore the age of the Alexandra Formation. Ab'Sáber and Bigarella (1961, p. 104) verified that the deposits of the Alexandra Formation were cut by the remnants of the P_2 pediment. This fact indicates that this formation was anterior to the mentioned pediment. The levels 27 to 30 m high which cut the top of the sediments and previously considered as marine came to be interpreted as remnants of erosion surfaces elaborated under a semi-arid climate.

A re-examination of the sediments indicated that they had possibly been formed during a semi-arid climate and deposited in a *bajada* environment, to a large extent in playa lakes. The sedimentary sequence shows the action of sheet transportation without a definite system of channels. In some places we noticed the action of mudstreams, which were able to transport boulders, especially close to the mountain zone.

PARIQUERA-AÇU FORMATION. This formation was deposited in a wide and dissected valley which came into existence after the development of pediplane Pd_2. Climatic changes occurred in this landscape. These changes originated an alternated predominance of processes of lateral degradation and linear erosion which were very important to the elaboration of the sediments.

The accumulation of sediments in the basin of the lower Ribeira where Pariquera-Açu was deposited may have several origins: drainage damming caused by faulting or some other phenomenon, or by the character of the transportation agent itself. We want to remark that valley filling is a normal process during semi-arid climatic phases.

The Pariquera-Açu sediments are dominantly fine-textured, consisting of irregularly alternated sandy-clayey silts and arkosic sands. Associated with the sands are pebble layers of small thickness. Usually the pebbles are angular to subangular and consist of quartz and quartzite. The thickness of these intraformational pebble layers generally is of some centimetres, normally less than half a metre. Thicker layers of pebbles and arkosic sands occur in the upper part of the lowermost section of the formation, where they represent the predominance of mechanical morphogenesis responsible for the elaboration of the pediplane Pd_1.

Primary structures and clearly developed stratification are practically absent in this formation. Cut and fill structures occur in great number both in silts and sands, indicating alternation of erosion and deposition. In some places granules and pebbles sparsely embedded in the fine sediments can be found. Sometimes the pebbles are concentrated in horizontal layers or fill channel depressions. In both cases the pebbles were transported inside a fine matrix, through mass transport, and the fine material was selectively eliminated, resulting in a concentration of the coarser material.

The structural and textural characteristics of the Pariquera-Açu Formation indicate depositional processes typical of a semi-arid climate. Among these the agents of mass transport (mudflows and sheetflows) play an important role.

During the elaboration of pediplane Pd_1, under semi-arid conditions, the debris was accumulated in the depressions. Successive reworkings resulted in incipient sorting. The fine clastics were disposed alternately in sandy and clayey-silty layers. They represent *playa* or *bajada* deposits. The debris formed when the marginal pediplanation of the basin was transporting material towards the interior of the basin in the direction of the evacuation trough. Coarser material eventually covered the finer sediments or in some instances made up lenses interbedded among the fine material. The predominance of phyllites in the area mainly produced fine clastics. Phyllite pebbles seldom occur in the rudaceous material (Figs. 17 and 18).

The transportation of eroded material to the basin by high-density flowing agents resulted in the aggradation of the valley and, consequently, in the rise of the local erosion base level. This aggradation went on until a balance was reached between the arrival of material from the slopes under pediplanation and the removal of deposits by the basin's evacuation trough. Reaching this equilibrium, the sedimentary fill of the lower valley of the Ribeira became a fully developed *bajada*.

The wide evacuation trough of this epoch left as remnants high terraces near the margin of the basin which corresponded in elevation to the level of pediplane Pd_1. The terraces are partially protected against erosion by layers of subrounded to rounded pebbles, indicating transportation. These pebbles are clearly different from those that are angular to subangular and found in the detrital pediment. The coarse

466

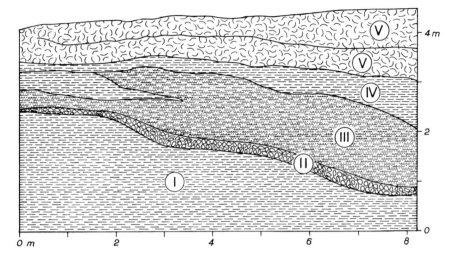

Fɪɢ. 17. Exposure in the Br-2 highway cut at 11.8 km from Jacupirango to
Registro (State of São Paulo). This exposure is truncated by the level P_2. Sediments of the Pariquera-Açu Formation I—silty-sandy sediments of grey colour
with violet spots in which was eroded a channel later filled by a gravel layer
20 cm thick (II), with pebbles around 5-8 cm in diameter, locally reaching 15 cm
in diameter. Over the gravels a sandy-silty-clayey layer of yellow-grey colour
(III) occurs. Above are silty-sandy deposits (IV) re-covered by two colluvial
layers, the lower one having reddish-brown colour and the higher having
yellowish-brown colour.

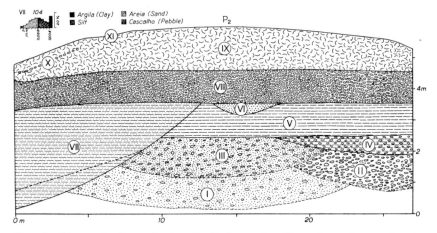

Fig. 18. Terrace level correlated to P_2. Pariquera-Açu Formation sediments. Road cut 3.2 km from Pariquera-Açu in the road to Cananeia (State of São Paulo). Sequences of lenses of grey colour, of variable texture, accompanied by a gravel deposit. I—arkosic sandy sediment, unstratified, with sparse pebbles; II—small pebbles in sandy silty-clayey matrix. A few pebbles 10 cm in diameter; III—arkosic sandy sediment, unstratified, with sparse pebbles; IV—gravel layer with silty-clayey sediments intercalated; V—silty-clayey layer; VI—arkosic sandy layer; VII —lens of silty-clayey sediment alternated with incipiently stratified sandy material. Sparse inclusions of subangular quartz pebbles having a diameter of 4-5 cm (Sample 104); VIII—gravel deposit formed by subangular pebbles averaging 5-7 cm in diameter, with some blocks 30 cm in diameter, many small pebbles 2 cm in diameter. In some places lenses of fine arenaceous detrital material occur; IX— brown colluvium with sparse granules and small pebbles; X—discontinuous detrital paleopavement; XI—brown colluvium with sparse granules.

angular debris resulting from mechanical morphogenesis removed to the evacuation trough was submitted to the action of sheet flows, becoming progressively rounded downstream.

The semi-arid Pd_1 period was followed by a humid epoch in which dissection and removal of great amounts of sediment laid down during Pd_1 time occurred. Several knickpoints developed as local base levels. The landscape regained a forest cover.

A new semi-arid epoch opened wide basins by pedimentation processes forming pediment P_2. Part of the Pariquera-Açu sediment (correlative to Pd_1) was reworked and redeposited in P_2 times. Between the two sequences an erosive unconformity occurs. The debris from the mechanical morphogenesis related to P_2 re-covered the previous sediments. Here again occurred a balance between the material produced by the pedimentation and that evacuated by the basin trough. A relation similar to that verified between Pd_1 and the high terraces (Tpd_1) is found between P_2 and its corresponding terrace (Tp_2). The pebbles found in the pediment are more angular, while those found in the terrace are more rounded.

After the formation of P_2, a new humid epoch again promoted dissection, accompanied by removal of a great amount of previously deposited material. Semi-aridity occurred again, resulting in the formation of the pediment P_1 and its corresponding terrace (Tp_1), similar to the previously described elaboration of older pediments. Few remnants exist from this pediment P_1. However, the terrace deposits of this P_1 epoch are more frequent.

The assemblage of the silty-clayey and sandy sediments, as well as the rudaceous deposits of the terraces deposited during Quaternary (between the elaboration of Pd_1 and the end of P_1) constitute the Pariquera-Açu Formation. It is divided into three parts (III, II, and I) corresponding respectively to the erosional surfaces Pd_1, P_2, and P_1. A similar scheme was proposed before for the Graxaim and Iquererim formations (Bigarella and Ab'Sáber 1964). The term Pariquera-Açu Formation (II) applies to all the sediments deposited during the elaboration of the pediment P_2.

IQUERERIM FORMATION. The assemblage of rudaceous material deposited during the several pedimentation epochs that fashioned the Atlantic side of the Serra do Mar, in Garuva, near the border of the States of Paraná and Santa Catarina, was named the Iquererim Formation (Bigarella, Marques and Ab'Sáber 1961). The sediments of this formation constitute the detrital pediments which present their dissected remnants slightly inclined.

According to the classical view, the detrital pediment consists only of a slight veneer of debris. However, in Garuva the rudaceous deposits have a greater development because of the exceptional character of the Serra do Mar slopes and the cyclic nature of the climatic changes, promoting alternately lateral degradation and relatively deep dissection with progressive inlay of the various pedimentary surfaces. In this way has been deposited not a thin veneer of clastics, but a significant stratigraphic sequence.

In the Garuva area the sediments unconformably overlie a very irregular surface. Above this surface the rudaceous material is deposited, usually without stratification, and varies in thickness from a few metres to more than twelve metres. This material is very coarse, angular to subangular, unsorted, and composed of pebbles and even huge blocks of heterogeneous composition (gneiss, granite, and diabase). Their size varies from few centimetres to more than four metres, and they are embedded in a sandy silty-clayey matrix.

The Iquererim Formation is composed of two separated sequences of deposition, each originating under a distinct epoch of pedimentation. They are related to the pediments P_2 and P_1 and were named phases II and I. Thus, the deposits of phase I are inset in the higher pedimentary level (P_2), referred to as phase II. Between these phases of pedimentation an epoch of humid climates occurred, promoting vertical erosion, interrupting the mechanical morphogenesis, and originating an erosive unconformity that can be found separating the semi-arid depositions I and II.

With the repetition of pedimentation epochs the pebbles and boulders were successively reworked, becoming each time a part of a new depositional phase. Thus, this material may be said to belong to more than one cycle, that is, it is polycyclical.

CANHANDUVA LAYERS. The deposits at the locality of Canhanduva (Br-59 highway cut between Itajai and Camboriu) were described by Bigarella and Salamuni (1961, p. 100). The stratigraphy consists of: (1) basement composed of Precambrian metamorphic rocks (Brusque Group); (2) erosive unconformity forming an irregular surface; (3) pre-Canhanduva layers; (4) Canhanduva layers; and (5) aggradational surface accomplished towards the end of the sedimentation, presently a remnant of the detrital pediment related to the pedimentary phase P_1.

Before the deposition of pre-Canhanduva layers a humid climate was conditioning the formation of a thick regolith and also promoting the dissection that gave origin to the erosive unconformity separating the basement from the pre-Canhanduva layers. When the climate changed progressively from humid to semi-arid, the vegetation was disturbed, facilitating the slope denudation. The regolith was then removed to the lower parts of the basin, filling the depressions mainly through mass movements. This sedimentation of variable thickness originated the pre-Canhanduva layers which have light grey colour. The sediments are predominantly fine textured and unsorted. The clayey and silty deposits are rich in sand, granules, and sparse pebbles of quartz and quartzite. The pre-Canhanduva layers are related to the initial phase of the pedimentation process.

The Canhanduva layers are representative of the mechanical morphogenetic epoch related to the elaboration of P_1. They are about 7.5 m thick and made up of a relatively coarse rudaceous reddish-brown deposit. Stratification is incipient. A succession of 50 to 70 cm thick layers corresponds to deposition from high-density flows. Angular pebbles, cobbles, and even boulders of quartz, quartzite, and phyllite are embedded in a sandy-clayey matrix. The abundance of pebbles and especially the great number of phyllitic ones (easily altered under humid conditions) confirm the prevalence of mechanical morphogenesis during their deposition. The same situation does not occur in the pre-Canhanduva layers. There the sparse quartz and quartzite pebbles represent residual elements of a previous, chemically-weathered regolith.

The deposits of this locality can be correlated geomorphologically with the Iquererim Formation, phase I.

CACHOEIRA LAYERS. The area named Cachoeira is located on the coast of Santa Catarina, some 20 km south of Tijucas, where dissected remnants of a sedimentary formation consisting of clays and arkoses, poorly sorted and practically without a clear stratification, are found. Outcrops can be seen in roadcuts along Br-59 and on the road leading to the locality of Ganchos.

The sediments are filling a north-south elongated depression of tectonic origin placed between two crystalline massifs at east and west. The remnants of the surface originated by the end of the local sedimentation seem, as a whole, to be inclined toward the centre of the basin. This geomorphic aspect, together with the sedimentological study of these layers, here named Cachoeira layers, allow an identification of the environment as being a *bajada* formed under semi-arid conditions. The stratigraphic sequence is similar in its general aspect to some features of the sediments of the Alexandra and Guabirotuba formations.

The Cachoeira layers, here considered *bajada* or bolsonplain sediments, would be contemporaneous with the elaboration of the local P_1 that can be found in the periphery of the basin. Thus, they could be correlated to the Iquererim Formation, phase I, while the surface originated by the closing of the sedimentation would correspond to the maximum sculpturing of the P_1 pediment.

The valley flat

The valley flat is defined as the low flat land between valley walls bordering a stream channel (*American Geological Institute* 1960, p. 311). In the valley flat are found many landforms, among which are included the gravel terraces Tc_2 and Tc_1 described elsewhere in this paper. The braided stream deposits, the *glacis* of colluvium, and the flood plain terraces, together with alluvial fill of the valley flat, constitute a problem in which a delicate balance between erosion and deposition is involved.

The valley flat consists basically of several fill terrace levels. The two highest levels (Tc_2 and Tc_1) are covered by *glacis* of colluvium inclined towards the centre of the valley ($3°$ to $4°$). The lowermost terraces T_1 (*terraços de várzea*, Port.) of the valley flat represent a complex of aggradation and degradation phases which occurred within the most recent humid phase. They are dissected remnants of previous valley bottoms. An inspection of the surficial and subsurface features indicates that the valley flat, although considered as a defined structural unit, is a rather complex one. It is made up of several genetically different types of sediments deposited under distinct climatic conditions: the basal gravels, braided stream sands, colluvium tongues, and flood plain deposits. The several colluvium sequences interfinger with some of the other valley flat deposits, as well as constitute *glacis* of colluvium (*rampa de colúvio* Port.).

The lower levels of the valley flat, corresponding to old flood plain deposits, are designated as flood plain terraces. The relation existing between these levels and the colluviation is still insufficiently known and presents a large field for later research. The colluviation may appear covering such levels and forming the *glacis* of colluvium. Normally, the influence of the colluviation is stronger on the periphery of the valley flat. In this way, larger valleys or those in which, for various reasons, the last colluviation phase did not advance so intensely towards the interior of the evacuation trough, show a clearer preservation of the original forms of the fluvial terraces.

Although in this paper the basic lines of the problem are considered, we do not have the amount of systematic study necessary to obtain a decisive stratigraphy of the colluvium tongues and a precise understanding of their relationship with the other sediments of the valley flat.

The formation of the valley flat lower terraces is directly connected to small changes in the hydrologic characteristics of the streams. A series of inlaid terraces was formed, all of them fill terraces. The scheme is rather complex in high-rank valleys. Since the lower terraces are related to small fluctuations in the processes of fluvial dynamics and, therefore, essentially to variations in the relation between load and discharge of the streams, it is quite possible, and even probable, that a perfect homogeneity in the evolution of this extensive studied area of Brazil in recent times has not happened.

In the study of a valley flat, the problem of deforestation of anthropic origin, which caused accelerated erosion in the slopes and changes in the hydrological regimen of the streams, must be considered. A first consequence of this problem is the difficult delineation between the actual flood plain and the lower terraces. Human activity caused an increase of the torrentiality of the rivers which began periodically to overflow terrace levels. Possibly the levels were out of reach of the floods when the previous hydrological equilibrium had not been artificially broken.

The problems connected with the interpretation of the elaboration of the valley floor today overlain by alluvial deposits are relatively complex. We do not yet know the complete form of this surface, which seems to be partly plane and partly irregular. Drillings indicate that it is covered by pebbles of heterogeneous lithology (quartz, quartzite, gneiss, and other metamorphics) resting unconformably over truncated gneisses (migmatites). The angular to subangular character of the phenoclasts indicates severe climatic conditions at the time of their sedimentation.

The valley floor was progressively enlarged, mainly after the dissection of the Tp_1 (terrace corresponding to the P_1 pediment). The climatic conditions under which occurred the emptying of the valleys are not clear. They do not seem to be similar to the present conditions nor identical to the semi-arid aggradation phase. Probably the processes involved are connected to particular phases of transition or climatic oscillations. It seems that the principal phase of valley widening happened before the low terraces Tc_2 and Tc_1 were formed.

Since then the valley floor may have been continuously refashioned. It is still not possible to establish precisely which phase of development is connected to the gravel deposits lying in erosive unconformity upon the Precambrian crystalline rocks. They may have different ages in different localities. We are fairly sure that the rocky floor underneath the alluvial fill of the valleys constitutes a surface developed during a semi-arid climatic phase, which was lowered and widened after the dissection of the pediment P_1 and fluvial terrace Tp_1.

Filling of the evacuation trough (present valley flat) with rudaceous and sandy material happened under climatic conditions more severe than the present one, since today these materials are only reworked in the river beds. These layers of pebble and sand lay normally in planes rich in primary structures and showing evidences of transportation as sheets rather than in channels. Presently, in the meandering rivers the sands are transported in channels, there being no evidence of sheet transportation. The meandering action of the rivers resulted in horizontal sand bodies disposed in irregular layers (Fig. 19). The stratigraphic profiles from the Mauricio River valley flat fill (km 30 of the Br-2 highway, south of Curitiba) show clearly the sedimentation irregularity and the fact that the meandering action of the river does not form sedimentary levels parallel to the surface. The deposition follows normally the vertical displacement of the river, upward in case of aggradation and downward when the channel deepened. A more recent sedimentary sequence covers unconformably the previous sequence and represents deposits formed under humid climatic conditions somewhat similar to the present. This whole assemblage is covered by a colluvial mantle.

In this way, the sedimentary ensemble of the valley fill represents at least two distinct climatic epochs—dry and humid. The transition from the last dry period to the humid took place about 2,400 years ago (Bigarella 1964, p. 219) according to data obtained from the alluvial plain of the "Estação Experimental do Trigo de Curitiba." This date cannot yet be generalized, since the alluvial fills of other areas show evidences of other climatic fluctuations not yet dated.

The general character of the valley flat deposits are relatively well known. However, their sedimentologic details are still not well understood. In the valley flat four different depositional features are individualized: basal gravel, braided stream sediments, colluvium deposits, and overbank and channel deposits. The gravel and sandy sediments of the braided stream channels make up the basal portion of the valley flat, resting unconformably over the Precambrian basement. The sandy deposits are usually crossbedded. They represent sediments deposited under more severe climatic conditions. The colluvium deposits are devoid of primary structures. The deposits of the meandering river channels present primary structures also. Here they are less frequently preserved. The structures described in this paper are those related to the braided stream deposits and therefore do not pertain to the present day deposition. They have been produced under different climatic conditions (dryer climate with concentrated rainfalls) when the river was intermittent.

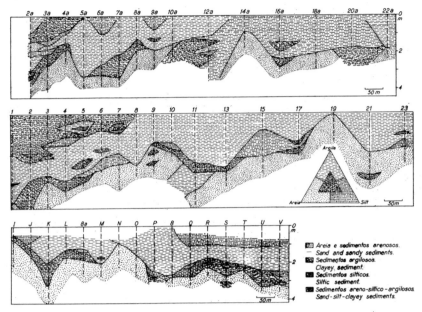

FIG. 19. Textural variations of the Mauricio River valley flat sediments. Highway Br-2, 30 km south of Curitiba (State of Paraná). The four fundamental types of sediments show a great variability, vertically and horizontally. The sandy-silty-clayey sediments correspond mainly to the colluvia tongues. In the lower profile, the colluvium is constituted of siltic material. The sandy sediments correspond to deposits from meandering channels, while the clayey sediments correspond mainly to sediments deposited during floods.

The details of the crossbedding have been obtained in sand pits in the vicinity of Curitiba, at the Iguaçu River valley flat. Figure 20 represents in tri-dimensional view a characteristic braided stream crossbedding; Figures 21 and 22 shows crossbedding patterns parallel and transverse to the transportation trend.

Although crossbedding patterns are not typical only of braided streams, they can be important if related to other stratigraphical data, like the colluvial tongues and the overbank and channel deposits, for the characterization of the valley flat environment.

The crossbeddings found are of the trough and planar types, small to medium sized according to McKee and Wier's (1953) classification. The trough type has a forward-dipping axis. The result of 188 cross-strata attitude measurements gave a direction of transportation S 58° W, parallel to the direction of the former and present valley trough, the consistency ratio being 0.61.

In the upper part of the braided stream sand deposits, thin layers of silty-clayey sediments occur which together with the sands form contorted bedding. In this part, ripple lamination is also present.

In sum, in the valley flat we have the following sequence of depositional events:

(1) Elaboration of the valley floor under severe climatic conditions.

(2) Deposition of pebbles contemporaneously to degradation of the valley bottom (semi-arid climate).

(3) Installation of anastomotic channels and deposition of sandy sediments. Braided stream phase, intermittent drainage under severe climatic conditions, not yet precised but being dry and having concentrated rainfalls.

(4) Entrenchment of the drainage, eroding part of the deposits of the anastomotic channels of the intermittent river.

(5) Fulfillment with fine silty-clayey and sandy sediments under conditions of humid climate somewhat different from the present (flood and channel deposits).

(6) Colluviation in various phases, starting at the end of the sand deposition in the anastomotic channels. These phases probably also reflect specific climatic conditions, possibly of dryer climate with concentrated rainfalls. Up to now we could not characterize this climatic type.

Textures

Grain-size analysis of samples from the weathering mantle, as well as from Quaternary sedimentary sequences of southern and southeastern

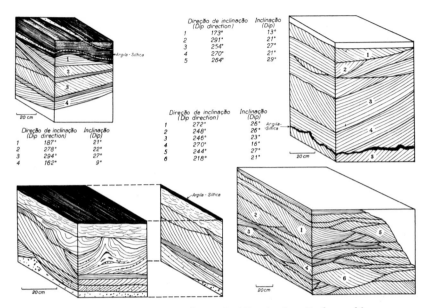

FIG. 20. Three-dimensional views of cross-bedding in deposits from old anastomosing channels of the Iguaçu River valley flat at Uberaba, Curitiba (State of Paraná). In the lower left block can be seen ripple cross-lamination, as well as sandy contorted strata.

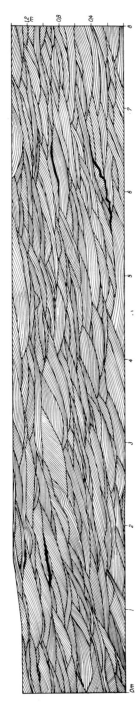

FIG. 21. Cross-bedding from old anastomosing channel (braided stream) of the Iguaçu River valley flat, at Uberaba, Curitiba. Section approximately longitudinal to the stream flow. Transportation trend from the right to the left side from the illustration.

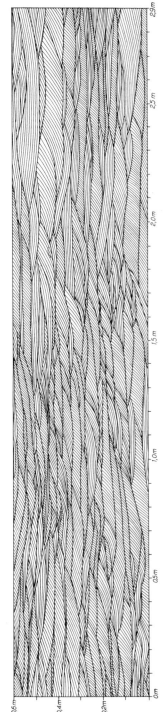

FIG. 22. Aspect of the cross-bedding found in the old braided stream deposits of the Iguaçu River valley flat at Uberaba, Curitiba. Section approximately transverse to the transportation trend.

Brazil, have been reported by Bigarella and Salamuni (1962) and Bigarella and Mousinho (1965 a, b).

The comparison of grain-size distribution curves and statistical parameters concerning samples from the regolith and from different formations and environments have shown characteristic variations which are closely linked to the processes involved in the sedimentation. Although these variations may have, to some extent, a genetic character, it seems convenient to recall that the factors which most affect the grain-size distributions are not related to the environmental changes, but instead, to the hydrodynamical properties of the grain submitted to the variations of velocity and density of the transporting fluid.

The sorting of a sediment mainly depends on the effectiveness of the involved agent and of the environmental conditions, and is therefore useful in helping the identification of the sedimentary processes. Samples of the weathering mantle, from the Guabirotuba and Pariquera-Açu formations and from the low terrace sediments, are usually poorly sorted. Only in the valley fill, especially in the braided stream deposits, do the sediments present better sorting.

Normally, in a grain-size distribution, the sorting, as well as the asymmetry, are functions of the sample median diameter. Inman (1949, p. 51) states that under normal conditions the samples which have median diameter close to 0.18 mm are the best sorted. A larger or smaller median diameter corresponds to a lesser degree of sorting.

If a sample with a median diameter close to 0.18 mm is poorly sorted, the agent is unable to realize a good sorting because of irregular transporting and depositional conditions. This is characteristic of high-density fluids (mudflows and mass movements). The correlation diagram between median diameter and sorting clearly points out some properties of the transporting fluid.

The sediments of the Iguaçu River valley flat show a close correlation between median diameter and sorting coefficient. The medians around 0.18 mm are those corresponding to the best sorting. For the Guabirotuba and Pariquera-Açu formations it seems there is no correlation between median diameter and sorting. The medians around 0.18 mm correspond to the most variable values of sorting, which means that the hydrodynamical properties of the fluids responsible for the deposition of the formations were different from those of the valley flat. The transporting agents of the Guabirotuba and Pariquera-Açu formations were dense fluids (mudflow) and were unable to sort the several grain sizes.

The samples of the weathering mantle do not present any correlation between median diameter and sorting.

479

In Figure 23 a comparison is made between the samples commented on above, and those from other areas and different geologic ages. The marine sediments off Hokkaido (Kato 1956) do not show any correlation between median diameter and sorting. A series of environment interferences causing mass movements in the sediments could be responsible for the lack of correlation. For the Baltic Sea and Straight of Davis sediments, the influence of floating ice was responsible for the absence of a good median diameter-sorting correlation. Mabesoone's (1959) and Nossin's (1959) analyses of sediments from northern Spain fluvial terraces do not present any correlation between the median diameter and the sorting coefficient. According to these authors the sediments were deposited in two different climatic phases (humid and semi-arid).

The Cretaceous deposits of the Bauru Group have the same characteristics with regard to the correlation between median diameter and sorting. They were deposited in a semi-arid environment.

Modifications in the hydrodynamical character of the transporting agent are marked by a difference in the statistical parameters obtained from the grain-size analysis. If a distinct contrast is verified, it is interpreted as a consequence of climatic change.

In Figure 24 the grain-size distribution cumulative curves are grouped and classified in several types according to their shapes.

The regolith samples from the weathered gneisses of the periphery of the Curitiba basin are represented in Figure 24A. The colluvium derived from the southeastern and southern Brazilian Precambrian Shield present two types of curve assemblages, one being more rectilinear and the other benched (Fig. 24B).

The valley flat deposits of the Iguaçu River near Curitiba present five types of curves (Figs. 24C, 24D) with different degrees of sorting. In Fig. 24C, the types I and II refer to samples of the braided stream phase of deposition. The sediments are usually sandy, sometimes with a small amount of clay or silt, and are better sorted. Type III of cumulative curve assemblages possibly correspond to the levées and part of backswamp deposits. Type IV (Fig. 24D) refers mostly to backswamp deposits, while type V represents, to a great extent, the deposits of the colluvium tongues interfingered with the flood plain deposits.

The Guabirotuba Formation presents three types of cumulative curve assemblages (Fig. 24E). Type I corresponds to the arkosic sands deposited in alluvial fan channels. Initially these sediments were transported in mudflows. Later removal of the finer material contributed to the best sorting degree presented by some of the sediments of this formation. Type III refers mostly to sheetflow deposits and partly to alluvial fan

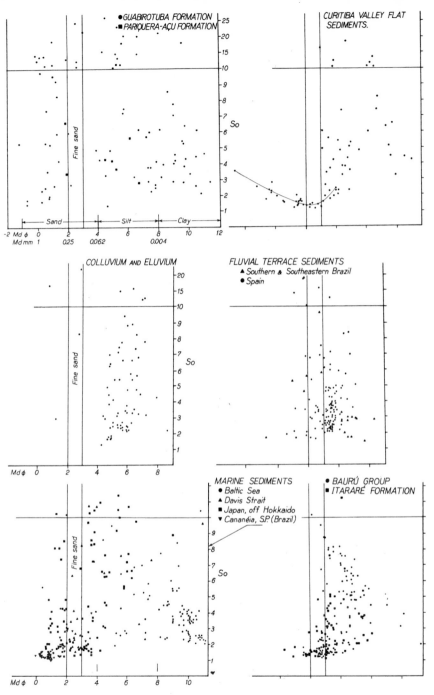

FIG. 23. Relationship between median diameter Mdφ and Trask sorting coefficient S_0. The continental formations (Guabirotuba Fm., Pariquera-Açu Fm., Bauru Group, Itararé Fm. and the terraces sediments) laid down under semi-arid conditions do not present any relationship between Md and S_0 because most of the sediments have been deposited from high density fluids. The same lack of Md-S_0 correlation occurs from some marine sediments, where turbidity flows and drift ice have been active. The valley flat deposits from Curitiba (mostly samples from the braided stream sediments) present a Md-S_0 correlation. The primary structures indicate normal hydrodynamical conditions for the deposition. The same is true for the marine lagunar sediments from Cananeia (State of São Paulo). For the elaboration of this diagram see Bigarella and Salamuni, Mabesoone, Nossin, Grinpenberg, Trask, Kato and Freitas (references in Bigarella and Salamuni, 1962). The Itararé Fm. mentioned above was laid down in a glacial and periglacial environment.

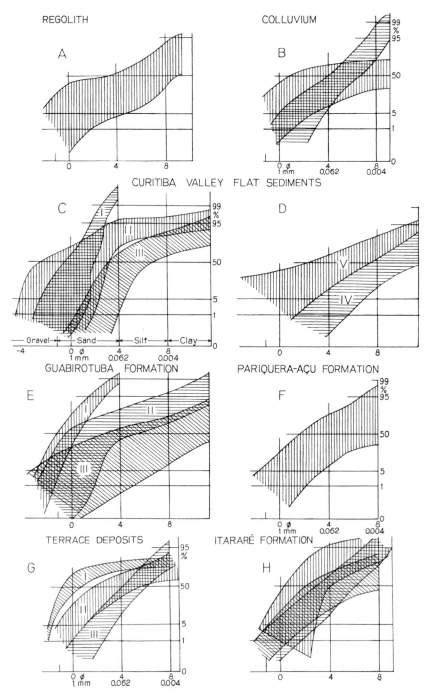

FIG. 24. Types of grain size distribution cumulative curves.

channels. Type II would correspond to the *bajada* or playa lake sediments. The curve assemblage relative to the Pariquera-Açu samples resembles very much the Guabirotuba type II.

The terrace deposits are grouped in three different types of cumulative curves of grain-size distribution. Type I refers mostly to channel deposits, while types II and III (Fig. 24G) correspond to sediments laid down from sheetflows.

The glacial and periglacial deposits of the Itararé Formation (Upper Carboniferous) show in the cumulative curves some resemblance to the semi-arid formations laid down in the Brazilian Pleistocene. There is also, in this case, a convergence of hydrodynamic conditions in which high density fluids played important roles.

There is a great contrast between the group of cumulative curve types corresponding to sediments laid down from high-density fluid, and those relative to normal water deposits. The sand-silt-clay content of the samples studied is shown in triangle diagrams (Figs. 25 and 26).

The Mauricio River valley flat localized at 30 km south of Curitiba, on highway Br-2, was studied with some detail. Three lines of borings were made, comprising forty-seven drillings. The holes were carried down to 5 m and were 50 to 100 m apart.

Figure 19 represents the grain-size composition of the 495 samples collected in the Mauricio River area. In the profiles of Figure 19 is shown the distribution of the several types of valley flat sediments. The great horizontal and vertical variability is clear. The deposition under humid climatic conditions differs greatly from the sheet deposition of the semi-arid environment. The colluvium tongues cover the overbank deposits and also interfinger with them. The sandy deposits of the meandering river follow, in zig-zag fashion, the valley aggradation or dissection.

SUMMARY

The study of the processes and environments of the Brazilian Pleistocene cold phases raised many questions about geomorphology, sedimentation, paleoclimates, and weathering.

The sedimentary textures show that in the past the operation of different processes of weathering in which mechanical disintegration was dominant, and, therefore, extremely different from those acting presently in the humid tropical or subtropical areas. In this paper a critical analysis of the weathering processes is made and from them the most probable were selected.

Sedimentary structures allow the recognition of processes involved

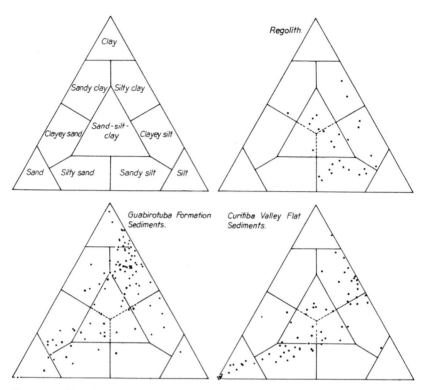

FIG. 25. Triangle diagram showing sand-silt-clay contents in samples of the regolith from the Curitiba area Precambrian gneisses, in samples of the Guabirotuba Formation and in samples of Iguaçu River valley flat at Curitiba. Nomenclature according to Shepard (1953).

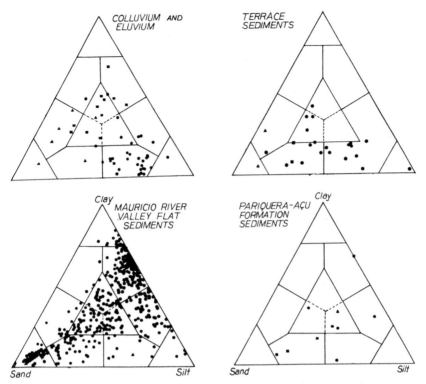

Fig. 26. Triangle diagrams showing sand-silt-clay contents in samples of colluvium and eluvium, terraces, valley flat deposits and Pariquera-Açu Formations sediments.

in the transport of debris into the basins, as well as in the mechanism of sedimentation.

Through the geomorphological survey of the area, pediplanes, pediments, *glacis* of colluvium, and fluvial terraces have been identified.

The study of the basins in most different geographical areas, close to the sea or in the high mountains, has shown equal number of erosion and aggradation levels. From these observations a new approach to the explanation of the land forms was made. Two different sets of processes have been visualized. One operated during the Pleistocene semi-arid climatic phases (= glacial times), producing lateral degradation (parallel retreat of slopes) forming pediments. The other acted during Pleistocene humid climatic phases (= interglacial times), promoting linear erosion causing dissection.

In the semi-arid phase the local base levels were more preserved, and when lowered the planated erosion surface (pediment) was constantly regraded. Meanwhile, in the humid phase, the local base levels dropped down causing deep incision and dissection of the topography.

The erosion levels have an alternated climatic control caused mainly by extreme climatic changes. These would be the reason why the same geomorphic picture is found in different basins at the most different geographical sites, regardless of uplift implications.

REFERENCES CITED

AMERICAN GEOLOGICAL INSTITUTE, 1960, Glossary of geology and related sciences, 2nd ed.: Washington, AGI, 325 p.

AB'SÁBER, A. N. and BIGARELLA, J. J., 1961, Consideraçoes sôbre a geomorfogênese da Serra do Mar no Paraná: Bol. Paran. Geogr., no. 4-5, p. 94-110.

ANDRADE, G. O. and LINS, R. C., 1961, O conglomerado do baixo Pirapama: Recife, Univ. Recife, Depto. Geogr., v. VI-2, fasc. XX-1, 121 p.

────── and ──────, 1963, Introduçáo a morfoclimatologia do Nordeste do Brasil: Recife, Cong. Nac. Geol., 17, Soc. Bras. Geol., 19 p.

BAULIG, H., 1956, Vocabulaire Anglo-France-Allemand de geomorphologie: Publ. de la Fac. de Lettres de l'Université de Strasbourg, 130, 230 p.

BIGARELLA, J. J., 1964, Variaçoes climáticas no Quaternário e suas implicaçoes no revestimento florístico do Paraná: Bol. Paran. Geogr., no. 10-15, p. 211-231.

BIGARELLA, J. J., SALAMUNI, R. and MARQUES, F°, P. L., 1959, Ocorrência de depósitos sedimentares continentais no litoral do Estado do Paraná: Curitiba, IBPT, Notas preliminares e Estudos no. 1, 7 p.

BIGARELLA, J. J. and FREIRE, S. S., 1960, Nota sôbre a ocorrência de cascalheiro marinho no litoral do Paraná: Curitiba, Bol. Univ. Paraná, Instituto de Geologia, Geol. 3, 22 p.

BIGARELLA, J. J., MARQUES F°, P. L. and AB'SÁBER, A. N., 1961, Ocorrências de pedimentos remanescentes nas fraldas da Serra do Iquererim (Garuva, SC): Bol. Paran. Geogr., no. 4-5, p. 82-93.

BIGARELLA, J. J. and SALAMUNI, R., 1961, Ocorrências de sedimentos continentais na região litorânea de Santa Catarina e sua significação paleoclimática: Curitiba, Bol. Paran. Geogr., no. 4-5, p. 179-187.

BIGARELLA, J. J. and SALAMUNI, R., 1962, Caracteres texturais dos sedimentos da bacia de Curitiba: Bol. Univ. Paraná, Instituto de Geologia, Geologia 7, 164 p.

BIGARELLA, J. J. and AB'SÁBER, A. N., Paläogeographische und Paläoklimatische Aspekte des Känozoikums in Südbrasilien: Z. f. Geomorph., v. 8, p. 286-312.

BIGARELLA, J. J. and ANDRADE, G. O., 1964, Consideraçoes sôbre a estratigrafia dos sedimentos conozóicos em Pernambuco (grupo Barreiras): Arquivos, Inst. Ciências da Terra, v. 2, p. 2-14.

——— and ———, 1965, Contribution to the study of the Brasilian Quaternary: Geol. Soc. America, Sp. Paper 84, p. 433-451.

BIGARELLA, J. J. and MOUSINHO, M. R., 1965a, Contribuição ao estudo da Formação Pariquera-Açú (Estado de São Paulo): Bol. Paran. Geogr., no. 16-17, p. 17-41.

——— and ———, 1965b, Consideraçoes a respeito dos terraços fluviais, rampas de colúvio e várzeas: Bol. Paran. Geogr., no. 16-17, p. 153-197.

BIROT, P., 1960, Le cycle d'érosion sous les différents climats: Rio de Janeiro, Centro de Pesq. Geogr. Brasil, Fac. Nac. Fil. Univ. Brasil, 135 p.

CAILLEUX, A. and TRICART, J., 1959, Zonas fitogeográficas e morfoclimáticas do Quaternário no Brasil: Not. Geomorf., v. 2, p. 12-15.

DAVIS, W. M., 1954, Geographical essays: London, Dover Pub. Inc., 777 p.

DRESCH, J., 1957, Remarques géomorphologiques sur l'Itatiaia (Brésil): Z. f. Geomorph., v. 1, p. 289-291.

HACK, J. T., 1960, Interpretation of erosional topography in humid temperate regions: Am. Jour. Sci., v. 258A, p. 80-97.

INMAN, D. L., 1949, Sorting of sediments in the light of fluid mechanics: Jour. Sed. Petrology, v. 19, p. 51-70.

KATO, K., 1965, Chemical investigations on marine humus in bottom sediments: Memoirs of the Faculty of Fisheries, Hokkaido Univ., v. 4, p. 91-209.

KING, L. C., 1956, A geomorfologia do Brasil oriental: Rio de Janeiro, Rev. Bras. Geogr., v. 18, no. 2, p. 147-266.

McKEE, E. D. and WEIR, G. W., 1953, Terminology for stratification and cross-stratification in sedimentary rocks: Geol. Soc. America Bull., v. 64, no. 4, p. 381-389.

MABESOONE, J. M., 1959, Tertiary and Quaternary sedimentation in a part of the Duero Basin, Plaencia (Spain): Leidse Geologische Medelingen, v. 24, p. 286-406.

MARTONNE, E. De., 1943, Problemas morfológicos do Brasil Tropical Atlântico (1.ª parte): Rio de Janeiro, Rev. Bras. Geogr., v. 5, no. 4, p. 523-550.

———, 1944, Problemas morfológicos do Brasil Tropical Atlântico (2.ª parte): Rio de Janeiro, Rev. Bras. Geogr., v. 6, no. 2, p. 155-178.

MURATORI, A., 1965, Geologia da Fôlha de Campo Largo: Inédito.

NOSSIN, J. J., 1959, Geomorphological aspects of the Pisurga drainage area in the Cantabrian Mountains (Spain): Leidse Geologische Medelingen, v. 24, p. 286-406.

ODMAN, O. H., 1955, On the presumed glaciation in the Itatiaia Mountains, Brazil: Eng., Min., Metal., v. 21, p. 107-108.

PENCK, W., 1953, Morphological analysis of land form: London, MacMillan and Co., 429 p.

PETTIJOHN, F. J., 1957, Sedimentary rocks, 2nd ed., Harper & Brothers, New York, 718 p.

RICH, J. L., 1953, Problems in Brazilian geology and geomorphology suggested by reconnaissance in Summer of 1951: São Paulo, Fac. Fil. Ciências e Letras da Univ. S. Paulo, no. 146, Geol. n. 9, 80 p.

RUELLAN, F., 1944, Evolução geomorfológica da baía de Guanabara e das regioes vizinhas: Rio de Janeiro, Rev. Bras. Geogr., v. 6, no. 4, p. 445-508.

SCOTT, G. R., 1960, Subdivision of the Quaternary alluvium east of the Front Range, near Denver, Colorado: Geol. Soc. America Bull., v. 71, p. 1541-1544.

SHEPARD, F. P., 1953, Sedimentation rates in Texas estuaries and lagoons: Am. Assoc. Petroleum Geologists Bull., v. 37, p. 1919-1934.